Enchanting
David Bowie

Enchanting David Bowie

Space/Time/Body/Memory

EDITED BY TOIJA CINQUE, CHRISTOPHER MOORE AND SEAN REDMOND

Bloomsbury Academic
An imprint of Bloomsbury Publishing Inc

B L O O M S B U R Y
NEW YORK · LONDON · OXFORD · NEW DELHI · SYDNEY

Bloomsbury Academic

An imprint of Bloomsbury Publishing Inc

1385 Broadway	50 Bedford Square
New York	London
NY 10018	WC1B 3DP
USA	UK

www.bloomsbury.com

BLOOMSBURY and the Diana logo are trademarks of Bloomsbury Publishing Plc

First published 2015
Reprinted by Bloomsbury Academic 2015

Library of Congress Cataloging-in-Publication Data
Enchanting David Bowie: space/time/body/memory / edited by Toija Cinque,
Christopher Moore and Sean Redmond.
pages cm
Includes bibliographical references and index.
ISBN 978-1-62892-304-9 (hardback : alk. paper) —
ISBN 978-1-62892-303-2 (pbk. : alk. paper) 1. Bowie, David–Criticism and interpretation.
2. Rock music–1971-1980–History and criticism.   I. Cinque, Toija.
II. Moore, Christopher (Christopher L.)   III. Redmond, Sean, 1967-
ML420.B754E53 2015
782.42166092–dc23
2015000515

ISBN:	HB:	978-1-6289-2304-9
	PB:	978-1-6289-2303-2
	ePub:	978-1-6289-2305-6
	ePDF:	978-1-6289-2306-3

Typeset by RefineCatch Limited, Bungay, Suffolk
Printed and bound in the United States of America

TC: *She'll come, she'll go. She'll lay belief on you.*
I hope [He'll] live forever . . .
CM: *You remind me of the Babe.*
SR: *I am only dancing. Give me more than one caress, satisfy*
this hungriness. The cop knelt and kissed the feet of a priest.
You, you will be Queen . . .

Contents

List of contributors

Amedeo D'Adamo was the founding dean and then president of the Los Angeles Film School, a floating graduate film-crafts conservatory in Hollywood, CA, USA. He is currently a visiting professor in the Cinéma MA at the University of Switzerland (It), teaches graduate-level film marketing and film directing at the Universita Cattolica, Italy and co-runs the Documentary Summer School at the Locarno Film Festival. He also co-founded The Traveling Film School, a non-profit organization that provides free film and theatre training to children in underdeveloped regions; it has built small tuition-free film schools in Cameroon and Sardinia. A filmmaker whose films have been in major festivals, he holds an MFA in film from Columbia University.

David Baker teaches cinema and cultural studies in the School of Humanities at Griffith University, Australia. He has followed David Bowie's work with considerable interest since his early teens in the early 1970s. He has published on popular cultural topics such as Elvis movies, lesbian vampire films of the 1960s and 70s, and Bob Dylan on screen.

Jennifer Otter Bickerdike is programme leader and senior lecturer in music and popular culture at Buckinghamshire New University. Jennifer's first book, *Fandom, Image and Authenticity: Joy Devotion and the Second Lives of Kurt Cobain and Ian Curtis* is published by Palgrave.

Will Brooker is professor of film and cultural studies at Kingston University, London, UK. His books include *Batman Unmasked*, *Using the Force*, *Alice's Adventures*, *The Blade Runner Experience* and *Hunting the Dark Knight*. His next monograph will be *Forever Stardust: David Bowie Across the Universe*.

Ian Chapman is a senior lecturer in music and convener of the Contemporary Performance Degree Programme at the University of Otago, Dunedin, New Zealand. A music iconographer and specialist in glam rock, David Bowie was the subject of both his PhD and masters theses.

Toija Cinque is a senior lecturer in the School of Communication and Creative Arts at Deakin University, Australia. She is working on the second edition of her co-authored book, *Communication, New Media and Everyday Life*, and a study of the changing media landscape in *Visual Networking*.

Glenn D'Cruz teaches drama in the School of Communication and Creative Arts at Deakin University, Australia.

Kevin Hunt is senior lecturer in design, culture and context in the School of Art and Design at Nottingham Trent University, UK. He has published articles in journals such as *Afterimage* and *Visual Communication* and his current research relates to eyes and seeing within visual culture.

Michael Mooradian Lupro is currently serving as an assistant professor and coordinator of the Senior Inquiry Program at Portland State University in Portland, Oregon, USA. Intermedia art, tourism, geography and culture studies are his broad fields of study and popular music, film, urbanization, mediation of genocide and faux-journalism have been the topics of his publications. His current research looks to Rocketman, Major Tom and Sun Ra to intervene in the development of space tourism.

Christopher Moore is a lecturer in digital communication and media studies at the University of Wollongong, Australia. His research interests include fandom, copyright, affect, materiality, online persona, the digital humanities and games studies, and he is a co-editor of *Zombies in the Academy: Living Death in Higher Education* (2013).

Tiffany Naiman is a PhD student in the UCLA Department of Musicology and the Experimental Critical Theory Graduate Certificate Program, USA, along with being an award-winning feature length documentary film producer. Her research focuses on a wide range of Anglophone popular music of the twentieth and twenty-first centuries, situating itself at the intersection of musicology, voice studies and media studies. She has a forthcoming chapter, 'Art's Filthy Lesson' which will appear in *David Bowie: Critical Perspectives* (2015).

Dene October is a research-oriented senior lecturer in the Department of Contextual and Theoretical Studies, London College of Communication, University of the Arts London, teaching 'Music Cultures', 'Fashion Body Identity' and 'Doctor Who by Design'. He is the founding editor of fbi-spy.com.

Daryl Perrins is a senior lecturer in film studies at the Cardiff School of Creative and Cultural Industries, University of South Wales, UK. He is also a PhD candidate at Royal Holloway College, University of London. His postgraduate research centres on the representation of the Welsh working class in film and television. He was educated at Coleg Harlech Adult Education College and the University of Glamorgan. He has published essays on the film *Twin Town* and working-class culture in South Wales, the Welsh in Ealing films and has co-authored a comparative study of the comedy stereotypes of Wales and Galicia.

Sean Redmond is associate professor in media and communication at Deakin University in Melbourne, Australia. He is editor of the journal *Celebrity Studies*, author of *The Cinema of Takeshi Kitano: Flowering Blood* (2013), and *Celebrity and the Media* (2013).

John Charles Sparrowhawk spent eight years as a Lloyds broker in the marine, oil, gas and North American markets. After a period as lecturer in political economy at the Shandong Finance Institute in Jinan, China, he moved to the University of North London (UNL), UK, as senior lecturer in arts and cultural management.

Tanja Stark is an artist from Brisbane, Australia. She has a background in research and social science and her work has been historically concerned with the interplay of psychology, philosophy and spirituality. She has had a series of creative installations exploring the manifestations of the Jungian shadow in suburbia.

Helene Marie Thian, a New Orleans native, graduated with distinction from the University of the Arts London/London College of Fashion Postgraduate Programme, UK. She is a Pasold Research Fund grant recipient. She spoke at London's Costume Society on Bowie and Japonism and at the V&A Museum during the 'David Bowie is . . .' exhibition, as mentioned in the acknowledgements of the eponymous book. Her work appears in Kyoto Costume Institute's *Dresstudy* journal and in the book *David Bowie: Critical Perspectives*. She welcomes enquiries on collaborative projects at helene.thian@gmail.com.

Introduction

David Bowie is one of the most influential artists of the last forty years and yet until recently has garnered minimal attention in terms of academic scholarship. This despite his: incredibly dedicated fan base; mainstream and global success; major influence in numerous cultural and artistic affairs; and the fact that he straddles the avant-garde and commercial nexus. His cultural and artistic currency is presently at an all time high with his first album in almost a decade, *The Next Day* (2013), reviewed as one of the greatest rock comebacks ever (Gill, 2013); the release of a series of portentous music videos that recall and reflect upon his artistic career; the record-breaking *David Bowie Is* global exhibition tour; and the recently released 'Sue (Or In A Season Of Crime)' from his compilation album spanning fifty years of recorded work on *Nothing Has Changed* (November, 2014).

Against this shimmering background the editors of this volume regard this to be a perfect moment to consider and reflect upon the cultural and artistic significance of 'David Bowie'. As such, this edited collection attempts to do justice to his considerable oeuvre, to fill that gap in scholarship on Bowie, at a time when he is again highly visible, releasing new music and continuing to raise complex and interesting questions about identity, stardom, nostalgia and belonging.

The question that has led and organized this edited collection on David Bowie draws provocative attention to the way his career has been narrated by the constant transformation and recasting of his star image and performative self. By asking the question, *who is he now?* the edition recognizes that Bowie is a chameleon-like figure, one who reinvents himself in and across the media and art platforms in which he is found.

This process of renewal means that Bowie constantly 'kills' himself, an artistic suicide that allows for dramatic event moments to populate his music, and for a rebirth to emerge at the same time or shortly after he expires. Bowie has killed Major Tom, Ziggy Stardust, Halloween Jack, Aladdin Sane and The Thin White Duke to name but a few of his alter-egos. In this environment of death and resurrection, Bowie becomes a heightened, exaggerated enigma, a figure who seems to be artificial or constructed and yet whose work consistently asks us to look for his *real* self behind the mask and to ask the question: is this now the real Bowie that faces us? Of course, the answer is always 'no' because Bowie is a contradictory constellation of images, stories and sounds whose star image rests on remaining an enigma, and like all stars in our midst, exists as a representation. Nonetheless, with Bowie – with this hyper-schizophrenic, confessional artist – the fan desire to get to know him, to immerse oneself in his worlds, fantasies and projections – is particularly acute, observable and most assuredly *real* in the experiential sense.

With the unexpected release of *The Next Day* on 8 January 2013, the day of his sixty-sixth birthday, Bowie was resurrected again. The album and subsequent music videos drew explicitly on the question of who Bowie was and had been, creating a media frenzy around his past work, fan nostalgia for previous Bowie incarnations, and a pleasurable negotiation with his new output. In this edited collection we seek to find Bowie in the fragments and remains of what once was, and in the new enchantments of his latest work.

The collected essays herein are both inter- and cross-disciplinary in approach, exploring David Bowie through four interlinking themes: (1) how he creates and exists in certain types of *spaces* – urban, alien, tourist and inter-galactic; (2) how he subverts and renegotiates *time* and the temporal, through anti-linearity, resurrection motifs, nostalgia and longing; (3) how he *embodies* gender, race and sexuality, opening up liminal and transgressive capacities of identification, and; (4) how his work generates, reproduces and calls upon *memory* and memorializes through sound, vision, allusion, remembering and forgetting. The selected chapters consider all aspects of David Bowie's oeuvre, from film, television, music video to live performance, including his early foray in theatre, and music output, to discuss his meanings and registers through gender, race, sexuality, song lyrics, music composition, memory and nostalgia, performance, commodity relations and the media industries that help promote him.

The title of the collection, *Enchanting David Bowie*, is meant to play out the numerous ways his work draws upon enchantment, fantasy, alter-egos and intensified forms of alienation. The authors all suggest, in different and sometimes contradictory ways, that Bowie enchants contemporary social and cultural life.

It is undeniable that David Bowie has influenced many aspects of cultural and artistic life including fashion, music, hair, and the politics and poetics of sexuality. In his art, he has long demonstrated an avid curiosity for the enduring patterns of modern life and Bowie's opus reflects the elements of ideological narratives around sexual (mis)adventure, expressivity and resistance to 'normative' behaviour. In terms of music, his work has had a profound and lasting affect on fans, and popular culture more generally. As McLeod (2003: 338) notes, his music is of fundamental importance because it:

> creates an embodied but imaginary space that mediates our internal space (feelings, desires, dreams) with external space (the physical, experienced) . . . Music takes us outside our bodies and place while simultaneously reminding us of our location and what it means to live there.

In grappling with Bowie's significance, Redmond (2012: 35) calls this a 'productive intimacy' where 'stars and celebrities feel they are an important and valued part of everyday life, and fans/consumers employ stars/celebrities to extend and enrich their everyday world . . .'. We opine then that such intertwined experiences afford indescribable, unlocatable sensation – even enchantment.

In the broader perspective, the book contributes to celebrity studies – a dynamic academic field that has become central to the work conducted by scholars across a range of disciplines and modes of enquiry. Celebrity studies has its own international, peer-reviewed journal and a growing body of writing that examines its cultural, political, economic, literary, digital, artistic footprints and sightlines. As an interdisciplinary academic field it is now widely taught across the university sector, and conferences and symposia are held around the world each year to assess its contemporary pulse and historical origins. Through an inversion of the usual teleological approach, this book offers an important circuition of David Bowie's creative output, and in doing so will introduce the reader to the key terms and concepts, dilemmas and issues that are central to the critical understanding of celebrity. The book, *Enchanting David Bowie*, is the first edited collection of scholarly essays to explore David Bowie's oeuvre from inter- and cross-disciplinary perspectives, drawing together the best writing that assesses music, performativity and identity through the circumnavigation of Bowie's various creative works.

The section summaries herein move across the interpretive themes of *space, time, body* and *memory*. Section one, 'Space', traces different conceptualizations of David Bowie through the ways in which he inhabits discrete and contradictory spaces, while creating spaces which fans can travel to, or recognize in their own personal and/or social lives. Bowie will be explored in terms of the urban, the tourist space, the space-in-between, spaces of alienation and transgression, and the alien, otherworldly space his characters and music often create or foster. The selected essays in this first section consider key aspects of David Bowie's work in this manner to make the considered claim that, in various ways, Bowie has made us aware of how we might understand the world around us not simply through visual and sonic representations but also via the space in between. Space then comes to represent the means by which we might understand what we see and hear, sometimes by what we do *not* see. In this context, space becomes the place of tension and the collapse of meaning.

Section two, 'Time', takes not a realist's view of temporality but considers its circularity wherein time folds back upon itself, allowing for the reinterpretation of memories, feelings and experiences, and all the intervals in between. Time is what we have, what we lose, a point we might look forward to or backward upon so the illation is made that it is simultaneously all and nothing, neither an event nor a thing. Bowie will be explored then through time and the temporal, as an artist who is futuristic and nostalgic, who draws upon resurrection and memorial motifs, and who 'bends' time so that an anti-linearity emerges in and through his work.

In Section three, 'Body', we consider Bowie through the carnal cartography of star embodiment. Bowie's charged and challenging body emerges in biography and auto-ethnography; song lyrics and music videos; film, theatre and television roles; in publicity and promotions; and in and across the threads and binds of his chameleon-coloured star trajectory. Bowie's body is its own meaty, sonic metronome; its movement and metric beat casting a glamorous shadow over much of the trends and fashions of contemporary rock and pop music. There are few others in the pantheon of higher-order iconicity that have done so much with their bodies to challenge the normative and bordered ways in which we are asked to survey and regulate ourselves.

In Section four, 'Memory', we explore the memorial as a bewitching site of remembering and forgetting, found in Bowie's work and in our own responses to his art, entangled as they are in the ghostly plasma of the personal. The personal memories one might have of Bowie, whether they be from a special performance, a key record, a heightened conversation or a pilgrimage to one of Bowie's sites of representation, are written into the shared and increasingly global histories of popular and subaltern cultures. Personal memories are very often collectivized and shared. Bowie becomes central to the way his fans story their lives: he is a metronome found in the beat of crisis, becoming, maturation, which are recalled in and through his lyrics, songs, performances and musings. These callings from the past are the sentient membranes that divide and memorialize both figuratively and literally; the spectres of half truths and semi-fictional contributions of Bowie as the subject of the celebrity biopic; and the experience of *Low* (1977) and its haunted figures of composer, performer and listener. This section also considers new memories shared online as the music industry becomes increasingly oriented around iTunes' downloads and YouTube views.

Summaries of each chapter in the collection can be found in the section Introductions. In preparing the manuscript, we also asked our contributors to reflect back upon their very thoughts and responses to our call for contributions, summarizing these for inclusion in the volume. We have included these personal accounts as part of the respective sections herein. This volume is a labour of love and our authors demonstrate this through the way they personally reflect upon the reasons they individually felt inspired to write about the enchantment of David Bowie.

References

Gill, Andy. 2013. 'David Bowie album review – track by track: The Starman pulls off the greatest comeback album in rock 'n' roll history with *The Next Day*', *The Independent*, 25 February, available at: www.independent.co.uk/arts-entertainment/music/reviews/david-bowie-album-review--track-by-track-the-starman-pulls-off-the-greatest-comeback-album-in-rocknroll-history-with-the-next-day-8510608.html, accessed 17 October 2013.

McLeod, Ken. 2003. 'Space oddities: aliens, futurism and meaning in popular music'. *Popular Music*, 22 (3), Cambridge: Cambridge University Press, 337–55.

Redmond, Sean. 2012. 'Intimate fame everywhere'. In S. Holmes and S. Redmond (eds), *Framing Celebrity: New Directions in Celebrity Culture*. Hoboken: Taylor & Francis, 27–43.

SECTION ONE

Space

Introduction

Resistance, alien, sacred, mythopoeic

In this section, Bowie will be explored through the way he inhabits discrete and contradictory spaces, while creating spaces that fans can travel to, or recognize in their own social life. Bowie will be explored in terms of the urban, the tourist space, the space-in-between, spaces of alienation and transgression, and the alien, otherworldly space his characters and music often create or foster. The selected essays in this section entitled 'Space' consider the aspects of David Bowie's oeuvre from such a perspective, broadly conceived, to argue that Bowie, in various ways, makes us aware of how we understand the world around us not simply through visual and sonic representations but also via the space in between. Space then comes to represent the means by which we might understand what we see and hear, sometimes by what we do not see. In this context, space becomes the place of tension and the collapse of meaning.

In the first chapter by **Michael Mooradian Lupro**, 'Keeping Space Fantastic: The Transformative Journey of Major Tom', Bowie's fictional astronaut's journey is tightly woven into the sonic fabric of space travel and considered to be associated strongly in the popular imagination with the human spacefaring future. For Lupro, dominant analyses of the song 'Space Oddity' elide the agency of the protagonist and assume forces like 'Ground Control' are indeed *in control*. Shifting the narrative analysis to include arrangements, instrumentation and recording technologies, among others, then, renders the controls on Major Tom contestable. Lupro argues that it is possible that Major Tom is not the passive victim of a catastrophic equipment failure, but rather an active participant in a costly act of rebellion against the forces of control, ground and otherwise. Since human spacefaring, and the labour that produces it, still exists more in the imagination than in material reality, the representations of contested space in texts like 'Space Oddity' represent an unprecedented opportunity to critique visions of space labour before a regime of real space labour is materially established. In personal contemplation of David Bowie, Michael passionately states that:

> David Bowie is the brightest star in the constellation of space-themed rock and 'Space Oddity' is a fixture in the popular imagination of space travel. As someone looking for models from which to construct the human future in space, Bowie looms large in my thinking and research as a glittering alternative to the normative constructions of space culture.

In his chapter, 'Ziggy's Urban Alienation: Assembling the Heroic Outsider', **Ian Chapman** identifies and explores an incarnation of alienation that has received comparatively little attention in critiques of the artist's work; specifically, urban alienation. Chapman uses a focused visual analysis of the Bowie persona of Ziggy Stardust to consider the iconography represented on the 1972 album cover for *Ziggy Stardust and the Spiders from Mars* that is, in Chapman's considered view, pre-loaded with established nuances of urban alienation, allied associations of the city, night, and space as frontiers, and heroic/anti-heroic identities. Chapman contests that Bowie constructed the liminal image of Ziggy Stardust alone at night on a London street as that of a quest-driven loner, tasked with surviving and/or taming the concrete frontier of threatening inner-city environs and suburbia. Ian's personal introspection revealed the special role that David Bowie played for him privately:

> I recognized in Bowie a champion for the marginalized, the alienated, the 'others' like myself. This quality existed in his music, certainly, but I felt it most keenly through his imagery and most particularly his album covers. From these many highly varied spaces he managed to convey his own alienation.

In **Jennifer Otter Bickerdike** and **John Charles Sparrowhawk**'s, 'Desperately Seeking Bowie: How Berlin Bowie Tourism Transcends the Sacred', the authors focus specifically on the ordinary sites in Berlin, East Germany, that David Bowie explored and lived in that have recently become significant for nostalgic fan-tourists who make the pilgrimage to the city because they are aware that he has touched that space, now rendered special. They argue that latterly, certain myths, narratives and folklore have subsequently arisen surrounding his time there. For Otter and Sparrowhawk, Bowie tourism perpetuates the rupture between such fetishized normality of his early years in the city to underscore the singer's contemporary legend. For the section author, Jennifer Otter Bickerdike, the broad concept of space to Bowie's work is important because:

Space is haunted with memories, myths and ideas of the past by those somehow connected to it, while simultaneously empty of meaning without prior knowledge or personal investment. When I approached Bowie, I realized how important place is to creating personal landscapes of value and importance of specific moments, people and things.

The final chapter in this first section is by artist/researcher, **Tanja Stark**. Her chapter, 'Confronting Bowie's Mysterious Corpses', presents David Bowie's entreaty for serious consideration; to: 'Confront a corpse at least once . . . the absolute absence of life is the most disturbing and challenging confrontation you will ever have.' Throughout this chapter, Stark critically examines Bowie's work to present the reader with the considerable number of cadavers to be found therein and the ontology they suggest. Stark argues that in Bowie's work, it is death as catharsis, as symbol, as mystery and revenge, but often wrapped in beautiful sounds that belie their darker content. Indeed, death has been an enduring companion to Bowie's creativity from the beginning; his earliest largely unknown songs from the 1960s include a quirky but murderous narrative about the death of a gravedigger and a poignant story of a lonely intellectual who jumps despairingly from a bridge. Ziggy Stardust, she argues, was virtually predicated on suicide, with genocide, homicide and crucifixion clawing their way into the oeuvre across many years. Together with the metaphorical deaths of love, faith, reason and identity, Stark contends that Bowie's corpses start piling up like some ideological morgue. Yet it is possible, Stark argues, to interpret the enduring presence of death in Bowie's creative expression as an instinctual drive for authenticity through confrontation and integration of the shadow. Tanja Stark explores here Bowie's palpable connection with mortality and the paradoxically transcendent impact this may have upon life through music and imagery, while drawing intriguing connections between Bowie and the nineteenth-century Symbolists and their mythopoeic approach to life and death. We asked Tanja about the ways in which space was an appropriate theme for her personal and scholarly views on David Bowie:

This piece plays imaginatively with poetic ideas around liminal spaces, of consciousness and mortality, themes Bowie explored so often as space became his metaphor for the psyche. Beneath Bowie's obsessions with death lie the existential questions of life that have always fascinated me. Perhaps these creative explorations around death are our way of letting our wondering minds rest in peace.

1

Keeping Space Fantastic:

The Transformative Journey of Major Tom

Michael Mooradian Lupro

What really mattered as an artist . . . was not what you did but what you were, and Bowie became a blank canvas on which consumers write their dreams.

FRITH and HORNE 1987: 115

I have been 'freak[ing] out in a moonage daydream', my entire conscious life. My earliest memory is of the broadcast of the first Apollo Moon landing. My earliest musical memory is a few years later, dancing around my yard singing the chorus of a Rolling Stones hit to my uncle's cat, Flash. So what if the original words to the song are not actually 'Jumping Cat Flash'? A full decade before the rise of Weird Al Yankovic, I had inadvertently begun engaging the flexible, customizable power of popular music.

My earliest space music memories are of Major Tom and Rocket Man. Their songs are great to sing along with, and they spurred me, born in this time when we humans were taking our first extraterrestrial steps, to imagine the potential cultural mundanity of this unprecedented technological accomplishment. These figures complicate popular visions of astronauts and, on an influential mass level, queered the narrative on human occupation of space. By tossing some oddity into the straightlaced world of the Right Stuff, these songs came to establish the foundations of the space music cannon.

Sun Ra, dreaming of a place of freedom and community, of discipline and equality, declared 'Space is the place'. Above all else, according to Sun Ra, space is a place made by music and accessed through music. As we shift into a new era of space travel, perhaps we should be working to ensure the places we make to labour and live in space will be the places of freedom and dignity to which Sun Ra aspired. I suggest here that it can be productive to consider how popular music has helped to premediate our imaginings of what life in space might be like.

As this volume amply attests to, David Bowie is a brightly shining star in the celebrity culture universe. I am interested here in how his star performances allowed those he inspired to dream up and occupy alternative spaces. Especially in the Ziggy Stardust era, Bowie aided his fans in transforming terrestrial alienation and outsider status from isolating curse to divine celestial calling. We see his playing with stardom most fully rendered in the character of Ziggy Stardust and circled back to throughout his career, but here I'd like to concentrate on how Major Tom, the figure that launched Bowie into rock star space, intertwines with our understanding of what it might be like to exist as a real human being in real space.

Bowie has used space as a place to locate difference, a place unbound by terrestrial norms of comportment and expression. Tom, as a celestial body created by and for someone willing, and able, to make themselves something liberating, powerful and influential, is worthy of a closer look in this era when private space development is returning our attentions skyward. While imaginings of space through popular music have proliferated broadly, actual human occupation of space has not kept pace. But as private space companies develop technologies with the potential to more broadly open space to human occupation, I have begun to wonder hard about the subversive potential of musical visions of space given that the production of space has shifted from military industrial to entertainment industrial corporations. In the next section, I ask the reader to think about the context of renewed efforts to put people in space and speculate on how these efforts might intersect with our popular productions of space. I'll then review the extant interpretations of 'Space Oddity' before sharing conclusions from my deep engagement with the lyrics, instrumentation, arrangements, vocalizations and production elements of the song.

The different stuff

As the private enterprise of real human spaceflight begins to take off, the question of what kind of place space might become is an open one. One of the salient differences between the new space race and the previous one is that entertainment-industrial transnational corporations are wresting the monopoly on human space travel from national governments and their military-industrial partners. Another significant development is that the astronaut corps of the near future will feature private citizens. The heroics of those who have made the journey out of Earth's atmosphere earn them the credentials to be called the Right Stuff, but identifying such a narrow part of the spectrum of humanity as the Right Stuff implies that most of us are the Wrong Stuff.

For those investing in and inventing new space technologies, technical and economic concerns override the cultural and social, so this is the time to intervene in the process of developing broader definitions of the Right Stuff for space, before space is actually occupied by real, working, people occupying spaces otherwise produced more technocratically than democratically. The developers of space do not see the probability of inequality as a problem, if they see it at all. There is a glaring disparity between frontier myths and frontier realities, specifically the socioeconomic inequalities elided by frontier myths.

Patricia Limerick is specifically interested in the frontier American West, but I believe the evidence of the race, class and gender disparities she brings to light in that historical location illuminate our understanding of frontiers generally (1987). In fact, Limerick has consulted with NASA, applying her analysis of the American West frontier to the frontier of space development. According to Limerick, despite the utopian nature of frontier discourses, the lived reality of frontier existence harshly replicates existing socioeconomic relationships, exacerbating existing inequalities and thoroughly dashing the hopes of those who come dreaming of a better life (1994). If we apply postcolonial analysis of previous frontiers to the precolonial stages of the space frontier it seems probable that without some precolonial intervention, there is little reason to suspect that the space frontier will be any different from previous frontiers when it comes to conditions for working-class labour. Should the traditional trajectory of terrestrial tourism development indeed hold true for space, then the first large groups of people to become citizens of the space frontier will be some combination of service workers staffing space tourism facilities and perhaps miners. Assuming that the treatment of this class of workers in the current conjecture is not fundamentally upended in the immediate future, broader space development would thus start off on an extremely inequitable footing, and from a labour point of view would replicate and extend the grossest terrestrial economic inequalities. Making matters potentially worse, the first space tourism facilities, including those that would house space labourers, may be completely privately constructed and controlled, far from terrestrial governments and unions and their attendant regulation of occupational health, safety and equity. There is little cause for optimism regarding the free market providing equal opportunity or sufficient protections to space tourism service workers. However, through Tom, and later Ziggy, Bowie helps to premediate the space frontier with more sociocultural freedom than previous frontiers.

Ground Control

Though I've painted a somewhat grim picture so far, it is far from too late to intervene in constructing space differently, or more specifically, to construct a space that is safe for difference. Since space is largely a cultural construction with, as of yet, relatively little materiality, it is not too late to intervene. I believe that the location of intervention is where music and space development meet and Bowie's 'Space Oddity' is a sign marking the trailhead.

Chris Hadfield, commander of the International Space Station, has actually lived in space. He has also made a critical contribution to global pop culture by becoming the first person to make a music video in space. The song he covers in the aforementioned video is 'Space Oddity'. By choosing this song in particular, Hadfield cements Major Tom's place as a significant contributor to the collective human construction of space. Back on Earth, Hadfield served as the voice of Ground Control but now he has used that same voice to certify the preeminent presence of oddity and difference in space. Hadfield also changed how space is mediated to the public, opening interest in space through his use of social media tools to promote the science taking place on the Station he commanded, the sartorial charge of space vistas, his musical collaborations and his 'Space Oddity' video. With his active participation in new media and his choice to give 'Space Oddity' a central place in his use of it, Hadfield also helps to strengthen the bridges between how space is culturally produced and how it might actually be colonized. Hadfield's oddity is somewhat tempered by conservative production, choices in lyrical changes, and the general rounding off of many of the original song's harder edges, but the video can still help the project of providing opportunities to keep space a frontier of possibility, inclusive of the odd and different.

The following examination of 'Space Oddity' centres on the proposition that the work of engaging with sound and music can play a role in creating a different space, or more precisely, different spaces in which our greatest hopes for the future and yearnings for freedom will move beyond utopian rhetoric and into material reality. Because of the role that entertainment and technology companies like Virgin, Amazon and PayPal are playing in the new private space race, I contend that the cultural production of space through pop music and pop culture more generally is part of what it will take to ensure that future space cultures are more equitable and more socially just than previous human frontiers. To 'boldly go' even further, because the political economy of the new space race is on the leading edge of the global shift from dominance of the military-industrial complex to entertainment-industrial relations, the sounds of space may represent an unprecedented opportunity to meaningfully intervene in the future of capitalist labour relations more broadly.

Music can and does create space. As Peter Doyle (2005), Delueze and Guatari (1987) and others have imaginatively demonstrated, the capacity of music to mark and map territory can have material consequences in place- and space-making. As Doyle (2005: 234) puts it in the conclusion to *Echo and Reverb*:

> Time and life might move on, and the current participants might go with it, but the fact of musical space-making, of territory-creating (rather than the specific attributes of any particular territory), once discovered, was there to be rediscovered and reinvented by others, in other places, at other times, for other purposes.

Space technology themes in music have been a consistent source of empowerment through which marginalized voices are given a safe forum for the exploration of new modes of identity (McLeod, 2003; Taylor, 2001). Music generates this empowerment by creating 'an embodied but imaginary space that mediates our internal space (feelings, desires, dreams) with external space (the physical, the experienced)' (McLeod, 2003: 337). In her examination of the late 60s counter culture of progressive rock, Whitely (1992: 3) concurs with McLeod on the function of space in relation to rock, specifically in regard to the relationship between popular music, cultural production and the liberatory potential of music as a symbolic act. The empowering potential of space in rock music, combined with the fact that these space themes have a long history of interaction with the real colonization of space (McLeod, 2003: 338), is the source of popular music's potential to help imagine and produce space.

Musical space interventions like 'Space Oddity' are created sonically as much as lyrically. As John Street (2001: 248) suggests, 'the politics lies in the sounds and their structures, in the way they refuse or embrace musical orthodoxies, in the way they follow and disturb expectations. The message can be in the mix'. The multivalent 'Space Oddity' narrative is thus more than the lyric or the song alone but also its performance, arrangement, recording, promotion, film, video and other expressions.

Many readings of 'Space Oddity' focus on 'the dangers of technological nihilism and alienation in a society that had increasingly become dehumanized' (Cagle 1995: 112). A focus on the technodystopic view of 'Space Oddity' leads Cagle to conclude that Major Tom is a suicidal Luddite:

In an act of technological treason, the major disconnects the transmitters in the spacecraft, purposely barring his communication with Earth. While the rocket spins uncontrollably, he proclaims that his situation is hopeless. Alone and absorbed in his suicidal destiny he mockingly screams the viewpoint of his commanders in charge, as if he is boasting about, yet damning, his act of anarchy. Such a message suggests an odd sense of irony in Major Tom's decision; he is to spend his last days of human existence differently from all those who have died before him, as he will terminate his life in space – by his own hand.

Cagel, 1995: 112

Auslander (2006: 128) also speaks of 'Space Oddity' as a statement of counter cultural technophobia, though his view is much less fatalistic:

A sense that the technology is in the hands of people who do not have Major Tom's best interests at heart emerges when the first thing he is asked after entering orbit is to endorse a brand of shirts; here, the song reflects the counterculture's general suspicion of commodity culture and its relationship to the military-industrial complex . . . The consequence is that Major Tom is rendered helpless to address the world's ills.

While the technophobia Auslander and Cagle see in 'Space Oddity' is certainly operative, I will show that the song can be more than a technophobic lament, or even a precursor to the questioning of normative sexuality, but rather an opening for a more thorough and generalized questioning of human existence in the space age.

The readings offered by Auslander (2006) and Cagle (1995) are reasonably derived conclusions from the lyrical narrative, but they do not explicitly question nor decentre identity, authority or the dominant narratives of space as would be suggested by a more expansive understanding of 'Space Oddity'. An alternative reading of 'Space Oddity' replaces the interpretation of Major Tom as a helpless victim of a technological mishap with a vision of him as an active participant in altering the conditions of his labour. What happens if we consider the possibility that when Tom steps through the door, freeing himself of Ground Control, he becomes Ziggy Stardust? Rather than a suicidal Luddite or hapless victim of space danger, Tom becomes a star. Tom's act of singular resistance makes possible a different space, space that has a place for the Wrong Stuff. His *celestial/musical* stardom emboldens the queer and sanctions the odd. Ziggy Stardust and his admirers cosmically travelled through the outer reaches of culture rather than be controlled by dominant authorities.

Commencing countdown, engines on

The song fades in at the beginning and out at the end, evoking a sense that the song is in orbit around the relatively fixed point of view of the listener. This bookended fade implies timelessness and perspectival relativity in that 'Space Oddity' precedes and endures the consciousness of the listener. As the deliberately paced percussive strum of a solo acoustic twelve-string guitar arrives, the faint martial rat-a-tat-tat of the snare drum becomes regular and grows louder. This spare funeral march is eventually joined by the wheezy strains of a mellotron.

With a discomforted and distant setting established, Ground Control declares its presence . . . pauses a beat . . . and then reiterates the declaration. The tone of the communication from Ground Control is bureaucratic and bored, as if issuing commands is a regrettable but required component of everyday official conduct. Mundanely authoritative, Ground Control speaks clearly in a single voice, mixed loud in this introductory section of the lyric to stand alone atop the other instruments.

Major Tom then receives his first set of instructions, a basic health and safety reminder to use his prescribed drugs and protective gear. The purpose and composition of his protein pills is left ambiguous but, given the sociocultural context, can be reasonably assumed to be standing in for psychedelic drugs and may also refer to the popular official drug regime of psychiatric rehabilitation. Either way, Ground Control is inciting its subject to alter his body chemistry. The coercive power in the incitement is revealed through a second, subservient voice of the Ground Control narrator, which is higher in pitch, softer, and mixed a little lower and behind the first. Two voices together remind Major Tom that the earlier single voice represents an institutional and social power greater than that of an individual.

The initial single voice of Ground Control then returns and reissues its declaration of presence, but this time the subordinated other voice counts backwards from ten. As the engines ignite on Ground Control's command, the parting note to Major Tom is a blessing of God's love.

Once the protagonist arrives in this space, the pace of the song picks up as signalled by the percussive strumming of the acoustic guitar and the slow driving boom-boom splash boom-boom splash of the drums. Major Tom's tin can is now in motion; the journey has been joined. Ground Control speaks in both voices at once all the way through this section of the song. Everything but the voices is mixed a little louder so that the noise of the engine competes equally with the basic track. Ground Control's tone is congratulatory, but seems slightly desperate as it informs Major Tom of his celebrity, consumer status and commercial potential. To complete the lucrative deal, Major Tom must dare to leave the safety and comfort of his capsule. The vocal tone of Ground Control sounds both confident of his compliance and cognizant that there are now limits to its power. The direct coercion available before take-off is no longer an option. Ground Control can't force Major Tom to leave the capsule, and so rather appeals to his sense of daring, promising to make him a celebrity if he complies.

We are nearly 40 per cent through the song chronologically before we hear from Major Tom. His voice is strong and double tracked to evoke a more powerful singularity, but not confident enough to mask unease and uncertainty. He first calmly follows communication protocol by announcing his identity as the speaker. He then declares that he indeed intends to leave the capsule, as Ground Control has dared him.

The stars look very different, today

Now we arrive at the point of peak multivalence. What might Bowie invoke when singing 'And I'm floating in a most peculiar way, and the stars look very different, today?' One reading centres on the rendering of celestial ethereality created by the backing instruments as they fill an extremely large range of the listening spectrum, big in the ear but still in the background. The voice shifts here from singular centred to multiple stereo, an unusual recording technique at the time which, according to Pegg (2000: 198), Bowie insisted on against the objections of his producer. The synthesized celestiality and the stereo vocals figure Major Tom as a universal cosmopolitan speaking uneasily for, of, and to, multiplicitous positions.

When Bowie pronounces 'in a most peculiar way' in a most peculiar way, he stumbles between 'most' and 'peculiar' so that it comes to the ear pronounced most a-peculiar (or most uh-peculiar). The a/uh utterance preceding 'peculiar' may work as a countering incitation of resistance. From this perspective, Major Tom's floatation is not strange or extraordinary at all, but a-peculiar, not-different, mundane, quotidian, everyday. Major Tom's experience of space becomes startlingly unremarkable. What then happens to the meaning of the next line, 'the stars look very different, today' in the context of his a-peculiar floating? The easy interpretation is that the stars look different because Tom's journey is a metaphor for a drug trip and so, at first reading, the line would seem (since 'very different' invokes the exceptional) to belie the supposition that Tom's peculiar floatation signifies the mundane. However, the strained force with which Bowie sings 'today' at the end of the line points to the possibility that these lines – those following 'stepping through the door' – do indeed mark Tom's turn towards resistance. 'Today' follows a micropause at the end of 'different'. Split out of both of the doubled vocal tracks, 'today' can be heard here like weary protest marchers answering to the staple: 'What do we want . . .? When do we want it?' (What do we want? Different stars. When do we want it? Today!)

So if the way Tom is floating is not peculiar but a-peculiar and 'today' marks a resistant immediacy, what is different about the appearance of the stars? From the perspective of the notion that Tom is performing some form of resistance, combined with the prospect that space travel turns out to be disappointingly regular, it is not the appearance of the stars themselves that is different, but rather Tom's altered consciousness and subsequent counter-hegemonic subject position after his epiphinal decision to resist his construction at the hands of Ground Control. His newly resistant consciousness transforms the way the stars register and how they are understood. Having broken free of Ground Control upon 'stepping through the door', Tom is seeing the stars, his environment, and perhaps even his own power to resist, in a new way. What is significant here is not the exact nature of this new way of seeing the stars but rather the fact of seeing them differently, of becoming different. New possibilities for seeing and experiencing space become possible and are animated by Tom's newly asserted agency. What might be producible in the territory Tom creates once he steps through the door?

Reinforcing this sense of liberated movement and difference is the manner of bass playing. Whereas the bass is a grounding presence in rock songs generally, the bass throughout the song, and with increased emphasis beginning in this section, is consistently irregular, as if searching for somewhere to be rooted. Throughout its kinetic journey, the bass remains solid, more confident than desperate, but completely unsettled at the same time. The bass simultaneously does its traditional job of holding down the low end of the overall sound while its place in the mix draws attention to the fact that the bass is keeping location mobile and indeterminate.

Tom's voice shifts from forcefully declarative when he is speaking defiance to Ground Control to sadly resigned as he turns to a more personal reflection on his own new status. Having defied Ground Control, Tom finds himself alone, 'sitting in a tin can, far above the world'. It is worth pausing for a moment to consider why Tom refers to his spaceship, an artefact of the leading edge of military-industrial/capitalist technological production, as a 'tin can'. Certainly, the shape and construction materials of his vehicle are associable to a tin can but in the context of his recent declaration of resistance, his diminished assessment of space travel technology can be read against the grain of the dominant ideologies of astrofuturism. Tom views his tin can not as a triumph of advanced engineering but a confining container for cheap meat.

In other words, stepping through the door, breaking from Ground Control and separating oneself from the dominant social structure entails a not insignificant personal cost. The first price paid by Tom, and anyone else who steps through such a door, is isolation – from those who remain inside and from the rewards of compliant acquiescence. So, contrary to the popular reading of the song that suggests Tom commits suicide, I suggest, rather, that he commits a metaphorical *social* suicide. Much like the end days of the 60s counterculture, against which Bowie positions himself at this early stage of his artistic career, placing oneself counter to the dominant culture severs connections with mainstream society. One's grounding in the material realities of the majority is lost. This critique of the cost of resistance, and of the shortcomings of 60s counterculture relative to the coming corporatization of rock (a project to which Bowie becomes a significant contributor), can also be read in the instrumental break that follows this section of the lyric.

The last new lyric in the song is a final transmission from Ground Control: 'your circuit's dead, there's something wrong'. As Ground Control repeats its final query, the voice sounds slightly confused or unbelieving, unable to come to terms with Tom's actions. 'Can you hear me Major Tom?' is repeated three times with diminishing presence in the mix, creating distance between Ground Control and Tom. The ground and control fade into the distance and the 'hear' in the final plea doubles as 'here'. Tom takes back the vocal and redeclares his presence in his tin can. The remainder of the song repeats the line from 'sitting in my tin can' to 'planet earth is blue . . .' and concludes with an extended version of the preceding instrumental break. Finally, the world turns, the listener remains behind, and Tom fades into the distance.

Message from the action man

Over the next several years, Bowie would continue to explore and develop the idea that those who live in or come from space are metaphors for popular culture productions of the notion of the rock star, always milking maximum multiplicity of meaning from the words 'star' and 'space'. The most relevant intertextualization of 'Space Oddity', besides Peter Schilling's direct homage, occurs in the lyric to 'Ashes to Ashes' from the 1980 *Scary Monsters* album. *Scary Monsters* comes at one of many significant turning points in Bowie's career. As Bowie moults his last fully formed alternate self he revisits Major Tom, only this time, Tom is more clearly standing in not only for humanity generally, but for Bowie the rock star as well.

The bass playing and percussion in 'Ashes to Ashes' is an early foray into the more danceable material to come from Bowie in the 80s when he avails himself of the R&B production aesthetics of Chic's Nile Rodgers. In the time between the recording of 'Space Oddity' and 'Ashes to Ashes' the methods used to produce sonic space shifted from out-there and experimental to standard popular music production practice. Rather cleverly, the synthesizers in 'Ashes to Ashes' rest comfortably within the contemporary range of their use while at the same time intertextualizing and updating the outlandish sounds of space on 'Space Oddity'. So while the sonic narrative of 'Ashes to Ashes' marks the 80s Bowie as a contemporary phenomenon in tune with the times, the lyrical narrative returns to the timelessness of space and Major Tom's place in it.

In the first stanza of 'Ashes to Ashes', Bowie hears 'a rumour from Ground Control' that he fears may be true. My contention that Major Tom is an active agent in resisting Ground Control is reinforced by Bowie's invocation of Tom as 'the action man' from whom a message filled with 'sordid details' is sent. An action man is not likely to have been a passive victim of a technological mishap, nor driven to suicide by technophobia. Though Tom does report that he is happy and aspires for the happiness of others as well, he does so in the form of a generic greeting that may be more perfunctory than revelatory. After all, there are 'sordid details' that he alludes to but does not share. 'I've loved all I've needed loving' can easily be folded into Bowie's bisexual mythmaking. On Tom's return journey, he sees a glowing earth rather than the blueness of the planet invoked in 'Space Oddity'.

This section of the song confuses point of view – who is speaking in this section? Tom, Major Tom, Bowie or a new character? More narrative possibilities are opened by confusing Bowie's self and his character from 'Space Oddity' – the 'guy that's been in such an early song' as Tom is referred to in 'Ashes to Ashes'. Tom/Bowie loving all needing love, when connected with Tom's parting salutation in 'Space Oddity', 'tell my wife I love her very much she knows', reiterates the possibility that Tom is figuratively leaving behind monogamous heterosexual normativity and that his peculiar floating is experimentation with sexuality as well as with drugs and autonomy. Read in this way, Tom/Bowie is creating space as a queered and open place for difference.

When the song reaches the chorus, we learn that 'Major Tom's a junkie, strung out on heaven's high, feeling that all time low' and this information is positioned as something 'we [all] know'. Revisiting Major Tom, the 'guy that's been in such an early song', Bowie treats the costs of resistance, of creating one's own space, as self-evident. As we've seen already in 'Space Oddity', Bowie consistently uses vocal performance, arrangement, instrumentation and recording to invoke multiplicity, and thus the caution incited in 'Ashes to Ashes' is more than one against the addictive pitfalls of narcissistic rock stardom. I suggest that he also offers the same rebuke to individual acts of resistance that take place outside the bounds of community. What good is Tom's resistance to Ground Control if the price is the loss of one's spouse and a descent to an 'all time low'? Tom suffers for his decision to defy Ground Control.

I think my spaceship knows which way to go

Though I have gone to great lengths to outline some of the subversive potential represented in Major Tom, it is worth considering a potentially contradictory meaning of the concluding section of 'Ashes to Ashes' in which Bowie repeats, mantra-like, the line 'my momma said, to get things done, you better not mess with Major Tom'. I see two main ways to interpret this. One is that the narrator is an apologist for Ground Control which views Tom as a subversive enemy of progress and that the song is a warning, launched in the early 80s by an established progenitor of corporate rock, against a return to the 60s politics of countercultural possibility. Another way to look at the lyric is as a more personal reconsideration of late 60s political action in which Major Tom is, like a weatherman for example, an impetuous individual actor who puts one's own need for immediate resistance ahead of a more considered long-term strategy developed with and in a broader community of stakeholders.

As evidence of this latter position, that Tom suffers adverse consequences from his lone resistant actions, I turn to Bowie's recapitulation of Tom as social actor in the final verse of 'Ashes to Ashes'. In the earlier verses of the song, the voice is performed in a strained and delicate falsetto with a twinge of sadness, whereas in the final lines transitioning into the bridge the voice is multiplied and stronger. By contrast, the final verse revisits the voicing Tom uses to declare that he was 'stepping through the door' in 'Space Oddity', a forced forcefulness that is powerfully resistant but that also presages a resignation to the social costs of political resistance. The lyrical narrative, though sung with force, is stuck between accepting one's past actions and wanting at the same time to alter the ultimate outcome. In this retrospective on his actions, Tom is neither hero to the counterculture nor petulant agitator against the dominant power structure. He has not done good or bad, but rather has acted the way anyone would have in his position and has, in his opinion, done so with consideration of predictable values and reason; he has done nothing 'out of the blue'. There are some additional possibilities to consider here given the polyvalent meaning held by 'blue' in 'Space Oddity'. Recall that blue was used to signify both sadness and the trope of spaceship Earth, the vulnerable and interconnected home to all humanity. Tom 'never did anything' outside the purview of the Earthbound values of humanity, except of course that he is floating out in space by himself; cold, alone, and increasingly frustrated by the impossibility of return, wanting to 'break the ice'. Whereas he sounded alternately defiant and melancholy in 'Space Oddity', in 'Ashes to Ashes' Tom sounds persecuted. And whereas he started this journey with the relatively passive action of stepping through a door, ten years on he is frustrated and lonely enough to consider picking up an axe to resolve his increasingly untenable situation.

As Bowie sings elsewhere (in the song 'Heroes' for example), heroism has a very short shelf life. Furthermore, when resistance and countercultural production is of an individual acting out their own sense of exceptionalism, as does Tom, the action will stand alone and the actor will be alone.

From Rocketman to Sun Ra, space is not a place for unproblematized heroes, but it is a place where problematized stars might open space that works against future 'social science fictions' (Nelson 2002: 1). For those interested in rendering space as a place Sun Ra would be welcome, an equitable frontier, hearing Major Tom is a productive place to begin.

References

Auslander, Philip. 2006. *Performing Glam Rock: Gender and Theatricality in Popular Music*. Ann Arbor: The University of Michigan Press.

Cagle, Van M. 1995. *Reconstructing Pop/Subculture: Art, Rock, and Andy Warhol*. Thousand Oaks, London, New Delhi: Sage Publications.

Deleuze, Gilles and Felix Guattari. 1987. Trans. Brian Massumi. *A Thousand Plateaus: Capitalism and Schizophrenia*. Minneapolis: University of Minnesota Press.

Doyle, Peter. 2005. *Echo and Reverb: Fabricating Space in Popular Music Recording 1900–1960*. Middletown: Wesleyan University Press.

Frith, Simon and Howard Horne. 1987. *Art into Pop*. London and New York: Methuen.

Limerick, Patricia Nelson. 1987. *The Legacy of Conquest: The Unbroken Past of the American West*. New York: W.W. Norton.

Limerick, Patricia Nelson. 1994. 'What is the cultural value of space exploration?' *What is the Value of Space Exploration?: A Symposium*. Sponsored by the Mission From Planet Earth Study Office, Office of Space Science, NASA Headquarters and the University of Maryland at College Park, 18–19 July. Washington, DC: National Geographic Society.

McLeod, Ken. 2003. 'Space oddities: aliens, futurism, and meaning in popular music'. *Popular Music*, 22 (3), 337–55.

Nelson, Alondra. 2002. 'Introduction: future texts'. *Social Text*, 71 (20/2), summer, 1–15.

Pegg, Nicholas. 2000. *The Complete David Bowie*. Richmond: Reynolds & Hearn.

Street, John. 2001. 'Rock, pop, and politics.' In *The Cambridge Companion to Pop and Rock*, edited by Simon Frith, Will Straw and John Street. New York: Cambridge University Press, 243–55.

Taylor, Timothy D. 2001. *Strange Sounds: Music, Technology, and Culture*. New York, London: Routledge.

Whiteley, Sheila. 1992. *The Space Between the Notes: Rock and the Counter-culture*. London, New York: Routledge, 1992.

Discography

Bowie, David. 1969. 'Space Oddity,' *David Bowie*. Mercury, 1969. Re-released on *Space Oddity*. RCA, 1975.

Bowie, David. 1972. *The Rise and Fall of Ziggy Stardust and the Spiders from Mars*. RCA Victor.

Bowie, David. 1977. "Heroes," *"Heroes"*. RCA.

Bowie, David. 1980. 'Ashes to Ashes,' *Scary Monsters (and Super Creeps)*. RCA.

John, Elton. 1972. 'Rocket Man', *Honky Chateau*. Uni. Reissued on *Elton John's Greatest Hits*. MCA, 1974.

Schilling, Peter. 1983. 'Major Tom,' *Error in the System*. Elektra.

Filmography

Space is the Place. 1974. Screenplay by Sun Ra and Joshua Smith. Dir. John Coney. Perf. Sun Ra and Raymond Johnson. North American Star System.

2

Ziggy's Urban Alienation: Assembling the Heroic Outsider

Ian Chapman

Introduction

Alienation is a thematic cornerstone of David Bowie's work, an observation frequently made by critics. This quality is frequently cited as something of a fait accompli, however, with little effort being made to unpack the nature of such alienation. Through iconographical analysis of a single image, the front cover of his 1972 breakthrough album, *The Rise and Fall of Ziggy Stardust and the Spiders from Mars*, this chapter seeks to determine with considerably more depth and specificity the nature of Bowie's alienation.

As a central component of his performative palette, Bowie has frequently taken the position of an outsider, and in so doing he has provided something of a rallying call for those who may themselves feel alienated. The manifestations of alienation evident in his work have fallen within a variety of categories including generational, psychological, technological, physical, and alienation based upon gender. Brief examples of each of these alienations include, respectively, the lyrics from 'All The Young Dudes': 'My brother's back at home with his Beatles and his Stones – we never got it off on that revolution stuff', where the artist emphatically distanced himself from the 60s countercultural generation; the depiction of schizophrenia on the cover of *Aladdin Sane* where his mask-like face was split by a lightening flash, thus indicating psychological disturbance; the hopeless isolation of astronaut Major Tom in 'Space Oddity', 'And I think my spaceship knows which way to go'; the cover of *Diamond*

Dogs where the obvious freakshow allusion introduced the concept of alienation through physical deformity; and the covers of the albums *The Man Who Sold the World* and *Hunky Dory* where gender was emphatically problematized.

Moore suggests that Bowie provides 'a focus, for the general public, of a whole range of cultural practices converging on rejection' (2001: 127). Frith purports, 'Bowie's fans have always identified with him particularly intensely, because no one else has captured so well their sense of difference' (1988: 136). Of this evident ongoing stance as an 'other', Bowie himself has said (in Miles 1980: 61–2):

> I do tend to stand on the outside sometimes. I don't know whether it's a failing or whether it's an advantage. My own feeling is that I hope very much that an outsider's viewpoint is as beneficial, if not more beneficial, than that of somebody who is completely involved.

On the front cover of the album at hand, Bowie is certainly an outsider. Extreme tension exists between his image and the surroundings in which he is pictured, creating a liminal space that requires much of the viewer if sense is to be made of the picture. Simply, he does not belong where he is found. Thomassen (2014: 1) suggests, 'Liminality refers to moments or periods of transition during which the normal limits to thought, self-understanding and behaviour are relaxed, opening the way to novelty and imagination, construction and destruction.' As will be seen through discussion of pertinent elements of the *Ziggy Stardust* cover image, this invitation to create one's own meaning from the picture is the quality that might best account for the ongoing fascination with this iconic image.

In order to critique alienation in Bowie's work, and to begin to identify and discuss its specific manifestation on the album cover at hand, it is first necessary to discuss alienation in a broader historical sense to provide a working definition appropriate to the task.

Alienation

Alienation within sociological theory was introduced by Karl Marx in *The Economic and Philosophical Manuscripts of 1844* (Kaufmann, 1971: xvi).[1] Originally employed as a term of economics, describing the process whereby production exploited workers under a capitalist system, Marx saw alienation existing in three variants: within the process of the production itself; from the actual objects produced; and from nature and humanity (Israel, 1971: 53). While the emphasis in this founding definition was placed on working conditions rather than personal psychological state (Israel, 1971: 207), as Horowitz points out, the term has since been the subject of much scholarly debate, undergoing many reinterpretations of meaning to ultimately become 'part of the tool kit of social psychology and social stratification' (1996: 17).

Despite Marx's original definition having been considerably broadened, many theorists agree that his fundamental dictum of separation remains largely sound, and that alienation 'in every variation suggests the loss or absence of a previous or desirable relationship' (Kenniston, 1972: 34). A working definition of alienation that fluidly acknowledges this debt to Marx and acknowledges the personal psychological effect of the condition is the proposition that industrialization and increasing technological advancement within society can result in a lack of individual identity and responsibility (Victor, 1973: 7). The common origins and the personal, psychological, impact of the condition is described as:

> . . . the loss of the natural condition of selfhood, that is, alienation from one's core being. Because this loss cannot be originated within the self – i.e. there is no reason for the human agent in his/her natural state to become self-alienated – the source of the deterioration is typically traced to the environment (e.g. defective economic or work conditions, urban life, consumerism, social influence).
>
> Gergen, 1996: 117–18[2]

Similarly, Israel suggests that effective analysis of alienation within its broadest, most common sociological meaning, should consider, 'The individual's experience of his own situation . . . against the background of sociological phenomena' (1971: 207).[3] In further explanation of how the condition manifests, Nevill believes, 'The fundamental characteristics of alienation involve feelings of loss, powerlessness, meaninglessness and estrangement from self and society' (2009: 135–6). I consider these descriptions to be entirely apt for the current investigation, as the portrayal of an individual somehow out of balance with both his personal and sociological surroundings is common to all of Bowie's multiple manifestations of alienation.

While alienation at large is a central component within Bowie's work, this chapter is concerned with a particular manifestation of alienation that has received relatively little attention: urban alienation.

Urban alienation

At times Bowie has visually and textually located his work within the city, a site preloaded with associations of emotional isolation and disassociation; a site of urban alienation. Both the *Ziggy Stardust* and *Diamond Dogs* albums are prime examples of this. The city and urban experience potentially acts to 'separate the self from imagination and creativity. Alienation is estrangement . . . [and is] the experience for many urban dwellers' (Bridge and Watson, 2000: 9).

Cities may be seen as either the epitome of humankind's achievements, or as being completely counterproductive to a healthy way of living. Some may regard them as 'the subjects of utopian imaginations and hopes for better futures . . . crucibles for potential enlightenment, democracy and freedom' (Pinder, 2005: vii).[4] As Von Der Thusen points out, 'The fact that utopias have often been given an architectural and urban form [suggests] . . . the city represents human existence in its most ideal form' (2005: 2). Equally, however, cities may be seen in a very negative light:

> Anti-urban imaginaries have been forcefully in play in literary, art, and political texts for as long as there have been cities. Here the associations are with the city as a site of anomie, alienation, corruption, ill health, immorality, chaos, pollution, congestion, and a threat to social order.
>
> Bridge and Watson, 2000: 15–16[5]

Williams neatly summarizes this duality when suggesting that the city offers the 'excitements and challenges of its intricate processes of liberation and alienation, contact and strangeness, stimulation and standardisation' (1985: 23).[6]

Silverstone suggests that some British popular music, and particularly Bowie's work, directly addresses the alienation felt by suburban youth. He suggests Bowie effectively offers deliverance through adventure, because 'The young are trapped and bored. They dream complex media dreams that shudder between the mundane and the apocalyptic' (1997: 24). Silverstone further sees Bowie's response to this as 'the turning of suburban alienation into aesthetic objects and cultural commodities' (1997: 24).

In order to arrive at a concise working definition of urban alienation appropriate to the current investigation, I have reduced its characteristics to just two widely agreed upon conditions: (1) the great size of population in big cities can result in depersonalization, and (2) the technology-dominated landscape is frequently seen as dehumanizing. Similarly summative, as

Fischer points out, alienation in all of its widely understood meanings has been linked to industrialization, mass society and the erosion of community, 'all forces seemingly epitomised by the city' (1973: 311).

The album

Released in June 1972, *The Rise and Fall of Ziggy Stardust and the Spiders from Mars* was the album that elevated David Bowie to the level of a preeminent popular music artist. Pegg's appraisal is typical of historical summations, describing it as 'Bowie's first hit album and his ticket to superstardom' (2002: 234).[7] Reaction at the time of the album's release was similarly enthusiastic, with *New Musical Express* reviewer James Johnson writing, 'There's nothing Bowie would like more than to be a glittery superstar, and it could come to pass . . . this latest chunk of fantasy can only enhance his reputation further' (1972: 12).

Not only was it Bowie's first commercially successful album, *The Rise and Fall of Ziggy Stardust and the Spiders from Mars* received widespread critical acclaim, dramatically increasing the size of his fan-base and providing the springboard to subsequent sold-out tours and unprecedented levels of media interest.[8]

Set in an urban scene at night, the cover shows David Bowie/Ziggy Stardust front-on to the viewer, located low and centralized within the frame. He is dwarfed by his surroundings, with industrial brick buildings looming above him to his left, while parked cars are situated to his right. At the rear, similarly-styled buildings are set against the dark, rain-heavy sky. The footpath where Bowie stands is wet and shiny, giving the impression that rain has been falling. Occupying the bottom right of the picture in the foreground is a collection of cardboard boxes and a large bundle of shredded or torn paper in a clear plastic bag. The front box is open at the top, the text L.I. CO. LONDON No. 2003 hand-written upon the front. Above and slightly behind, occupying the centre of the cover, is a large yellow sign with the lettering K. WEST. Lights glow yellow from windows, while a large streetlight above Bowie's head illuminates both him and the green door at his left. The bright colouring of Bowie's costuming and hair set him apart in stark contrast to the dominant browns and greys of the bricks, concrete and sky. His exposed chest and light mode of dress seem completely incongruous in the seemingly wet and presumably cold conditions of what we might justifiably contend to be a winter's night. Dressed in a light blue jumpsuit open at the front and exposing his chest, he has his left leg raised and bent at the knee. His right arm rests easily there, while his purple left boot is positioned upon a rubbish bin. Bowie's hair is an unnatural bright yellow hue. He holds an electric guitar against his side at waist height, supported by a wide black strap across his shoulder.

The clear incongruity between Bowie and his environment is a disparity noted by commentators, with Moriarty suggesting 'The album's cover depicted Bowie, clad in a futuristic jumpsuit with guitar slung low, looking as though he had just beamed down from his mother ship to a dark London street' (2003: 99). Buckley too has commented upon this in suggesting that, such is Bowie's apparent displacement, the scene might well be set in a parallel universe populated by aliens rather than in London (1999: 136). Auslander suggests 'Bowie seems not to belong to the urban landscape in which he appears' (2006: 126), while Gillman and Gillman regard the scene as 'an image of urban loneliness' (1986: 280). Simply, Bowie's presence is jarring; he clearly does not belong. The album cover image is one of urban alienation.

Because Bowie's location is urban-industrial rather than suburban-residential, and clearly identified as England's capital city, inferences of both industrialization and mass society are inherent to the image. The erosion of community, suggested by Fischer earlier as a central component of alienation, is here an absence of community – given that Bowie is the only visible figure. Certainly the lights shining in the buildings suggest the unseen presence of others, yet the fact that these hidden protagonists are indoors, presumably warm, dry and safe on this dreary night, serves to further underline Bowie's isolation within the scene.

The city at night

Cities undergo a marked change after darkness falls. Throughout the daylight hours, or the 'working day', the city streets are the hub of industry and commerce, bustling with workers who day after day carry out their myriad labour roles to ensure the city fulfils its primary reason for being. Indeed, for a capital city such as London, a recognized global leader of capitalism, expectations of its performance on the stage of world commerce are as high as they can possibly be. As Blum describes it, 'The city which is at the centre of a civilization is the capital precisely because it can make the dissemination of the question of worldly desire its capital concern' (2003: 163).

At night, however, those same city streets that during the day held industry and commerce sacrosanct become the playground for the workers who enabled that daytime function. The streets become sites for entertainment, for stress-release and the exploration of imagination, or as Blum puts it, public stages for the 'nocturnal liberation' of the populace (2003: 160). While the daytime city is epitomized by order and control, the night offers uncertainty and possibility, a complete transformation of 'a realm where ordering tendencies are often ascendant but various counter-processes erupt and are displaced to the night or the margins' (Edensor, 2000: 137). At night the city's workers ostensibly become of equal status, both management and rank-and-file alike freed up from their prescribed daytime roles and imposed hierarchy to be suddenly, with the movement of a clock-hand, egalitarian. They have leisure time on their hands; time to do as they please. Night-time in the city offers them the opportunity to put into practice that which they may have imagined during the confines of their working day, because 'even in the spaces of alienation, shackled to the production line, acts of the imagination like daydreams form sites of resistance' (Bridge and Watson, 2000: 9). In this guise then, although it may be perceived as drab and dreary, the city scene in which Bowie appears can be read less as a site of oppression and control than a site of transformation, excitement and unknown potential.

Further, while night-time in the city offers release from constraint through the entertainments and distractions that are available to all those with leisure time at their disposal, the lack of daytime order and control and the potential for concealment within the surrounding darkness in which these activities take place also creates the potential for danger. If actual danger itself is not present, then certainly the atmosphere still elicits the suggestion of danger (Melbin, 1978: 11).[9] Blum believes that 'night is typically talked about in terms of crime and security or deviance and governance . . . free time releases "destructive" temptations as idleness exacerbates the natural vulnerabilities of people, exposing them to conditions that bring out their worst' (2003: 146). Individuals experiencing leisure time at night within inner-city environments have historically enjoyed opportunities for unscripted, heightened experience outside the safety and control of the working day. Bailey, drawing upon the work of sociologist and philosopher Georg Simmel, suggests that through a combination of chance, accident and necessity, such leisure time in the big city has always offered adventure based upon, to varying degrees, the presence of an inherent risk (2004: 4).

In addition to workers adopting different roles when remaining in, or returning to, the city at night, the altered function of the central urban space attracts other protagonists from suburbia. This includes those who work outside the inner city, certainly, but also, and crucially, it draws a large contingent of youth seeking respite through adventure to relieve them from the mundane nature of life in suburbia. As Silverstone sees it, 'The city is the lamp around which suburban moths flutter: camp, elegant, marginal and modestly dangerous, and in all of these things resolutely other than dully suburban' (1997: 23). Frith regards Bowie as 'the quintessential suburban star' (1997: 271), further remarking that the artist conveys to his fans:

> . . . the lure of the city – the metropolis at the end of the local railway line, a metropolis not to occupy but to visit . . . at the weekend, for the occasion, in a gang. In pop terms London is a peculiar place . . . Suburban sensibility here concerns the enactment of escape (rather than escape itself) and the domestication of decadence.
>
> 1997: 272

In this sense then, on the front cover of the *Ziggy Stardust* album Bowie can be seen to be providing a visual enactment of the night-time flight of an alienated 'other' (Ziggy Stardust, or perhaps Bowie himself), to the inner city in search of, or already in the midst of, an adventure. Lehan describes the presence of the 'other' in a major city as 'a disturbing presence . . . an urban element, usually a minority, deemed "outside" the community . . . the mysterious stranger – the Dionysus figure . . . the mysterious man from nowhere who disrupts the city from within' (1998: 8). Clearly, such a description resonates with Bowie's picture, as there is no evident explanation for his out-of-context presence; he is 'a mysterious man from nowhere' indeed. Equally, there is a widely held perception that night is 'the haunt of weirdos and strange characters' (Melbin, 1978: 10). This view is backed up by Thomas, who suggests the nocturnal environment of the city is 'the preserve of "alien" groups' (1992: 61).

Such notions have been well considered in other forms of art, including, and most especially pertinent to this current discussion, within film noir.

Film noir

The *Ziggy Stardust* cover has been hand-coloured, thereby adding a layer of artificiality to the scene that 'exaggerates the strangeness of his appearance' (Auslander, 2006: 239).[10] This is a filmic allusion, 'The unnatural, hand-tinted hue [giving] the impression of a noirish, Hollywood stage set' (Paytress, 1998: 91). This quality also exaggerates the effect upon Ziggy of the streetlight positioned above him, creating a mask-like over-saturation that eliminates individuality and imbues his face with mystery.

Indeed, the composition of the cover picture shows a marked similarity to the visual characteristics of film noir, a filmic style that is primarily concerned with the expression of urban alienation (Dimendberg, 2004: 7).[11] In film noir, 'lonely characters in empty, urban spaces evoke a sense of urban alienation. The city is usually shown at night and in the rain' (Mennel, 2008: 47). Further outlining a typical city scene for film noir, Spicer suggests, 'Film noir's iconography consists of images of the dark, night-time city, its streets damp with rain which reflects the flashing neon signs' (2002: 48). This is a scenario echoed by Vincendeau, who identifies the primary visual motif for film noir as a city scene at night, 'illuminated by shiny cobblestones and pierced by gleaming neon signs' (1992: 54).

The plot of the album, too, has commonalities with film noir. Vincendeau outlines the genre's essential characteristics, suggesting the on-screen action was designed to match the off-screen emotions of the audience by 'Mirroring anxiety . . . [a] sense of hopelessness, of destructive forces . . . The myth of escape, from country, identity or circumstances . . . [where] the dream of escape is thwarted. Endeavours are doomed and heroes will be destroyed' (1992: 55).[12] Such a description is directly applicable to the *Ziggy Stardust* album, where Ziggy, overcome by the destructive forces of rock and roll excess, fails in his quest to deliver to the Earth and its inhabitants an escape from the doom predicted in the album's opening track, 'Five Years'. Ziggy's quest bears a close relationship to Muller's observation that 'Film noir pointed toward the black core of corruption in our "civilized" society and our primitive essence. The struggle of the individual to transcend or escape provided the emotional tension' (1998: 11).

Glam rock

Locating the *Ziggy Stardust* album cover within the time in which it was released provides considerable further insight as to its potential for social impact. Glam rock, circa 1971–5 (approximately) offered its followers an escape from the confinement, drudgery and physical, mental and emotional restrictions of the inner city and suburbia. The wider reinventive promise of glam rock was that one could transcend one's immediate physical, social and even sexual environment to construct a new idealized version of the self.[13] This notion is in alignment with Norman's (1990: 7) description of the heroic vision:

> Whereas man perennially trembles in the face of Paradise Lost – of chaos, uncertainty, destruction, alienation, night and death – but also of overwhelming ecstasy, life and day, what is of the highest concern is the possibility that a heroic vision may dawn within each of us, to be assimilated – beyond theory or intellectualization – into our everyday lives.

Such a notion illustrates the desire for transcendence from the world of the mundane through becoming a rock and roll hero, and is therefore fully in keeping with glam rock's fundamental 'dream of common people promoted to stars' (Lenig, 2010: 11). The following lyric line from 'Star', the seventh track on the *Ziggy Stardust* album, sums this desire up perfectly: 'I could make a transformation as a rock 'n' roll star'. Such a declamation is consistent with the notion of embarking upon a quest; that Bowie, as Ziggy, is facing a frontier that must be conquered at all costs. If Ziggy Stardust is indeed set to embark upon a frontier, however, then what is its nature?

Frontiers

The American western frontier has been seen as a readily transferable concept; a location for hopes and dreams (Aquila, 1980: 415). As McLure puts it in her contextualization of the internet as the newest frontier, 'The perceived virtues and heroic figures of the American West have always provided familiar, inspiring models for current conditions and problems, particularly during times of economic transition, rapid cultural changes, or social stress' (2000: 458).[14] And as Aquila points out:

> The new westerner might be a surfer, skier, hippie instead of a cowboy, miner or farmer, but he is still searching for the same thing. His West, like the mythic West of the nineteenth century, is a promised land of immediate, personal, physical enjoyment, fulfilment, or escape.
>
> 1980: 432

The sense of threat or risk that exists in a city at night, as encapsulated in film noir, is consistent with the challenges of a transferred frontier. There exists around every corner, in every darkened doorway, the potential for adventure, a quality also intrinsically linked to the potential presence of 'others'. As Blum puts it, 'night has evoked an aura of ferocity and unruliness, personified in the notion of "the last frontier"' (2003: 141). Melbin too has regarded night in the city as a frontier, suggesting 'Both land frontier and the nighttime have reputations as regions of danger and outlawry' (1978: 10). As Bowie stands alone on the wet concrete of a nondescript, urban industrial London street, his countenance purposeful and alert despite a studied casualness, he might well be regarded as a kind of futuristic frontier hero. His diminution in the frame highlights the enormity of the task ahead of him; he is alone and small, pitted against both the daunting city and the challenges of the night.[15] In addition, implications of space and science fiction introduce a further frontier allusion.

Space as frontier

Space provides a further variant of the transferred American western frontier and has been a commonly used analogy. Deudney suggests, 'Space is humanity's high frontier. Like all frontiers, space has produced unexpected treasures, generated strong enthusiasts, spawned wild speculations, and been enshrouded in myth and false promise' (1982: 5). In popular entertainment, space has been trumpeted as the ultimate modern frontier, epitomized most particularly perhaps through the well-known spoken voiceover from the theme of the popular US science fiction television series, *Star Trek*: 'Space – the Final Frontier'.

Space had figured previously among Bowie's thematic concerns. Padel is just one of many commentators who have aligned Bowie to the space-as-frontier notion, regarding him in his role of Ziggy Stardust to be a tragic hero and suggesting '[he] is the astronaut, who dares . . . to boldly go where no man has gone before. David Bowie turns this into a psychonaut, inventing a persona, Ziggy Stardust, an alien hermaphrodite messianic pop deity' (2000: 238–9).[16]

Space is not represented overtly within the cover image, as, notwithstanding the grey sky above, the picture is very much an earthbound scene. Yet Bowie's jumpsuit and boots are to a degree similar in style, if not in colour, to clothing worn by astronauts in popular science fiction representations such as Kubrick's *2001: A Space Odyssey*, and television series such as *Lost in Space* and *Buck Rogers*, thus providing a strong visual inference. Crucially, the album's title and other written text on the cover provide a strong paratext that significantly strengthens that inference. The words 'Ziggy Stardust and the Spiders from Mars' on the front, in conjunction with song titles on the rear cover including 'Moonage Daydream', 'Starman', 'Lady Stardust', 'Ziggy Stardust' and 'Star', ensure that space is a prominently highlighted element.[17] These paratexts serve to (re)direct with more contextual focus the viewer's eye towards Bowie's unlikely presence within the scene, collectively bearing out Pegg's view that the image conveyed the 'adventitious impression that the guitar-clutching visitor to this unglamorous twilit backstreet has just touched down from another dimension altogether' (2002: 241). Bowie, or Ziggy, might well have materialized on the spot, much in the manner of the Star Trek crew teleporting down to the surface of an alien planet, or Dr Who's Tardis materializing amid who knows what or where. As Cato candidly put it, 'Bowie looking like a stranger from an unknown land, leaning against the wall, Gibson hanging nonchalantly against hip, outside K. West furriers on a deserted and rain-swept London backstreet, was just so fuckin' out of this world' (1997: 30).

Hero/antihero

By virtue of his diminution within the frame and the clear alienation from his dominating surroundings, Bowie might well have appeared vulnerable in this image. However, his countenance is strong, even confident, thereby transcending the threat. His stance is seemingly that of a hero.[18] Indeed, Dawson has described Bowie as 'a modern heroic figure' (1994: 276).

The traditional hero is, by nature, a figure alienated from the frontier in which he or she operates. As Victor puts it, 'In exploring origins of hero myths, alienation emerges as an essential feature' (1973: 22). As a would-be heroic figure then, Bowie's alienation too is exactly as it must be, for as Tasker also purports, the hero is 'a figure who lacks a place within the community for which he fights' (2002: 77). His stance on the Ziggy Stardust cover is certainly similar to the manner in which British military heroes are frequently depicted, as can be observed in London statues of military luminaries such as Lord Horatio Nelson (Trafalgar Square), Major General Sir Henry Havelock (Trafalgar Square), Major General Robert Clive (Whitehall) and General Charles James Napier (Trafalgar Square). As is the case with each of these heroic depictions, Bowie too is positioned squared-up and front-on to the viewer, his gaze fixed and his expression serious and unsmiling as if in acknowledgement or contemplation of the enormity of the quest that lies before him.[19] There are parallels to be drawn too with the tradition of the British swagger portrait, a theatrical style of portraiture that emphasizes bravado and ostentation, implying 'a degree of self-consciousness . . . which causes the portrait to transcend the private statement and address itself to the public at large. There is therefore an element of rhetoric in it, even of challenge' (Wilton, 1992: 17). The military heroes and Bowie are both positioned with one foot forward of the other, as if beginning the act of stepping into the frontier that awaits them, 'implying past and future movement' (Summers, 1996: 783). Bowie's pose, with the weight of the body borne on one leg while the other bends, approximates a positioning termed *contrapposto* in art historical terminology, and is considered an ideal male heroic pose.[20] In addition, each of the military heroes is depicted carrying weapons or other tools of their trade at their side, with each of them carrying a sword and two of them carrying rolled-up documents. Bowie's guitar therefore becomes highly symbolic as the weapon with which he will tackle his quest; the preeminent symbol of rock and roll, the electric guitar or 'axe'. Padel exemplifies this idea when describing Jimi Hendrix as 'A guitar hero, brandishing the magic weapon that turned him into a god' (2000: 81).

That Ziggy ultimately fails in his quest to save the earth, and particularly noting the nature and means of his demise, invites one to ponder his status as hero or antihero. Both the story and the album cover picture bear a strong thematic resemblance to the 1969 movie *Midnight Cowboy*, the qualities of transferred frontier and urban alienation common to both. The plot of *Midnight Cowboy* tells the story of a young Texan man, Joe Buck, who leaves his home to find his fortune in New York City. Once there, however, the naïve adventurer becomes swallowed up by the impersonality and street-savvy ways of the vast city, totally failing in his attempts to hustle for a living. During his quest, however, he finds friendship with another societal outcast, the physically handicapped Enrico Rizzo. Ultimately they escape the city by bus for Miami, but Rizzo dies en route. At the movie's end Buck is left sitting with his arm around his dead friend, gazing out of the bus window. The city is seen to have won the battle; the would-be heroes vanquished, their alienated status absolutely confirmed.

In the movie posters for *Midnight Cowboy*, Buck's cowboy attire renders him completely out of place within the inner-city New York surroundings that encircle him, whether framed by the steel girders of the Brooklyn Bridge under a heavy, oppressive and smog-laden sky, or surrounded by the bright lights of a vibrant night-time scene downtown. His western frontier image should rightly be located in rural, wide-open-spaces locales and not in the inner city, which accordingly takes on a sinister aura of a kind that a cowboy is not traditionally equipped to combat. Effectively, *Midnight Cowboy* takes the American western frontier legend and transports it to a new location, treating the city as frontier.

> Like the traditional western hero, Joe sets out to conquer a daunting, dangerous frontier. But he faces, again, not a landscape of open, unsullied, 'natural' possibility but the metropolis, a center of global capitalism, a well-trodden landscape of abundant riches and misery alike.
>
> Floyd, 2001: 109

Rizzo too, limping badly from the effects of polio, dressed all in black with his long overcoat pressed tightly to his frame, projects a lonely figure that is similarly 'alienated, uncertain, and agitated' (Bapis, 2008: 100). Indeed, the two figures are as alienated by their surroundings as the blue jumpsuited Bowie/Ziggy appears to be in his London scene.

That Buck and Rizzo's quest as outsiders aspiring to make their fortune in New York City should fail so dismally and completely is in keeping with Clapp's observation that, in movies addressing the theme of urban alienation, 'It is a rarity that the city is conquered. Survival of self or one's values is perhaps the best that can be achieved by those with conquest in mind' (2005: 9). Bowie/Ziggy's quest to save the Earth from destruction also fails, his redemptive zeal and transformative ardour blunted by the all too urban excesses of rock stardom, sex, substance abuse and ego. In this light, then, and as was the case with Buck and Rizzo, Bowie is far more antihero than hero, a flawed being who cannot measure up to the primary expectation of a true hero; that is, 'The hero of legend always overcomes tremendous odds' (Steckmesser, 1963: 173).[21] In his quest, Ziggy Stardust clearly succumbs rather than overcoming.

A further contemporaneous antihero comparison might be drawn between *Ziggy Stardust* and the 1976 movie, *Taxi Driver*, in which a psychologically unstable ex-Vietnam War veteran struggles to cope with the challenges of being a night-time taxi driver in New York City. The taxi-driver, Travis Bickle, a survivor of the transferred western frontier of the Vietnam War and thus a military hero of sorts, fails to cope with the new version of the frontier he faces in the city-at-night back in his home country, a challenge full of decadence, sleaze and corruption that he single-handedly attempts to right. The advertising poster for the movie, with the city rising up dark and foreboding behind him, epitomizes urban alienation and is highly reminiscent of the Bowie image from four years earlier.[22]

Bowie has also long acknowledged his admiration for the work of Stanley Kubrick, most particularly the movies *2001: A Space Odyssey* (1968), and *A Clockwork Orange* (1971):

> For me and several of my friends, the seventies were the start of the twenty-first century. It was Kubrick's doing on the whole. With the release of two magnificent films, *2001* and *A Clockwork Orange*, within a short period, he pulled together all the unarticulated loose ends of the past five years into a desire of unstoppable momentum.
>
> Bowie and Rock, 2002: 12

As was Anthony Burgess' original novel upon which the movie was based, Kubrick's work too was set in London. As McDougal puts it, the location was a London 'of the near future' (2003: 7). Farber, meanwhile, regarded the urban setting for Kubrick's work as 'the nightmare city of tomorrow' (1972: 288). In his 1971 review of the film, Robert Hughes described the location as a 'subtopia . . . [with] alienating décor' (2003: 131). And, beyond the similarity in location, the costuming worn by Bowie/Ziggy bore significant resemblance to costuming seen in the movie. Bowie has candidly admitted this influence: 'I had just seen *A Clockwork Orange* and had been galvanised not only by Kubrick's startling visualisation of Burgess's novel but also his take on functional-chic youth outfits' (Bowie and Rock, 2002: 17).

The title track, 'Ziggy Stardust', is the moment on the album when Ziggy becomes irreparably consumed by his fame; the point where his quest to save the Earth ultimately, irreconcilably, fails. Written from the perspective of a jealous band-member, the lyrics document the rift that developed between the star and his backing musicians, as Ziggy 'took it all too far'. Describing Ziggy as a 'leper messiah', the rise and fall element of the album's title is here brought to life, the descriptor clearly laying out the triumphant and tragic extremities of the hero's failed quest and confirming his antihero status. With 'messiah' representing the very essence of one who promises salvation, epitomizing the very peak of fame and influence, and 'leper' then instantly and completely undercutting it to the lowest possible level of societal hierarchy, the term juxtaposes opposites; hero with antihero.

The inclusion of the word 'droogie' in the song 'Sufragette City' is a clear reference to *A Clockwork Orange*, the central protagonists of which were termed droogs. Of this, Paytress makes a telling observation: 'It was impossible to listen to the urban rush of "Suffragette City" in the summer of 1972, especially in the wake of the *Clockwork Orange*-inspired panic over mugging, without imagining that cities were places where only the strong could survive' (1998: 87).

Aspects of the plot of the Kubrick film can also be gleaned in the plot of *Ziggy Stardust*, a point noted at the time of the album's release, with Watts, for instance, suggesting the apocalyptic scenario outlined in the album's opening track, 'Five Years', was 'exactly the sort of technological vision that Stanley Kubrick foresees in *A Clockwork Orange*' (1972: 19). The protagonist in the song 'Star' opts for reinvention as a rock star in outright rejection of the conventional career choices on offer for a young man in London, 1972, having earlier distanced himself from the world of parents/adults in 'Starman' through the line 'Don't tell your Papa or he'll get us locked up in fright', and from conventional faith in the belief systems of religion and politics during 'Soul Love'. Similarly, in *A Clockwork Orange*, Alex too 'has a cynical view of his parents, clearly rejecting their jobs, their care, and their aesthetics . . . The institutions of the family, industry, and politics are seen as corrupt and unsatisfying' (Gabbard and Sharma, 2003: 89). Further, Gabbard and Sharma regard Alex, who chooses violence as his means of expressing this dissatisfaction, as a hero figure, suggesting, 'The artist-as-hero rejects older systems of belief . . . The arbiter's consciousness functions as the arbiter of society and as the only index of change' (2003: 89). Ziggy Stardust, while similarly disillusioned, chooses not violence but rock and roll as his agent of change. Unlike the weapons of violence borne so casually in the hands of the four droogs in *A Clockwork Orange*, Bowie instead clasps an electric guitar as his weapon of choice.

Conclusion

The front cover of *The Rise and Fall of Ziggy Stardust and the Spiders from Mars* is a powerful, liminal and multi-faceted depiction of urban alienation. David Bowie as Ziggy Stardust is pictured in heroic guise, an obvious outsider who bravely, even casually, faces the tripartite threat provided by the transferred frontiers of the city, of night, and of space. Armed with an electric guitar as his weapon, he is alone in the city, alone in the night, and alone as a spaceman/alien-being figure; his estrangement emphatically rendered. As has been shown, each of these locations carries with it inherent inferences of alienation, while the hero – or antihero – figure is itself, by its very nature, a naturally highly marginalized entity. With his extreme diminishment in the frame acting as a representation of the size of the quest that lies ahead of him, the image borrows established and heavily loaded iconography from film noir while also evoking comparisons to contemporaneous and highly successful movies of the late 60s and early 70s that each in turn have urban alienation at their core. Thematically contemporaneous also with glam rock – the preeminent popular music style of the day – the image conveys the central promise of that style; of transcendence from the humdrum of urban/suburban existence through an invitation to dream of escapism and betterment through personal reinvention. As claimed in the title of this chapter, through his careful assemblage of visual componentry centred upon urban alienation, Bowie indeed claimed for himself the status of heroic outsider.

Notes

1   See also Israel, 1971: 2–5 and Finifter, 1972: 3.

2   See also Geyer, 1996: x.

3   See also Seeman, 1959: 783.

4   See also Hindery and Reiner, 1984: 133.

5   See also Lehan, 1998: 8, and Von Der Thusen, 2005: 2.

6   For further discussion of city duality, see Pinder, 2005: vii, and Briginshaw, 2000: 109; also Von Der Thusen, 2005: 5.

7   This view is shared by a majority of critics. See Edwards and Zanetta, 1986: 159. Also Sandford, 1996: 90–2.

8   For an overview of Bowie's newfound success and increased popularity, see Buckley, 1999: 147–8. Also Pegg, 2002: 234–42.

9   See also Dixon, 2007, 243.

10 See also Pegg, 2002: 239.

11 See also Clapp, 2005: 14, and Silver and Ward, 1979: 5. Also Silver and Ursini, 1999: 51.

12 See also Hibbs, 2008: xv.

13 See Hoskyns, 1998: 3–8 and Hebdige, 1979: 59–62. Also Auslander, 2006: 234.

14 Also see Smith, 1970.

15 Mark Paytress is one of few critics to have discussed Bowie's diminution within the frame on this album cover, but rather than considering it to be a representation of urban alienation or having any sort or heroic implication(s), he suggests it is an important device designed to dissolve the distinction between David Bowie and Ziggy Stardust, the performer and the role. See Paytress, 1998: 91.

16 See also Cagle, 1995: 146–7, and Paytress, 1998: xi.

17 Providing yet further support, the rear cover picture of Bowie in a phone box is highly reminiscent of a peculiarly British form of space transport, a police phone box called the Tardis, favoured by Time Lord, Doctor Who, the central character in the BBC science fiction television series, *Dr Who*.

18 Although, as will be discussed shortly, Ziggy assumes more an antiheroic role as the story of the album unfolds.

19 A point made by several Bowie biographers is that the neon sign, K. West, situated above Ziggy on the album cover, acts as a metaphor for his quest to save the Earth. While I have not been able to find any evidence that this was at all intentional on Bowie's part, and indeed it seems unlikely, it is certainly a point to acknowledge. See Paytress, 1998, 91: and Pegg, 2002: 239.

20 See Sheehy, 2010: 37. Also Wills, 1997: 18.

21 See also Simmons, 2008: ix.

22 *Taxi Driver* is widely seen as a late example of film noir. See Hibbs, 2008: 107–16. Also Naremore, 2008: 34–7, and Schwartz, 2005, 33–6.

References

Aquila, Richard. 1980. 'Images of the American West in rock music'. *The Western Historical Quarterly*, 11 (4), 415–32.

Auslander, Philip. 2006. *Performing Glam Rock: Gender & Theatricality in Popular Music*. Ann Arbor: University of Michigan Press.

Bailey, Peter. 2004. 'Adventures in space: Victorian railway erotics, Or taking alienation for a ride'. *Journal of Victorian Culture*, 9 (1), 1–21.

Bapis, Elaine M. 2008. *Camera and Action: American Film as Agent of Social Change 1965–1975*. Jefferson: McFarland & Company Inc.

Blum, Alan. 2003. *The Imaginative Structure of the City*. Montreal: McGill-Queens University Press.

Bowie, David and Mick Rock. 2002. *Moonage Daydream: The Life and Times of Ziggy Stardust*. Guilford: Genesis Publications Ltd.

Bridge, Gary and Sophie Watson. 2000. 'City imaginaries'. In *A Companion to The City*, edited by Gary Bridge and Sophie Watson. Oxford: Blackwell Publishers Ltd, 7–17.

Briginshaw, Valerie. 2000. 'Dancing bodies in city settings: construction of spaces and subjects'. In *City Visions,* edited by David Bell and Azzedine Haddour. London: Pearson Education Ltd., 107–20.

Buckley, David. 1999. *Strange Fascination: David Bowie: the definitive story.* London: Virgin Publishing Ltd.

Cagle, Van M. 1995. *Restructuring Pop/Subculture: Art, Rock, and Andy Warhol.* Thousand Oaks: Sage Publications.

Cato, Philip. 1997. *Crash Course for the Ravers: A Glam Odyssey.* Elkton: S.T. Publishing.

Clapp, James. A. 2005. '"Are you talking to *me?*": New York and the cinema of urban alienation'. In *Visual Anthropology*, 18, 1–8.

Dawson, Graham. 1994. *British Adventure, Empire and the Imagining of Masculinities.* London: Routledge.

Deudney, Daniel. 1982. *Space: The High Frontier in Perspective.* Washington, DC: Worldwatch Institute.

Dimendberg, Edward. 2004. *Film Noir and the Spaces of Modernity.* Cambridge: Harvard University Press.

Dixon, Wheeler W. 2007. 'Night world: New York as a noir universe'. In *City That Never Sleeps: New York and the Filmic Imagination,* edited by Murray Pomerance, Piscataway: Rutgers University Press, 243–57.

Edensor, Tim. 2000. 'Moving through the city'. In *City Visions,* edited by David Bell and Azzedine Haddour. London: Pearson Education Ltd., 121–40.

Edwards, Henry and Tony Zanetta. 1986. *Stardust: The David Bowie Story.* New York: McGraw-Hill Book Company.

Farber, Stephen. 1972. 'The old ultra-violence'. In *The Hudson Review* 25 (2), 287–94.

Finifter, Ada F. 1972. 'Concepts of alienation'. In *Alienation and the Social System,* edited by Ada F. Finifter. New York: John Wiley & Sons Inc.

Fischer, Claude S. 1973. 'On urban alienations and anomie: powerlessness and social isolation.' In *American Sociological Review* 38 (3), 311–26.

Floyd, Kevin. 2001. 'Closing the (heterosexual) frontier: *Midnight Cowboy* as national allegory.' In *Science & Society Color, Culture and Gender in the 1960s,* 65 (1), 99–130.

Frith, Simon. 1988. 'Only dancing: David Bowie flirts with the issues.' In *Zoot Suits and Second Hand Dresses: An Anthology of Music and Fashion*, edited by Angela McRobbie. Boston: Unwin Hyman Inc., 132–40.

Frith, Simon. 1997. 'The suburban sensibility in British rock and pop.' In *Visions of Suburbia*, edited by Roger Silverstone. London: Routledge, 269–79.

Gabbard, Krin and Shailja Sharma. 2003. 'Stanley Kubrick and the art cinema.' In *Stanley Kubrick's 'A Clockwork Orange',* edited by Stuart Y. McDougal. Cambridge: Cambridge University Press, 85–108.

Gergen, K. J. 1996. 'Postmodern culture and the revisioning of alienation.' In *Alienation, Ethnicity, and Postmodernism,* edited by Rudolf F. Geyer. Westport: Greenwood Press, 117–25.

Geyer, Rudolf F. 1996. Introduction in *Alienation, Ethnicity, and Postmodernism*, edited by Rudolf F. Geyer. Westport: Greenwood Press.

Gillman, Leni and Peter Gillman. 1986. *Alias David Bowie.* London: Hodder & Stoughton.

Hebdige, Dick. 1979. *Subculture: The Meaning of Style.* London: Methuen & Co. Ltd.

Hibbs, Thomas S. 2008. *Arts of Darkness: American Noir and the Quest for Redemption.* Dallas, Texas: Spence Publishing Company.

Hindery, Michael A. and T. A. Reiner. 1984. 'City planning: images of the ideal and the existing city'. In *Cities of the Mind: Images and Themes of the City in the Social Sciences*, edited by Lloyd Rodwin and Robert M. Hollister. New York: Plenum Press, 133–47.

Horowitz, Irving Louis. 1996. 'The strange career of alienation: how a concept is transformed without permission of its founders'. In *Alienation, Ethnicity, and Postmodernism,* edited by Felix Geyer. Westport: Greenwood Press, 17–19.

Hoskyns, Barney. 1998. *Glam: Bowie, Bolan and the Glitter Rock Revolution.* London: Faber & Faber Ltd.

Hughes, Robert. 2003. 'The décor of tomorrow's hell.' In *Stanley Kubrick's 'A Clockwork Orange'*, edited by Stuart Y. McDougal. Cambridge: Cambridge University Press, 131–3. Originally published in *Time,* 27 December 1971.

Israel, Joachim. 1971. *Alienation: From Marx to Modern Sociology.* Boston: Allyn & Bacon.

Johnson, James. 1972. '*David Bowie: The Rise and Fall of Ziggy Stardust and the Spiders from Mars.*' In *New Musical Express*, 10 June.

Kaufmann, Walter. 1971. 'The inevitability of alienation.' In *Alienation* by Richard Schact. London: George Allen & Unwin Ltd., xiii–lvi.

Kenniston, Kenneth. 1972. 'The varieties of alienation: an attempt at definition.' In *Alienation and the Social System*, edited by Ada F. Finifter. New York: John Wiley & Sons Inc., 32–44.

Lehan, Richard. 1998. *The City in Literature.* Berkeley and Los Angeles: University of California Press Ltd.

Lenig, Stuart. 2010. *The Twisted Tale of Glam Rock.* Santa Barbara: Praeger.

McDougal, Stuart Y. (ed.). 2003. *Stanley Kubrick's 'A Clockwork Orange'.* Cambridge: Cambridge University Press.

McLure, Helen. 2000. 'The Wild, Wild Web: the mythic American West and the electronic frontier'. In *The Western Historical Quarterly*, 31 (4), 457–76.

Melbin, Murray. 1978. 'Night as frontier.' In *American Sociological Review*, 43 (1), 3–22.

Mennel, Barbara. 2008. *Cities and Cinema.* New York: Routledge.

Miles, Barry. 1980. *Bowie in his own Words.* London: Omnibus Press.

Moore, Alan. 2001. *Rock: The Primary Text.* Aldershot: Ashgate Publishing Ltd.

Moriarty, Frank. 2003. *Seventies Rock: The Decade of Creative Chaos.* Lanham: Taylor Trade Publishing.

Muller, Eddie. 1998. *Dark City: The Lost World of Film Noir.* London: Titan Books.

Naremore, James. 2008. *More than Night: Film Noir in its Contexts.* Berkeley: University of California Press.

Nevill, Annemarie. 2009. 'Over 60 and beyond . . . the alienation of a new generation: exploring the alienation of older people from society'. In *Theorising Social Exclusion,* edited by Ann Taket, Beth R. Crisp, Annemarie Nevell, Greer Lamaro, Melissa Graham and Sarah Bert-Godfrey. New York: Routledge, 134–42.

Norman, Dorothy. 1990. *The Hero: Myth/Image/Symbol.* New York: Anchor Books.

Padel, Ruth. 2000. *I'm A Man: Sex, Gods and Rock'n'Roll.* London: Faber & Faber Ltd.

Paytress, Mark. 1998. *Classic Rock Albums: The Rise and Fall of Ziggy Stardust and the Spiders from Mars.* New York: Schirmer Books.

Pegg, Nicholas. 2002. *The Complete David Bowie.* London: Reynolds & Hearn Ltd.

Pinder, David. 2005. *Visions of the City.* New York: Routledge.

Sandford, Christopher. 1996. *Bowie: Loving the Alien.* London: Warner Books.

Schwartz, Ronald. 2005. *Neo-Noir: The New Film Noir Style from Psycho to Collateral.* Lanham: Scarecrow Press Inc.

Seeman, Melvin. 1959. 'On the Meanings of Alienation'. In *American Sociological Review,* 24 (6), 783–91.

Sheehy, Coleen J. 2010. 'Bruce's Butt: masculinity, patriotism, and rock's ecstatic body.' In *Coverscaping: Discovering Album Aesthetics,* edited by Asbjorn Gronstad and Oyvind Vagnes. Copenhagen: Museum Tusculanum Press, 21–42.

Silver, Alain and James Ursini. 1999. *The Noir Style.* New York: The Overlook Press.

Silver, Alain, and Elizabeth Ward. 1979. *Film Noir: An Encyclopedic Reference to the American Style.* New York: The Overlook Press.

Silverstone, Roger. 1997. Introduction to *Visions of Suburbia,* edited by Roger Silverstone. London: Routledge, 1–25.

Simmons, David. 2008. *The Anti-Hero in the American Novel.* New York: Palgrave Macmillan.

Smith, Henry N. 1970. *Virgin Land: The American West as Symbol and Myth.* Cambridge: Harvard University Press.

Spicer, Andrew. 2002. *Film Noir.* Harlow: Longman Press.

Steckmesser, Kent L. 1963. 'The Frontier Hero in History and Legend'. In *The Wisconsin Magazine of History,* 46 (3), 168–79.

Summers, David. 1996. 'Contrapposto'. In *The Dictionary of Art: Volume Seven,* edited by J. Turner. London: Macmillan Publishers Ltd., 783.

Tasker, Yvonne. 2002. *Spectacular Bodies: Gender, Genre, and the Action Cinema Comedia.* London: Routledge.

Thomas, Deborah. 1992. 'How Hollywood deals with the deviant male'. In *The Book of Film Noir,* edited by Ian Cameron. New York: Continuum, 59–70.

Thomassen, Bjorn. 2014. *Liminality and the Modern: Living Through the In-Between.* Farnham: Ashgate.

Victor, George. 1973. *Invisible Men: Faces of Alienation.* Englewood Cliffs: Prentice Hall.

Vincendeau, Ginette. 1992. 'Noir is also a French Word: the French antecedents of film noir.' In *The Book of Film Noir,* edited by Ian Cameron. New York: Continuum, 49–58.

Von Der Thusen, Joachim. 2005. 'The city as metaphor, metonym and symbol'. In *Babylon or New Jerusalem?: Perceptions of the City in Literature,* edited by Valeria Tinkler-Villani. New York: Rodopi, 1–11.

Watts, Michael. 1972. 'Oh You Pretty Things'. In *Melody Maker*, 22 January.

Williams, Raymond. 1985. 'The Metropolis and the emergence of modernism'. In *Unreal City: Urban Experience in Modern European Literature and Art*, edited by David Kelley and Edward Timms. Manchester: Manchester University Press, 13–24.

Wills, Garry. 1997. *John Wayne's America*. New York: Simon & Schuster.

Wilton, Andrew. 1992. *The Swagger Portrait: Grand Manner Portraiture in Britain from Van Dyck to Augustus John 1630–1930*. London: Tate Gallery.

3

Desperately Seeking Bowie:

How Berlin Bowie Tourism Transcends the Sacred

Jennifer Otter Bickerdike and
John Charles Sparrowhawk

Introduction

In this chapter we broadly explore the relationship between celebrity and landscape, how it was that David Bowie came to live in Berlin in the 70s and the subsequent cultural impact of his arrival and stay both then and now. We discuss Bowie's Berlin years as a means for developing an insight into what is described as 'cultural pilgrimage' within the wider process of secularization; we raise the questions as to how space becomes sacred and how places themselves are transformed from being seen as ordinary to becoming culturally important; finally, we investigate Bowie's relationship with the landscape in terms of our perceptions of authenticity and everyday life.

The relationship between tourism and pilgrimage is not new and has been explored over a number of years by numerous scholars. It was Dean MacCannell (1973, 1976, 1992), however, who first suggested tourists go on holiday to seek, create and experience imagined mythical structures from their past which had been demolished by the processes of modernity. As tourists, we look to escape from our everyday lives, not simply as pleasure-seekers, but, as MacCannell suggests, as pilgrims trying to reclaim what is lost through the search for what is authentic.

When David Bowie came to Berlin from Los Angeles, via Switzerland, in late 1976, he was, according to *Observer* columnist Kate Connolly 'exhausted by drugs and fame' (2013). Bowie craved escape from his 'everyday' life of celebrity excess, and wanted to encounter what he saw as the 'ordinary' existence of average people. In this manner, Bowie becomes what Eric Cohen (1988) defines as an 'existential tourist' in the sense he is clearly committed to '. . . an elective spiritual center external to the mainstream of [his] native society'. Thus, Bowie as tourist, according to Cohen, becomes a pilgrim himself in so far as he is searching for something that may be defined as meaningful to him – something more 'real'. Following MacCannell, Bowie in this sense is searching for the authentic – thus, he is not so much a tourist as he is a pilgrim. We suggest this works, as rigid distinctions between pilgrimage and tourism have become much harder to define; indeed, some would argue that as such these distinctions do not exist at all. It is not impossible to suggest there must inevitably exist a close interaction between people and places that ultimately work together to socially construct the landscape as sacred. It is often the actions of fans themselves who create, maintain and evolve the meaning of specific spaces, underscoring and often validating the same behaviour in others. Reijinders (2011: 105–6) believes this is in part because, '. . . there is unmistakeable recognition of a definite structural analogy between media tourism and the pilgrimage'. He goes on to point out that it is crucial to:

> . . . [interpret] both phenomena as the externalization of an underlying need. What people in both cases strive for is to make tangible that which is not tangible in the first place. By coupling imagination or religion (both being complex imaginary systems) to specific locations and material objects, something that is fundamentally immaterial can be pinned down, appropriated and consumed.
>
> 2011: 105–6

In this way, Bowie's time in Berlin supplies a rich canon of places, spaces and physical items for the fan to cobble together their own meaning of the city, the singer and their personal identity both from the real and the imposed.

In 1947, the man who was to become Bowie was born David Jones in Brixton, South London. He moved with his family to suburban Bromley in 1953 where he latterly studied art, music and design. Jones formed his first band, The Konrads, in 1962. He changed his name to David Bowie in order to avoid confusion with the Monkees lead singer of the same name. Bowie's commercial breakthrough came in 1969 with the UK top five hit 'Space Oddity'. Following the albums *David Bowie* (1967, 1969), *The Man Who Sold the World* (1970), *Hunky Dory* (1971), *The Rise and Fall of Ziggy Stardust and* the *Spiders from Mars* (1972), *Aladdin Sane, Pin Ups* (1973), *Diamond Dogs* (1974), *Young Americans* (1975) and *Station to Station* (1976), Bowie was an influential international rock star. By this time, he had bound his art to a series of personas that he had created to act as the focus for the narrative of his music. The effect of this was twofold. Firstly, Ziggy Stardust and The Thin White Duke acted not only as unique selling points for the brand that was David Bowie but, secondly, they provided a means by which to deflect attention away from the artist himself and onto an imagined other, an entity who masked the man, his human crises and vulnerabilities.

By 1976, Bowie had become addicted to cocaine, affecting his behaviour so profoundly that playwright Alan Franks later wrote in *The Times* that the singer 'was deranged'. As Bowie himself later agreed, he was at the time 'functioning on mythology' (Jones, 2013), and blamed his substance abuse and the character of The Thin White Duke for his flirtations with Hitler, King Arthur and a passing interest in right-wing political movements. His drug-induced delirium culminated in a widely reported incident at Victoria Station where, in his Duke persona, he allegedly waved to fans in a manner reminiscent of a Nazi salute (Buckley, 2005).

Bowie's need to clean up dovetailed with his emerging attraction to collecting modern art. He visited galleries in Geneva, and crucially the Brücke Museum in Berlin. His growing interest in the contemporary Berlin music and art scene coupled with his need to beat his drug addition made the German capital appealing.

Bowie was interested in Berlin because the city represented much of what he saw was important to who he was, and possibly what he had lost through his success and celebrity. In a sense, the move to Berlin was a nostalgic expression of returning home: though Bowie himself is not German, coming from South London rather than Berlin, the city uniquely offered him the opportunity to covertly rediscover his inspirational roots, something which would have been much harder to find living in the soft parade of a Los Angeles celebrity limelight. The West Berlin of the 1970s was a stripped down, bare, frontier town. It was an isolated part of the new German Republic, a former capital city coming to terms with its recent unpleasant past and seeking a redefined postwar identity. Just as Bowie was trying to understand who he was, the same could be said of post-Nazi Berlin. In this regard, Berlin was ideal for Bowie, as he was trying to escape his recent volatile lifestyle; he was keen to rediscover his artistic mojo; Berlin, on the other hand, was reconnecting with its more liberal artistic traditions. The city itself had long been a place associated with the cultural avant-garde, having been the centre of the experimental Bauhaus architecture movement in the 1920s as well as home to expressionist painters Paul Klee and Wassily Kandinsky, the playwright

Bertholt Brecht and the composer Arnold Schoenberg. The West Berlin of the 1970s was a Cold War capitalist outpost in hostile communist territory, and, like the Weimar Republic of the 1920s, and Bowie himself for that matter, it had an uncertain future. Bowie was not the only artist or musician to move to Berlin during this period. Ever since the postwar division of Germany, the city had developed a reputation as a place, upon which, as John Czaplicka (Assmann and Czaplicka, 1995) suggests, artists, architects, historians and writers converged to come to terms with human loss through art and architecture in an attempt to reconfigure the recent past. This makes Berlin, then and since, a natural destination for artists and bohemians such as Bowie.

The eastern part of the city is now being transformed to a place of art galleries and cafes reminiscent of Greenwich Village, New York, with artists such as Olafur Elison, Stan Douglas, Tacita Dean and Bojan Sarcevic having located there from Iceland, Canada, England and Serbia respectfully. Likewise, Hansa Studios, once frequented by Bowie, Iggy Pop, Lou Reed and Brian Eno, has in recent times been the home to musicians such as Nick Cave and the Bad Seeds, Killing Joke, U2, REM and the Manic Street Preachers, who themselves were drawn there by the stories, history and folklore attached to the place.

When Bowie moved into his flat at 155 Haupstasse in unfashionable Schöneberg, he sought an opportunity, albeit briefly, to live an ordinary life, far from the media spotlight and the photographer's lens. Back in 1976, Berlin was a rather distant, almost frightening place, hard to reach, difficult to fathom, grey in architectural design – a place often viewed by the West as unattractive, peripheral and slightly alien. Within this extraordinary landscape of modernist 60s architecture and bullet-hole-ravaged buildings, Bowie found himself living with 'ordinary' people simply trying to live 'ordinary' lives. And it was, above all else, this fascination with the ordinary that so marked out Bowie's time in Berlin.

In a sense, Bowie moves to Berlin to strip away and lose his identity as hero and icon. He comes to fetishize the everyday lives of the Berliners he finds himself amongst as much as his own artistic heroes of the past who partially inspired his stay in the city. The irony here is David Bowie, the pilgrim/tourist, cannot escape who he is – or rather, who he is perceived to be. His observations on the everyday become evermore apparent in his art and are reflected in songs such as 'Subterranean', 'Art Decade' and 'Heroes'. The more he tries to be inconspicuous – wearing a boiler suit, riding his bicycle about town, living in his modest flat – the more his everyday activities become part of folklore and myth which latterly give rise to a whole tourist industry focused around Bowie's Berlin years.

Today, several tours of 'Bowie's Berlin' bring visitors to a handful of key spots credited to have influenced the artist during his time living in the city.

While fans can literally walk the streets of their hero, the places that Bowie celebrated in his music for their very commonness are transformed into sacred spaces; in essence, the everyday landscape is transformed into a location that is both mystical and spiritual for the diehard Bowie fan. It should be noted that such a 'sacralization' process is today compounded and further reinforced by the unstoppable force that is the rise of Web 2.0, E-Word of Mouth and the growth of networked communities and blogs in general which augment existing narratives about sacred places and people's experience of them. Thus, even before the tourist visits the site, he or she will have an imagined set of imprinted expectations of the place. In essence, the myths, narratives and folklore surrounding Bowie's time in Berlin form the basis of a collective imagination, to use Stijn Reijnders' (2011) term, that is shared by the anticipating tourists. The importance and meaning of each space is thus reaffirmed and strengthened with each Google search for 'Bowie' and 'Berlin', via the stories shared in online communities of fans who will never meet in real time, and through the dual shared experience of placing meaning on not only the Bowie songbook and myth, but upon the physical locations associated with the performer. In this way, fans are already knowledgeable and familiar with the key sites of 'Bowie's Berlin' long before ever – or if ever – setting foot on German soil.

The Dutch scholar, Stijn Reijnders, whose own research is primarily focused on media tourism, has written extensively on the subject of collective imagination, a term which he coined, *'Lieux d'imagination'*. Drawing on the theories of Pierra Nora's work on collective memory, Reijnders concludes that *Lieux d'imagination* is a mechanism by which physical locations, '. . . serve as a symbolic anchor for a society's collective imagination' (2011: 234). For Reijnders, a 'new' cultural memory of value thus replaces the original meaning of the locality despite the reality that the spatial entities in question have often experienced a physical transformation over time. In other words, 'Bowie's Berlin' no longer exists in reality precisely as it did back in the 70s; in fact, the Berlin often recounted as part of the Bowie myth may never have actually been a place, just as Brecht's Berlin of the 20s that attracted Bowie never truly was. The time Bowie spent in Berlin, however, is brought to life by the reinforcement of narratives that serve to collectively legitimate certain sites and places as sacred. Of course the irony here is that when Bowie the pilgrim/tourist walked those Berlin streets himself looking for the authentic places where once Brecht or Kandinsky lived, his own expectation was nurtured on the very same narratives, myths and stories, albeit unaided by social media, as the contemporary sonic pilgrim is who is in search of the singer's ghost today.

The ordinary places that Bowie explored, visited and lived in, as those visited by Schonberg, Brecht or Gropius, have, however, become endowed with spiritual mystique not originally inherent to the specific spots but to which contemporary tourists are attracted. This new importance dovetails with Lynch's argument for a cultural shift away from dominant forms of religious practice towards a '. . . view of life [where] people seek meaning that feels personally authentic to them rather than being prepared to accept pre-packaged truths provided by religious, political or corporate organizations' (2002: lx). Within this framework, Cobb (2005: 3) notes, 'Symbols once inseparable from religious myth and ritual . . . began to wander . . . into other cultural spheres, carrying with them their inherent aura and an authority that once derived from religion but became autonomous.' Where once the road to Mecca would be a revered and sought-after destination for a traveller, it is now the streets Bowie walked during the recording of the albums that have been come to be referred to as the 'Berlin trilogy' – *Low* (1977), "*Heroes*" (1977) and *Lodger* (1979) – that move mere pedestrian byways to roads of mythologized inspiration. As Bowie once famously attempted to encapsulate the sights, sounds and smells of 70s Berlin within the triad of records, the modern traveller tries to capture that same 'authenticity' which has become at once central and intertwined to this period of both the artist's and the city's history.

The inclusion of the word 'authentic' can be counted on to appear in references to Bowie's time in the German capital. The concept of 'authenticity' is itself not unproblematic and has been a much-discussed area of enquiry since MacCannell (1973, 1976) first applied the concept to the study of tourism motivation (Wang, 1999). Within this framework there is an assumed understanding as to what 'authentic' is when encountered in a context about the singer or the city. Yet it is imperative to unpack exactly what it inferred from and pinned upon this seeming innocuous characterization when used in conjunction with this specific rock moment. The term 'authentic' itself is loaded – not just with meanings placed upon it but those which are attributed to its binary – the 'inauthentic' or 'fake' – both immediate danger zones in the marketing and perpetuation of art (see today's arguably fabricated celebrities from the *X Factor* 'machine' or a completely plastic cityscape like Las Vegas). Therefore, one informs and shapes the other, as the opposite creates the definition of its alternate.

In this way, authenticity, when used to describe 70s Bowie and Berlin, is defined by this very normality, a normality of harsh and conflicting political conditions (Berlin) and unglamorous, 'everyman' existence (Bowie), and the work in the forms of the images and hailed recorded masterpieces which emerge from within such a setting. This inscribes an equation where the earnest, stripped-down means-based standards – as prescribed in Bowie's transportation, dress and even his choice of Berlin – the stark, wild city in glaring contradiction to the voluptuous glitter of Hollywood – come to define truth, thus creating and buttressing authenticity. For Bowie fans, this offers a new perception of the singer, one who during his time in Berlin was seen to be living a normal and recognizable existence – one not dissimilar to many a listener – in the sense that he lived in an average flat, drank coffee in regular cafes and wore workman's overalls, becoming part of the Berlin cityscape of the time and the community itself.

Such contemporary folklore and narrative provide the tourist/sonic pilgrim with an image of Bowie's 'everyday' life in Berlin which can be easily understood, accessed and seen to be much more meaningful in terms of the tourists' own lives. Bowie's time in the city, on the surface, presented him as somebody who was simultaneously extraordinary but also normal. Perhaps a more appropriate term to use here would be 'real'. He could be encountered like anyone else, and potentially more likeable because of it. These ideas have thus been fetishized via the work which Bowie produced, for himself and housemate Iggy Pop, during the Berlin years. The continued circulation in contemporary culture of the pictures taken and songs created from the time now offer a symbiotic vision between the then creativity, poverty and bare aesthetics of the space.

This creates a specific manner of endless mirroring, as Bowie travels to Berlin to manifest his own idols and the modern tourist attempts to conjure Bowie. Yet Bowie's own attraction to the adopted normality he practises during the 'Berlin Years' is a reflection not of the very authenticity which he wished to embrace, and fans want to touch; instead, it illustrates Bowie's chameleon nature of continual reinvention. For as he casts off the drug-addled hazy persona tied to his Los Angeles days, Bowie wraps himself in the new identity of everyman – an 'everyman' ideal which he will never be able to truly embody, as he is *David Bowie*. His very glance and interest in a space, place or person transforms them from the unnotably average to inherently valued and often exulted in both worth and meaning to the extent that, 'whenever he [Bowie] went into a record store, the word would spread and people would gather outside, and when he came out with his purchases they would rush in and ask the sales person what he had bought' (Connelly, 2013). As time has passed, the myth around the star, the songs and the worth and meaning attached to them has continued to substantially grow and evolve. Cobb (2005: 7) notes that this is an example of how such pop culture fodder allows '. . . whole generations . . . [to] attempt through bricolage to invest life with meaning and find a justification for their lives' – through rock music and visiting places of historical importance to a particular artist or album instead of traditional hymns, prayers and Hail Marys. Bowie's own behaviour during his Berlin years both underpins Cobb's theory while prescribing a foundation for future fans to repeat the same behaviours and practices of secular pilgrimage to the city. Yet the very meaning is tethered to the exact authenticity of the artist during this period – an ideal that never truly existed. For Bowie as chameleon, it makes it impossible for him to ever be fully authentic because the very ordinariness that he seemingly longs for so desperately can never be his. Indeed, his shedding of looks and gestures, moving from Los Angeles to Berlin to New York to London, clashes with the very base value of the ideal of authenticity – even his ability to fluidly transcend such diverse destinations and identities clashes with the very commonality which has come to be an integral part of the 'Berlin trilogy' myth. For authenticity hinges not only on a specific, founding truth but also on a continuity of such truth, a persistence of presence which Bowie's ever-changing persona – from Ziggy Stardust to The Thin White Duke, then Berlin resident – conflicts with at the most base level. Fans going to Berlin with the purpose of pursuing this veritable version of Bowie are chasing a spectre who never lived, investing in a mythologized moment which never actually happened – once again repeating the way Bowie himself imagined Berlin during his stay. And yet, as Ning Wang (1999: 365) suggests that 'even if toured objects are totally inauthentic, seeking otherwise is still possible, because tourists can quest for an alternative, namely, existential authenticity to be activated by tourist experience'. For Wang, even if the toured landscape or object is essentially fake, this does not preclude the tourist experiencing a state of 'Being' in the moment or an emotional space that they perceive themselves to be truly authentic.

Cobb notes, 'a great number of people are finding solace in popular culture, solace they find lacking in organized religion' (2005: 6). Retracing the steps of one's own idols allows for participation by individuals in such bespoke and personal practices described by Cobb. Pilgrimage, according to Reader and Walter (1993: 3):

> . . . is one of the most common phenomena found in religious culture, occurring in just about every major religious tradition. Islam, Christianity, Buddhism, and Hinduism . . . have all developed complex pilgrimage cultures ranging from overarching and unifying sites that transcend any national or cultural boundaries, to regional and localized sites that may conversely affirm cultural belongings, perhaps even over and against universalizing ones.

The current tours of 'Bowie's Berlin' fold back on both the traditions found across such a wide swath of familiar belief systems while expressing Bowie's own desire during his turn in the city to at once escape the trappings of celebrity pinned to him via fame while simultaneously tapping into and revisiting the very wells of artistic productivity that his own idols had found within Berlin. These two principles are what make Berlin as much a place for the reinvention of Bowie and as it is a current space for sonic pilgrimage. For Bowie himself chose the city, it would seem, for the very same reasons that fans now go to drink at S036, the venue Bowie and roommate Iggy Pop used to haunt: such travel fulfils the emotional longing to connect to something deeper and more meaningful than the everyday.

Going to such spaces provides a way to touch and embody the very celestial essence, if even for a moment, which inspired their heroes, in much the same way that more traditional practices of religious pilgrimage have assumed such journeys for centuries – an act which was often 'a central tenet of . . . faith and sanctioned as a religious duty' (Reader and Walter, 1993: 3). In an ever-more complicated and fast-paced world, such visits allow for the 'tourist and pilgrim alike go out from the familiar world (their own home) to seek something (that enriches their lives, and stands outside and in contrast to the normal modes of their existence), and then return home again to the familiar world' (Reader and Walter, 1993: 9), becoming a manifestation of the very individualistic means of practising traditional behaviours. Each new person going on the tour of 'Bowie's Berlin' not only justifies and adds to the importance placed on the Bowie myth and the specific sites included on the excursion, but normalizes and rationalizes the transformation of the spaces from overlooked to revered. This also provides a compelling example of the power of selective memory, and the rupture between the real and the remembered, as it is only a handful out of the possible countless areas, sites and establishments that Bowie visited during his time in the city that are now considered crucial to the 'Berlin trilogy'. This illustrates once again how it is the traveller/pilgrim who makes the space of interest, not necessarily the location itself; necessary are the symbols and cultural connotations that act as the conduit for keeping fans returning to specific destinations.

Reader and Walter (1993: 227) argues that journeys of these sorts have often been defined by 'the manifestation of signs that mark out a particular location, and that signify that it is somehow special, a place where people may encounter powers and experience feelings that cannot be found in the normal flow of life'. The idea of such spaces inherently being imbued with such esoteric significance underscores why such trips are symbolic, as they provide, 'the notion of rebirth and return: rebirth to a new life after the pilgrimage, rebirth of the shattered community, rebirth and reaffirmation of the recreated community and communal identity' (1993: 222). This ties back to Bowie's own seeking of refuge and renewal within the borders of Berlin: his very musical productivity and healthy recovery after arriving in the city in a very fragile condition provides support for Reader's assertions while simultaneously adding to the mythos of such trips. The modern Bowie fan is thus pursuing a similar form of transformation and inspiration, both by individual participation in such ritual and within the larger set of meanings inherent in such practices. Thus, every visitor to 'Bowie's Berlin' interacts not only with the other members of the tour group, but with the myths and ideas surrounding the singer's time in the city. Here once again Bowie's original interest in the place contrasts with the very basic characterization of the act of being a visitor, for his fascination with basic normality dovetails with the action of seeking such guidance from a physical space, as 'pilgrimage . . . [provides] a vehicle through which to encounter and access the extraordinary, transform[ing] . . . the ordinary and everyday' (Reader and Walter, 1993: 236). The irony here lies in that Bowie's very presence, action and beliefs in the power of place – his own attempts at simultaneously tapping into the phantoms of his own heroes while seeking to exist in an arguably contrived version of undistinguishable existence – are what now endow the city with the very traits of glimmering celebrity that the singer was originally trying to escape. Bowie's own participation in such pilgrimage clearly illustrates what Reader argues is the act of pilgrimage, allowing for the

> . . . creat[ion], albeit temporarily, [of] an alternative and idealized order and transient community of pilgrims . . . [in] this transitional state, in which the individual gives up his/her normal social status and its resultant constraints, [the pilgrim can] . . . enter a state of freedom and of equality with all others.
> Reader and Walter, 1993: 236

It is the pursuit of the levelling effect associated with such journeys that compelled Bowie to stay in Berlin, as he attempted to become one such of many.

Bowie's embrace of the rented tenement apartment which he shared with Iggy Pop and the war-ravaged Hansa Studio where he finished *Low* provide isolated and, in some ways, romanticized ideas of bleakness which serve as key sites of importance for modern-day Bowie fans. In essence, these are contemporary secular sacred sites that draw the secular pilgrim. Bowie was at once removed from the very ordinariness he sought by being David Bowie – yet this aided in elevating many places related to his years in Berlin from their commonness to exalted destination. This creates a tension between the sought-after 'authentic' experience for the tourist and actuality in the present time: the buildings which are currently standing in the new, remodelled city versus the gritty, dark and often desolate presence the metropolis played as inspiration for Bowie's music in that period. The very characteristics that Bowie found so compelling have now been stripped of their founding value – either literally by their demolition, overt-restructuring or via this shift from common to celebrated – making the search for any remnants of Bowie's genuine inspiration a mission impossible.

Bowie tourism perpetuates the rupture between such fetishized normality, further underscoring the singer's legend. The modern-day visitor on a Bowie tour is left with having to imagine a city in which Bowie is riddled with bullet holes and filled with fear on the verge of renaissance. The pilgrim embarks on the endless loop of secular pilgrimage, as Bowie himself did during his stay in the city, looking to (re)capture the greatness attributed to Berlin by their heroes. Fans embarking on David Bowie Berlin walking tours provide a clear example of the discrepancies between 'old' paradigms predicated on the assumption that pilgrimage is a religious experience.

Bibliography

Assmann, Jan and John Czaplicka. 1995. 'Collective memory and cultural identity'. *New German Critique*, 65, Cultural History/Cultural Studies (spring – summer), 125–33.

Beaudoin, Tom. 1998. *Virtual Faith: The Irreverent Spiritual Quest of Generation X*. San Francisco: Jossey-Bass.

Buckley, David. 2005. *Strange Fascination: David Bowie: The Definitive Story*. London: Omnibus Press.

Cobb, Kelton. 2005. *The Blackwell Guide to Theology and Popular Culture*. Malden: Blackwell Publishing.

Cohen, Erik. 1988. 'A phenomenology of tourist experiences'. *Sociology*, 132, 179–201.

Collins-Kreiner, Noga. 2010. 'Researching pilgimage: continuity and transformations'. *Annals of Tourism Research*, 37 (2), 440–56.

Connolly, Kate. 2013. 'Bowie's Berlin: a time of Sturm und Drang in the shadow of the Wall'. *Observer*, 13 January.

Foley, Malcolm and John Lennon. 2000. *Dark Tourism: The Attraction of Death and Disaster*. London: Continuum.

Jones, Lucy. 2013. 'David Bowie takes on the NRA & Charlton Heston?'. NME. com, available at: www.nme.com/blogs/nme-blogs/david-bowie-takes-on-the-nra-charlton-heston, accessed 31 July 2014.

Lewis, Lisa. 1992. 'Fandom as pathology: the consequences of characterization'. In Lisa A. Lewis (ed.) *The Adoring Audience: Fan Culture and Popular Media*. London: Routledge.

Lynch, Gordon. 2002. *After Religion: Generation X and the Search for Meaning*. London: Darton, Longman & Todd Ltd.

Lynch, Gordon. 2007. 'What is this "religion" in the study of religion and popular culture?' In Gordon Lynch (ed.) *Between Sacred and Profane: Researching Religion and Popular Culture*. New York: Palgrave Macmillan.

MacCannell, Dean. 1973. 'Staged authenticity: arrangements of social space in tourist settings'. *American Journal of Sociology*, 793, 589–603.

MacCannell, Dean. 1976. *The Tourist.* New York: Schocken Books.

MacCannell, Dean. 1992. *Empty Meeting Grounds.* London: Routledge.

Reader, Ian and Tony Walter. 1993. *Pilgrimage in Popular Culture.* London: Palgrave Macmilllan.

Reijnders, Stijn. 2011. 'Stalking the Count: Dracula, fandom and tourism'. *Annals of Tourism Research*, 38 (1), 231–47.

Sandford, C. 1997. *Bowie: Loving the Alien.* Los Angeles: Time Warner.

Seaton, A. 1999. 'War and thanatourism: Waterloo 1815–1914'. *Annals of Tourism Research*, 261, 231–47.

Seaton A.V. 2002. 'Thanotourism's final frontiers? Visits to cemeteries, churchyards and funerary sites as sacred and secular pilgrimage'. *Tourism, Recreation Research*, 27 (2), 27–33.

Vermorel, Fred and Judy Vermorel. 1985. *Starlust: The Secret Fantasies of Fans.* London: Comet Books.

Wang, N. 1999. 'Rethinking authenticity in tourism experience'. *Annals of Tourism Research*, 26 (2), 349–70.

4

Confronting Bowie's Mysterious Corpses

Tanja Stark

Introduction

'Confront a corpse at least once' Bowie implored, '. . . the absolute absence of life is the most disturbing and challenging confrontation you will ever have' (Bowie, 2004). His words accompanied a haunting photographic recreation by Steven Klein of Michelangelo's *Pieta* set inside a prison cell, a strange androgynous figure draped, like the lifeless body of Christ, across Bowie's lap while he made a Latin benediction gesture with the ink-stained fingers[1] of his left hand (see www.npg.org.uk/collections/search /portraitLarge/mw129577/David-Bowie). A decade later, Bowie's 2013 album *The Next Day* contained more than just one cadaver; indeed the album dripped death like a bleeding beehive of blood, a honeycombed-catacomb of cryptic mystery, rage and resignation. This was no safe space for neophytes or necrophobes, but for those with the 'terror of knowing', bright light casts dark shadows and the eternal paradox lies in discerning which one is which. *The Next Day* ain't rock 'n' roll, as much as art on suicide watch, with last observations taken at 9.25.[2]

Death has been an enduring companion to Bowie from the beginning, giving creative form to that most existentialist Kierkegaardian obsession:

As soon as a human being is born, he begins to die. But the difference is that there are some people for whom the thought of death comes into existence with birth and is present to them in the quiet peacefulness of childhood and the buoyancy of youth; whereas others have a period in which this thought is not present to them until, when the years run out, the years of vigor and vitality, the thought of death meets them on their way.

Kierkegaard, 1844: 280

Born in the shadows of World War II, the first corpses emerged when Bowie was barely out of his teens. Amongst Bowie's earliest songs was a murderous narrative about a child killer who kills a gravedigger ('Please, Mr Gravedigger', 1967), cannibalistic 'Hungry Men' threatening mass extermination (*David Bowie*, 1967) and the heartbreakingly poignant 'Conversation Piece', the story of an intellectual who jumps despairingly from a bridge, a brilliant mind no compensation to the despair of loneliness[3] (single B-side of 'The Prettiest Star', 1970). These songs mark the first taste of Bowie's ongoing fascination with liminal spaces, control, consciousness and the extinguishment of life, foreshadowing a lifetime of deathly intrigue that led inexorably to *1. Outside. The Ritualistic Art Murder of Baby Grace – a Non-Linear Gothic Drama Hyper-Cycle* (1995) and later, to *The Next Day* and the dark torment of 'You Feel So Lonely You Could Die' in 2013.

'My head's full of murders where only killers scream' the tripped-out singer confessed on 1970's 'Unwashed and Slightly Dazed'. It was on the same album he introduced us to 'The Man Who Sold the World' who thrust Bowie deep into the mysteries of death and consciousness as he found himself amongst millions of undead in a song with echoes of Saint-Exupéry's novella *The Little Prince* and the jazz standard 'Nature Boy', with their tales of enchanted wanderers, magical encounters and the revelation of wisdom[4] (*The Man Who Sold the World*, 1970).

On the apocalyptic *The Rise and Fall of Ziggy Stardust and the Spiders from Mars* (1972) Bowie was a 'Rock 'n' Roll Suicide', a 'leper messiah' resigned to a sacrificial (albeit hubristic) slaughter at the hands of the ignorant masses. Two years later, *Diamond Dogs* (1974) pushed into stranger territory. Melodramatically opening the album with the dystopian spectre of Hunger City, its gruesome urban decay splattered with decomposing bodies '. . . and in the death, as the last few corpses lay rotting on the slimy thoroughfare . . .' it gave way, amid a primal, pulsating force of wailing guitar, to one of rock's darker manifestos '. . . this ain't rock and roll, this is genocide'. ('As they pulled you out of the oxygen tent' pumped up on nihilistic hedonism, cultural cleansing had never sounded so damn sexy.) Conceived as an interpretation of Orwell's 1949 book *Nineteen Eighty-Four*, Bowie's *Diamond Dogs* hypnotically entranced us with fatalistic resignation on 'We Are the Dead': 'Oh dress yourself my urchin one, for I hear them on the stairs / Because of all we've seen because of all we've said / We are the dead' – and reinforced our inevitable fate, conjuring the macabre spectre of death in the strangely shamanic funk rhythm of 'The Chant of the Ever Circling Skeletal Family'.

Homicide and crucifixion continued to claw their way into the oeuvre wherever they could take hold, adding to the metaphorical death of love ('Up the Hill Backwards', 1980), death of faith ('I Would be Your Slave', 2002), reason ('I'm Deranged', 1995) and identity ('Heat', 2013). Even during his most commercially popular incarnation as the suave yellow-suited star of the *Let's Dance* (1983) era, Bowie's death complex never abated, that most commercial of albums masking dark references to spiritual struggle and death. Among the themes of colonialism, race, identity and morality, the album's iconic lyrics 'put on your red shoes and dance the blues' also seem to recall Hans Christian Andersen's tale *The Red Shoes*[5] in which the little girl was vainly tempted to wear them only to find they could not be removed, dancing the wearer insane and separating her from God's grace – 'let's dance for fear your grace should fall'.[6] In Andersen's tale, the holy pictures on the church wall glared at the girl in divine judgement, a weight of condemnation echoed in 'Ricochet' (1983) with its injunction to '. . . turn the Holy Pictures so they face the wall' amidst its spirit-crushing lyrics and the 'sound of the devil breaking parole'. 'So you train by shadowboxing, search for the truth'[7] Bowie had sung three years earlier on 'Scream Like Baby' (1980). On the cover of *Let's Dance* Bowie continued this fight with shadows and spiritual tricksters with 'no sign of life . . . just the power to charm'.

Symbolist death

Bowie's aforementioned 'Please Mr Gravedigger' track is a significant marker of the symbolic centrality of death that permeates his career. In this strangely dramatized *a capella* tune he sings as a child murderer haunting the churchyard where his victim is buried, planning in his world of twisted vengeance to kill the old gravedigger who dared snatch a locket from her grave. In this story of a murderer killing a thief (possibly set in the real West Norwood Cemetery, where V-1 bombs hit the chapel during World War II), the bombing of the churchyard speaks of the death of the spiritual and the sacred, of memory and ritual; deathly layer upon deathly layer as fall dogs bombed the tombs.

The song could almost be a creative interpretation of Carlos Schwabe's[8] 1895 Symbolist painting *La mort du fossoyeur – The Death of the Gravedigger* (see Figure 4.1) – an evocative image of an old man cowering with his shovel inside a freshly dug grave while a dark angel of death coolly steals his soul. Indeed, Bowie's career so deeply aligns with the tradition and tone of the

FIGURE 4.1 La mort du fossoyeur – The Death of the Gravedigger *by Carlos Schwabe, 1895*

nineteenth-century Symbolists and their mythopoeic fascination with mysticism, esoteric spirituality, mortality, ideals, dreams and symbols that it is easy to see a synchronistic manifestation of their thematic concerns throughout his work, particularly in the quest to transcend duality – spirit/ flesh, male/female, life/death – through the integration of polarities.

The iconic cover of *Diamond Dogs* (1974) that showed a naked Bowie morphed with a dog (see www.davidbowie.com/news/diamond-dogs-album- 39-today-51731> for instance), has curious parallels with Belgian Symbolist Fernand Khnopff's 1896 image of the hybrid leopard woman in *L'Art ou Des Caresses* or *The Caress* – a painting filled with erotic overtones, androgyny and hermetic symbolism (see Figure 4.2) (Khnopff was a close collaborator with the poet Joséphin Péladan, grandmaster of the Rosicrucian Mystic Order of the Rose + Croix, a society exploring esoteric spirituality and ritual that had

FIGURE 4.2 *Symbolist artist Fernand Khnopff's 1896 painting* L'Art ou Des Caresses

once fascinated Bowie). Painted by another Belgian artist, Guy Peellaert in 1974, both Bowie's dog-man and Khnopff's cat-woman are theriomorphic figures, human-animal hybrids that appear throughout history as symbols of mystery and magic. The androgynous figures in these images seem to reflect the symbolic conjunction of sexual opposites, evoking an unsettlingly seductive tension. *Diamond Dogs* was the first album on which Bowie utilized the chaos magician William Burroughs' infamous cut-up method to allow for the unconscious creation of lyrics. When Bowie sang 'Oh caress yourself my juicy' on 'We are the Dead' one can almost imagine the sphinx in Khnopff's *Caress* purring this to the youth with the magic staff.

The fascination with the interior, unconscious worlds of dreams and ideas that arise and percolate in artists like Bowie – and deeply resonate with the ideas of Carl Jung (Stark, 2015) – often sees them drawn to and reflecting the themes of the Symbolists. When Bowie slipped in a reference to Belgian Symbolist poet and writer Georges Rodenbach (who wrote of murder and melancholy, doppelgangers and death)[9] on 2013's *The Next Day* album, he gave an unmistakable acknowledgement to this art movement with its strong parallels to the content and processes of his creative life.

We need to talk about David

There is a deliberate dissonance permeating Bowie's reappearance in 2013. *The Next Day* brims with dead men hanging, walking, packing guns and Bibles, surrounded by swirling ideas of death and resurrection, possession, deception, judgement and retribution. It's death as catharsis, as symbol, as mystery and revenge, but so often wrapped in beautiful sounds that belie their dark content: such as the disturbing 'Valentine's Day', a sway-along song about a deluded shooter who has confided in the singer his dreams of massacre and dominion'. . . Valentine told me how he feels / If all the world were under his heels / or stumbling through the mall' ('Valentines Day', *The Next Day*, 2013).

It is not the first time Bowie has sung of the macabre, visceral reality of slaughter and assassination. On 1970's 'Running Gun Blues' (*The Man Who Sold the World*) for example, Bowie sings as a Vietnam veteran who unleashes his violent demons upon society on his return: '. . . For I promote oblivion, And I'll plug a few civilians I'll slash them cold, I'll kill them dead I'll break them gooks, I'll crack their heads I'll slice them till they're running red'. He soaked up vicarious TV violence on Tin Machine's 'Video Crime' (*Tin Machine*, 1989): '. . . Trash Time Bundy, Death Row Chic (chop it up) . . . Blood on video-video crime . . . Late night cannibal-cripples decay, Just can't tear my eyes away'.

'Day In Day Out' (*Never Let Me Down*, 1987) culminates in a woman contemplating her own gun crime, worn down by abuse and injustice before a mysterious angelic intervention shoots her down instead. 'She's gonna take her a shotgun – Pow, spin the grail spin the drug, She's gonna make them well aware she's an angry gal' Bowie sings as the film clip shows him playing a 'headless' guitar-as-gun as he would repeat in the 'Valentines Day' film clip twenty-five years later. Death psychopathically stalked Bowie in the video to 1997's 'I'm Afraid of Americans' (*Earthling*) where Trent Reznor, an assassin with spiritually dark undertones, relentlessly pursues a paranoid Bowie through the streets with a virtual gun, before finally appearing in the guise of Christ on his way to crucifixion in a strange Mexican 'Day of the Dead'-like procession.

But perhaps the most cryptic corpse was on 1995's *1. Outside: the Ritualistic Art Murder of Baby Grace – a Non-Linear Gothic Drama Hyper-Cycle*, a conceptual detective mystery set in the future where murder is a legitimate form of artistic expression. Woven through song, video and liner notes, Bowie confronted his audience with bizarre themes of detachment, derangement and bodily desecration, decapitated minotaurs and mannequins, dark pagan rituals and Bacchan last suppers: 'The Limbs of Baby were then severed from the torso[10] . . . then hung upon the splayed web, slug-like prey of some unimaginable creature[11] . . . It was definitely murder – but was it art?' (Diary of Nathan Adler, *1, Outside* 1995). Bowie would describe the macabre project as an exploration of society's spiritual hunger for meaning and authentic inner spirituality: 'The one continuum that is throughout my writing . . . is a real simple, spiritual search', he confessed (Bowie in III, 1997). Bowie's search, however, was hardly simple, as many have pondered (see Ball, 2013; Cinque, 2013; Dery, 2010; Savage, 2010) and the album brought his God and death complexes to the fore. On *Outside* it appeared he was ritually dismembering old religious strictures and social restraint, metaphorically burning them to ashes, singing of 'a fantastic death abyss, It's the hearts filthy lesson'. Amongst the gruesome layers, Baby Grace arguably alluded to the holy child of grace, whose own body was also violently impaled through crucifixion.

In an article by Ian Penman, 'The Resurrection of Saint Dave' for *Esquire Magazine* (Bowie, 1994), Bowie said:

> My input revolved around the idea of ritual art – what options were there open to that kind of quasi-sacrificial blood-obsessed sort of art form? And the idea of a neo-paganism developing – especially in America – with the advent of the new cults of tattooing and scarification and piercings and all that . . . people have a real need for some spiritual life and I think there's great spiritual starving going on. There's a hole that's been vacated by an authoritative religious body – the Judeo-Christian ethic doesn't seem to embrace all the things that people actually need to have dealt with in that way – and it's sort of been left to popular culture to soak up the leftover bits like violence and sex.

Bowie's linking of violence, spiritual belief and death, and the lack of contemporary, culturally resonant frameworks to meaningfully process these powerful energies, as explored on *Outside*, is intriguing, particularly when considering why people are attracted to violent expressions of belief, such as 'Islamic State'. (Bowie had previously explored the ancient clash of religious ideology in his 1985 song 'Loving the Alien', singing of terror and torture from the crusades through to modern times: 'Watching them come and go, the Templars and the Saracens . . . Torture comes and torture goes . . . terror in the best laid plans . . . Christians and the unbelievers, hanging by the cross and nail'.) Grace's corpse on *Outside* seemed the end result of the convergence, subversion and dysfunctional channelling of these primal drives. Bowie sang in several guises across the 1995 album, from detective Nathan Adler, who had undertones of a cryptic 'grand inquisitor' figure (Dostoyevsky, 1880),[12] to murder suspect Leon Blank, a reversal of Noel, herald of emptiness, a Holy Fool cutting esoteric zeroes into the fabric of time and perceiving hidden mysteries through 'these architect's eyes', a name for God in the mystery traditions.[13] Deliberately ambiguous, the project possibly intimated that the detective himself could be the 'Minotaur' serial killer who murdered Baby Grace, a theological implication perhaps cryptically reflected in 'The Next Day' single and film clip with its contempt for exploitative religious leaders who 'work with Satan while they dress like saints' and corrupt institutions of power that exploit and destroy the Grace they should protect and illuminate.

Shadows of *The Next Day*

For several years prior and subsequent to the release of *The Next Day* in 2013, Bowie remained as silent as Rosenbach, giving no public interviews or appearances to promote his work. It was unsurprising then that like some virtual vivisection, Bowie's digital resurrection was forensically picked apart for meaning in symbol and verse in the notable absence of a real body. The iconoclastic title track 'The Next Day' which emerged like a nine-inch nail to the eye was carved up in all its histrionic glory as many conducted spiritual autopsies on the controversial film clip temporarily banned by YouTube. Yet, there are also some very interesting and subtle visual nuances in the iconography and cryptic images around Bowie's latest incarnation. For those whose imaginations are 'not quite dying', it seems Bowie has been perpetually confronting us with the mysteries of mortality and death, even in the still photography.

The first photograph to appear in 2013 was 'Three Men in Hats', a black and white portrait by Jimmy King of Bowie seated under an earlier Terry O'Neill portrait of the artist as a young man, back to back with synchronistic beat poet and chaos magician William S. Burroughs (see http://tanjastark.com/2014/10/20/confronting-bowies-mysterious-corpses-2/). It was Burroughs who infamously coined the 'seminal' phrase The Thin White Rope in his 1959 book *Naked Lunch* that would morph into one of Bowie's more sexually potent yet emotionally detached personae. The stark black and white portrait portrayed Bowie presiding intensely from an oroborous ring of steel, hinting at mysteries of circularity, repetition and prescience, casting shadows between two columns that recall the twin pillars Jachin and Boaz in Solomon's temple seen in Khnopff's '*The Caress*' (see Figure 4.2) that feature heavily in esoteric mystery traditions (2 Chronicles 3:15–17). The image also evoked synchronistic associations with Father Time or three-headed Chronos of antiquity, mythically connected with the birth of chaos, the prima materia and magical semen, that perhaps Bowie had cryptically alluded to as he infamously sang '*Time . . . falls wanking to the floor*' in his youth ('Time', *Aladdin Sane*, 1973).

The image emerged with the launch of 'Where are We Now' (*The Next Day*), the ghosts of Bowie's Berlin bringing the circularity of his life to the fore. Released on his sixty-sixth birthday, it always seemed as interesting that the '. . . man lost in time near KaDeWe, just walking the dead' shared his birth date with Stephen Hawking, that intellectual master of 'chaos' that is quantum theory, as much as he does with the king of Rock 'n' Roll, Elvis Presley. The Tony Oursler-directed film clip was a cornucopia of archetypal imagery, the double-headed mannequin suggesting the sacred marriage of opposites, Heiros Gamos; the diamond of the self, a philosopher's stone, sun, rain, fire, you, me – the alchemic mysteries of the inner journey literally spelled out on screen.

Death's door

Shortly after the release of the 2013 album another fascinating image appeared, this time taken by Jimmy King in the Magic Shop studio in New York where the album was covertly recorded (see http://tanjastark.com/2014/10/20/confronting-bowies-mysterious-corpses-2/). It's a stunning portrait of a glowing, white-shirted Bowie full of vitality, standing over the mixing controls. But this image, too, continues the theme of the eternal cycle of life and death, for if one looks closely behind Bowie's left shoulder there is a ghostly pareidolic image of a skeleton formed by the grain of the wooden door, Shroud of Turin-like, with a Claddagh crown. It brings to mind Bowie's iconic rendition of Belgian Jacques Brel's 'My Death' the night he killed Ziggy – a song sung by one who lives in the knowledge of mortal fragility and the other world behind the door: 'My death waits like a Bible truth at the funeral of my youth . . . But whatever lies behind the door there is nothing much to do, angel or devil, I don't care . . .' ('My Death', 1973). In light of 'The Next Day' film clip, with its contempt for duplicitous religion, the spectre of a holy relic in King's photograph is as elegant as the camera angle that creates the illusion. Bowie holds a Faustian homunculus in his hands as time itself, symbolized by his watch, disappears up a 'magician's mysterious sleeves'.

The angels of life and death, that most classic duo of Symbolist iconography, recur throughout the decades in Bowie's work, foreshadowing liminal spaces and transitions; new angels of promise, angels of lead, angels in these golden years, angels for life, angels that have gone. In 'Look Back in Anger' (*Lodger*, 1979) the Angel of Death seemingly comes to Bowie, heralding his mortal end: 'You know who I am, he said / The speaker was an angel / He coughed and shook his crumpled wings . . . It's time we should be going / Waiting so long . . .' But the Angel of Death didn't take Bowie in 1979; the visitation was yet another dispassionate reminder of the inevitability of his eventual demise. If a deal had been struck, someone across the years apparently reneged on the terms.

In 'Bring Me the Disco King' (*Reality*, 2003) Bowie laments his slow drawn-out ending, addressing one who had led him through trails of money and sex to an impotent dark ending. It was arguably the same crumpled winged angel of 'Look Back in Anger' watching over a life reduced to worthless, crumpled paper in 'Bring Me the Disco King': 'You promised me the ending would be clear / You'd let me know when the time was now / Don't let me know when you're opening the door / Stab me in the dark, let me disappear' ('Bring Me the Disco King', *Reality*, 2003).

A hauntingly beautiful film clip[14] accompanies the track: Bowie standing over his lifeless body in a dark, twisted forest after a desperate search for water. Often mystically associated with the spirit (living water, baptism, rebirth, chaos) this quest for water is a recurring symbol for spiritual sustenance or thirst in his oeuvre, a theme exemplified in 'Looking for Water' (*Reality*, 2003): 'Take my hand as we go down and down / Leave it all behind nothing will be found / I'm looking for water'[15] (2003), in the frantic search by Bowie's tiny glass spiders for spiritual nourishment in the face of maternal abandonment – 'Gone, gone the water's all gone / Mummy come back 'cause the water's all gone / If your mother don't love you then the riverbed might' ('Glass Spider', 1987) – and Mishima's black dog that blocked the flow of the waterfall in 'Heat' (*The Next Day*, 2013) – a stunning metaphor for the dark psyche that can impede spiritual nourishment.

Bowie's search for water in the chthonic earth is a stark counterpoint to his ungrounded space jaunts. Frustratingly, the water he uncovers quickly transforms into a thousand fractured 'reflectors' – a mirrored disco ball, its shards of light tauntingly hinting at gnostic release of the pneumatic sparks of life . . . but not quite. It is a concept that would reappear a decade later in his collaboration[16] with Arcade Fire, another band navigating the turbulent seas of mystic spirituality.

Intriguingly, in the closing moments of the film clip to 'Bring Me the Disco King' we see Bowie in a recording studio, candidly remarking on an apparent paranormal experience around death, with knowing assurance: '. . . you hear all these sounds that have just emerged since we started talking about the supernatural? That's the sound of death . . . that's what it sounds like when you're dead . . . doors opening'.

There's a distinct familiarity as he speaks of death as a doorway, evoking Janus, the ancient Roman god of beginnings and ends, change and transition, the keeper of gates, doorways and the passage of time. Bowie and the twin-faced god looking eternally to the future and the past seem well acquainted. Yet dark as Bowie's death complex seems, swirling with fears of being forgotten and invisible, perhaps the enduring presence of death can be as much a force for liberation as melancholic burden. According to Carlos Castaneda, the famous twentieth-century anthropologist turned mystic, Yaqui seers, believed that to fully grasp life one must live knowing death stands eternally behind your left shoulder, only ever a backwards glance away (Castaneda, 1968). The skeletal apparition of death on the Magic Studio door behind Bowie's own left shoulder seems a profoundly uncanny manifestation of this precept.

The haunting shadows continued in the still images. Jimmy King's bizarrely striking Silver (death) Mask portrait created for *NME* (see www.nme.com/news/david-bowie/68907) conjured up Bowie's early mime performance 'The Mask' (from the 1969 promotional film *Love You till Tuesday*), the tale of an actor who dons a persona for his audience until it subsumes his underlying self, smothering his identity with its unrestrained dominance and kills him. This reference seemed to signal the enduring struggle with persona and shadow seen in Bowie's creative work, foreshadowing archetypal manifestations such as Ziggy Stardust and The Thin White Duke so seemingly disintegrated they split off and took on lives of their own. Inside the magazine, a dimly-lit Bowie stood beside a curtain, the hint of a negative image evoking a ghostly skull behind his left shoulder. Once more Bowie was accompanied by an ethereal doppelganger, staring back from the pages like a glitch in the material matrix.[17]

A corpse hanging from a beam

Undoubtedly one of the most disturbing corpses in Bowie's recent work is the one hanging from a beam in the vicious invocation of suicide found on 'You Feel So Lonely You Could Die' (*The Next Day*, 2013). With chilling contempt Bowie, possibly singing as a dark Angel of Death, seems to be sociopathically willing a soul into the abyss, his dark, wolverine lyrics cloaked in a disarmingly accessible sheep's-clothing ballad: 'I see you as a corpse, hanging from a beam / I could read you like a book, I can feel you falling . . . please make it soon'. His swinging corpse brings to mind yet another nineteenth-century Symbolist, Belgium painter James Ensor, whose creative expression abounds with the same archetypal images that fascinate Bowie: masks and skeletons, mannequins, pierrots, corpses, death, Christ and religious iconography. In Ensor's *Skeletons Fighting for the Body of a Hanged Man*, painted in 1891, Death itself is split as 'ever-circling skeletal' figures fight for '. . . a corpse hanging from a beam' while a crowd of grotesque archetypal theatrical characters watch fixated from behind opening doors (see http://jamesensor.vlaamsekunstcollectie.be/en/collection/skeletons-fighting-for-the   body-of-a-hanged-man). As Bowie had so assuredly observed at the end of 'Bring Me the Disco King': '. . . that's the sound of death . . . doors opening'.

Significantly, Ensor's corpse is marked with the word 'civet' – a dish of stewed hare. With hares/rabbits a traditional symbol of Easter, scholars have noted Ensor was associating this corpse both with the persecuted Christ (Acts 10:39 – Christ slain and hung on a tree), and the artist himself (Vervoort, 1990). Ensor's convergence of Christ/hare/corpse symbolism throws up interesting comparisons with Bowie's most recent corpses and mirrors the Ziggy/hare/corpse dynamic seen in the incarnation and crucifixion of the 'leper messiah' Ziggy Stardust in his Yamamoto jumpsuit emblazoned with . . . a white hare.[18]

In one way, 'You Feel So Lonely You Could Die' could be the tortuously dark shadow to Ziggy's 'Rock 'n' Roll Suicide' forty years earlier, whose passionate declarations of support against the horror of loneliness, alienation and abandonment in 1972 were the counterpoint to the tormented, lacerating voices coldly spat out in the later song: 'Oh no love! you're not alone / You're watching yourself but you're too unfair/ All the knives seem to lacerate your brain, I've had my share, I'll help you with the pain' ('Rock 'n' Roll Suicide', 1972). All who have stared into the existential abyss of self-annihilation have heard the tormenting voice in 'You Feel So Lonely You Could Die' or the baying crowd taunting the suicidal in 'Jump They Say'[19] *(Black Tie White Noise*, 1993), desperately craving the salvation offered in 'Rock 'n' Roll Suicide'. But things may not be this simple when attempting to discern the difference between incarnated projection and spiritual direction. What if aspects of ourselves, like Bowie's mime mask, need to die or be killed in order to be released or resurrected?

Curiously, the corpse Bowie saw 'hanging from the beam' in 2013 was lyrically prefigured by punk band Scaterd Few in 1990's 'Kill the Sarx',[20] singing of Bowie's persona Ziggy Stardust. '. . .Weird and Gilley wasting away in the trance of their chameleon's Messiahcal gaze, the spirit is willing the flesh is still weak, Corpses lay rotting corpses still reek . . . Kill the sarx, Hang him from your rafters'('Kill the Sarx', *Sin Disease*, 1990). Three years later Bowie reflected:

> There was a theory that one creates a doppelganger and then imbues that with all your faults and guilts and fears and then eventually you destroy him, hopefully destroying all your guilt, fear and paranoia. And I often feel that I was doing that unwittingly, creating an alternative ego that would take on everything that I was insecure about.
>
> Bowie, 1993

In this way, the instinct behind the carnage is an attempt to manage powerful shadow forces before they subsume the light, both on the personal and collective level. The corpse hanging from a beam in 'You Feel So Lonely You Could Die' who 'stole their trust, their moon, their sun' – images with archetypally spiritual and hermetic connotations – could then arguably be representative of the shadow self, as well as the deceptive figures in 'The Next Day'.

Quid est veritas?

Years earlier Bowie had played Pontius Pilate in *The Last Temptation of Christ*, a movie exploring the dilemma of discerning truth when darkness masquerades as light. Handing Christ over to his own crucifixion, his character asks Christ to perform a miracle, enquiring whether this is 'good magic or bad magic?' (*The Last Temptation of Christ*, 1988). After a lifetime of shadowboxing, Bowie was still exploring spiritual dialectics, closing his 2013 album with 'Heat', one of the most tortuous songs he has ever written: '. . . And I tell myself, I don't know who I am . . . But I am a seer, I am a liar. . .' (*The Next Day*, 2013).

It's a song that seems to come from a lifetime staring deep into the abyss '. . . waiting for something, looking for someone, Is there no reason? Have I stared too long?', the lyric from 'The Rays' (2002) echoing Symbolist Odilon Redon's 1896 painting *St Antoine: What Is the Point of All This? The Devil: There Is No Point!* It's the death of surety, the '*quid est veritas?*' – 'What is truth?' – Pilate remarks, confronting Christ in the Gospels, 'the horror of knowing' that perceptions may only be projections, reflections or self-delusory deception. It's the seer's curse, that lies can bleed truth; the gnostic dilemma, trapped in the black iron prison of matter by the wrong god; or is that yet another illusion? It's a Mobius strip of confusion as many see symbols but read them so very differently.[21]

Which brings us to yet another intriguing Jimmy King image of Bowie overlooking New York like Mishima's peacock in the snow (see http://tanjastark. com/2014/10/20/confronting-bowies-mysterious-corpses-2/). He salutes, fingers hinting, again, of the Latin benediction gesture he displayed in his prison cell *Pieta*. Performed with the right hand, this iconic gesture is associated with the papal blessing seen in religious paintings and statues; performed with the left, it can be indicative of the Left Hand Path of esotericism that so intrigued Bowie's portrait companion, William Burroughs. Inverting the image, his scarf apophenically functions as a hangman's noose emblazoned with Rorschach-like inkblot skulls – an ever-circling skeletal family around his neck, an archetypal 'Hanged Man' swirling with themes of death and resurrection.

Synchronistic shadows often seem to swirl around Bowie, but they are only one part of the whole. Look again at King's balcony photograph searching for light and, with a dash of imagination, it seems the angels haven't gone. Death may lurk behind Bowie's left shoulder, but in King's image a serendipitous snowflake gives the illusion of an angel on his right one – a tiny 'word on a wing'.[22] As Fyodor Karamazov might wonder: 'Was it symbolic of something, or what?'[23]

Everybody gets got

'Seek and you will find', promises the old spiritual principle.[24] If we look for death we see her everywhere and Bowie is confronting us, as she confronts him, with all her guises. Death stalks us all and 'everyone gets got' in the end ('I'd Rather Be High', 2013). But Bowie's corpses are but one polarity – for where there is shadow, there is also light. Where there is crucifixion there can also be resurrection. In Bowie's tumultuous dance with religion, death and mysticism, his art wrestles with the possibility, and impossibility, of worlds and concepts beyond the material veil. As Saint-Exupéry's fox in *The Little Prince* wisely observes, 'One sees clearly only with the heart. What is essential is invisible to the eye.' When the ever-circling skeletons approach and death finally opens the door, may the wisdom of mystic St John of the Cross transcend the angels and devils, and in the evening of life may we be judged on love alone.

Notes

1   Recalling the poisoned, stained fingers of the monks in Umberto Eco's novel *The Name of the Rose*, (1980) who worked on forbidden manuscripts.

2   'Time he's waiting in the wings / He speaks of senseless things. His script is you and me, boy . . . Oh well I look at my watch, it says 9:25 and I think Oh God I'm still alive' ('Time', *Aladdin Sane*, 1973).

3   'I took this walk to ease my mind / to find out what's gnawing at me / wouldn't think to look at me, that I've spent a lot of time in education / It all seems so long ago / I'm a thinker, not a talker, I've no one to talk to, anyway . . . And the world is full of life / Full of folk who don't know me . . . And my hands shake, my head hurts, my voice sticks inside my throat I'm invisible and dumb / And no one will recall me' ('Conversation Piece', 1967).

4   Saint-Exupéry's classic novella *The Little Prince* (Saint-Exupéry and Howard, 2000) and 'Nature Boy' – a Jazz standard from 1948, covered by Bowie in 2001 – are two tales of mysterious encounters between enchanted wanderers and wise strangers that seem to have some overlap with the concepts in 'The Man Who Sold the World' (1970). The magical Little Prince from another planet who falls to Earth on a curious search, seeking water (a spiritual metaphor) and wisdom, learning the mysteries of life, love and death also parallels Bowie's far more detached character in *The Man Who Fell To Earth* [1976] – an alien on a quest for water. The lyrics of 'Nature Boy' too, speak of a strange enchanted boy wandering afar until '. . . one magic day He passed my way, and while we spoke of many things, fools and kings this he

said to me / the greatest thing you'll ever learn is just to love and be loved in return'.

5   Kate Bush also sang of Hans Christian Andersen's tale on 'The Red Shoes' in 1993. Her film clip features Lindsay Kemp, Bowie's (and Bush's) early mime teacher as a demonic trickster; a cautionary tale about the seductive 'power to charm' of the dark side and the heavy price one can pay for dancing with the devil.

6   Despite severing her own legs to stop the red shoes dancing, the dismembered limbs in Andersen's tale continued their cursed dance, blocking the little girl from getting '. . . to the church on time' – a concept referenced in 'Modern Love', leaving her alone, pleading for mercy.

7   'Scream Like a Baby' (*Scary Monsters and Super Creeps*, 1980).

8   Almost a homonym for CoCo Schwabe, Bowie's long-term friend and assistant.

9   Rodenbach's opus was the novel *Bruges de Mort*, a tale of death, melancholia and a fatal obsession with a doppelganger that results in a deranged murder – all themes touched upon by Bowie in his work.

10   Echoing the severing of the legs that wore the cursed red shoes in Hans Christian Andersen's fairy tale.

11   '. . . A glass-like spider / having devoured its prey it would drape the skeletons over its web in weeks creating a macabre shrine of remains . . . One could almost call it an altar' ('Glass Spider', 1987).

12   See Dostoyevsky's 'The Grand Inquisitor' from his novel *The Brothers Karamazov*.

13   The Great Architect – God in the mystery and Masonic traditions etc.

14   The original film clip from the *Reality* promotional media suite.

15   The Old Testatment also speaks of Hagar desperately 'looking for water' for her dying son Ishmael, Islamic patriarch.

16   The film clips to both songs feature black and white imagery of the woods at night, fractured pieces of mirrors and disco balls scattering rays of light, and hints at conceptual ideas of gnostic mysteries, psyche reflections, shadows and paradox.

17   Recalling the Kirlian 'energy' photography that once fascinated the Duke, featured in the *Station to Station* tour material, and again in the film clip to *Seven Years in Tibet*.

18   Animals traditionally thought to have hermaphrodite traits.

19   '. . . My friend don't listen to the crowd / They say "Jump" / Got to believe somebody / Got to believe' ('Jump They Say', 1992). Said to be influenced by his brother's suicide, the song has interesting parallels to Satan tempting Christ to throw himself from the temple found in the New Testament.

20   *Sarx*: Greek for flesh.

21   Bowie may be 'a seer' and 'a liar' but perhaps some of the tumult in 'Heat' is in part, rare confirmation of Picasso's intriguing observation, 'We all know that Art is not truth. Art is a lie that makes us realize truth at least the truth that is given us to understand. The artist must know the manner whereby to convince others of the truthfulness of his lies' (Picasso, 'Picasso Speaks,' in *The Arts*, 1923).

22 'Lord, lord, my prayer flies like a word on a wing . . . does my prayer fit in with your scheme of things? ('Word on a Wing', *Station to Station*, 1975).

23 See Dostoyevsky's 'The Grand Inquisitor' from his novel *The Brothers Karamazov*.

24 Gospel of Luke, Chapter 11, Verse 9.

Bibliography

Ball, Norm. 2013. *Red Book Red Sail*. http://redbookredsail.wordpress.com.

Bowie, David. 1993. Interview by Tony Parsons. *Arena Magazine*, spring/summer.

Bowie, David. 1995. 'Diary of Nathan Adler'. CD liner notes, *Outside*, Arista/ BMG.

Bowie, David. 2004. 'What I've learned: David Bowie'. *Esquire Magazine*, 29 February.

Burroughs, William S., James Grauerholz and Barry Miles. 2001. *Naked Lunch*. New York: Grove Press.

Castaneda, Carlos. 1968/1996. *The Teachings of Don Juan: A Yaqui Way of Knowledge*. New York: Simon & Schuster.

Cinque, Toija. 2013. 'David Bowie: dancing with madness and proselytising the socio-political in art and life'. *Celebrity Studies Journal*, 4 (3), 401–7.

Dery, Mark. 2010. 'Leper messiah: a Jesus freak's search for the meaning of Bowie'. In ReligionDispatches.com, http://religiondispatches.org/leper-messiah-a-jesus-freaks-search-for-the-meaning-of-bowie-a-critical-novella/ (see also www.markdery.com).

Dostoyevsky, Fyodor. 1880/2007. *The Brothers Karamazov*, translated by Constance Garnett. Hertfordshire: Wordsworth Classics.

III, Paul. (1997). 'The search starts with a simple abundance of enthusiasm'. *Music Paper*, March, www.algonet.se/~bassman/articles/97/mp.html, accessed 10 February 2014.

Kierkegaard, Soren. 1844. *Eighteen Upbuilding Discourses*. Translated by Edna Hatlestad Hong and Howard Vincent Hong. Princeton: Princeton University Press.

Mishima, Yukio. 2010. *Spring Snow*. New York: Random House.

Penman, Ian. 1995. 'The resurrection of Saint Dave.' *Esquire Magazine*, October.

Saint-Exupéry, Antoine de and Richard Howard 2000. *The Little Prince*, 1st edition. San Diego: Harcourt.

Savage, Steele. 2010. *The Hearts Filthy Lesson / David Bowie, Alastair Crowley and Holy Grail*. www.parareligion.ch/2010/bowiegrail.htm.

Stark, Tanja. 2015. 'Crashing out with Sylvian: David Bowie, Carl Jung and the Unconscious.' In Eoin Devereux, Martin Power and Aileen Dillane (eds) *David Bowie: Critical Perspectives*. London: Routledge.

St John of the Cross and Kathleen Jones. 2001. *The Poems of St John of The Cross*. 1st edtion. Tunbridge Wells: Burns & Oates.

Vervoort, P. 1990 'Reinforcing the image: Ensor's use of signs in works 1886 to 1896'. In Theo d' Haen (ed.) *Verbal/Visual Crossings*, 1880–1980. Amsterdam: Rodopi.

SECTION TWO

Time

Introduction

Echo, cover, play, mash

Time is what we have, what we lose, a point we might look forward to or backward upon – it is simultaneously all and nothing, neither an event nor a thing. This section takes not a realist's view of time but considers its circularity wherein time folds back upon itself, allowing for the reinterpretation of memories, feelings and experiences and all the intervals in between. In this section Bowie will be explored through time and the temporal, as an artist who is futuristic and nostalgic, who draws upon resurrection and memorial motifs, and who 'bends' time so that an anti-linearity emerges in and through his work.

In **Will Brooker**'s chapter, 'Time Again: The David Bowie Chronotope', Bakhtin's theory of the chronotope is used to explore the nature of time, story and character in David Bowie's work across several decades, with a focus primarily on the textual analysis of lyrical content. Brooker has applied Bakhtin's concepts of narrative and chronological structure to key themes in Bowie's oeuvre, such as time, age, identity and the exotic Other, and traces these themes across texts from the early 'The London Boys' (1966) to the more recent and retrospective 'Where Are We Now?' (2013). Brooker takes notable individual songs such as 'The Man Who Sold the World' (1970) as the focus of sustained case study, drawing out their intertextual links and cultural echoes to suggest the broad dialogic matrix in which they function. Overall, Brooker makes the strong case for the utility and potential of this literary theory as applied to his examination of Bowie's extensive, complex output, and suggests the ways in which this approach could be usefully continued. We asked Will about what drew him to this approach to Bowie's work over time:

My concern with, or interest in, or relationship with Bowie seems inseparable from ideas of time. As a Bowie fan since 1983, his albums and singles, his various styles and shifts in direction are bound up in memories of my own life and its landmarks. As episodes in my life seem to echo Bowie songs and videos, and find parallels with other memories and experiences, so his lyrics and the images he constructs seem to speak backward and forward to each other, across the decades – sometimes self-consciously, sometimes accidentally. I use Baktin in this essay as a tool for beginning to structure and explore this huge, complex landscape of sounds and visions. It is an academic piece, but also personal. I feel it also begins to explore my feelings for Bowie and pay tribute to his importance in my life, through the medium – scholarly writing – most easily available to me.

The chapter by **David Baker**, 'Bowie's Covers: The Artist as Modernist', is primarily concerned with considering some of the key ways in which Bowie's work contextualizes itself in a relationship with other artists, partly through what we might call the 'tribute song' but principally through the cover version. While accepting that a certain postmodern thematic is clearly present in certain aspects of Bowie's work, particularly in the 70s (artifice, play, camp, for example), Baker's contention, motivated by his dissatisfaction with postmodern analyses of Bowie's work which he argues tend to read Bowie's intertextuality in partial and tendentious ways, is to temper postmodern enthusiasm by considering the ways in which Bowie's work has maintained a certain distance from postmodernity. In order to consider some of the strategies by which Bowie's work draws out intertextual relations with other artists, Baker makes a strategic decision to adopt an analytic approach to Bowie which considers his work as *both* postmodern and modern, thus problematizing easy distinctions between artifice versus authenticity, play versus seriousness, or camp versus straight as exemplars in Bowie's corpus. Baker's critique makes no claims to completion, but considers three specific aspects of Bowie's oeuvre: firstly, a close examination of Bowie's transitional 1971 album *Hunky Dory* to tease out the ways in which the 'tribute' songs on the album point in both a modernist and a postmodernist direction; secondly, that on the two Bowie albums which arguably trade strongly in cover versions – *Pin Ups* (1973) and *Tonight* (1984) – modernity not only underpins but in fact circumscribes postmodernity. Thirdly, in considering Bowie's cover versions more generally across his opera, Baker suggests that a postmodern approach that would consider Bowie's covers in terms of their deconstruction of the opposition between fan/consumer and creator/interpreter is not thoroughgoing enough. He contends instead for the efficacy of an approach that considers Bowie's covers in terms of the system of gift exchange as outlined by the French sociologist Marcel Mauss (1966). In his own auto-ethnographic reflection of what led him to begin his essay, David recalls that:

I was delighted to contribute an essay considering time in relation to Bowie because of a long-held interest in Bowie's cover versions. Bowie's covers, it seemed to me, were very much concerned with establishing his relationship with other artists – both in terms of establishing his own relationship to various traditions of pop/rock music as well as acknowledging the ways in which other artists had not merely influenced him but were in fact part of the bricolage or ensemble of elements that made up Bowie himself. There was a strong temporal dimension to this, both in terms of the way Bowie related to both past and present in developing a persona, as well as continually taking on board new influences while developing/ transforming that persona.

The very first Bowie album I was old enough to be conscious of its release was *Aladdin Sane* which contains the song 'Time' ('His trick is you and me, boy'), which always intrigued me for the way in which the song personified time. Bowie's very next album was the album of covers, *Pin Ups*. I wonder whether the association between time and covers began for me there?

Film-maker scholar, **Amedeo D'Adamo** questions in his chapter, 'Ain't there One Damn Flag that Can Make Me Break Down and Cry?: The Formal, Performative and Emotional Tactics of Bowie's Singular Critical Anthem "Young Americans" ', whether, of all the fabulist baubles of five decades comprising David Bowie's work, there might be just one damn song that consciously tries to make us break down and cry; one that is uniquely political and uniquely emotionally real. The answer for D'Adamo is an unequivocal 'Yes'; there is his hit song 'Young Americans'. By no coincidence, 'Young Americans' is also Bowie's singular foray into the rich tradition of the American anthem, that long chain of storytelling songs that set out to portray the state of the nation. D'Adamo argues that the great songbook opens with the classical American anthem itself but of course the pro-nationalist tradition takes a critical, modernist turn in the 1950s as the folk movement writes critical anthems for the civil rights and anti-war movements. He considers systematically that suddenly, the tree begins producing strange fruit at this time; the anthem's formal choral nature, featuring many people pursuing many objectives and faiths but all united by a certain pursuit of happiness, is suddenly ironically appropriated; in the critical anthem, a myriad of American characters are all lost in a morally empty American landscape, their naïve faiths shattered. D'Adamo further contends that the pop-chart debut of 'Young Americans' in 1975 marked the withering end not only of the folk dominance of the critical anthem but even of both New Left utopian hope and perhaps of the modernist critical anthem itself. For here, according to D'Adamo's thesis, Bowie's unparalleled skills as a vocal, lyrical and character menagerist peoples a materialist landscape with no myth left from the ghetto, no hope to be found in marriage or sex, no way to tell emotion from alienation. The chapter declares that, whereas other critical anthems use many personal stories to express a political problem, Bowie brilliantly flips this to make the political personal, using the political exhaustion of the US after president Richard Nixon (from 1969 to 1974) as a metaphor for the country's exhausted gender-roles and paralysed pop-cultural hopes. Finally, D'Adamo examines this critical point in time in the US to draw attention to its swirling choral cacophony of unsatisfied desires, an intimacy of narrator slippage and 'dissolving self', but notes that, consequently, the period also bore witness to the opening of the postmodern chapter – the liquid inner turn – of the critical anthem songbook. In personal consideration of 'why Bowie' and specifically, 'why "Young Americans?" ' as a chosen theme, Amedeo remembers that:

As a kid in the 1970s I think I always related to pop singers as adopting the particular festiveness of American holidays, and for me Bowie was always like a child running around on Halloween night. He's not a balladeering lover declaiming on Valentine's Day like Elton John and so many others were. And he's never a folk-singer delivering homilies on Thanksgiving Day or (like Dylan or Springsteen) playing concerned citizen in a denim jacket on the Fourth of July or meditating on the sacrificial meaning of Memorial Day; there's no obvious civic or romantic lesson, no hard-gained wisdom in Bowie's work, no striving for authenticity, no squeezing of the heart for tears, no sympathies and no celebrations of ideals, events, situations and historical sacrifices in the classic, modernist, folk or rock mode. That's for another day – tonight it's Halloween; this is a night of enchantment.

Except for this one damn song. Today I'm a feature and documentary filmmaker who works extensively with actors, and perhaps that's why I love how in 'Young Americans' Bowie's ability to carve mannered netsuke-like characters and his Gatsby-like precision of singing and acting comportment is colliding with specific and traumatic American national-historical moments, somehow joining studio-time's precision of affect with socially-shared time and memory, creating a paradox of solidly-fixed forensic documentary-time and liquid studio-time. This crazy mix in the song has resonated with me personally in three different ways. First there was this Brit-in-America singing about 1975; I initially heard the song as a young American growing up in the Bronx during Vietnam, the son of an upper-class British-South African mom of impeccable manners and Brooklyn-born working-class Italian-American dad, a pair tenuously united through their work in the civil rights movement. Later, when we moved from the raucous Bronx to a 'McMansion' in the all-white suburbs, the song's sense of being trapped suddenly mirrored my own sense of life in the Reagan (-led government) era. And in 2014, probably because I now work with so many young Europeans who've no shared EU identity and no myth left from the marketplace, Bowie's anxious affect now sounds like a beseeching shout-out to our widespread global precarity. Misery, boredom and anxiety; the song has it all.

In **Christopher Moore**'s chapter, '2004 (Bowie vs Mashup)', the 2004 'mashup' competition conducted by David Bowie, as part of the promotional strategies for the American component of his 'A Reality Tour' in the same year, is revisited. Moore's work frames this specific encounter within remix subculture using Sinnreich's account of the mashup's musical 'figure' and 'ground' to consider Bowie's own appropriation of the subgenre that is consistent with his pre-digital history of bricolage. Moore critically explores Bowie's history as a celebrated bricoleur whose revisionist performance of the public presentation of the self was richly demonstrated in the early 1960s through participation in mod subculture and later with his Ziggy Stardust persona in 1972. Moore considers the 2004 competition as characteristic of Bowie's bricoleur business strategies, demonstrating his ability to complicate the music industry's key domains of devaluation of the mashup through intellectual property restrictions. Moore addresses three domains of devaluation in terms of Bowie's appropriation of the mashup: firstly, the domain of the individual, the primary point at which mashups are restricted by the music industry's legal and technical forms of governance; the secondary domain of devaluation, where general audience-level access restrictions and copyright-based contracts are intended to limit the potential for transformative responses to creative works; and the tertiary domain of devaluation that is established broadly by the organization of copyright law to regard works based on samples as 'derivative', and where mashups are reserved by artists and record labels as non-serious, ancillary content that is suitable only for promotional products and fan consumption. It is clear that Chris is passionate about this aspect of study as his personal chronicle attests:

David Bowie entered my life at a very formative time. I was neck deep in the history of intellectual property in the early days of my PhD candidature and thoroughly, fannishly obsessed with the copyright 'hackers' including Richard Stallman, Lawrence Lessig, Aaron Swartz and others who were actively challenging the neoliberal agenda at the centre of trade-based harmonization of international copyright law that would criminalize file-sharing, reduce open culture and ultimately lead to the erosion of the public domain. Bowie entered this scene in early 2004, a time when remix culture was being heralded as a subcultural response to the restrictive permission culture of the music recording industry, which had engaged in decades of grossly exorbitant copyright litigation against the unauthorized use of audio samples. The mashup competition co-sponsored by Bowie and the auto manufacturer Audi was, on the surface, an audacious move, but the fine print in the terms and conditions of entry revealed a complex iteration and translation of the mashup to a more commercial-friendly culture. I was determined to include Bowie and the mashup competition as a case study alongside the Open Source, Creative Commons and Free Software movements in my thesis and began to investigate what mashup producers were saying about this mainstream industry figure co-opting the subculture for purely promotional purposes. Two distinct conversations were immediately apparent, the first was concern over the commercialization of the culture, but the second was the incredible regard for Bowie and the extensive use of his work in mashups. There was in some sense a little payback in terms of counter-appropriation in this encounter, but unfortunately Bowie never made it to the thesis.

The mashup competition remained only small note in the history of remix culture, which deserved much greater attention. When the editors approached me to submit an abstract for the collection I knew exactly what I wanted to pitch, possibly before they had finished asking the question.

5

Time Again:

The David Bowie Chronotope

Will Brooker

'One day,' David Bowie promised in 1984, in his song 'Blue Jean', 'I'm gonna write a poem in a letter.' In 1997, he effectively kept that promise, releasing 'Battle For Britain (The Letter)', which explicitly offers the song and its lyric as a correspondence with the listener ('don't you let my letter get you down . . .'). But he, or another, earlier version of himself, had already ticked this commitment off his list, long before 1984.

In 1969 Bowie had written 'Letter to Hermione', a poem addressed to a former girlfriend, which of course (despite its own lyrical promise that he was writing 'just for you') became a public document and an open, one-sided correspondence when it was released as an album track. Already, through this simplest of examples, any sense of chronology in Bowie's work and career begins to break down, as texts seem, through their connections, to speak to each other across time.

One day. I'm gonna. Where, when and how does Bowie's statement from 1984 operate? Is it a vow to the listener, or a vague note to himself? If the latter, then which self? The *Let's Dance* album of 1983 is usually seen as Bowie's return to (or invention of) a fitter, happier, healthier self, stripped of all the personae he'd adopted in the previous decade (Ziggy Stardust, Aladdin Sane, The Thin White Duke, Hallowe'en Jack, Major Tom); sexually straighter, in business suits and with an easy laugh, poised to reach a mainstream, international audience. The Bowie of 1984, of 'Blue Jean' and the *Tonight* album, occupies the same period and the same role, the same clean, athletic image. No masks, no costumes, no fake names: except of course, for the tan, the suit, and 'David Bowie'. Could an aside made in 'Blue Jean' ever be seen genuinely as an artistic footnote for David Jones, the man who was born in Brixton on 8 January 1947 and who has his own, private biography, progressing slowly now towards his own seventieth birthday? Should we see that line as 'David Bowie' talking to himself, to us, to the character Blue Jean; or is the Bowie of 'Blue Jean', despite the lack of explicit persona, himself a character from that specific song – a man hung up on a girl who is never mentioned in any other track?[1]

One day. I'm gonna. How does it complicate our sense of chronology and historical moment when we remember that Bowie performed the song, made that promise, or murmured that aside, to live audiences on his 1987, 1990 and 2004 tours? If I play the song again now, in April 2014, is the line renewed again, and the promise deferred once again into the future? Should we see it in context, as a historical artefact from a specific period, or is Bowie's dialogue with us, with himself, always 'live', revived as a conversation whenever we play the song (on vinyl, on cassette, on CD, on iTunes and YouTube) and play it again into a million different moments and as many unknowable contexts as there are listeners?

How do we begin to answer these questions? Not through a poem or a letter, but a chapter, or better, an *essay*, with its inherent sense of *attempt*. We should, at this stage, begin with questions, rather than a complete solution; we should anticipate and even embrace exploration and negotiation. A scholarly piece about Bowie should, I believe, also try to capture – not in the sense of *contain* and keep, but catch and communicate, borrow from and pass on – some of his energy, experiment and novelty. In this chapter, then, I draw on Mikhail Bakhtin's ideas of time and space in the novel, not in an attempt to box up Bowie within theory, but to suggest some ways in which this approach can offer new entry points, draw lines of continuity through a career associated with change, and start to map routes through the vast, complex chronology and territory of his work. Rather than providing all the answers, it is intended to mark a beginning.

Bakhtin's 'Forms of Time and Chronotope in the Novel' was written in 1937–8, though its concluding remarks – a lengthy and significant section – were added in 1973, two years before Bakhtin's death and in the year of *Aladdin Sane*'s release.[2] It explores several different types of *chronotope* ('time-space'), a term Bakhtin himself borrows from mathematics to describe the means through which the time-space relation is expressed in art (Bakhtin, 1981: 85). Though his named focus is the novel, his use of that term, too, is so broad – stretching back far beyond and before the conventional eighteenth-century landmarks of Defoe, Richardson, Fielding and Sterne to include the ancient Greek romance – and his gestures towards other forms such as oral storytelling and song are so suggestive – 'we always arrive', he proposes, 'in the final analysis, at the human voice' (253) – that his theory seems to actively invite an application to narratives in other media.[3] While his categories of chronotope are presented as distinct and specific to a particular genre, Bakhtin stresses, in his powerful concluding remarks, that they also overlap, intersect and enter into dialogue with each other (and with both author and reader/listener) (252).

Bakhtin (102) also draws on the metaphor of a space filled, in the Greek romance, with 'isolated curiosities and rarities that bear no connection to each other . . . self-sufficient items – curious, odd, wondrous . . . they are congealed "suddenlys," adventures turned into things'. In a different historical and formal context, he describes the fusion of time and space in the 'new territory' of the seventeenth-century Gothic novel as a castle, filled with 'the traces of centuries and generations . . . furnishings, weapons, the ancestral portrait gallery, the family archives . . . the traces of time in the castle do bear a . . . museum-like character' (246). We might think here not just of the cluttered store-rooms, both interior and exterior, conjured by the lyrics of 'Five Years' (1972) ('my brain hurt like a warehouse, it had no room to spare') and displayed in the video for 'Where Are We Now?' (2013) but also of the vast and comprehensive David Bowie exhibition, first hosted by London's V&A Museum in 2013.

Time, too, is given flexible flesh, made both fluid and concrete, through Bakhtin's chronotope: it seems to gain form like one of the elastic-bodied superheroes in comic books, stretching while remaining solid. It becomes, in Bakhtin's words, 'in effect, palpable and visible; the chronotope makes narrative events concrete, makes them take on flesh, causes blood to flow in their veins' (250). In the chronotope, 'spatial and temporal indicators are fused into one . . . concrete whole. Time, as it were, thickens, takes on flesh, becomes artistically visible; likewise, space becomes charged and responsive to the movements of time, plot and history' (84). In Bowie's work, time also takes on physical form, a silent, mime-like companion who, in 'Rock 'n' Roll Suicide' (1972), 'takes a cigarette . . . [and] puts it in your mouth'; in 'Time', also from 1972, time is a figure who waits in the wings and, in a vivid image of chronology taking on flesh and thickening through the rush of blood, 'falls wanking to the floor'.[4]

This is not the time, and there is not the space, to fully demonstrate the affinities that Bakhtin's theory has with Bowie's oeuvre. But if we can accept, as a starting point, that Bowie's two poems-as-letters-as-songs and his hypothetical letter of 'Blue Jean' exist, metaphorically, somewhere within or between the head-like-a-warehouse of 1972's 'Five Years' and the crowded memory-room of 'Where Are We Now?', and that Bakhtin's intersecting, overlapping models of time and space can help us to analyse the complex relationship between the artefacts of Bowie's songs and performances, the various masks, costumes and voices that surround them, the historical moments that link and contextualize them, the various authors and characters that circulate around David Jones, and the reader-listeners who receive and interpret his stories at different times in different places, then where are we now? We are at the beginning of an exploration, an investigation, an explanation.

Across the diverse forms of 'novel' in his study, Bakhtin returns repeatedly to a model that posits a horizontal and a vertical. In the 'adventure novel of everyday life' (111), the horizontal maps the protagonist's life, tracing his overall growth in experience and, often, a progress towards redemption. Commonly, this progress is represented within the story by an 'actual spatial course or road . . . thus is realized the metaphor "the path of life" ' (120). This road both provides the metaphorical map for the character's pilgrimage and progress, and provides the arena for the chance meetings and choices that structure his narrative and shape his life. 'On the road', from Chaucer to Kerouac,

> the spatial and temporal paths of the most varied people . . . intersect at one spatial and temporal point . . . people who are normally kept separate by social and spatial distance can accidentally meet; any contrast may crop up, the most various fates may collide and interweave with one another.
>
> Bakhtin, 1981: 243

The individual scenes, encounters and episodes of his story occupy a vertical axis, intersecting the horizontal and chopping up the primary narrative into single episodes (128). He later identifies the vertical intersections that cross 'the horizontal axis of time' as 'a superstructure for reality . . . other-worldly, idealistic, eternal, outside time . . . simultaneous with a given moment in the present' (148).

This 'other-worldly, vertical axis' is

> subject to symbolic interpretation . . . time is utterly excluded from action. This is a 'vision,' after all, and visions in real time are very brief; indeed the meaning of what is seen is itself extratemporal (although it does have some connection with time).
>
> Bakhtin, 1981: 156

In Dante, Bakhtin confirms, this vision-time intersects with 'the specific biographical moment (the time of a human life) . . .' (56); it is, literally, a step out of time, off the 'road' of linear chronology, into an alternate space. In Dante, this results in a struggle between 'living historical time and the extratemporal other-worldly ideal' (158):

The temporal logic of this vertical world consists in the sheer simultaneity of all that occurs (or 'the coexistence of everything in eternity'). Everything that on earth is divided by time, here, in this verticality, coalesces into eternity, into pure simultaneous coexistence. Such divisions as time introduces – 'earlier' and 'later' – have no substance here; they must be ignored in order to understand this vertical world; everything must be perceived as being within *a single time*, that is, in the synchrony of a single moment; one must see this entire world as simultaneous.

Bakhtin, 1981: 157

We can draw from this, then – before we factor in other, more complex axes – a simple geometric model of a horizontal – which carries the values of 'living historical time'; the road, progress, evolution, development, biography and chronology – intersected with verticals, which in turn represent sidesteps, alleys, choices, episodes and visions. To borrow from children's literature, the horizontal is the biographical lives of the Pevensie children in C.S. Lewis' novels, as they age and experience the twentieth century; the vertical intersections represent their adventures in Narnia, during which little or no 'real time' passes.

On 'Never Get Old', from the significantly-named *Reality* album of 2003, Bowie declares that he is 'running down the street of life': an advertisement for Vittel water, starring Bowie alongside tribute act David Brighton as the singer's earlier incarnations, opens boldly with that line. If we take the career of David Bowie (leaving to one side for now the biography of David Jones) as the horizontal 'street of life' – the advert clearly depicts this Bowie, older and simply-dressed, sceptical of his earlier forms, as the 'real' one, in contrast to the CGI and impersonation of the earlier versions – then the other incarnations are the characters we and he meet on that road. The advert shows us the Pierrot of *Ashes to Ashes*, the half-canine beast of *Diamond Dogs* and the red-haired profile from the cover of the *Low* album, but we could also include The Thin White Duke, Ziggy Stardust, Aladdin Sane and other named characters such as Hallowe'en Jack and Nathan Adler. These other figures lead us down the side-roads of adventure-time, which intersect the main 'street of life' on a vertical axis.

David Bowie's career can be mapped through time: the singer himself visibly (and audibly) ages, and is generally considered to evolve through stages from one album to the next; from the eponymous 1967 debut album, announcing his name and brand,[5] to 2013's *The Next Day*, with its inherent titular sense of chronological progression and its conceptual themes of nostalgia and age (most obviously in 'Where Are We Now?' and the video of 'The Stars Are Out Tonight'; but even the lighter rock of 'Valentine's Day' is based around a calendar date). However, Ziggy Stardust lives again whenever we revisit the 1972 single, The Thin White Duke returns with the first line of *Station to Station* (1976) and Nathan Adler's investigations begin once more with every replay of the 1995 *Outside* album. Of course, even the more personal and confessional Bowie of *Reality* also represents a side-step out of chronology to reflect on a specific moment (2003), but *Outside* steps further, into a then-imaginary future (the year 1999, now history) and into the personae of several characters, of various ages and genders. This alternate-universe adventure about Art Crime and its detection represents, against the linear horizontal of Bowie's career, what Bakhtin calls the 'other-worldly . . . outside time . . . simultaneous with a given moment in the present'. We can regard the stories of Thomas Newton in *The Man Who Fell To Earth* (Nicolas Roeg, 1976), Jareth in *Labyrinth* (Jim Henson, 1986), even Nikola Tesla in *The Prestige* (Christopher Nolan, 2005) similarly as sidesteps off the main road into a different world and different time.

Within this model, we can then approach Bowie's individual songs and videos as 'visions', 'adventures'; small pilgrimages, stories or, in the case of concept albums like *Diamond Dogs* and *Outside*, story-cycles made up of shorter episodes.[6] These metaphors acquire a particular resonance with Bowie's many songs that involve a form of narrative, however dreamlike, and a cast, however vague, of characters. 'The Man Who Sold the World' (1970), for instance, describes a meeting and dialogue with a spectre from the past, presumed long dead – though the narrator, too, 'wasn't there', implying a trance-state – followed by a journey in the mythic tradition. 'I searched for form and land, for years and years I roamed.' Obviously, this narrative, which seems to take place over eras (the narrator's travels end with him gazing at millions who 'must have died alone, a long long time ago'), operates in its own time-scheme. The song 'The Man Who Sold the World' is exactly four minutes long – its narrative takes that time to tell, as an album track, and occupies that precise temporal space in the listener's life – and we can date its composition, first recording and release to specific months and days in 1970.

On one level, 'The Man Who Sold the World' takes place in its own chronotope, a dreamlike time/space where years pass and millions die, and yet, at the end of the song, nothing has changed; it is as though we wake up, or return from Narnia, to find the world almost entirely as it was, only four minutes later. This chimes with the 'adventure-time' Bakhtin identifies in the Greek romance, where, for all the incidents and accidents of the narrative, the story ends at almost the same point as its beginning. The adventure is a hiatus between start and finish, taking up almost no 'real' time (91):

In this kind of time, nothing changes: the world remains as it was, the biographical life of the heroes does not change, their feelings do not change, people do not even age. This empty time leaves no traces anywhere, no indications of its passing. This, we repeat, is an extratemporal hiatus that appears between two moments of a real time sequence, in this case one that is biographical.

The hero of these stories, Bakhtin goes on, 'endures the game fate plays. And he not only endures – he keeps on being the same person and emerges from this game, from all these turns of fate and chance, with his identity absolutely unchanged' (105).

Clearly, this interpretation does not apply to Bowie himself, the public performer and recording artist, and even less so to the private individual David Jones; it describes only the narrator of that song, and that specific adventure off the main road. We emerge from that dreamlike story to find that nothing has changed, and, revisiting it at any point between 1970 and the present day, find ourselves back at the start, immersed again in a narrative that lasts both four minutes of real time and eras of adventure-time. We could compare the trancelike episode of 'The Man Who Sold the World' to the comic books studied by Umberto Eco, which, in that period – known to fans and scholars as the Silver Age, prior to tighter and more consistent 'continuity' in the superhero universe – exist in an 'oneiric climate' (Eco, 1984: 114) where each adventure makes little difference to the overall history of Superman, and can be either forgotten, rewritten, vaguely remembered or revisited and developed in future stories.

As such, each adventure down these side-streets into the other-worldly fictions of Bowie's songs, films and videos could be seen as self-contained, operating according to a specific chronotope where events take place and time passes, but nothing changes. However, as Bakhtin notes in his later concluding remarks, chronotopes are rarely if ever fully self-contained. Just as the various models of time-space he describes can be identified in the work of a single author, or even combined in a single work, so we may notice 'complex interactions among them', though one often dominates the others (252):

Chronotopes are mutually inclusive, they co-exist, they may be interwoven with, replace or oppose one another, contradict one another or find themselves in ever more complex interrelationships . . . the general characteristic of these interactions is that they are dialogical (in the broadest sense of the word).

'The Man Who Sold the World', then, like all the side-road adventures that intersect the horizontal real-time of Bowie's career, must be seen not as an isolated dead end but as part of a far more complex dialogic matrix. To trace only a few of the extra lines that extend from it, the song can be seen in the context of the album to which it lends a name, and with whose other tracks, in one interpretation, it shares Lovecraftian themes (Carr and Shaar Murray, 1981: 38). Its title speaks forward in time to *The Man Who Fell To Earth* (1976), also anticipating Bowie's later line 'I'll give you a man who wants to rule the world' ('China Girl', 1983) and backwards to Heinlein's novel *The Man Who Sold The Moon* (1951), to the William Hughes Mearns poem of 1922 about meeting 'a little man who wasn't there' and the World War II song it inspired, to the 1954 DC comic 'The Man Who Sold The Earth' and the 1968 Brazilian political satire *The Man Who Bought The World* (Doggett, 2012: 92). To David Buckley, Bowie's intonation echoes The Lord's Prayer (Buckley, 2001: 100); to Chris O'Leary, the song can be interpreted as a conversation between the unassuming David Jones who, in an alternate timeline, never left Bromley, and the Bowie of 1975, world-famous at the expense of his sanity. O'Leary (2010) sketches further links in the dialogic matrix in which the song operates, identifying not just its 'score of fathers', listed above, but also its 'symbolic twin', the Nicolas Roeg film *Performance* of the same year, and noting that the encounter described in the lyrics resonates with 'everything from Wilfred Owen's "Strange Meeting" to Conrad's "The Secret Sharer" to Ray Bradbury's "Night Meeting", in which a man and Martian cross paths . . . each convinced that the other hails from the distant past'.

As these multiple interpretations suggest, the matrix of meanings also includes reader-listener responses to the text. Bakhtin embraces this further dynamic, noting that (254):

> However forcefully the real and the represented world resist fusion, however immutable the presence of that categorical boundary line between them, they are nevertheless indissolubly tied up with each other and find themselves in continual mutual interaction; uninterrupted exchange goes on between them . . . The work and the world represented in it enter the real world and enrich it, and the real world enters the work and its world as part of the process of its creation, as well as part of its subsequent life, in a continual renewing of the work through the creative perception of listeners and readers.

Those who respond to a Bowie track such as 'The Man Who Sold the World' – and Bakhtin constantly seems, despite his ostensible focus on the 'novel', to gesture towards music in these concluding remarks, referring not just to readers but also to 'listeners', extending his discussion of the text to include 'epic songs' (254), 'songs, chapters and so on' (254), and identifying the author as, in 'the final analysis', nothing more than 'the human voice' (253) – help to shape and create the track and its continued meaning, keeping it alive. 'If it is torn out of its environment, it dies' (254). This continued interaction with listeners, readers and interpreters, from casual first-time encounters (a song played at a club, covered at a gig, overheard while shopping) to the long-term love affair Bowie fans have with his music, constitutes, in Bahktin's terms, 'a special *creative* chronotope . . . which constitutes the distinctive life of the work'.

The concept of Bowie's individual tracks, videos and films as 'adventures', or 'episodes', which frequently relate directly to each other and combine into longer, more complex cycles – whether explicitly, as with a concept album like *Outside*, or more subtly, as in the 'Berlin trilogy' of albums and their connection in turn to *The Man Who Fell To Earth*, or with the long narrative of Major Tom that can be traced from 'Space Oddity' through 'Ashes to Ashes' to 'Hello Spaceboy' – enables us to clarify Bowie's role as author of these adventures and distinguish between Bowie as creative artist, and the characters he plays within the story-episodes.

Of course, 'Bowie' is a public persona and to an extent a fictional construction, born in January 1966, and must be distinguished from David Robert Jones, born in January 1947, whose private life remains relatively obscure; but there is a further important distinction to be made between Bowie and 'Ziggy Stardust', 'Aladdin Sane' and all the other, often-unnamed, characters of his songs and videos. Though the boundary is sometimes blurred by reviews and articles that use character names such as 'The Thin White Duke' as synonymous for 'Bowie', the difference is immediately clear through a quick study of publicity and promotional images.[7] Just as the poster for *The Man Who Fell To Earth* presents 'David Bowie in Nicolas Roeg's film', positioning him unambiguously as actor, distinct from the character 'Thomas Jerome Newton', so it is obvious from the cover of *Aladdin Sane* that 'David Bowie' holds a different position to 'Aladdin Sane'. If there was any ambiguity, it would be settled through a glance at the preceding and subsequent albums, which are similarly and evidently branded 'David Bowie', and mark him as the longer-term creator (and perhaps curator), rather then the short-lived character. The *Ziggy Stardust* album is not authored by Aladdin Sane, and vice versa: both are by David Bowie. So while 'Bowie' certainly occupies an ambivalent, complex and fluid position between the worlds of reality and fiction, that position is different from the level occupied by Ziggy, Aladdin Sane, Major Tom, The Thin White Duke and *Outside*'s Nathan Adler; and it is different, too, from that of the unnamed narrator of 'The Man Who Sold the World', the man he meets on the stair, the man who 'met a girl named Blue Jean' and arguably, every 'I' who tells a story in Bowie's episode.

Naturally, we are inclined to assume that the 'I' who makes the fractured confession in 'Breaking Glass' (1977) that he's been 'breaking glass in your room again . . . don't look at the carpet; I drew something awful on it' is in some way reflecting on Bowie's experiences of the time ('Is Bowie commenting on the doomy, fetishised existence he'd led in Los Angeles?' asks Hugo Wilcken (2014: 76)). Similarly, it is tempting to read Bowie's musing 'I should have been a wiser kind of guy . . . I miss you' and his quietly anguished 'you're the great mistake I never made' from 1999's 'Survive' (*Reality* album) as, if not analogous with 'reality' itself – not an unvarnished, autobiographical statement from David Jones, or even a direct expression of David Bowie's millennial state of mind – then closer to 'reality' and 'truth' and further from fiction than other lyrical confessions such as 'I just met a girl named Blue Jean' or Jareth the Goblin King's 'You remind me of the babe', from 'Magic Dance' (1986).

If, then, for the purposes of argument, we take David Jones' inner life and private thoughts as our baseline of 'reality', and a performative, provocative statement by David Bowie such as 'It's true – I am a bisexual' (*Playboy*, September 1976) as our next level of fictional construction, then Bowie's various characters occupy different positions in the 'other-worldly', vertical superstructures (adventures, or episodes) that intersect with his horizontal, chronological career-line. As in Dante's vision of Hell, we could place characters like Jareth – though clearly inhabited by and promoted as a performance of 'David Bowie' – towards the 'fiction' end of the spectrum, with Bowie's stage and screen interpretation of historical figures (Nikola Tesla; the 'Elephant Man' Joseph Merrick) at a different position on the scale, closer to the 'real'.[8] Figures like Ziggy Stardust and The Thin White Duke, who are essentially titles for Bowie's performance at the time rather than 'characters' in the conventional literary sense, are closer to expressing and revealing 'David Bowie', while the unnamed, relatively unadorned narrators of songs like 'Survive' and 'The Man Who Sold the World' are surely closer still to serving as transparent vehicles for the author. Yet these last speakers, too, are not necessarily analogous to or identical to the 'David Bowie' who discusses his intentions in interviews, and again, this public face and voice, however confessional, should be considered as quite distinct from the inner life of David Jones. To what extent 'David Bowie' has come to encompass, perhaps to engulf, David Jones, and whether, and in what form, the man who was born David Jones can still be said to exist, is another matter.[9]

David Bowie, despite the consistency of his themes and the dialogic echoes that run through his work from 1966 to the present day, clearly changes, evolves and develops. There is a marked difference between 1967's *David Bowie* and 2013's *The Next Day* in terms of performance, authorial position, musical composition, vocal tone and lyrical concerns, and two songs from each period could not simply swap places in time without significant revision – as confirmed by the difference between the thin, cracked 'London Boys' of 1966 and Bowie's weary but rich cover of the same track on the unreleased *Toy* album, recorded in 2001.

As such, he – unlike the characters who occupy and narrate his songs – pushes beyond the chronotope Bakhtin identifies in the Greek romance, whereby the middle section of a story is merely a hiatus, and the protagonist emerges unchanged, like a superhero in a Silver Age comic book, ready to repeat the adventure (or set off on a similar one) again. Bowie changes, though not as much as the popular stereotype of a chameleonic artist suggests.[10] The 'road', the horizontal chronological progression of his career, does involve a journey, a progression, a gaining of perspective and experience through a series of encounters and progressions. Bowie's career, rather than a weightless hiatus – in science fiction terms, a hyperspace jump – from 1966 to the present – embodies a long-term transformation, such as we would expect in the evolution of any serious artist who remains active and engaged for so many decades. However, this gradual change – this 'Slow Burn', to borrow his song title from 2002's *Heathen* album – is quite distinct from the multiple, shorter-lived and more superficial transformations he embraces during his episodic 'adventures'. If we see Bowie as a traveller on a long road, then he regularly and frequently adopts masks and costumes and dips into various spheres of life, inhabiting them temporarily before rejoining the main path.

In Bakhtin's (154) terms, we could see Bowie in the role of:

> the *rogue* and the *adventurer*, who do not participate internally in everyday life, who do not occupy in it any definite fixed place, yet who at the same time pass through that life and are forced to study its workings, all its secret cogs and wheels.

Bakhtin identifies other, similar roles with similar functions, opportunities and limitations, their special access and understanding balanced against their lack of settled home and sense of belonging: the *servant* (124), the *parvenu*, the *procurer*, the *prostitute* and *courtesan* (125). These characters are eavesdroppers, spies, 'exposing and portraying all layers and levels of private life' (126):

> This is the philosophy of a person who knows only private life and craves it alone, but who does not participate in it, who has no place in it – and therefore sees it in sharp focus, as a whole, in all its nakedness, playing out all its roles but not fusing his identity with any one of them.

This is the world of the criminal, the detective, the investigation – 'as specific forms for uncovering and making private life public' (124) – yet the crime itself is only a plot device, for 'what matters are the everyday secrets of private life that lay bare human nature' (124). The titles of Bowie's songs alone, spanning his entire career, confirm his consistent fascination with this world and its stories, without immediate need for further evidence: 'Criminal World' (1983), 'Queen Bitch' (1971), 'The Voyeur of Utter Destruction (as Beauty)' (2005), 'The Secret Life of Arabia' (1977). At a later point, Bakhtin also introduces 'the clown and the fool' to this group of characters who 'create around themselves their own special little world, their own chronotope'. They are, Bakhtin argues, 'life's maskers', carrying 'a privilege – the right to be "other" in this world . . . they see the underside and the falseness of every situation. Therefore, they can exploit any position they choose, but only as a mask' (159). Again, even a superficial survey of Bowie's personae – The Thin White Duke, the Pierrot of the 'Ashes to Ashes' video, the artist/Minotaur who, according to the sleeve-notes, narrates 'The Voyeur of Utter Destruction (as Beauty)', even the wanderer of 'The Man Who Sold the World' – confirms his career-long association with outsider figures, with costumes, archetypes and folk characters. Just as Bakhtin adds the 'crank' to his cast of clowns – compare with Bowie's identification of himself and his then-wife Angie as a couple of 'Kooks' (1971) – so we could perhaps add the term 'Bowieism' to the 'Shandyism' and 'Pantagruelism' Bakhtin lists as literary examples of 'personalized eccentricity'.

Again, we can only note here in passing that this outsider role – a 'foreigner who does not understand' the world through which he moves, like Gulliver on his travels (164) – could, if not justify and excuse, then at least contextualize Bowie's Orientalism and the stereotypical exoticization of the cultural Other in much of his work. If his 'visions of Jap girls in synthesis' from 'Ashes to Ashes', the description of Blue Jean's 'Latin roots', and his cover of the Mauritanian song 'Don't Let Me Down and Down' (1993) in a cod-patois accent are at best ill-considered, then it could be argued that they are part of a broader (even Brechtian) making-strange, a naïve, alienated approach to the world that, homeless and wandering, sees everything as Other. In the Los Angeles of 'Black Tie, White Noise' (1993), despite living in the city during the riots, Bowie admits he is 'getting my facts from a Benetton ad, staring through African eyes'. In 'Strangers When We Meet', presumably set – if its original release on the 1993 *Buddha of Suburbia* album provides any geographical clue – within Greater London, he is equally 'bewildered' and 'dazzled by the new', describing the lifestyles of his affluent British friends in fragmented, 'foreign' terms: 'no trendy *rechauffé* . . . humming Rheingold . . . we trade by *vendu*'.

As Bakhtin observes, although the masks of the clueless clown, the adventurer and the investigator 'come to the aid of the novelist' (161), enabling him to inhabit and move between various spheres of society in various guises and, through his work, make those private lives public, the relationship between the author and the characters is not straightforward (254):

> We find the author *outside* the work as a human being living his own biographical life. But we also meet him as the creator of the work itself . . . we meet him (that is, we sense his activity) most of all in the composition of the work . . .

But, 'a more general question arises: from what temporal and spatial point of view does the author look upon the events that he describes?' (255) These questions help us to draw distinctions between David Jones (private individual), David Bowie (public author) and personae such as Ziggy Stardust (a character in described and performed events).

For Bakhtin, the author's position with regard to the fictional world is complex, neither outside nor within (256):

> He represents the world either from the point of view of the hero participating in the represented event, or from the point of view of a narrator, or from that of an assumed author or – finally – without utilizing any intermediary at all he can deliver the story directly from himself as the author pure and simple.

But even in this last instance, 'he can represent the temporal-spatial world and its events only *as if* he had seen and observed them himself, only *as if* he were an omniscient witness to them'. As the creator, he 'remains outside the world he has represented in his work.'

This is not the occasion to do more than identify the complexity of the relationship between Bowie as narrator of the song 'Ziggy Stardust' and Ziggy Stardust, the character who is regularly associated with Bowie himself, played (even inhabited) by him on stage, yet described by the song in the third person and the past tense; or the relationship between Bowie and the unnamed narrator-character who seems to confess his destructive tendencies in 'Breaking Glass', and the author-figure who, seemingly with less artifice, muses on his regrets, decades later, in 'Survive'. What this model does offer us is a structure that acknowledges and enables further investigation into this dynamic: and also, importantly, it allows us to distinguish between Bowie-as-author and his less obviously constructed characters, such as the man who just met a girl named Blue Jean. Within this reading, the narrator-characters of 'Blue Jean', 'Modern Love' and 'Let's Dance', from the period when Bowie became an international superstar and supposedly dropped the masks and costumes along with much of his subversive play and provocation, are revealed as simply another persona: the businessman, the straight man, even the return of 'The Man Who Sold the World', glimpsed by an earlier Bowie narrator in 1970.

Once more in conclusion, we cannot, in a chapter, fully unpack the complexities of the matrix activated by a single line in a single song like 'Blue Jean', with its promise, or recollection, that one day Bowie (or a version thereof) will write a poem in a letter. Even a longer investigation cannot hope to fully map this network, in part because it is our own interpretations of Bowie's previous, current and future work that continue to keep those meanings alive, to reactivate and extend the chain of signifying echoes, integrating them with our own life landscapes and our own personal responses; it is, in a sense, we as listener-readers who continue to keep Bowie 'novel', forever new and changing. But an investigation must start somewhere, and we have begun.

Notes

1 Unless we link her with the 'Jean Genie' of 1974.

2 Of course, this is coincidence, but it is interesting to note that Bakhtin's career did overlap with Bowie's.

3 Compare Bakhtin's broad historical use of 'the novel' with the more conventional discussion in, for instance, Lennard J. Davis, *Resisting Novels* (London: Routledge, 1987). For an application of the chronotope to cinema, see for instance Alexandra Ganser, Julia Pühringer and Markus Rheindorf, 'Bakhtin's chronotope on the road: space, time, and place in road movies since the 1970s', in *Linguistics and Literature*, 4 (1) (2006), 1–17.

4 In 1987, Bowie suggested another physical embodiment of history and future, in the title and chorus of 'Time Will Crawl'.

5 David Jones adopted the stage name David Bowie in January 1966 and released songs under that name in 1966, but his first album as 'Bowie' was released in 1967. See David Buckley, *Strange Fascination: David Bowie, the Definitive Story* (London: Virgin Books, 2001), 34.

6 *Outside* is subtitled 'a non-linear Gothic Drama Hyper-Cycle'.

7 See for instance several online articles that refer to Bowie's 2013 comeback as 'the Return of The Thin White Duke': *The Digital Fix Music*, last modified 8 January 2013, accessed 6 August, 2014, http://music.thedigitalfix.com/content/18301/blog-the-unexpected-return-of-the-thin-white-duke-news-flash.html, *Eleventh Stack*, last modified 13 March 2013, accessed 6 August 2014, http://eleventhstack.wordpress.com/2013/03/27/return-of-the-thin-white-duke/, *The Tin*, last modified 28 March 2013, accessed 6 August 2014, http://blog.thetin.net/post/2013/03/28/The-return-of-the-Thin-White-Duke.

8 We might want to distinguish further between cinema and stage appearances; Thomas Newton might be located in between Bowie's Nikola Tesla (Bowie playing a named and distinct role, written by Jonathan and Christopher Nolan from a novel by Christopher Priest, and based on a historical figure) and his Thin White Duke (a title for Bowie's performance), as a distinctly-authored fictional character who nevertheless seems to develop from, and in turn develop, Bowie's contemporary persona.

9 Buckley notes that David Robert Jones exists legally, at least – 'David Bowie' was never adopted by deed poll and remains a stage name – and that all financial and contractual information is still issued to Jones in his legal name. Buckley, *Strange Fascination*, 34.

10 The *Rolling Stone* biography entry, accessed 6 August 2014, describes Bowie as 'the consummate chameleonic artist' – http://www.rollingstone.com/music /artists/david-bowie/biography; *AllMusic*, accessed 6 August 2014, lists him as 'the original pop chameleon', http://www.allmusic.com/artist/david-bowie-mn0000531986; *Wired*, last modified 5 August 2011, accessed 6 August 2014, headlines him as a 'musical chameleon', http://www.wired.com/2011/05/david-bowie-artist/.

Bibliography

Bakhtin, Mikhail. M. 1981. *The Dialogic Imagination*. Translated by Caryl Emerson and Michael Holquist. Edited by Michael Holquist. Austin: University of Texas Press.

Buckley, David. 2001. *Strange Fascination: David Bowie, the Definitive Story*. London: Virgin Books.

Carr, Roy and Charles Shaar Murray. 1981. *Bowie: An Illustrated Record*. New York: Avon Books.

Davis, Lennard. 1987. *Resisting Novels*. London: Routledge.

Doggett, Peter. 2012. *The Man Who Sold the World: David Bowie and the 1970s*. London: Vintage.

Eco, Umberto. 1984. *The Role of the Reader*. Bloomington: Indiana University Press.

Ganser, Alexandra, Julia Pühringer and Markus Rheindorf. 2006. 'Bakhtin's chronotope on the road: space, time, and place in road movies since the 1970s'. *Linguistics and Literature*, 4 (1), 1–17.

O'Leary, Chris. 2010. *Pushing Ahead of the Dame*, https://bowiesongs. wordpress.com/2010/01/27/the-man-who-sold-the-world.

Wilcken, Hugo. 2014. *David Bowie's Low*. London: Bloomsbury/Continuum.

6

Bowie's Covers:
The Artist as Modernist

David Baker

Introduction: *Hunky Dory*

Hunky Dory (1971), David Bowie's highly regarded third album, may perhaps best be viewed as a kind of ground-clearing operation, the opening up and making available of the space for Bowie's extraordinary 'breakthrough' concept, character and album *The Rise and Fall of Ziggy Stardust* released the following year. The most well-known tracks on *Hunky Dory* are appropriately vague and allusive songs which articulate ideas and themes which Bowie would continue to develop: 'Changes' with its oblique reflections on time, youth and the transitive artist; 'Oh You Pretty Things' which develops the Nietzschean *Übermensch* thematics apparent on Bowie's previous album *The Man Who Sold the World* (1971) with a vague and suggestive focus on the brokenness of current paradigms and an androgynous and uncharted future; 'Life on Mars?' covering similar terrain with both its female protagonist as well as its artist/narrator literally bored with the same 'film' running again and again, seeking some point of differentiation in the wistful interplanetary question 'is there life on Mars?'

Although the only cover version on the album is Bowie's take on Biff Rose's light-hearted and decidedly non-ironic 'hippy' paean to love, freedom, and happiness – a recognition perhaps of the hippy ethos from which Bowie's earlier work, in particular the *Space Oddity* (1969) album – it emerges that four of the original songs on *Hunky Dory* are 'about' Bowie's relationship with other stars/artists who have particularly impacted his work in one way or another. These songs have the function of placing Bowie's work in two starkly contrasting American rock/pop musical traditions – looking in one direction to the bisexual camp of the New York 'Factory' ethos, and in the other to a 'straight' American rock/country/folk tradition.

On the one hand 'Queen Bitch' and 'Andy Warhol' recognizably point to Bowie's androgynous future. 'Queen Bitch', in its evocation of transvestitism and gay sex, features, as Philip Auslander suggests, 'a replication of Lou Reed's songwriting and singing styles' (2006: 109). The chorus of 'Andy Warhol' – 'Andy Warhol, silver screen / Can't tell them apart at all' – wittily and concisely summarizes the point of the song as well as some of the postmodern uses Bowie would make of Warhol's aesthetic.

On the other hand, two other 'tribute' songs place Bowie in a straight rock /country/folk tradition: 'Kooks' and 'Song for Bob Dylan'. The pretty children's song, 'Kooks', addresses and offers advice to a newborn child entering a kooky but decidedly nuclear family strongly resembling Bowie's own; David Buckley suggests the song was a gift for his newborn son Zowie. The song borrows heavily from Neil Young's then recent song 'Till the Morning Comes.' (Buckley, 2005: 91; Doggett, 2011: 114).

In 'Song for Bob Dylan', Bowie directs a question to Robert Zimmerman, asking him to return to his earlier politically charged songs, songs with words of 'truthful vengeance' that will 'give us back our unity, give us back our family'. Bowie's Zimmerman had been a unifying figure who 'sat behind a million pair of eyes and told them how they saw'. By 1971 Dylan had entirely abandoned this role; in Bowie's view, by abdicating the role of 'Voice of a Generation', Dylan had failed his art, failed his duty as star and betrayed his audience: 'Then we lost your train of thought the paintings are all your own / While troubles are rising we'd rather be scared together than alone.' In effect Dylan had forsaken his leadership role and placed himself outside the ties of alliance and commonality that form what we might call the imagined rock community. Under these circumstances Bowie, in the song's chorus, introduces the enigmatic 'same old painted lady', who will 'scratch this world to pieces as she comes on like a friend'.

It's not possible to pin down exactly who 'she' is: an ageing hooker, catty and destructive; she's flirty but she dissimulates. Wilfred Mellers is probably roughly correct in suggesting she is 'in a general sense an agent of moral and social corruption' (1996: 57). Bowie may well be remarkably prescient here, foreshadowing a perhaps postmodern 'culture where façade and impact are kings, and a belief in oneself regardless of talent or accomplishment is no longer regarded as impudent, genuine modesty, humility and balance have become handicaps to achievement,' (Rojek, 2012: 184), a culture in which, as Nick Couldry's 'Public Connection' project makes clear, there is no clear link between celebrity culture and citizens' sense of matters of public concern

(Couldry, 2006; Couldry and Markham, 2007). In 'Song for Bob Dylan', Bowie nostalgically, non-ironically and emphatically seeks a return to a moment before the latest return of the 'painted lady'. Just a couple of songs from Dylan's 'old scrapbook' – he wistfully muses – 'could send her home again'.

Postmodern and modern

There is no doubt that David Bowie is routinely considered in entirely different terms to what for argument's sake we'll name the 'modernist' singer-songwriters, for example, Bob Dylan and Neil Young, whose values of authenticity, depth, reality, immediacy and unity are central to the artists' self-formation. There is little argument that 'postmodern' Bowie is far more clearly identified with the figure of Andy Warhol than Bob Dylan; Nick Stevenson neatly outlines what he describes as Bowie's 'postmodern' thematics as developed in the 1970s: identity as plastic, artifice as opposed to 'authenticity and a 'deep self', playful sexual ambiguity and androgyny, Nietszchean 'superman' individualism and/or alien messianisism, camp, pop art and trash aesthetic, the embrace of commodification and so on (Stevenson 2006: 38–81). Van M. Cagle suggests that the 'Warholian tradition' (1965–69) provided "glitter-rock" performances with the primary themes of flamboyance, style and image construction, polymorphous sexuality, and multi-media montage as performance art' (1996: 96). This would seem to be the Bowie who in 1976 stated, emphatically, 'I have no message whatsoever. I really have nothing to say, no suggestions or advice, nothing' (Brackett, 2005: 279); the Bowie who stated in a 1972 interview 'sometimes I don't feel as if I'm a person at all . . . I'm just a collection of other people's ideas' (cited in Doggett, 2011: 129); the Bowie whose own contemporaneous analysis of *Hunky Dory* was to suggest (in Cagle 1996: 139): 'I'd rather retain the position of being a photostat machine with an image, because I think most songwriters are anyway. I don't think there are many independent-thinking songwriters. They're all heavily influenced, far more than any other form of writing.' What would this arch, ironic, postmodern Bowie make of the earnest, authentic, modernist Bowie of 'Song for Bob Dylan'? The postmodern response would be to suggest 'Song for Bob Dylan' is Bowie's own restless farewell to Dylan, the last gasp of old school 'modernist' Bowie; that whatever lingering sentiment Bowie may have had for the self-consciously authentic modernist artist on *Hunky Dory*, by 1972's *Ziggy Stardust* he had fully embraced the concept of performer/performance as artifice: 'fundamental to this redefinition was Bowie's assertion that he was using rock-and-roll, that he was pop's first self-avowed poseur, showing no allegiance to any one style of music or to any single visual presentation' (Buckley, 1996: 4). That the very voice Bowie adopts in 'Song for Bob Dylan' is an inhabited, theatrical voice; Bowie is 'playing at' being a folkie Dylan fan abandoned and disappointed by his idol.

Another analysis, however, would suggest that postmodernity is also a pose; that in posing as postmodern, Bowie never leaves modernism behind. There has always been an ambivalence in Bowie; Bowie as both postmodern and modern: the two terms don't necessarily oppose one another in his work. Bowie has always looked both ways. Indeed the Bowie of 1969's 'Space Oddity' – which predates the opposition between the two songs 'Song for Bob Dylan' and 'Andy Warhol' – fuses acoustic guitar playing singer-songwriter with electronics aficionado; wide-eyed hippy communalist with detached, post-hippy alien.

From this point of view Bowie was and remains first and foremost a singer-songwriter; his value in relation to performativity, stardom and visual aesthetics is underpinned by his capacity as a writer of original songs. Chris Rojek may be entirely accurate in suggesting that in the 70s Bowie 'through dress, use of cosmetics, spoken values and mannerisms . . . challenged not merely heteronormative domination, but all types of established cultural rule' (Rojek, 2012: 129; for a similar point see Cagle, 1995: 3), but Bowie's authentic status as a singer-songwriter penning original songs was precisely that which authorized his performative and political capacities. Bowie as postmodernist required absolutely the imprimatur of Bowie the modernist. Cagle suggests that 'glitter rock . . . [demonstrated] . . . that to effectively transmit oppositional ideas, one had to be at the centre of popular culture' (1996: 217). One of the key ways Bowie positioned himself as central to popular culture and thus capable of transforming it was precisely because he demonstrated his songwriting kudos as an engaging, creative and authentic singer-songwriter. Bowie's individual long-play releases, in the main, have over time (and in particular during the 1970s) aspired to and largely satisfied the normative canonical criteria for rock albums as outlined by Carys Wyn Jones: the albums have been coherent bodies of work as a whole (as opposed to a couple of singles with filler), they possess the 'canonical criteria of originality, complexity and truth . . . that is associated with an autonomous artist/genius', they demand 'repeated listening and can sustain multiple interpretations', and they have 'stood the test of time and influenced subsequent albums' (Jones, 2008: 42).

Bowie has 'played the game' in terms of rock's employment of the figure of the romantic artist/genius who composes material in a prescribed format (the album). As David Tetzlaff puts it, in the context of modern art in the twentieth century, 'even overt attempts to explode the idea of individual creativity, of the aura of the work, have been incorporated into the romantic ideology of Art, are taken as signs of the auteur's Genius'. Tetzlaff suggests further that 'this is how Bowie's fans . . . understood all his self-conscious posturing – as proof that he was an artiste, possessed of both a more unique intelligence and a more authentic creative vision than the guys in Bachman-Turner Overdrive' (1994: 104).

Postmodernity circumscribed by modernity

Bowie's postmodernity is not only predicated upon his modernity, his postmodernity is circumscribed by his modernity. On occasion, Bowie has attempted to step outside of modernism and fully engage his postmodernity, but instructively critical discourses around rock have not enabled him to do so. Two albums in particular stand out in this regard, *Pin Ups* (1973) and *Tonight* (1984). Stuart Lenig usefully provides an overview of the 'lacklustre reception' accorded *Pin Ups*, Bowie's album consisting entirely of cover versions released at the height of his Ziggy stardom but serving as a marker between the canonical albums *Aladdin Sane* in 1973 and the 'post-Ziggy' *Diamond Dogs* (1974). Lenig points out the way in which *Pin Ups* 'puzzled the critics and the public', and surveys the ways in which reviews, particular that by Greg Shaw for *Rolling Stone* magazine, 'criticized every aspect of the work' (Lenig, 2010: 130–2; for further examples see Peraino, 2012: 177, n. 7).

There is considerable critical agreement that a period of creative decline began for Bowie with the release of the *Tonight* album in 1984; Kurt Loder describes the album as 'a throwaway' and an 'uninspired disappointment' (Loder, 1996: 198, 199). Although an apologist for the argument that Bowie's contribution to culture was postmodern, Nick Stevenson's discussion of *Tonight* is telling: a

> decline in creative energy was evident in the first genuinely disappointing musical contribution to his career . . . What is most noticeable about it was that it included little new material, and much written by other people . . . so many cover versions and old songs leave Bowie's creative involvement open to question.
>
> Stevenson, 2006:101; cf. Spitz, 2009: 329–31

We will leave to one side the merits of the argument that *Tonight* may well be one of Bowie's weakest albums; our interest in it here is the way in which the album demonstrates quite precisely the limits of the 'postmodern' argument in the popular music context: 'Bowie attacked the idea of the work of art expressing the uniqueness of the author. What happens in this process is that art loses its autonomy and becomes mere commodity' (Stevenson,

2006: 102). The paradox here is that *Tonight* can be understood easily as engaging in a kind of Warholian critique of the (modernist) rock album. In its case the album is more akin to commercial art than the autonomous and authentic modernist artwork, and by implication the design, rather than the figure of the artist, lies at its centre. The ironic Bowie, so often a detached persona in a song lyric ('Ziggy played guitar': Bowie's persona in the song 'Ziggy Stardust' is as a member of the backing band the Spiders from Mars, not Ziggy himself), is, on *Tonight*, detached from Bowie the modernist artist. The argument further implies that, and is unable to shake, the critique that the authenticity of the artist can only be undertaken by an authentic artist, otherwise art is reduced to mere commodity. Bowie, unlike Warhol, is working in a popular cultural rock/pop idiom, and is thus unable to 'abdicate' his position as creator; he could not, for example, have an assistant undertake and complete a work in his name. Under such circumstances it is perfectly acceptable for Bowie to collaborate – his work with, for example, Mick Ronson, John Lennon, Carlos Alomar, Brian Eno, Nile Rogers certainly attests to this. The collaborations arguably renovate, innovate and invigorate Bowie the auteur, but the reception of *Tonight* demonstrated that Bowie as pop/rock performer could not be allowed to become pure 'signature' in the Warholian sense.

Both *Pin Ups* and *Tonight* produce critical anxieties because of their reliance, or at least emphasis upon, the cover version; the 'other-authored' cover version works against the grain of the notion of Bowie as artist/genius. Cover versions are highly problematic for critical rock discourse – the cover version runs the risk of being a sign of decadence, a sign perhaps that the authentic artist has lost his way, has some sort of creative blockage. The artist is merely performing covers, understood explicitly as 'filler'. In discussing the hierarchy among types of popular music performers, Roy Shuker points out that the common view among musicians, fans and critics is that the 'cover band' resides at the base of the hierarchy, on grounds that 'reliance on someone else's material concedes that you have nothing of your own to say' (Shuker, 2008: 62). Bowie's insistent use of the cover version thus becomes a problem for one seeking an artist/genius. Certain postmodern thematics may be possible for Bowie in the 1970s, but as *Tonight* attests, there are clear limits to what Bowie, in the rock/pop idiom, can achieve as a postmodern/deconstructive artist.

Bowie's covers

Although the cover version causes problems for Bowie's attempts at a throughgoing postmodernity, the point remains that cover versions have fundamental work to do in his corpus. On the one hand, as George Plasketes points out, 'the process of covering a song is essentially an adaptation, in which much of the value lies in the artists' interpretation' (Plasketes 2010: 27). Bowie does not in fact perform postmodern deconstructive work with cover versions, rather he demonstrates his skill as an authentic artist by making cover versions his own; precisely by recontextualizing them. Bowie's unique modernist self is already a kind of bricolage: as Lenig neatly puts it (circa 1973): 'a unification of pop, crooner vocals, Jacques Brel art song, and hard rock rolled into a new synthesis' (2010: 135). Through Bowie's career he transforms this bricolage and recontextualizes other people's songs into and by means of this synthesis.

On the other hand, covers always serve to connect Bowie's work with specific and particular popular musical traditions. Bowie's covers are emphatically not equivalent to Warhol's paintings of say Campbell's soup cans precisely because he is self-consciously not creating art out of the banal, the mass-produced. Bowie is always careful and motivated in his choice of covers; covers have meaning in relation to Bowie's status as a popular artist/star, not as an artist invested in foregrounding the banality or mass-produced foundations of his own artistic production. Bowie is never ironic in his choice or performance of cover versions; Bowie could never be accused of holding, say, a patronizing attitude toward his material.

In the course of his career, Bowie has released over seventy versions of other people's songs. An analysis of the list of songs (see below) reveals systematic and coherent patterns; taken as a whole the cover versions proffer a self-conscious and perhaps even well-rounded portrait of Bowie the artist (there are, of course, significant gaps; for example there is no cover of any 'krautrock' material, so significant for Bowie's work in the late 1970s. That said, however, the song 'V-2 Schneider' (1977) stands as a 'tribute' to Kraftwerk). Each of Bowie's cover versions falls into one of six main categories, five of which are concerned with Bowie self-consciously entering into an authentic relationship with a specified popular musical tradition: songs which relate his work directly to the 'swinging sixties', in particular mod London 1964–7; songs from what might be variously described as mainstream, 'classic' rock or even *Rolling Stone* magazine rock history; 'art' songs (including for example artists connected to Warhol's Factory, Scott Walker and Berthold Brecht); songs from the soul/R&B catalogue; songs perhaps best described as 'new wave' and 'post-glam'; and what might appear at first to be a loose, miscellaneous category best captured in terms of the concept of the 'gift'. I want to begin my brief discussion of Bowie's covers by considering the small group of songs which can best be understood as specific gifts, and go on to consider the remaining categories in the light of the concept of the gift.

The gift

Bowie's explicitly 'gift' songs include the beautiful 'Don't Let Me Down and Down', a cover of a song performed by Tahra Valmont which Bowie's wife Imam suggested to him and whose recording presumably is a gift to her (Thompson, 2006: 96); 'I Took a Ride on a Gemini Spaceship' which honoured a debt to the Legendary Stardust Cowboy for the 'Stardust' part of Ziggy (Thompson, 2006: 246–7); the 1977 televised duet with Bing Cosby 'Peace on Earth/The Little Drummer Boy', both a Christmas gift and an extraordinary and moving moment of intergenerational solidarity; and Bowie's cover of Paul Simon's 'America' for the 9/11 benefit concert for New York, which functioned as a gesture of solidarity with the US in the wake of the twin towers tragedy, perhaps also as an olive branch from an artist who had released the song 'I'm Afraid of Americans' (*Earthling*, 1997) just a few years earlier.

The category of the gift is not, as might appear, a marginal one. Rather, the notion of the gift stands central to Bowie's art as a whole. In order to appreciate this point, the notion of the cover as 'gift' needs to be clearly contrasted with a recent postmodern analysis of the cover version in Bowie. Judith Peraino seeks to utilize the work of Judith Butler in order to interrogate Bowie's covers. Peraino asks what she calls the 'Butlerian' (postmodern) question. What Peraino seeks is a vocabulary whereby the cover version might stage a work of deconstruction, wishing it to 'trouble the concepts of "original" and "copy" '. What she encounters in this staging is an extraordinary resistance on the part of the cover version; the cover version stubbornly refuses deconstructive analysis, forcing the conclusion that in the realm of popular music, 'probing the relationship between "original" and "copy" results in sharp distinctions rather than ambiguities' (Peraino, 2012: 152). After surveying some of the difficulties of deconstructing the sharp distinction, Peraino, seeking to maintain a postmodern project, shifts to a seemingly more moderate argument which suggests that in the act of covering songs Bowie 'places himself in the role of consumer and fan as much as creator or interpreter' (153).

However, the suggestion that Bowie is consumer/fan as much as creator/ interpreter simply does not go far enough; it fails to appreciate the function of stardom in Bowie's work. The key point here is that although Bowie has been routinely identified with Ziggy Stardust, his specific form of stardom is precisely not that of Ziggy Stardust, and in fact stands as oppositional to it. Ziggy functions as a cautionary tale; Bowie 'himself' counteracts Ziggy's unbounded rock star narcissism and egoism with a conception of rock stardom as akin to something like that which eminent sociologist/anthropologist Marcel Mauss describes in his classic essay 'The Gift' as 'noble expenditure' (Mauss, 1966: 66).

Bowie as rock star/artist functions in a pop/rock economy of alliance and commonality. The cover version is central to understanding this economy. Within the gift economy the artist creator/interpreter is obliged to give and receive; indeed, by virtue of his stardom is obliged to return more than he receives. In such an economy, where the rock artist is under an obligation, to refuse to give or receive would be to place the artist outside the ties of alliance and commonality that form what we might call the imagined rock community:

> If things are given and returned it is precisely because one gives and returns 'respects' and 'courtesies.' But in addition, in giving them, a man [sic] gives himself, and he does so because he owes himself – himself and his possessions – to others.
>
> Mauss, 1966: 44–5

My contention is that in the conceptualization of cover version as gift, Bowie is considerably more than simply fan and consumer; rather Bowie, as artist and star capable of 'noble expenditure' willingly places himself in a system of obligatory gift exchange within a system of alliance and commonality. Indeed, Bowie's status as star and artist is dependent upon his place in this system, and the various categories of cover versions he performs make sense in terms of his 'noble expenditure' within this system of alliance and commonality. Each of the remaining categories can be best understood in terms of Bowie 'giving back'.

Mod/'swinging sixties'

In the mid-60s, when his own work was indistinguishable from many other mod wannabes, Bowie recorded several cover versions of Mod songs (for example 'Liza Jane' and 'Louie, Go Home'). Once he had achieved stardom, Bowie's relationship to 'the swinging sixties' is demonstrated by *Pin Ups* (1973), his sole album made up entirely of covers: a tribute to bands such as The Who, Pink Floyd, The Yardbirds, The Kinks, Them, The Pretty Things and others. As tributes these songs are homage and acknowledgement to the specific music that influenced and formed 'glam' Bowie, placing him obviously within a system of alliance and commonality: 'Pin-Ups melds camp, acid-pop, crooner, hard rock and mod influences as a codex to Bowie's glam style' (Lening, 2010: 130). Lenig, rightly in my view, suggests that the tracks chosen for *Pin Ups* 'were so influential to Bowie that they spurred his own work, and the similarity of Bowie's work to the originals serves to illustrate that in many ways, glam existed as simply a hyperbolic form of sixties mod pop' (Lening,

2010: 132). Mod subculture, itself a bricoleur culture, is reworked in the service of glam; mod rebellion, again following Lening, is re-placed 'in the context of gender and identity politics' (2010: 135).

Ray Davies assumes particular significance in the Bowie oeuvre. Aside from the direct personal relationship – Bowie's early band Manish Boy were a support act for The Kinks in 1965 (Spitz, 2009: 59) – there is the manner in which Bowie acknowledges the way in which he himself sits neatly in the 'white, middle-class autodidact' tradition of British rock star to which Davies (along with Pete Townshend and Jagger and Richards) so clearly belong (Buckley, 2005: 14). Bowie clearly derived aspects of his own artistry, in particular the emphasis on the British music-hall tradition as well as the employment of the song-cycle or 'concept' album from Davies' work with The Kinks (e.g. The Village Green Preservation Society, 1968). 'Where Have All the Good Times Gone' appears on *Pin Ups*. In 2003 Bowie recorded 'Waterloo Sunset' during the sessions for the *Reality* album. By being covered on multiple occasions Davies is thus a clear recipient of Bowie's respects and courtesies.

Mainstream 'classic' rock

Through the course of his career Bowie has evinced a strong tendency to cover songs by artists routinely considered absolutely central to mainstream rock history, Songs by Chuck Berry and Lieber and Stoller representing 50s/early 60s rock and roll; while Bowie has performed and recorded covers of songs by 60s (and after) luminaries The Beatles, The Rolling Stones, The Beach Boys, Cream, Neil Young and Bob Dylan. This group of covers clearly suggests he has considerable stake in this lineage and is entirely conscious that his own legacy stands in commonality with mainstream rock and owes considerable debt to it; a debt which the covers repay.

'Art' songs

Bowie has also recorded various 'art' songs by performers who have had considerable and lasting influence on both his music and star image. I have already mentioned those Bowie-penned songs that cement his relationship with the New York Factory ethos: 'Queen Bitch' and 'Andy Warhol'. Bowie has at various times covered Lou Reed songs: 'I'm Waiting for the Man', 'White Light/White Heat' and 'Dirty Boulevard', though interestingly has never released any of these on any of his major studio albums. Bowie's cover of 'Pablo Picasso' on *Reality* (2003) functions in part to align him with key Velvet Underground 'disciple' Jonathan Richman, but also forms an intertextual chain with former Velvet John Cale's 1975 version. Bowie has also of course had several collaborations with Iggy Pop (for an outlining of the multiple personal and conceptual connections between Pop and the Factory ethos see Cagle, 1995: 103–7) – in particular Pop's 1977 albums *The Idiot* and *Lust for Life*, but has also at various times covered Pop's songs such as 'I Wanna Be Your Dog', 'Bang Bang' and 'Don't Look Down'. Although Bowie was never himself directly affiliated with the Factory, the various personal connections and chains of association clearly imbricate him within the system of alliance and commonality that constitutes the Factory network and sphere of influence.

If Bowie looks to New York in one direction, he looks to Europe in another. Bowie references the pervasive influence of Scott Walker née Engel, both through Walker's own 'Night Flights' as well as through a couple of Jacques Brel songs Walker performed, 'Amsterdam' and 'My Death'. Berthold Brecht in collaboration with either Kurt Weill or Dominic Muldowney is clearly also a significant musical influence; Mike Garson's Berlin-cabaret piano and Bowie's theatrical vocal performance on 'Time' (*Aladdin Sane*, 1973) is a really clear example here. Brecht is referenced, via The Doors, by the 1978 live version 'Alabama Song' (*Stage*) as well as by Bowie's reverent performance of Brecht songs for the 1982 BBC Television play *Baal*. In each of these cases Bowie clearly returns respects and courtesies to artists whose work has enriched his own work and persona.

Soul/R&B

Bowie's 'blue-eyed soul' period (1974–6) was anticipated by the self-penned '1984' on *Diamond Dogs* (1974), combining, as Peter Doggett points out, elements from Blaxploitation soundtracks: the 'chattering wah-wah guitar' and 'percussive blend of bass and piano' drawn from Isaac Hayes 'Theme from Shaft' and use of strings evoking Curtis Mayfield's *Superfly* soundtrack (Doggett, 2011: 198). Bowie also utilized cover versions to draw him into the soul/R&B tradition. Eddie Floyd's 'Knock on Wood' and the Ohio Players' 'Here Today and Gone Tomorrow', both appearing on *David Live* (1974), an album otherwise made up of soul reworkings of tracks from *Ziggy Stardust, Aladdin Sane* and *Diamond Dogs* are clear examples. Bowie's cover of The Flares minor 1960 doo-wop hit 'Footstompin', televised on the Dick Cavett Show in 1974 led, through the incorporation of Carlos Alomar's guitar line, directly to his 1975 hit 'Fame'. ('Footstompin' is, interestingly, performed as a medley with 'I Wish I Could Shimmy Like My Sister Kate', which probably references Betty Grable's performance of the song in the motion picture *Wabash Avenue* (1950) diegetically screened in *The Girl Can't Help It* (1956), a movie highly influential in the dissemination and popularization of early rock and roll in Britain, and thus foundational to mod.)

Further connections with soul/R&B include Bowie's very early (1965) cover of 'I Pity the Fool', which foreshadows his later move into R&B while emphatically endorsing the connection between R&B and mod. 'Wild is the Wind', via Nina Simone, allowed Bowie to develop a 'melange of chanson and soul' (Buckley, 2005: 271), Nat King Cole's 'Nature Boy' featured in the *Moulin Rouge* soundtrack in 2002, while the 1985 Jagger/Bowie cover of Martha and the Vandella's 'Dancing in the Street' drew a direct and obvious line to Tamla Motown.

'New wave'/'post glam'

The above four categories of cover version represent the acknowledgement of various strands and influences that Bowie has utilized in constructing his own persona and sound. Since the end of the 1970s Bowie has covered songs which function to align him with more contemporary 'alternatives' and 'new waves': Tom Verlaine's 'Kingdom Come' in 1980, Morrissey's 'I Know it's Gonna Happen Someday' in 1993, and The Pixies 'Cactus' in 2002 are clear examples. I would suggest Bowie's recording of a couple of Bruce Springsteen songs around the time of *Diamond Dogs* might be considered part of this lineage, Springsteen at the time being an up and coming artist who now forms part of the 'classic' rock tradition. Further, Bowie has also invested in covers of 70s 'glam' tracks: in particular Roxy Music's 'If There is Something' on *Tin Machine II* (1991), as well as post-glam: Metro's 'Criminal World' on *Let's Dance* (1983) and Sigue Sigue Sputnik's 'Love Missile F1-11' in 2003.

Alongside Bowie's work with much younger bands such as TV on the Radio and Arcade Fire, Bowie's covers of 'new wave' and 'post-glam' can be understood in terms of Bowie participating in and being open to the development of rock history as a kind of two-way street, acknowledging music that has been influenced by Bowie himself, but also demonstrating one of the ways in which Bowie's career has constantly developed and been renovated by taking on new influences and collaborations.

Conclusion

My conclusion is that a postmodern analysis of Bowie's work has a definite but limited value; particularly in assessing certain thematics associated with Bowie's Ziggy Stardust period. However, any postmodern analysis of Bowie's work needs to be supplemented by the manner in which postmodern and modern coexist and intermingle in Bowie's ouevre. Bowie's postmodernity is underpinned and circumscribed by his modernity, indeed those moments where Bowie pushes too strongly in a postmodern direction demonstrate the very limits of the postmodern achievement in the rock/pop sphere. Futhermore, the postmodern attempt to deconstruct 'original' and 'cover' does not work in the popular music sphere. Rather, the cover version is central to Bowie's art considered in terms of a gift economy. The cover version provides quite a clear portrait of the elements that make up the Bowie synthesis and offers respects and courtesies to the appropriate artists: 'swinging London mod, classic rock, New York Factory and Euro art song (Brel and Brecht), along with soul/R&B. The cover version also provides recognition for and of the ways in which Bowie's art has developed and renovated. Importantly, the cover is what brings the alien back to earth; it is what prevents the space voyager from floating away. The rock star/artist as superman/*Übermensch* – capable of 'noble expenditure' – does not stand outside or above the system of alliance and commonality of the imagined rock community of which he functions as something like a treasurer to his fellow-citizens. The cover version is one of the key ways in which the artist returns his obligations.

References

Auslander, Phillip. 2006. *Performing Glam Rock*. Ann Arbor: University of Michigan Press.

Brackett, David (ed.). 2005. *The Pop, Rock and Soul Reader*. Oxford: Oxford University Press.

Buckley, David. 1996. 'Still pop's faker?' In Elizabeth Thomson and David Gutman (eds), *The Bowie Companion*. London: Da Capo, 3–11.

Buckley, David, 2005. *Strange Fascination: David Bowie: The Definitive Story*. London: Virgin Books.

Cagle, Van M. 1996. *Reconstructing Pop/Subculture: Art, Rock and Andy Warhol*. London: Sage.

Couldry, Nick. 2006. 'Culture and citizenship: the missing link?' *European Journal of Cultural Studies*, 9 (3), 321–39.

Couldry, Nick and Tim Markham. 2007. 'Celebrity culture and public connection: bridge or chasm?' *International Journal of Cultural Studies*, 10 (4), 403–21.

Doggett, Peter. 2011. *The Man Who Sold the World: David Bowie in the 1970s*. London: The Bodley Head.

Jones, Carys Wyn. 2008. *The Rock Canon: Canonical Values in the Reception of Rock Albums*. Aldershot: Ashgate.

Lening, Stuart. 2010. 'David Bowie's *Pin-Ups*: past as prelude'. In G. Plasketes (ed.), *Play it Again: Cover Songs in Popular Music*. Farnham: Ashgate, 127–38.

Loder, Kurt. 1996. 'Tonight.' In Elizabeth Thomson and David Gutman (eds), *The Bowie Companion*. London: Da Capo, 198–9.

Mauss, Marcel. 1966. *The Gift: Forms and Functions of Exchange in Archaic Societies*. London: Cohen & West Ltd.

Mellers, Wilfred. 1996. 'Still Hunky Dory, after all these years'. In Elizabeth Thomson and David Gutman (eds), *The Bowie Companion*. London: Da Capo, 51–8.

Peraino, Judith A. 2012. 'Plumbing the surface of sound and vision: David Bowie, Andy Warhol and the art of posing'. *Qui Parle*, fall/winter, 21 (1), 251–81.

Plasketes, George. 2010. 'Further re-flections on "the cover age": a collage and chronicle'. In G. Plasketes (ed.), *Play it Again: Cover Songs in Popular Music*. Farnham: Ashgate, 11–42.

Rojek, Chris. 2012. *Fame Attack*. Gordonsville: Bloomsbury.

Shuker, Roy. 2008. *Understanding Popular Music Culture*. London and New York: Routledge.

Spitz, Marc. 2009. *Bowie: A Biography*. New York, Crown Publishing Group.

Stevenson, Nick. 2006. *David Bowie: Fame, Sound and Vision*. Cambridge: Polity.

Tetzlaff, David. 1994. 'Music for meaning: reading the discourse of authenticity in rock'. *Journal of Communication Enquiry*, 18 (1), 95–117.

Thompson, Dave. 2006. *Hallo Spaceboy: The Rebirth of David Bowie*. Toronto: ECW Press.

Bowie cover songs

Ahbez, Eric. 2002. 'Nature Boy'. *Moulin Rouge* soundtrack.

Arnold, Billy Boy. 1973. 'I Wish You Would'. *Pin Ups*.

Asher, Tony and Brian Wilson. 1984. 'God Only Knows'. *Tonight*.

Barrett, Syd. 1973. 'See Emily Play'. *Pin Ups*.

Barrett, Syd. 2007. 'Arnold Layne'. *Remember That Night: Live at the Royal Albert Hall* (with David Gilmour).

Berns, Bert. 1973. 'Here Comes the Night.' *Pin Ups*.

Berry, Chuck. 1982. 'Round and Round'. *Rare*.

Berry, Chuck. 2000. 'Almost Grown'. *Bowie at the Beeb*.

Bonner, L., M. Jones, R. Middlebrooks, D. Robinson, C. Satchell and G. Webster. 1974. 'Here Today and Gone Tomorrow'. *David Live, 1974*.

Brecht, Bertholt and Dominic Muldowney. 1995. 'Baal's Hymn'. *Christiane F/Baal/Rarities*.

Brecht, Bertholt and Dominic Muldowney. 1995. 'Dirty Song'. *Christiane F/Baal/Rarities*.

Brecht, Bertholt and Dominic Muldowney. 1995. 'The Ballad of the Adventurers'. *Christiane F/Baal/Rarities*.

Brecht, Bertholt and Kurt Weil. 1978. 'Alabama Song'. *Stage*.

Brecht, Bertholt and Kurt Weil. 1995. 'The Drowned Girl'. *Christiane F/Baal/Rarities*.

Brel, Jacques. 1973. 'Amsterdam'. *Pin Ups* (Rykodisc re-release).

Brel, Jacques. 1982. 'My Death'. *Ziggy Stardust and the Spiders from Mars: The Motion Picture Soundtrack*.

Browne, Duncan, Peter Godwin and Sean Lyons. 1983. 'Criminal World'. *Let's Dance*.

Bruce, Jack and Pete Brown. 1993. 'I Feel Free'. *Black Tie White Noise*.

Collins, Aaron/Clarence Williams and Armand Piron. 1995. 'Footstompin/I Wish I Could Shimmy Like My Sister Kate'. *Rarest One Bowie*.

Conn, Lesley. 1991. 'Liza Jane'. *Early On: 1964–66*.

Crouch, Nicky, Bob Konrad, Stu James, Keith Karlson and Simon Stavely. 1973. 'Everything's Alright'. *Pin Ups*.

Davies, Ray. 1973. 'Where Have All the Good Times Gone'. *Pin Ups*.

Davies, Ray. 2007. 'Waterloo Sunset'. *David Bowie Box*.

Davies, Ron. 1972. 'It Ain't Easy'. *Rise and Fall of Ziggy Stardust and the Spiders from Mars*.

Dee, Johnny. 1973. 'Don't Bring Me Down'. *Pin Ups*.

Degville, Martin, Anthony James and Neal Whitmore. 2007. 'Love Missile F1-11'. *David Bowie Box*.

Duncan, Jimmy and Bill Farley. 1973. 'Rosalyn'. *Pin Ups*.

Dylan, Bob. 1994. 'Like a Rolling Stone'. *Heaven and Hull* (Mick Ronson).

Dylan, Bob. 1995. 'Maggie's Farm'. *Alternative Biography*.

Engel, Scott. 1993. 'Nite Flights'. *Black Tie White Noise*.

Feldman, Bob, Jerry Goldstein and Richard Gottehrer. 1973. 'Sorrow'. *Pin Ups*.

Ferry, Bryan. 1991. 'If There is Something'. *Tin Machine II*.

Floyd, Eddie and Steve Cropper. 1974. 'Knock on Wood'. *David Live*.

Francis, Black. 2002. 'Cactus'. *Heathen*.

Fraser, Ian, Larry Grossman and Alan Kohan/Katherine Kennicott Davis. 1995. 'Peace On Earth/The Little Drummer Boy'. *Christiane F/Baal/Rarities*.

Gaye, Marvin, Williams Stevenson, Ivy Jo Hunter. 2002. 'Dancing in the Street'. *Best of Bowie*.

Gershwin, George and Ira. 1998. 'A Foggy Day in London Town'. *Red Hot + Rhapsody: The George Gershwin Groove*.

Gilmour, David. 2007. 'Comfortably Numb'. *Remember That Night: Live at the Royal Albert Hall* (with David Gilmour).

Harrison, George. 2003. 'Try Some Buy Some'. *Reality*.

Jagger, Mick and Keith Richards. 1973. 'Let's Spend the Night Together'. *Aladdin Sane*.

Legendary Stardust Cowboy. 2002. 'I Took a Trip on a Gemini Spaceship'. *Heathen*.

Lennon, John. 1989. 'Working Class Hero'. *Tin Machine*.

Lennon, John and Paul McCartney. 1975. 'Across the Universe'. *Fame*.

Lennon, John and Paul McCartney. 1996. 'This Boy'. *Radio Hype*.

Lieber, Jerome and Mike Stoller. 1984. 'I Keep Forgettin'. *Tonight*.

Lieber, Jerome and Mike Stoller. Late 1990s. 'I'm a Hog For You Baby'. *Divine Symmetry*.

Lindsay, Mark and Paul Revere. 1991. 'Louie, Go Home'. *Early On: 1964–1966*.

Malone, Deadric. 1991. 'I Pity the Fool'. *Early On: 1964–1966*.

Migliacci, Francesci. 1996. 'Volare'. *Absolute Beginners Original Soundtrack*.

Morrissey and Mark E. Nevin. 1993. 'I Know it's Gonna Happen Someday'. *Black Tie White Noise*.

Pop, Iggy. 1988. 'I Wanna Be Your Dog'. *Glass Spider*.

Pop, Iggy and Ivan Kraal. 1987. 'Bang Bang'. *Never Let me Down*.

Pop, Iggy and James Williamson Jr. 1984. 'Don't Look Down'. *Tonight*.

Reed, Lou. 2011. 'Dirty Boulevard'. *Birthday Celebration: Live in NYC 1997* (with Lou Reed).

Reed, Lou. 2000. 'I'm Waiting for the Man'. *Bowie at the Beeb*.

Reed, Lou. 2000. 'White Light/White Heat'. *Bowie at the Beeb*.

Richman, Jonathan. 2003. 'Pablo Picasso'. *Reality*.

Rose, Biff. 1971. 'Buzz the Fuzz'. *The Forgotten Songs of David Robert Jones*.

Rose, Biff and Paul Williams. 1971. 'Fill Your Heart'. *Hunky Dory*.

Samwell-Smith, Paul, Jim McCarty and Keith Relf. 1973. 'Shapes of Things'. *Pin Ups*.

Simon, Paul. 2001. 'America'. *The Concert for New York City*.

Springsteen, Bruce. 1973. 'Growin' Up'. *Pin Ups* (Rykodisc re-release).

Springsteen, Bruce. 1989. 'It's Hard to Be a Saint in the City'. *Sound + Vision*.

Tiomkin, Dmitri. 1976. 'Wild is the Wind'. *Station to Station*.

Townshend, Pete. 1973. 'I Can't Explain'. *Pin Ups*.

Townshend, Pete. 2001. 'Pictures of Lily'. *Substitute: The Songs of the Who*.

Townshend, Pete and Roger Daltrey. 1973. 'Anyway, Anywhere, Anyhow'. *Pin Ups*.

Traditional. 1995. 'Remembering Marie A'. *Christiane F./Baal/Rarities*.

Valmont, Martine, Michel Valmont and Tahra Valmont. 1993. 'Don't Let Me Down and Down'. *Black Tie White Noise*.

Vanda, Harry and George Young. 1973. 'Friday on My Mind'. *Pin Ups*.

Verlaine, Tom. 1980. 'Kingdom Come'. *Scary Monsters*.

Young, Neil. 2002. 'I've Been Waiting for You'. *Heathen*.

7

Ain't there One Damn Flag that Can Make Me Break Down and Cry?

The Formal, Performative and Emotional Tactics of Bowie's Singular Critical Anthem 'Young Americans'

Amedeo D'Adamo

Introduction

In this chapter I focus on one song among all of David Bowie's music that is singularly – and idiosyncratically – both political and emotional; his hit 'Young Americans', written in 1974 and released on the album of the same name in 1975. Among all of Bowie's massive output, 'Young Americans' is a unique expression of protest against conservative politics, racism, and – less-uniquely for Bowie – the oppressive nature of gendered roles and social institutions such as marriage. The song also has another singular aspect – among the many shining baubles of this fantasist's work, 'Young Americans' has a powerful socially- and emotionally-grounded, intimate urgency that surprises and moves us even today. And the song is, finally, also singular in its approach to time; here Bowie eschews both nostalgia and futurism, refusing to look backwards or forwards to a better or worse America, choosing instead to play with both music time and storytelling tense as his voice's affect travels from story affect into the immediate, experiential present, moving anxiously and performatively towards the listener's subjectivity while linking it to tales of lost lives, disempowered subjects and the performer's own despair (Auslander, 2004, 2006; Cinque, 2013; Frith, 1996; Holmes and Redmond, 2012). In these ways the song is, among this master enchanter's oeuvre, uniquely disenchanting and yet singularly emotional.

The chapter has two parts. The first takes the song's title seriously; this is a song about Americans and thus relates directly to the rich tradition of encoding enchanting social visions of America in song (Anderson, 1991; Babha, 1990; Biddle and Knights, 2007). Thus Bowie's song relates directly to the rich American tradition of anthems, and so I trace this tradition from the American national anthem 'The Star-Spangled Banner' down through a responding song tradition that I label the critical anthem and that I argue shapes 'Young Americans'. I then offer a formal definition of this genre and use this definition to explain the aesthetic, political and performative strategies of 'Young Americans'.

The second aspect of the analysis concerns the other rather unique aspect of the song – its authentic, vivid and grounded despair and emotion. Here I situate the song in the context of Bowie's own experience of America, of its social, economic and political chaos in 1974–5, and of his own precarity at that moment. Then I examine verse-by-verse Bowie's masterful manipulations of musical and performative time, songwriting craft, vocal inflection and sound design, relating these choices to his own much-storied anxieties about his bisexuality, his self-definition as a rock performer, and his own pop-cultural hopes and disenchantments.

In the conclusion I examine the lessons we might learn from this one song about how Anthems can inscribe and dissolve social bonds. I think that Bowie's own lyrical, performative and contextual tactics all throw light on how performance can enchant or disenchant an audience in ways that form and shape social identity, and that furthermore, his example might illustrate a specifically democratic form of anthem, one that differs from the dangerous collective bonding of most national anthems because it bonds us to the experience of a social group while simultaneously preserving the boundaries of individual experience. This is the real agenda of the chapter; though disenchanting, Bowie's 'Young Americans' may in fact point a way forwards, like other anthemic performances by Beyoncé, Roberto Benigni and others, towards a progressive re-enchantment of our social world of the kind that we urgently need (Bennett, 2001).

Does David Bowie ever cry?
Is he a serious man?

First we should see how this one damn song stands out in such stark contrast to David Bowie's other work. As diverse as his productions have been, those of us whose teen years were deeply inflected by Bowie's astonishing output can all generally agree on a few particulars. First of all, in view of the rich formal literary and songwriting traditions of 'high seriousness', I think we can agree that he is not a serious man.

Instead, Bowie generally is an enchanter. He is a gestural, storyteller, a mask-wearer who creates a sense of danger and freedom by enacting poetic fantastic performances that inhabit and explode iconography and gender boundaries (Auslander, 2006). He is also generally a story miniaturist, a puppeteer and provocateur who seems to have no overt commitment to any ideology besides the brave libertarianism of the radical aesthete, ethically committed only to a freedom of play, expression and gender (Goodlad and Bibby, 2007; Hebdige, 1979, 2005).

Bowie's lyrical tactics usually mirror this mayfly aesthetic; wherever possible he prefers a slippery obscurity over weighted clarity in his lyrics. Likewise he often avoids certain earnest emotional poses and vocal techniques of authenticity and sincerity; he is never an authentic torch singer or emotional confessionist. He lives within consumerism, within fandom, within theatre's playful round, creating fantasies and science fiction stories. Even at his most daringly transgressive, he rarely steps out from play into an affect of grounded ethics such as panegyric, protest or memorial. If he ever plays a social Cassandra his prophesies are so strange and eel-like that we'll never know if they've come true. Those of his songs that might be described as science fiction haikus are never instructional in any ordinary sense – while often dystopic, he is less diagnostic and more a fantasist, more like William Burroughs than H.G. Wells. We often hear writers and even songwriters saying they write what they know, or they sing from the heart, but Bowie never does, opting instead to tell tales of gnomes, Ziggy and spacemen while inhabiting the personae of geishas, puppets and decadent nobles. He is transmutative, Bacchic, a fantasist. Bowie's only manifesto, if it can be called one, is perhaps to engender a specific sense of liberation in people by encouraging them to explore the characters that now lie incipient and asleep within their own fantasy.

This is not to say that Bowie is not simply a pure aesthete fighting boredom; his dark clowning, bold transgressive stances and puckish situationist actions do in fact express a transgressive social mission. Seen from one angle, he is essentially a Gramscian clown working all the points of Kosofsky-Sedgewick's homosocial triangle. He knows there is a dominant cultural and sexual hegemony and that sexual roles and expectations somehow gird and underpin it, that these hegemonic forces prefer to remain hidden or appear in the guise of common sense and convention; thus they are perfect subjects to be dragged puckishly into the limelight. But even this mission is not announced; it must be inferred from Bowie's gestures and poses.

Lastly, issues of a nation and of genuine politics are something he clearly and completely rejects. Nationalism in Bowie is always temporarily borrowed and purely performed; he has inhabited the German and Japanese popular cultures in complex ways but this has meant adapting only their visual tropes and some shiny fragments of their pop-cultural stories, mannerisms, affect and ambiance – a bit of geisha, a snatch of cabaret. He never strives to create a political point of view on any real topic and never really comments on a nation or national identity. And he never directly speaks, the way that for example folk and R&B singers often do, for a recognized marginalized group or a politicized but suppressed social voice.

In all these ways he set the terms of the 1980s postmodern period that he – perhaps more than anyone – helped to create in pop culture. And yet. There is at least one exception to these tropes, poses, aesthetic fantasies, political dodgings and cultural bricolage: Bowie's beautiful and authentically moving ballad 'Young Americans'. This I think is the only moment when the unearthly David Bowie did not go off-planet, did not try to add to our gender imaginary-menagerie, the moment when he fell to Earth, put aside his normal fascinations and was moved to write and sing about the existing cultural and social scene of the USA. The disenchanted, political song 'Young Americans' critiques stardom and fandom and the pop and sexual culture of America.

At the same time this song is sung not by a clown nor a mask nor an invented persona. It is not the sound of fantasy or the spell of enchantment but a portrait of social and political realities performed in a voice of disenchantment, and it features a singular vocal 'intimacy corridor' that Bowie carefully constructs between himself and the listener. Why? How is this American oddity different and how can it be understood in his overall oeuvre, which it departs from on so many fronts?

I will argue here that 'Young Americans' presents a moment of making the personal political. This song, written from a time of personal, professional, economic and artistic crisis, is different from his other work in many ways, but most strikingly because it feels grounded in an authentic fear, insight and bleakness. Perhaps, I will argue at the end, this is Bowie writing what he knows – about the flatness of gender roles, the empty trap that institutions like marriage can be, and the exploitative passive-inducing nature of the pop star-fan system. Interestingly, he chose an unusual – for him – song genre to express this; a form usually associated with 'serious' American singer-songwriters which we might call the critical anthem.

The challenge of tracing the nation in song

Since we are focusing on what *America* is in 'Young Americans' we should note at the outset the archaeological distance between us and Bowie's song of 1974–5, and especially one particular phenomenon that has been commented on in studies of popular music: the disappearance of the nation as a critical concept in the past four decades. Since 1974 we have instead passed through a phase of thinking of ourselves as late-capitalist nomads, suspended, fractured subjects dancing between the local and the global. As Biddle and Knights argue (2007: 8–9):

> Popular music studies in the anglo-American tradition is dominated still by two ideological orientations, neither of which has dealt terribly constructively with nationalism or the conceptualization of the nation-state. The first, essentially Marxist in orientation, has tended to view the nation-state as an antiquated bourgeois construction and scholars touched by this tradition have found it difficult to track the ideological fluidity of nationalist sentiments and their implications in popular musical practices. . . . the second, essentially a liberal tradition, has tended to view the nation-state as a sovereign but pragmatic unit . . . [and reduces] national sentiment in popular music to an array of beguiling and seductive differences, available for consumption on the global market. . . . [As a result,] In seeking to articulate the 'national' dimension in music, scholars are met with an extraordinary set of complex problems.

But of course the nation and nationalism were a far more contested and debated category in the songs of the 1960s and 1970s. The nation was not then understood as an 'Imagined Community' (Anderson, 1991), nor was it understood as an almost-ephemeral epiphenomenal shadow of the frisson between local and global forces (Biddle and Knights, 2007). Instead the nation shows up in top-chart pop and R&B songs like 'American Pie', 'Living For The City' and 'Inner City Blues' as an overwhelming force that might destroy one's life, community, neighbourhood and the planet itself. As Guthrie, Dylan, Gaye, Wonder, Bowie and so many other singers then treated it, the nation was not only a construction in the social imagination but a powerful aesthetic construct causally connected with racist police riots and hot (and possibly nuclear) war. Thus it was a worthy object of urgent aesthetic attack, a dangerous enchantment that must be unmade and, perhaps, remade.

Therefore in this chapter I seek to articulate a specific set of frames for understanding how America is present in Bowie's song. Here I first propose a frame of interpretation that I root in the American national anthem and argue is then re-appropriated by the 'anti-American' musical activist tradition. This frame of the critical anthem – a series of tropes of portraiture and dramatization – is intended to help make visible what Zizak and others argue is elided – the national in its aesthetic force.

Here, in trying to understand techniques for inscribing the national, I argue we must go beyond the idea of an imagined community if we want to unpack the specific inscriptions of an anthemic act, which is not simply the shared imagining of a collection of texts but is dynamically inscribed in us through specifically dramatized and performed rituals of community. This frame is a tool for pointing out certain rhetorical commonalities; it is also a device for highlighting the point, made by many, that because the nation is so constituted by culture, it is therefore a very unstable and contested form of identity (Babha, 1990). Bowie wants to join this contestation with 'Young Americans', and so in this chapter I will ask: what are some of the rhetorical and performative techniques that have not only contained the collective imagining of this imagined community but have in fact repeatedly dramatized it? This means trying to deconstruct in Bowie's case, and in other anthemic performances, not only what is sung but also *how* it is sung, what makes it anthemic, and how its textual, recording and performed context, as well as the personae and affect of the singer, all help grant or deny its inscribing power.

Let's begin however by focusing on *what* is sung, treating the anthem first as a text and as an intertextual form and tradition.

What makes Americans so young? The American anthemic tradition

America generates many critical anthem-like songs, especially in times of national crisis. Suddenly story-based portraits of the American landscape appear in songs like 'This Land Is Your Land', 'A Hard Rain's A-Gonna Fall', 'American Pie', 'Inner City Blues', 'Living For The City', 'Tangled Up In Blue', 'Young Americans', 'Streets Of Philadelphia', 'Sign o' The Times', 'All I Wanna Do' and others. There is in fact a massive songbook of songs, including a great number of punk, rap and hip hop songs that ask us to reconsider the American nation as a whole, its core ethics, its basic health, its needs and aspirations, its existential dreads and concrete conflicts and pain.[1]

But how did the USA end up with such a rich tradition; is there anything especially American about it? This complicated anthemic tradition actually starts, unsurprisingly, in our slightly peculiar American national anthem, 'The Star-Spangled Banner'. However clunky and impossible to remember, our anthem possesses a rather specific dramatic structure that, enriched by the epic free-verse work of our most publicly-celebrated poets, then sets the tone for the whole genre of later critical anthems. It is a storytelling structure that comes down into popular music through the folk movement, exploding in Dylan and the protest period just before David Bowie's 'Young Americans' and now enriching all of today's popular musical genres.

Let us examine its specific form; it is a story with a dramatic premise and an open-ended ending. The tale begins with a narrator rather nervously asking us to look out at dawn to survey the grand landscape of a long terrible night battle to find out if our flag is still waving or if it has been captured. Then, after describing the battle, the terrible character of our adversaries, their cowardly flight, and finally the ongoing defence of our homes by brave Americans, the song's narrator eventually answers the question with reassuring clarity – yes, Our Flag is Still There; we still fight on for our freedoms.

This is in fact a rare call-to-arms among the world's old-school industrialized nations. Though some national anthems – such as France's 'La Marseillaise' and China's and Italy's two modern-era anthems – have strident exhortations that we all must fight for freedom, many modern anthems – for example, the British, German, Russian, Japanese and the Late-Mao Chinese and Savoy-era Italian anthems – still spend their verses blindly, baldly and clunkily extolling the king/emperor/leader and insisting we have faith in the wonderful mother- or fatherland. There are other varieties; for example Australia's, which is essentially a series of stanzas that exhort us to protect the land and raise the nation. But few anthems are really stories, and fewer pose a dramatic question as their central dramatic drive, and so are not portraits of an imagined community that we are invited to imaginatively project ourselves into. None are specifically stories with such an open-ended ending – is America won or is the battle going on into my own generation? – and thus offer two alternative enchantments as does 'The Star-Spangled Banner'.

This is interesting for our analysis of 'Young Americans' because the American national anthem's structure – a song that asks us questions and then invites us out into a blasted landscape where we are to find the answer among the stories and the experiences of different characters – does not only describe 'Young Americans' but in fact defines a subgenre of both epic poetry and songwriting in America. We might call this the critical anthem, songs that utilize the form of our anthem for the purpose of re-appraising America itself.

The critical anthem song cycle is a boxing ring for American social politics, and 'The Star-Spangled Banner' itself inscribes that contested site, not least because it can itself be heard differently by – and thus casts a different enchantment upon – different political persuasions. Those enchanted on the political right hear the song singing that the war for freedom has itself been won, the land is now ours and we must keep it as it is. To American progressives, by contrast, the song is about a battle and not a war; it sings to us to be brave and steadfast as we go into future battles to finish the project of America. In this reception the nation's free citizens must always fight to keep that flag waving, and so the truthful cliché expressed here is that America is an incomplete ideal and that every generation has to work to further complete the democratic project.

There is also an interesting historical tension in the anthem. At the start of our Civil War some new verses defending the anti-slavery cause were penned by a leading literary figure of the time and were reprinted in many songbooks.[2] With that move the national anthem itself was temporarily turned into a critical anthem, though this step was successfully contested after the Civil War; the new verses eventually disappeared from collective memory and the far-less-challenging, comfortingly nationalistic version returned. Americans now ritually sing that older version at sporting events and public rituals.

In short, this anthem itself shows how the American anthem genre at its origins was clearly an activist site of critical commentary – a battleground over what the term 'America' actually means – well before its form was re-appropriated by the American protest movement.

A parallel lyrical debate over the definition and enchantment of America developed in our epic poetry. Consider just one short poem from Walt Whitman's *Leaves Of Grass*, that epic poem cycle which comes closer than anything else to being the national epic poetry of the United States. 'I Sit And Look Out' hits nearly every dark theme of Bowie's 'Young Americans'. Whitman's other work fills in the one large gap; his other poems famously indict the anti-gay puritanism of American life.[3]

These two traditions fed into the American folk-music movement, which began to create similar landscape-like portraits of the state of the nation often anchored by a Whitmanesque narrating figure walking across the land and reporting on the political and social injustices to be found there.[4] Probably the most famous example is Woody Guthrie's classic folk song 'This Land Is Your Land', written in anger after hearing Irving Berlin's nationalistic 'God Bless America' played one too many times on the radio.[5]

And then came Dylan. In his clever hands Guthrie's frame of the critical traveller's eye – a kind of activist landscape-painting of the nation – became a refined, rich tactic to ask fundamental existential questions about what it means to be an American, what kind of flag we want to see waving up there. With Dylan the era of the critical anthem truly entered popular music in America; without him we would not have Arlo Guthrie, Don McLean, Springsteen, Tracy Chapman, *et al.* And we would not have 'Young Americans'.

Hopeful hymnal anthemic affect

But 'The Star-Spangled Banner' does not only help define the 'Americans' in Bowie's title for 'Young Americans'; the anthem also helps keep all Americans 'young'. When foreigners like David Bowie visit America they are often impressed with the remarkably earnest intensities of American self-identification with the nation, often connecting this hopeful patriotism with a charming, alarming innocence. All hopeful enchantedly-American Americans seem 'young' to the non-enchanted.

There are many socialization activities that encode this affect, but one is certainly and intentionally our anthem. We might define any song as anthemic if it is ritually performed by a group to invoke and deepen a common social bond around a rousing intent, but national anthems always encode and project a certain *positive* national identity; in this way they are specifically agents of mass enchantment. For example, our American anthem is ever-present in national life, performed endlessly at social and sports gatherings throughout the country, a ritualized epic enacted with intent to rouse and bind. It is rousing and binding specifically because it must only be sung with a specifically hopeful and earnest affect, and through our sharing a performance with a performing singer this affect is inscribed in us. In view of the anthem's appropriation of the hymnal's vocal and performative affect of respectful solemn hopefulness and joy, it is no coincidence that the song's meta-textual message is very Christian and very romantic; a new democracy is born in this fiery night of war, a new age is ushered in, and we know this because the flag is still up there atop the hill bathed in the sunrise like a positive crucifix, a revelatory vision of the death of the false, dark English prophets whose blood anoints the founding of our new Jerusalem. The emotional reality of this situation is brought alive in us by the shared performed affect. The American anthem *requires* this affect for it to function as what it is; a positive, apocalyptic communication, something that implicates and intends to change the listener into a believer and to unite the affirming fold. Scandal and outrage always result if it is perceived that this affect is not being respected (as Jose Feliciano, Roseanne Barr, Macy Gray, Beyoncé and many others have learned to their professional peril).[6]

Of course all national anthems are machines designed to inscribe this earnest hopeful affect in us through performance; they in fact require this affect if they intend to bind one's allegiances and align one's emotions and ethics with the national interest. All national anthems implicitly inscribe what Oakeshotte (2008) called the national *societas* (the community's commonly accepted moralities) and its *universitas* (the community's broadly accepted sense of purpose) and thus they are designed as enchantments in the sense defined by Jane Bennett (2001), conceived by those who believe in them as enriching life, informing our ethical actions while expanding our sense of social identity. The American anthem works this way also on a lyrical level, telling of many people unified in a moment of war, united against a common enemy, illustrating *universitas* in the same way 'La Marseillaise' does. And like 'La Marseillaise', our national anthem also contrasts the *societas* of the American fighters against the non-*societas* of the amoral non-virtuous invaders.

Thus on both a lyrical and a performative level, this anthem successfully inculcates a myth and a vision of a future that tells us our lives and land are special and unique; it offers a kind of innocence, a childlike horizon of promise and approval. Its ritual re-enchantment endlessly re-enacted is at least partly responsible for the American social affect; our young enthusiasms for our young country, inscribed in us anthemically as well as socially, is what keeps us Americans so young.

Defining the critical anthem genre

And so in a sense, for anyone who wants to change America – be it Guthrie, Dylan, Gaye or Bowie – this deeply ritualized enchantment – a concrete cultural emblem of the phantasmagoria of nationalism – is a primal presence against which the American critical anthem is cast as a kind of metaphorical counter-spell, sung to wake those dreamers who believe they now live in that land of beguiling promise. All critical anthems make a specific disenchanting argument; that the promises implicit in the national anthem are false and so you must now wake and look at the land as it is, face the truth of the lived stories all around you, hear, see and feel the real, actual, existing nation. Critical anthems do this usually with the intent of setting up an alternative vision of communal *societas* (through offering one or more social moralities) and its *universitas* (although the community does not always have a broadly accepted sense of narrative purpose).

Critical anthems borrow many lyrical characteristics from 'The Star-Spangled Banner' and are marked by certain common thematic, formal, emotional and storytelling strategies. For example, like our national anthem their texts attempt a kind of literary high seriousness as they convey an urgent account of the state of the nation. They tend to do this by taking the wide-angle scope usually associated with the epic form, acquiring the aura of being about the nation as a whole by showing a series of individual lives in their specificity. Often some characters are entangled in nationally-sanctioned ethical values or exhibit a certain faith in certain ideals, and those ideals and ethics are then either strengthened or undercut by events by the end of the song.

Like 'The Star-Spangled Banner', the texts of critical anthems also often possess certain narrative strategies for conveying and combining a sense of both individual perspective and national perspective. Often this is achieved formally by changing from different forms of address and different points of view, sometimes moving back and forth from first- to second- and third-person singular and plural pronoun perspectives in different verses.

Such songs often adopt another lyrical element of 'The Star-Spangled Banner'; their formal and emotional shape may include a window onto the singer's or narrator's own soul, a soul provoked or affected by these stories into some strong emotional expression. Often there is also an emotional or ethical appeal directly to the listener as well.

As we will see, all of these aspects are also present in the text of 'Young Americans', but it is far from the first critical anthem. For a young nation of uncertain social centre such as the USA, the epic form was often pressed into the service of defining, interrogating and confronting national identity and our social, political and ethical conflicts.[7] Consider for example a critical anthem from 1962, Bob Dylan's 'A Hard Rain's A-Gonna Fall', which features a narrator asking a boy who wanders the US what he has seen and the boy telling of many specific people in many situations. This song, highly Whitmanesque and disenchanted in tone, is also a clear forefather of 'Young Americans' in that it features an overall hopelessness in the face of a paralysis and pollution of the land of America. Hopefully a hard rain will wash all the pollution away. The song not only tells of many people of many ages in many situations but also features every pronoun except 'we'. Don McLean's 'American Pie', a hit song in 1970, is even more potently disenchanting, a despairing landscape portrait of the country that we will compare to Bowie's. Note how these disenchanting examples show that critical anthems often are better at disenchantment than at re-enchantment, and also that disenchantment by itself is neither amoral nor dissolving of social bonds; though all three songs do not propose a new *universitas*, they *do* each propose an alternative or expanded *societas* or social morality.[8] Sharing this specific form of disenchantment means they also share a resulting formal trait; portraying a society which has lost its *universitas* means of course a resulting loss of narrative unity, but this also allows their narratives to be much more diffuse, polyvalent and multivocal, far more likely to allow contrasting or otherwise marginalized voices, and are thus a closer homological fit with a conflicted, multicultural nation like Vietnam-era (and present-day) America.

1974–5: the year of 'Young Americans' examined

I think I'm a fairly good social observer and I think that I encapsulate areas; maybe every year or so I try and stamp that down somewhere, what that year was all about. . . . it's about trying to capture the quintessence of that year. . . . My job is as an observer of what is happening.

DAVID BOWIE in an interview with *Toppop* in 1977

Now that we have situated the song in a formal aesthetic frame, we can historicize the song to some degree in its historical moment, reminding ourselves of both Bowie's sense of America and of his own words and situation in 1974–5. This contextualization will help inform not only the song's text but also our analysis of Bowie's shifting performance in the song.

In his youth, Bowie had imbibed the spirit of the American rock pioneers Chuck Berry and Little Richard; their energies made him imagine the USA as a land of pop song promises, almost a teen paradise of freedoms, experimentation and adventure. But while he'd found this spirit in New York City and Los Angeles, he also discovered the puritanical, conservative heartland as he crisscrossed America on his early 1970s tours. For example, at one point in Texas he was threatened with murder by a man in a pickup truck with a rifle because of his clearly gay clothes.[9] In addition to an often-hostile reaction to his bisexuality, he'd also gained a sense of American racial politics through his long-term romantic relationship with Ava Cherry, the black singer who leads the Gospel choir on 'Young Americans'. So by 1974, Bowie understood something of the homosocial cruelties and racial prejudices of American culture. That year he was also broke thanks to a formerly-trusted American who'd cheated him of nearly all the profits of his recent albums and tours.

He unveiled 'Young Americans' to the US in a live interview and performance on *The Dick Cavette Show* in late 1974.[10] He explained his new aesthetic as follows: he had just completed the highly-theatrical *Diamond Dogs* tour and said he was done with doing 'productions' and wanted to just perform with a band doing songs; in fact he could not afford to stage any theatrics, so this new aesthetic made a virtue of his sudden poverty. Bowie then also insisted his work was about nothing, meant nothing, that he was not an intellectual and that he couldn't stand politics and political meaning.

On the face of it, we have to doubt Bowie's insistence on hating politics because 'Young Americans' is, first and foremost, clearly about the political state of the USA in 1974. It is there in the lyrics; references to Nixon, the House Un-American Activities Committee and racism would all evoke the last twenty years of song from the American civil rights and protest movements in listeners.

As the song portrays, America in 1974–5 was quite a mess; the country had just lost the Vietnam War and was trying to move beyond the extra-legal presidency of Richard Nixon who would step down just as Bowie's album came out. Americans were also suddenly forced to ask fundamental questions of the country's much-vaunted dedication to freedom, processing revelations about the CIA's anti-democratic initiatives around the world, the aftershocks of years of widespread racial violence and generations of radical inequality. For the first time, broad cultural insights about widespread gender oppression and the limitations of such institutions as the Church, the family and marriage also entered the public consciousness.[11] There was a sense in the air that, as Michelangelo Antonioni had claimed, 'eros is sick'.

Meanwhile Bowie's own sudden personal financial precarity was mirrored in the nation's economic state. Because of the OPEC oil embargo the price of oil had quadrupled in 1974; states were asking Americans not to string Christmas lights to save energy – one state even outlawed them. Gasoline not only jumped radically in price but a shortage triggered national rationing, long lines of cars stalled at gas stations and a sudden anxiety that natural resources might run out. These energy shocks deepened the phenomenon of stagflation, in which inflation combined with the worst recession since the Great Depression. In 1974–5, for Bowie and for Americans, bills had become very hard to pay.

With all this in view, and after some twenty-plus years of hard organizing, this might have been a celebratory moment for the American Left. After all, just as Nixon stepped down the last bleak lies about the Vietnam War were exposed, the war itself was ending with a humiliating capitulation while right-wing antidemocratic terror campaigns were finally revealed in Congressional hearings on the CIA's dark history.

And yet despite these apparent victories, a political and moral emptiness reigned, simply because in this would-be triumph of democracy there was no one and nothing left to take Nixon's place on the national stage. By 1975 the Old Left was long since debunked, the New Left fragmented by identity politics, marred by terrorist escapades and crippled by extra-legal FBI campaigns, the union of the SDS world and the Panthers were all a thing of the past, and any hopes of inner-city racial rage being a revolutionary force were now extinguished; whatever political energies had existed there in the days of rage were now replaced by the problems of heroin and escalating crime.

This was the moment David Bowie penned and recorded his critical anthem, his only foray into what by late 1974 had become not only a staple of the American songwriting scene but was by then in its sunset period, having peaked in the protest movements of the 1960s that were now proving to be politically, culturally and artistically exhausted.

The tactics of 'Young Americans' verse by verse

Let's now examine Bowie's 'Young Americans' verse by verse on both a textual and a performative level to see just how he is re-imagining the American community, or rather how he is dramatizing its very lack of community.

From the outset we recognize the American anthemic form that quickly sketches many lives *in media res*. Similarly, 'Young Americans' starts in the third person describing a young married couple having quick and unsuccessful sex behind their refrigerator. This couple's strange choice of location for sex immediately invites comparison to Chuck Berry's 1964 classic 'You Never Can Tell'[12] which tells of a happy, recently-married teenage couple who love amorously in an apartment with a bounteous refrigerator.[13] And yet Berry's infectious youthful American optimism, his pure pop sensibility, is here marred by ignorance and sexual misfire; Bowie's couple end their sex quickly and unsatisfyingly. And so right away we know we are not in an ordinary pop song; already something is broken in the land of pop song promises.[14]

Note how Bowie's vocal affect changes on each of the song's first three lines, switching from singing to narration to performance. The first line is sung, with each word falling on a musical beat. But in the second line Bowie changes into a storyteller; as he sings 'he lays her down' he stretches out the time signature so that the words 'lays', 'her' and especially 'dooown' cross many beats as they are sung with a gentle tone, conveying the physical act of our young boy gently laying our young girl down. Now Bowie has become a bard or a griot telling a tale; this will be a story, not just a song, and when 'frown' is rhymed with the three-beat-sustain of 'down', we hear the bard invoke dark foreshadowing.

Then in a quick rubato shift in the third line we have the appearance of Bowie the actor sunnily delivering the line of this boy: 'Gee! My life's a funny thing, am I still too young?'. Here Bowie, in occupying the boy's role, gooses the word 'Gee!' to convey this boy's naivete, emphasizing that European sense of Americans as selfish naifs. But then with his voiced worry at the end of the line – 'Am I still too young?' this boy reveals an insecurity that makes him sympathetic.

The verse ends by describing the girl's desperateness for contact and affirmation from this shallow and dumb young boy; both seem utterly inexperienced, uncertain about life, and tricked by models of conventional maturity into marrying in order to become adults. We also know she is desperate – 'she'd have taken anything' – and that all night her desire will be unfilled – the marriage just dooms her to dissatisfaction.

Note also a small and apparently technical detail here that will I think open out the complex social agenda of this song. Bowie delivers the two ironically-quoted lines of the young American boy by ending each line on a tiny breathy, gaspy exhale. This exhale does two specific things: first it subjectively performs the boy's sense of real surprise; second, this gasping breath starts us on a rhythm of tiny exhales that will punctuate the next five lines and then grow into a performative trope – from surprise to sex to anxiety to desperation – that will extend and build through the entire song and lead finally to his panicked and breathless performative breakdown in the final verses.

Note too the way Bowie, master lyricist, writes and sings the first lines as a smoothly-travelling bed of vowels; at first everything is vocally rounded-off and flowing, a soothing, optimistic accompaniment to the smooth, happy-sounding sax. This pop music optimism, which takes us all the way to the question 'Am I still too young?' is then consonantly broken, starting in the emphasized consonants of the word 'kissed', which sets up a roll of breaking 'k' and 't' sounds. Now a rhythmic series of sharp, hard 't' and nearly-hissed 'k' sounds will come four more times, a sharp change that emphasizes this interruption of the couple's dream by the realities of bad, empty sex. This too is handled very artfully; the breaking of the dream, through the 't'-'k' consonant-breaks in four repetitions of the word 'take', will now become a crucial pattern that sets up the song's social themes; this America is a land of takers and taken, of sexual alienation and failed, empty desires.[15]

The second verse features the odd appearance of a Slinky Vagabond who betrays a woman who then cries out 'Where have all Papa's heroes gone?' Following the sexual disenchantment of the first verse, we are already seeing that every verse will contain at least one person who is 'taken'; frustrated, lost, shorn of hopes and illusions, a victim lacking any wisdom or awareness. Toija Cinque has pointed out (Cinque, 2013) how Bowie is often concerned with agency in his work, but note how different these young Americans are from the self-conscious agents that she highlights, such as the children in 'Changes' who are 'quite aware of what they're going through' or the world-weary proto-punk kids in 'All The Young Dudes'. By contrast, Bowie gives these young Americans no self-awareness; they lack agency because they lack any awareness of other possibilities. That lack of agency is twinned with a complete lack of community. The optimistic kids in 'Changes' and the nihilistic ones in 'All The Young Dudes' are at least unified among themselves, and there is also the promise of community Bowie offered in 'Rock 'n' Roll Suicide', when he screams out 'Gimme your hand!' to his audience. But these young Americans have no such unity; they are atomized individuals, too bombarded by consumerist media to think beyond passing wants. It is as if pop has popped, as if in the guise of this bewildered, betrayed woman, a newly-rudderless Bowie is really asking, 'Where have all pop-*music's* heroes gone?' And in fact this song is a kind of pivot-point for Bowie's own oeuvre from an occasional mild communitarianism to his radically alienated individualism of the Berlin period and *Scary Monsters*.

Now we have a verse that takes us out to the national stage for the first time, but does so in a way that comments on the youth culture of the mid-70s. The final line 'We live for just these twenty years, Do we have to die for the fifty more?' is of course a direct bonding address to Bowie's young fans, but it also comments on the American New Left's slow maturity and loss of innocence. This was a mass movement that at its inception often warned its members 'Don't Trust Anyone Over 30' and then moved this age upwards as the movement itself aged. By 1975 it was clear that this youth movement's idealism had changed to despair – campus radicalism was dying down and the hopes of Woodstock and communalism had been replaced by Altamont, drug addiction and the beginnings of the punk movement.

The chorus now comes back in with one change; the woman who longs for the young American has now switched genders, pluralizing the song's sense of subjective longing. This takes us into the verse about lost faith, disillusion and quotidian anxieties. This for me is the most potent social critique – I never stop admiring the line: 'Not a myth left from the ghetto'. In 60s popular culture and in New Left hopes the black inner-city ghettos were going to produce a liberating force in the nation's politics. But by 1975 much of that Marxism-based hope was gone; by then the FBI had destroyed the Black Panthers and nothing had replaced their social vision. As a result, the black inner cities were now overwhelmed by crime, drug addiction, apolitical cynicism and the insular racial politics of the Nation Of Islam – any idea of a united front with white radicals or with the left wing of the Democratic Party was clearly out of the question.[16]

The next verse portrays America as a land of pimps, hustlers and suckers, of performers and consumers, of rich pop stars like Bowie and poor fans who passively watch them, a place of car-owners and of suicides. In fact the quoted Beatles' line is about a man who shot himself in the head in a car, but the other three cars in the song – the Cadillac, the Chrysler and the Mustang – are also worth mentioning.

The very first rock and roll song is a celebration of fast cars and from the very beginnings of rock and pop such cars are used as engines of freedom and emblems of success and possibility, central objects in the Geertzian symbolic system that constituted the American Dream. But in the nationwide gas shortage and economic crisis of 1974–5, these American cars would hum with a new Bachelardian air of loss and a class-status anxiety quite different from their older presence in pop and rock. That year car use dropped sharply and a common media image was of long lines of cars lined up for hours at empty gas stations. In a real sense cars in 1974 had suddenly become psychic burdens, emblems of lost liberty, engines of promise now out of gas, inert and too expensive to refill, reminders of the sudden widespread sense of national and personal precarity.

Bowie now poses a series of open questions about love that mix up national political disasters, fandom, pop cultural passions, real-life heartbreak and two different fatal cures for suicidal depression. At the end of this list come increasingly intimate, demanding questions addressed to the listener, all capped by Bowie's powerful solo self-interrogatory plea: 'Ain't there one damn song that can make me break down and cry?'. This line is the emotional nexus of the song, and we should examine it from a few different angles.

First, there is the technical design here. This final belted-out question reveals a tension in the song between 'clean' elements and less crisp ones which are manipulated now to give this line its strong dramatic impact. The line is far more immediate, present, bright and foregrounded than any of Bowie's other lines throughout the song. Why is this?

In large part this comes through a sudden, canny manipulation of the song's four-point sonic envelope and the rather unique positioning of the lead singer's voice within it. In the sound design of 'Young Americans' we have a clear distinction of sonic presence; from the song's very first notes the sax, the piano, the choral voices and the drums have been arranged and mixed to be up front, alive and present, and are all generally panned to the centre, with some varying panning to stereo right and left. All of these sounds are very full and bright.

But this three-dimensional acoustic envelope – front, right and left – is in sharp contrast to Bowie's voice which, though it dominates in volume, has from the start been artificially flattened, slightly muted so that it is coming from a different, further-back sonic space. This position in that four-dimensional sound-design pattern runs nearly throughout the entire song. This muffling of Bowie's voice, 'burying the lead' by putting it into the back, is very remarkable. Usually the frontman wants to be in front and up front, with a backup band in the sonic background,[17] but Bowie has reversed this, which is especially unusual since he is also playing both a performative and a storyteller's role. That distancing choice, certainly a dominant material realization of the intended 'plastic' element in Bowie's plastic soul, also helps him disguise his own voice's desperate message and delivery behind the sonically-dominating happy 'cherry pop' instrumental soundscape.

But this all changes on this crucial line. With the shout of 'Ain't there one damn song . . .' Bowie's vocal suddenly turns from 'plastic' to 'soulful', heightening the strong dramatic and emotional effect of this question. The shift comes through two sonic changes; first, the muffling filter is suddenly gone and, second, Bowie's voice on this one line is suddenly mixed into the front. As a result we are hit with clarity and presence. Suddenly Bowie's voice becomes authentically present the way the gospel choir has been, and the difference is emotionally and affectively very important – we are now affectively 'with' Bowie as if this actor has quickly moved from upstage to direct downstage, just as he has his emotional catharsis and the song hits its highest dramatic rise.[18] His long extended 'Cryyyy?!!' then stands lonely and alone, given a brief, singular, full instrumental silence as his voice starts bright stereo centre and then echoes out right and left to fully fill the evacuated acoustic envelope that formerly had been occupied by all of the song's other elements.

Consider the dramatic effect of this change in the soundscape. Throughout the song we have a massively complex acoustic environment with many competing elements running alongside each other. There is a funk-like democracy of arrangement here that overwhelms our ears, as if we are hearing the voices of a great gathering of individuals all talking at once; the elements have been melodically independent, layered with numerous spontaneous jazz riffs but yet strangely-synchronous, thus filling our attention without allowing us any primary attention to any specific dominant element, melody or performance.

But now that polyphonic group – perhaps standing in for the nation of 'young Americans' – falls back, fading out so that Bowie's lone voice can rise to meet us in a newly-intimate sonic space as he demands this imperative question of himself. In dramatic effect it feels as if the listener personally meets Bowie in a sonic close-up at a moment of his most bare soul-searching. This plea, this existential question, is met by a short but powerfully dramatic beat of silence. The answer is . . . no, it seems there is no such song; if this acidic account of innocence and hope destroyed won't provoke real authentic emotion, then nothing will.

Another songwriter-singer, Don McLean, had already used this very same structure in his own famous critical anthem 'American Pie'. Bowie would certainly have known the song – 'American Pie' had hit number one on the American pop charts in 1971 and number two in England in 1972.[19] In fact this is only one of many striking parallels between the two songs; not only do we have similarly depressing narrative depictions of many different lost Americans, we also have self-address and self-questioning, audience-address and audience-questioning, quotes from famous rock songs, a fixation on specific brands of cars, and even obscure references to an injured trickster character. We also have a narrator expressing personal emotional exhaustion, who then questions whether music could save our souls in the face of national political exhaustion, followed by a demand for a song of comfort and psychical guidance, followed by a silent musical beat as the resounding, disenchanting answer. Here again a lost narrator portrays a lost generation of American kids, then asks to be helped out of his own portion of the shared emotional despair by asking for a musical antidote. But things have gotten so bad in America that his need for a meaningful song is met by a silent and dramatic beat.[20]

The parallels are striking and the structure seems highly appropriated, but Bowie is not McLean and is not a fellow political folk singer, he's not even an American, and most importantly 1975 is not 1971. Although both songwriters deploy similar lyrical tactics, each is using this metaphor – of the death of music's ability to move and bind – to describe a very different kind of national and internal despair and disenchantment.

For McLean in 1970, the energies of renewal were still roiling the industrialized world, the battles over Vietnam between police and protestors were still raging, and the promises of May 1968 still shone on the cultural horizon. But many had already read the end of the New Left symbolically in the assassinations of Martin Luther King, Malcolm X and Robert Kennedy, and McLean was right to connect this despair to Manson's madness and to Altamont; in 'American Pie', as in 'Young Americans', the land is blighted by a malaise of depression and exhaustion. As left-wing bombing campaigns continued and as Manson's clan was cast in the media as a hellish version of an intentional community, the New Left had already begun to lose the media war. In 1970 their social enchantment, a crucial part of their song, was alive if fatally wounded.

These, however, were not Bowie's concerns in 1974–5, a moment when that particular enchanting social dream was dead. For Bowie at that point, America's problem was quite different; one of deep inauthenticity, somehow created by consumerism and by being forced into outdated gender roles, expectations, institutions and hopes, longing after cars and whatever everyone else wants, and by an overall social atomization.[21]

In other words, the nature and causes of the country's malaise are very different for the two songwriters. McLean is more directly and traditionally political and so more modernist than Bowie – in 'American Pie', pop cultural emotions and exhaustions are caused by and are metaphors for national emotions and exhaustion. McLean has also experienced real political struggle and we hear this in his drama, which features social groups battling for the field, a generation searching together for solutions, and a trickster who sings in our collective voice. Most of the bands he references – Dylan, The Rolling Stones, The Byrds – held a clear leftist political opposition and represented a unified social promise.

By contrast the music referenced in 'Young Americans' is not political at all – it is largely pop and soul music backed by a salsa beat. Similarly, for Bowie the malaise in 1974–5 America is not primarily political; for him the problem is reversed from 'American Pie' in that the emptiness of America and the exhaustion of its politics is somehow actually *caused* by the limits of its pop culture. Marriage is full of false expectations, there is no myth left from the ghetto, we blush at the afro-sheeners and our only connection to the national trauma of racism comes from watching the TV show *Soul Train*. Now, like the girl in the song's bad marriage, each American is socially and existentially isolated but no shallowly-held beliefs in false flags and faded utopian-left myths will help.

Bowie's own personal history in the mid-70s reveals some of these themes; consider his failed marriage, his love for a black transvestite and for a black woman, his endless sexual escapades that, while often abusive, were marked by a polyvalent experimentation and a different, outlier form of masculinity. By 1974–5 that long orgy was coming to a close; Bowie had personally been there and done all those things and yet found himself battling depression, poverty and a sense of spiritual destruction. The bleakness of Bowie's experiences and his sense of the traditional gender institutions informs this song's characters, and in that sense he is enacting the phrase that was being batted about in 1975 by the new philosophers of gender and racial oppression – the personal is the political.

In this way Bowie is unlike both McLean and the rest of the folk movement's earnest, grounded politics; he is uninterested in political history and meaning but is endlessly fascinated by transgression, by gender, by breaking the oppression of everyday roles, and by pop music with its endless proposals to combat boredom with new pleasures. That is Bowie's great weakness and also his great strength; he is far more savvy about consumerist, postmodern cultural concerns and the oppression of gender but has repeatedly declared – and shown – his cluelessness about actual politics; he is perhaps best described as an individualist with a deep suspicion of all social glue.

These concerns of Bowie's find voice in the song's final verses, which run the chorus over the narrator as he confronts/accuses the listener and then himself. This long list of interrogatives triggers a breakdown of structure; Bowie reveals that 'I want what you want', that in a consumer society desire is not exploratory but only imitative, and then he rushes on with somehow even greater emotional energy into this final whirlwind of broken lines, finally descending into a bewildering loop of subjective pronouns attached only to wants – 'I want you, you want I'. His narrative, emotional, and performative tactics now swirl all into chaotic shifting desires as the last linking desire between narrator and listener dissolves into the song's final subject; objectless, raw want. Formally speaking, this is an elegant, quintessentially postmodern end where the aesthetic machinery and structure of the piece has finally led to its own revelatory undoing; what was solid in the modern period has turned 'liquid' (Bauman, 2000).

Bowie personalizes this turn into chaos, turning it into the breakdown of a subjectivity. He emphasizes this subjective turn through deepening the formal development of vocal stances that he introduced in the song's first three lines. We have already noted how – by contrast to folk's melancholic, backwards-looking, measured and constant singer's vocal affect common to Dylan, McLean and most folk-songs – Bowie instead enacts this song with three radically evolving vocal stances. First, he moved from singer to griot, singing calmly in the first verse and then anxiously narrating the middle verses, then punctuating this by playing the voices of certain characters and their emotions. Then in the next verses he knitted us into this landscape by addressing us directly, trying to get us to see that we share the desires and problems of the characters he's been playing/telling us about. Now in this final verse Bowie-the-narrator begins desperately confessing his own needs and emotions. This concludes the song's emotionally rising and increasingly intimate journey from a verse about a he to one about a she to a verse addressed directly to us listeners, a development ending here with the narrator interrogating himself. And then, either under pressure of this self-analysis or just of being a young American, the narrator's own subjectivity finally dissolves. All four of these performative affects – singing, narrating, acting in character, and this final confessional direct address – can each be shaped by different acting-directing techniques. This is important to point out since it is always wise to ground your methodology in the actual practices of the creators of culture. Nowhere is this more true than in performance studies.

Metalepsis, threatened narrator breakdown and personal prophetic voice

We briefly focus further on Bowie's emotional and vocal breakout introduced by the line 'Ain't there one damn song . . .?' This dramatic, resonant shift in the song can be heard as a kind of metalepsis, as if the narrator has left the story and now addresses us directly in the 'real' world: 'The basic function of Metalepsis remains a crossing of the border between the fictional world and (a representation of) the real world' (Kukkonen and Klimek, 2011: 6).

This eruption happens on three levels. First, Bowie's now-intense anxiety is an affect of the immediate present and so marks a shift from the earlier reflective narrative time of Bowie's singing and storytelling affects. It is as though Bowie had rushed on stage in one of Shakespeare's tragedies to tell of an off-stage battle, only to begin telling of himself, then confessing, then berating himself, then becoming lost in an emotional breakdown. This rise in emotional register is supported by an overall rise in musical register, a conventional technique for creating musical progression and dramatic tension. The second change is in an interruption of reflective narrative time; we are now in the immediate present in both our verb tenses and in the first-person singular of self-address. The third change, building upon the first two, is in the dropping of the tropes of professional singing and storytelling. The singer loses the singer's mask as if it has slipped off because the singer, presumably Bowie himself, is now so overcome with the events he is telling us. After this beseeching confessional, the song slides towards cacophony, with Bowie singing increasingly out of synch against the chorus, his lines growing increasingly broken, apparently bewildered, forgetful and distracted. It seems we are to believe that the singer/narrator/confessionist is lost, his earlier controlled delivery now losing its coherence under pressure of the emotions that are unexpectedly welling up in him.

As consumers of narratives we know how to read such metalyptic breaks from various documented breakdowns – one can think of the Hindenburg tragedy's eyewitness announcer, 'Oh the humanity!', or more recently of the 2014 interview of UNRWA Christopher Gunness breaking down in tears on live TV unable to tell us of an Israeli attack on a UN school in Gaza.[22] We also see such breaks risked by singers in specifically powerful moments; think of Roberto Benigni's emotional performance of the unofficial national anthem by Verdi, or Beyoncé's emotional performance of 'At Last' at President Obama's first inauguration.[23] Many of us remember the final moments of that astonishing performance where Beyoncé seemed on the edge of crying, a performance that helped transform this R&B standard into a dramatic and famously moving national moment. This apparently spontaneous welling up of her emotions combined with the performance's historical and racial context to transform this romantic song into a kind of realized critical anthem of historical significance, a dynamic spectacle that was both imbued with and that reinscribed a mass collective progressive vision and hope for the country.

We are moved in moments of narrator slippage in ways we often long remember; as a form of narrative breakage, it hammers home the emotional truth of a narration in ways that little else can. But we might ask ourselves, why are these forms of narrator slippage, moments in which both the fourth wall and song time begins to crumble, one of the most powerful forms of the machinery of sympathy in narrative performance?

Because they suddenly and crucially bond the text and its referents with the person delivering it in the very moment of delivery. In narrator slippage we slip too, and into the emotional; our normal psychic distance collapses and instead we respond on a non-narrative, animalistic level to the sufferings or joys being experienced in the present by the person who suddenly and unexpectedly might lose the ability to go on.

This break, and the emotive rush it triggers, works on two separate levels. First, there is what we might call *event slippage*; the break quickly brings this moment in the narrated story vividly into our own immediate present. Before this moment, the events were being told with the detachment of the narrator (be she newscaster, spokesperson, storyteller or singer). But now, suddenly, because they are being remembered and experienced right in front of us by the teller, we begin emotively mirroring what we perceive as the narrator's actual emotions. Thus the narrated events become epistemically real on an entirely new level.

Second, there is what we might call *threatened narrator breakdown*; this break also brings the actual existence of the teller, as an actual living, experiencing being, suddenly into a new focus. Narrator slippage depends on us believing in the documentary truth of the narrator's emotional breakdown, in his or her suddenly-halting trouble to complete the script because of an emotional slippage into the narration, in a moment of emotional mirroring where the narrator's emotions are enmeshed and entangled with those of the narrated subjects. The narrator's self, entangled in this way, then also becomes a conduit of emotional entanglement for the audience. It is this moment of apparently unplanned and unintentionally shared intimacy and humanity, backed by the apparently authentic emotions of the overwhelmed teller who is struggling against them to continue narrating, that grants the performance its epistemic and emotive force. There is also the excitement of abandoning the performative frame of the rehearsed. In breaking the frame of the scripted and rehearsed, the moment opens the performance out in an alarming and exciting way; no one, not even the performer, knows quite what will come next, and this newly-shared uncertainty brings the performer more intimately closer to the audience. Intimacy is also created with the element of embarrassment and even shame by the narrator over having this moment-by-moment struggle; we can admire the struggle of the professional to master his or her human, vulnerable self. Lastly, we assume the message must matter a lot if the person is struggling so hard to continue to tell it in the face of this obvious inner conflict and public exposure. And so we admire the person while enjoying the sudden gift of intimacy now slipping out from behind the narrator's torn facade.

Thirdly, when narrator slippage events involve famous celebrities – as opposed to previously unknown UN spokespersons or ordinary people whom we've never seen before – we may experience an intense flash of what Redmond (2012: 35) calls 'productive intimacy', that phenomenon of fandom in which 'fans/consumers employ stars/celebrities to extend and enrich their everyday world'. This is the further binding nature of an intimacy corridor when opened for us by a celebrity; in this specific performance I can feel that in this moment I am being addressed by Bowie himself, who is apparently putting aside his pop stardom to address me directly and honestly from 'within himself'. Such moments are really also about entangled intimacy, since my emotions in such a moment are self-perceived to be not only directly triggered by his, but to be a perfect mirror of his, bringing me emotively close to the object of my fan adoration so that I can share in his hopes, vulnerabilities and travails.[24]

The affect of narrator slippage is powerful when brought into any speech or song, but it holds a special power in songs like 'Young Americans' that are contextualized within larger social conflicts. At such moments the intimacy corridor becomes also a social corridor. When a performer breaks down in an Oscar speech or a love song we can be moved by their situation and may even identify with their personal struggles and broken-hearted sentiments, and be reminded of our own lost loves, and so we are linked with the performer's own life. But when a performer breaks down while referencing a social group's misery, we are then brought via the performer into a further binding identification with that group's sufferings. This fact grants such performances a special power to inscribe a new form of social unity into us, one that unifies us with a group while recognizing individual experience.[25]

Compare Bowie's and Beyoncé's singing performances to Martin Luther King's speech 'I Have A Dream' which has been said to be performed in the prophetic voice, a moment when a speaker is experienced by an audience as speaking for a nation.[26] Bowie is boldly attempting here what Beyoncé clearly achieves, a rhetorical moment that goes beyond celebrity intimacy and even beyond prophetic voice into what might be called personal prophetic voice, into a moment where one singer or speaker is simultaneously experienced by an audience as not only speaking *for* a social group but as *personally and socially emoting*, as embodying and projecting, the emotions of and for that social group. In all narrator slippage we care for the narrator and for the events being narrated in a parallel and mutually reinforcing fashion; a subjectivity in a vulnerable moment is joined to the emotions of the narrated experiences. In moments of grand historical narratives, however, such narrator slippage can achieve personal prophetic voice by bringing alive great struggles in a way that no simple narration about a nation can.

For all of these reasons, narrator slippage is in fact a form of vocal affect with large implications for anthemic speech-acts, a point that returns us to the concept that an intimacy corridor opens in this song in the final verses between 'Bowie himself' and the listener. This is the epic hope of certain critical anthems such as Bowie's which not only strive to marry the social experience with individual experiences, the story to 'the real', and in some cases the celebrity to the fan, but which further strive to actually turn the performer's own subjectivity and emotional experience into a conduit, inducting listeners simultaneously into his or her own subjectivity *and* into broader social experiences.

Perhaps these are paradoxical hopes; can we really experience moments when an individual's experience is married to the social without losing its own claim to singularity? The example of Beyoncé's enchanting anthemic appropriation, and its inculcation of a progressive political vision, suggests that yes we can. If so, these may be the best social nodes for creating meaning in anthemic form in progressive democracies without risking a fall into the dangers of fascist emotivism that seem ever-present in so many national anthems and grand epic speeches by political leaders.

Conclusion: the many lives and deaths of social enchantments

We began this chapter by asking: ain't there one damn song among all the fabulist baubles of five decades of David Bowie's work that consciously tries to make us break down and cry, one that is uniquely political and uniquely emotionally real? Yes, I've argued; there is his 1975 hit song 'Young Americans' in which Bowie paints a sympathetic view of young Americans trapped in their country's historical, social and economic mess and which provides an intimate corridor to Bowie's own feelings. By no coincidence, 'Young Americans' is also Bowie's singular foray into the rich tradition of the American anthem, that long chain of storytelling songs that portray the state of the nation through the eyes of an emotionally affected narrator.

This great songbook opened with the classical American anthem itself. But that anthem's pro-nationalist origin, already complicated by a nationally contested rewrite in the American Civil War, took a decisively critical, modernist turn in the 40s and 50s as the folk movement wrote critical anthems for progressive movements. Now the tree begins producing strange fruit; the anthem's formal choral nature, featuring many people pursuing many objectives and faiths but all united by a certain pursuit of happiness, is suddenly ironically appropriated; in the resulting critical anthem, a myriad of American characters are all lost in a morally empty American landscape, their naïve faiths shattered. But the folk movement by its very existence gives a contextualizing enchantment; its own social and political successes promise that a new land is possible.

As the 60s ended and that communitarian enchantment began to fade, the later critical anthem tradition became marked by songs that decry the death of music itself. McLean's is the most famous example but even Bob Dylan's 1975 pop-chart hit and critical anthem 'Tangled Up In Blue' tells of how in the past when the narrator lived in a community, 'there was music in the cafes at night and revolution in the air'. By 1975, as his song notes, that music and revolutionary social promise was gone. Dylan's tangled emotion in 1975 is not a nostalgia for a lost youth so much as a bitter acceptance that the grand social promise of the folk movement was made but not met.

But Bowie was not part of this movement. So then what social promise in 'Young Americans' has not been met? What specific music has died for Bowie? To answer that, we retell our tale as a one of spells of enchantment, disenchantment and counter-enchantment. We begin with the primal American enchantment with its spangling stars. Here as always, nationalism is a powerful and dangerous dream that enfolds the listener in a mantle of positive energies and victories, a seductive social identity that ameliorates one's alienation while aligning one's ethical behaviour and commitments with an apparently unerring compass that always points up the hierarchy to those who hold power. A national anthem, to the extent it is effective, throws a shadow of enchantment across the land, and it is also of course deeply committed to shaping time, since a nation is a vehicle of time, a form of narrative self-identity that makes sense of one's transit through life. The promise of nationalism is that whatever else I experience, whatever failures or successes, loves and losses, whatever unrealized prides, at least I am and will be an American; should I fail at all else, should I starve on the streets, I can take pride in that one noble if phantasmagorical pursuit of my nation's grand timeline of achievements. Anthems in their exhortatory role tend to lay out the demands of that pursuit; be loyal, obey the laws and requisitions of the nation's leaders, and fight in its wars – do these things and you can participate in the enchantment of its enduring greatness.

In calculated reaction, a critical anthem tries to dispel and delegitimize this powerful national enchantment in order to unleash forces of change. It tries to alienate the listener from the anthem's false image of the land, and sometimes tries to replace this new alienation with a newly-minted enchantment, a new ethical and political vision and sense of community. The folk critical anthem exemplifies this concerted contestation of the dream of America, but that folk enchantment – and the entire New Left vision of a future community – had been broken by 1974–5, as McLean and Dylan themselves attest. That particular music had died.

The pop-chart debut of 'Young Americans' in 1975 marks the withering end of the modernist critical anthem and the beginning of the postmodern one. Here, in typical critical anthem style, Bowie used his unparalleled skills as a vocal, lyrical and character menagerist to people a bleak materialist landscape with no myth left from the ghetto, no hope to be found in marriage or sex, no way to tell emotion from alienation. But, whereas other critical anthems use many personal stories to express a political problem, Bowie brilliantly flips this to make the political personal, using the political exhaustion of the US after Nixon as itself a metaphor for the country's exhausted gender roles and paralysed hopes about pop music, sex and consumerism. Bowie's specifically evolving four-point sound design amplifies these remarkable lyrical and vocal progressions, and all these techniques together create the song's temporal progression from reflective singing time into specific narrative time and then into a subjectively present time that links us directly and intimately to the singing narrator's emotions as they are experienced, bringing Bowie ever closer to us listeners through the steps of singer, narrator, actor-performer, and finally in-the-moment confessor.[27]

All of these formal choices helped Bowie dramatize and self-identify with the subjective anxieties and alienations of wide-eyed young Americans without having to offer any history, solidarity or social solutions to this alienation. Bowie thus completes the turn away from folk's and R&B's social projects – both of which depict America in disenchanting ways in order to mobilize forces to combat its misery, and also offer positive reimaginings of how the social can be reconstituted. But Bowie's song marks a cultural turn away from this demanding social solidarity towards a music that at its most evocative can only express late capitalism's social atomization and at its best can only combat boredom and personal and sexual anxieties. By the song's last note, America's enchantments are exploded, its affects oddly unaffecting, but the song by itself offers no compensatory nationalism to replace that enchantment. It differs from Bowie's other work which argues for a kind of compensatory nationalism; come join the nation of the nomad, you too can become an imaginative node who can hook into any nation's identity, aesthetic, tropes. But this song makes no such argument – instead it seems to argue forcefully that this is exactly the way that soul itself becomes plastic. And so, as his vocal portrait personalizes this bewildering swirling choral cacophony of unsatisfied desires, it also opens the postmodern chapter, the inner turn, of the critical anthem songbook.

But apart from being a critic of this process of capitalist emptying – a process that he himself practises with exceptional élan – Bowie the disenchanter is not necessarily in good political or ethical territory. Disenchantment, while a necessary antidote to nationalistic romanticisms, is primarily destructive and does not provide us with any positive vision to face our problems, and so by itself it tends to only further feed our alienation. Giving voice to a generation's nihilism and despair can be personal and prophetic, perhaps even innovative for the world of 1970s pop music, but the Reagan era would trigger a chorus of such disenchanting voices, and they have not gone silent since. And faced as we are with the current situation it is hard to celebrate the combined effect of such voices on their generation's political and social action. An honest clear point of view is clearly not enough to demand of our atomized and atomizing culture, just as critique and analysis is not enough to demand of our critical thinkers.

Instead we may all now have to meet that powerful challenge laid down by Jane Bennett in *The Enchantment of Modern Life*, where she argues for the need for some form of enchantment for any ethical actions: 'It is too hard,' she says rightly and prophetically, 'to love a disenchanted world.'

And perhaps it is too easy to hate anthems. Certainly there are excellent historical reasons for the commonly-held fear of national anthems as emblems of false consciousness. But while it is true that old-school national anthems usually stress issues of liberty, loyalty and faith over issues of fairness and the elimination of cruelties, the example of critical anthems in general and of 'Young Americans' itself shows that anthemic form, context and affect can be reappropriated and remixed to create all kinds of ethical messages.

We have in this chapter reframed not only the history of American anthems but have also briefly traced one long wave from marginalized slave narratives of social misery through MLK's speech to Beyoncé's national performance of the R&B standard 'At Last'. Beyoncé's 2008 performance is an excellent counter-example to Bowie's song, one of progressive *universitas*. Contrasting Bowie's properly destructive strategies with our hunger for the nationalistically unifying experience of Beyoncé's performance suggests that decades of disenchantment may have at last given way to a time for generating new unifying or reunifying anthems. Beyoncé's and other examples show that an anthemic prophetic voice can not only be fashioned from the experiences of the dispossessed but can, while singing of its own social group's history and hopes, then also powerfully speak to a larger social group and thus even help inscribe new forms of *universitas*, of national identity and progressive and democratic energies.

I would argue that this is a very urgent project. At the real risk of sounding like a young American, I propose that the postmodern phase of the critical anthem is over, that today a new generation of anthems, one informed by its own long performative and social history, can help us re-enchant our atomized social world without risking the same hegemonic performativity of standard anthemic enchantments. We need songs that create and strengthen social bonds, songs that do not instil forgetfulness and do not crush subjectivity but that will somehow bring people together to solve our gigantic contemporary problems. Here we see how redeeming Bowie's song is, just as we argue that the critical anthem must go beyond 'Young Americans', by recalling the words of Frantz Fanon: 'National consciousness, which is not nationalism, is the only thing that will give us an international dimension.' Perhaps in a social sense, Bowie's acidic, disenchanting Plastic Soul helps clear the way for a re-enchantment of Soul.

Notes

1   I'd like to dedicate this chapter and to thank my old friend Andy Bienen, screenwriter of the Oscar-winning film *Boys Don't Cry*. It was in a conversation with him about Dylan that I first proposed that Bowie's 'Young Americans' should be understood as an anthem and then had to formally define an anthem. Thanks also to Vincenzo Satta for his enlighting comment that this song is set to a Salsa beat, to my wife Nevina Satta for her unflagging critical thinking, and to Toija Cinque for her boundless patience, help and enthusiasm.

2   Oliver Wendell Holmes Sr added activist verses, popular during the Civil War, highlighting the fact that the anthem sings about freedom, reminding the listener that the republic was founded upon the idea of equality and so was opposed to slavery in all its forms.

3   A hundred years later Allan Ginsberg continues this critical and epic portraiture of America in his own works 'America' and 'Howl'.

4   The civil rights freedom songs were highly activist and many became anthemic at countless protest movements.

5   Guthrie's politically potent critical anthem was sung – with its angry social verses included – at the 2009 inauguration of President Obama. In a 1985 performance, Bruce Springsteen gave a moving acknowledgement that critical anthems define an America that may no longer be able to live up to its promises – www.youtube.com/watch?v=1yuc4BI5NWU:

6   See www.today.com/entertainment/beyonces-national-anthem-scandal-why-all-outrage-1C8087094.

7   Many of these characteristics of the critical anthem are also realized in, for example, the American novelistic tradition, the paintings of James Rosenquist or such movies as Robert Altman's 1975 *Nashville*.

8 And of course the national anthem's use of war as a narrative tactic for bonding the community in *universitas* makes proposing a new *universitas* in a time of war much more challenging.

9 Russell Harty, *PlusPop* interview, 17 January 1973.

10 The Dick Cavette Show, ABC TV, US 45 mins, taped in New York, 2 November 1974. Broadcast 4 December 1974.

11 For example, Ingmar Bergman's 1974 *Scenes From a Marriage*, which portrays marriage as a dated soul-sucking trap for men and women, is credited with raising divorce rates. Robert Altman's film *Nashville*, a harsh critical anthem of a somewhat similar bitter taste, came out in the late spring of 1975.

12 The song, sometimes called 'Teenage Wedding', tells of a teenage American couple. When the man finds work, he buys lots of rock and roll albums and a car that they use to drive to New Orleans to celebrate their anniversary. There is a mention of a refrigerator as a sign of their new independence and bounty as a couple living together. We hear in the song's second line that 'The coolerator was crammed with TV dinners and ginger ale'.

13 Connecting the two songs is not so far-fetched; not only is Bowie a lifelong Berry fan and dreamed of America through hearing his songs, but on this album Bowie worked closely with Carlos Alomar who had worked with Chuck Berry.

14 The verse has also been heard in the somewhat nonsensical version printed in the album's lyric list as 'They pulled in behind the bridge'. But Bowie clearly sings 'fridge' in the song premiere on *The Dick Cavette* show, and subsequent remakes such as The Cure's have followed this version.

15 Note the second and third uses of 'took' – the boy taking his orgasm and her, taking nothing from the short experience, is then followed by the first desperate revelation – 'heaven knows she'd have taken anything'. This line marks a rise of perspective into third-person storytelling which marks the appearance of our narrator's more knowing presence.

16 This arc from hope to despair is also clearly audible in a string of number one R&B hits from this period: consider such critical anthems as Marvin Gaye's 1972 'Inner City Blues', the longings in the Staple Singers' 1972 'I'll Take You There', or the harshness of Stevie Wonder's 1973 hit 'Living For The City'.

17 Burying the lead vocals was a common tactic for famed 1960s music producer Phil Spector; it foregrounded his own Wagnerian 'Wall Of Sound' instrumentation over the presence of the lead singer.

18 In a sense, Bowie uses the studio's mixing possibilities to recreate his dramatic stage entrances in his stage shows. Unfortunately, this original, dramatically motivated mixing strategy is almost entirely eliminated in the indiscriminate 'brightening' process of the 2007 remixed version, an artistic crime committed with commercial intent which removed much of the muffling process as if it were simply an artefact of old recording technology, which it clearly isn't.

19 It stands as the fifth greatest song of all time in the RIAA Song of the Century ranking.

20 In 'American Pie' the narrator/singer meets a girl who once sang the blues, and he asks her for some happy news, 'But she just smiled and turned away'. The he heads down to the 'sacred store' where he used to listen to music, but there discovers that the music has stopped.

21 The sense in this song of characters substituting pop music for being lost and alone reflects comments that Bowie has made elsewhere, where he connects his music and rock in general to America's socially atomized and socially hungry subjectivities: 'In just about every country except England and America there are strangely strong family ties,' he said. 'Very few countries need rock & roll. Very few. It's America and England that need it, and probably Germany. But France and Italy, no way. They don't need it. Rock provides a family life that is missing in America and England. It provides a sense of community.' in Timothy Ferris, 'David Bowie in America: The Iceman, Having Calculated, Cometh'. *Rolling Stone*, 121 (9), November 1972, www.rollingstone.com/music/news/david-bowie-in-america-19721109.

22 See www.youtube.com/watch?v=iFd8jVrbf0A.

23 See www.youtube.com/watch?v=JU-fs4yvT_M.

24 Pure celebrity narrator slippage is an art form practised in many moments; for example, we see it unveiled continually in the Oscar acceptance speech or the politician's apology for his role in a sexual scandal.

25 For example, when Beyoncé finishes 'At Last' at the 2009 inauguration, I cannot but be moved by her own feelings, but I am also emotionally impacted by the realization that her feelings of hope reflect not only millions of other Americans but also centuries of African-American miseries and dreams in America, and thus even as a white subject I can experience a fierce urgency to back a more inclusive vision of the country.

And note that neither her emotional struggle nor it in the context of the song's lyrical content alone creates this effect. Instead, her performance stood upon a powerful greater performative context; in a brilliant stroke of Gramscian articulation, 'At Last' acquires critical anthemhood here specifically because the context of the national stage in this moment of racial transformation, the song's title and refrain, and lines such as 'I found a dream that I can speak to, that I can call my own' all so perfectly evoke MLK's famous 'I Have A Dream' speech from the March On Washington, that famous speech event of Whitmanesque critical anthemic significance, a litany of African-American misery which ended with MLK's enunciation of his dream of a future liberation. Beyoncé's performance of 'At Last' in these circumstances amplifies the powerful affect of a specific earlier moment in MLK's performance, that final moment of his speech – which receives much airplay in American mediatizations of the civil rights era – when he emotionally belted out the lines (drawn themselves from an old slave-era spiritual) 'At Last, At Last, We are Free At Last!'

And it is exactly because we and she knew something of all of this powerful metatextuality of performative affect, and not at all because of the romantic lyrics of 'At Last', that Beyoncé's own emotions in this national ritual then danced so unforgettably along the border of narrator slippage, giving the performance that further terrific emotional force that made it such a binding social moment between the hopes of past struggles, a present moment of civil rights triumph, her joy, African-American exuberance, our participation in hers, MLK's and Obama's celebrity, and our own joyful sense of participating in a community that is releasing itself of some bitterness and finding a hope and affirmation in a new vision of possible future community.

26 See Vail, Mark. 2006. 'The "Integrative" Rhetoric of Martin Luther King Jr.'s "I Have A Dream" Speech'. *Rhetoric and Public Affairs*, 9.

27 We also note the postmodern contradiction of lyrical and instrumental affect in 'Young Americans'. Bowie has replaced the folk anthem's melancholic, backwards-looking instrumental form (usually a prominent guitar sometimes quietly backed by harmonica, drums and/or piano) with a fresh pyrotechnical cheerful-sounding mix of samba, gospel, jazz, rock and pop. This tactic of using a happy-sounding song to deliver a dark existential vocal message, a contradiction in aesthetics borrowed from pop art and funk music, also helps distinguish Bowie's work from the far simpler unities in folk critical anthems. Bowie's oppositional techniques will reappear in later critical anthem songs. Consider the countervailing happy-affect and bleak lyrics in the critical anthem to Los Angeles by Sheryl Crow, 'All I Wanna Do'. In its purposefully-contradictory aesthetic strategy, 'Young Americans' is a pop analogue of the great critical anthem paintings of James Rosenquist and of the shattered narratives of shallow Americans in both Tom Wessleman's and Roy Lichtenstein's paintings.

Bibliography

Anderson, Benedict R. 1991. *Imagined Communities: Reflections on the Origin and Spread of Nationalism*. London: Verso.

Auslander, Phillip. 2004. 'Performance analysis and popular music: a manifesto'. *Contemporary Theatre Review*, 14 (1), 1–13.

Auslander, Phillip. 2006. *Performing Glam Rock*. Ann Arbor: University of Michigan Press.

Babha, Homi. 1990, 2013. *Narrating The Nation*. Abingdon: Routledge.

Bauman, Zygmundt. 2000. *Liquid Modernity*. Cambridge: Polity Press.

Bennett, Jane. 2001. *The Enchantment of Modern Life*. Princeton: Princeton University Press.

Biddle, Ian and Vanessa Knights (eds). 2007. *Music, National Identity and the Politics of Location: Between the Global and the Local*. Burlington: Ashgate.

Buckley, David. 2005. *Strange Fascination: David Bowie: The Definitive Story*. London: Virgin Digital.

Carawan, Guy and Candie Carawan. 1990. *Sing for Freedom: the Story of the Civil Rights Movement Through its Songs*. Bethlehem: Sing Out Corporation.

Cinque, Toija. 2013. 'David Bowie: dancing with madness and proselytizing the socio-political in art and life'. *Celebrity Studies*, 4 (3), 401–4.

Cray, Ed. 2004. *Ramblin Man: The Life and Times of Woody Guthrie*. New York: W.W. Norton & Co.

Fanon, Franz. 1959, 1968. *The Wretched of the Earth*. New York: Grove Press.

Frith, Simon. 1996. *Performing Rites: On the Value of Popular Music*. Cambridge, MA: Harvard University Press.

Frye, Northrop. 1957. *Anatomy of Criticism*. Princeton: Princeton University Press.

Goodlad, Lauren M.E. and Michael Bibby. 2007. *Goth*. Durham: Duke University Press.

Hebdige, Dick. 1979, 2005. *Subculture: The Meaning of Style*. London: Routledge.

Holmes, Su and Sean Redmond (eds). 2012. *Framing Celebrity: New Directions in Celebrity Culture*. London: Routledge.

Kukkonen, Karin and Sonja Klimek (eds). 2011. *Metalepsis in Popular Culture*. Berlin: Walter de De Gruyter.

Oakeshotte, Michael. 2008. *The Vocabulary of a Modern European State: Essays and Reviews 1952–88*. Thorverton: Imprint Academic.

Pegg, Nick. 2011. *The Complete David Bowie*. London: Titan Books.

Plan C. 2014. 'We are all very anxious'. Creative Commons, http://www.weareplanc.org/we-are-all-very-anxious#.U3zV8i94xmo.

Redmond, Sean. 2012. 'Intimate fame everywhere'. In S. Holmes and S. Redmond (eds) *Framing Celebrity: New Directions in Celebrity Culture*. Hoboken: Taylor & Francis, 27–43.

Sanger, Kerran. 1995. *When the Spirit Says Sing! The Role of Freedom Songs in the Civil Rights Movement*. New York: Taylor & Francis.

Weston, Judith. 1999. *Directing Actors: Creating Memorable Performances for Film & Television*. Studio City: Michael Wiese Productions.

Whitman, Walt. 2013. *Leaves of Grass*. New York: Signet Classic.

Discography

Berry, Chuck. 1964. 'You Never Can Tell'. Chess Records.

Bowie, David. 1971. 'Changes'. *Hunky Dory*, produced by Ken Scott and David Bowie, RCA Records.

Bowie, David. 1975. *Young Americans*. David Bowie RCA Records.

Bowie, David. 1975. 'Young Americans'. *Young Americans*, produced by David Bowie, Harry Maslin, and Tony Visconti, RCA Records.

Dylan, Bob. 1962. 'A Hard Rain's A-Gonna Fall'. Columbia Records.

Dylan, Bob. 1975. 'Tangled Up In Blue'. Columbia Records.

Keyes, Francis Scott (lyrics, 1814) and Smith, John Stafford (music, 1780). 'The Star-Spangled Banner'. Public domain.

McLean, Don. 1971. 'American Pie'. United Artists.

Filmography

Nashville. 1975. Directed by Robert Altman. DVD Paramount, 2001.

Scenes From A Marriage. 1974. Directed by Ingmar Bergman. The Criterion Collection, DVD.

8

2004 (Bowie vs Mashup)

Christopher Moore

Introduction

The aim of this chapter is to revisit the 'mashup' competition David Bowie conducted as part of the promotional strategies for the North American leg of his 'A Reality Tour' in early 2004. In order to understand Bowie's relationship to the remix subculture of the mashup, the investigation follows two lines of inquiry connected to the observation of Bowie as a bricoleur. The first begins with the audio mashup producer's arrangement of the sounds of others to create a complex new integration, which Sinnreich (2010) argues acts to disrupt attempts to fully comprehend the resulting polysemic assembly. This is achieved with the digital technologies of samplers and synthesizers, plugins, sequencers and filters that enable the melodic reorganization of a song's 'figure' – it's melody, hook or key vocals – so that the 'ground' – the instrumentation and musical textures – begins to disappear or transform (Sinnreich, 2010). The result is a complex aural experience with obvious connections to the elements' previous forms. A successful mashup requires the listener to attend to multiple, competing and complementary figures often above a shifting and changing ground. It is these notions of figure and ground that will be used to consider Bowie's interaction with mashup subculture, which is consistent with his pre-digital remix practices as a bricoleur. The chapter then examines Bowie's bricolage in terms of the celebrated revisionist approach to the public presentation of the self that he demonstrated in the early 1960s mod subculture and later with his Ziggy Stardust persona in 1972. It pursues a second line of inquiry that considers Bowie's relationship to the mashup expressed by the conditions of entry in the 2004 competition where Bowie's business strategies are characteristic of the bricoleur; David Bowie is able to remix the music industry's own key domains of devaluation of the mashup as an unauthorized, illegal and subaltern practice. Three domains of industrial devaluation of the mashup will be addressed: the domain of the individual is the primary site at which mashups are restricted by the music industry's legal and technical forms of governance, including code-level implementations of digital rights management (DRM) designed to prevent copyright infringement; the secondary domain of devaluation occurs at the general audience level where access is restricted by click-and-enter conditions, end-user licence agreements and other copyright-based contracts that are intended to limit the potential for transformative responses; the tertiary domain of devaluation is established broadly by copyright that regards works based on samples as 'derivative' and where, at best, mashups are reserved by artists and record labels as non-serious, ancillary content that is suitable only for promotional products and fan consumption.

Bowie and the mashup

A mashup is created through the isolation and reintegration of an object's components with the isolated elements of other objects. Mashups are pure science fiction; they disassemble Bowie and transmit him into parallel worlds where performances with Rihanna, Bruno Mars, MGMT, Katy Perry, Genesis, Coldplay, Grace Jones, Placebo, Adele or Santana,[1] individually or simultaneously, are all virtually possible. The mashup demolishes the boundaries of time and space, subverting our expectations, messing with our understanding of the structures and strictures of popular music. The audio mashup producer, simply referred to as a DJ, uses a variety of software tools to extract and weave the selected audio samples together. The results are variously known as bootlegs, booties, blends, smashups, mashes, mashups and the 'bastardized' form of popular culture. Some mashes feature hundreds of audio samples intricately layered into sonic tapestries and Vallee (2013) describes these as 'rhizomatic' in their assembly strategies, made possible by digital technologies requiring a musical aesthetic and technical literacy that can be difficult to fully acquire.

The focus in this chapter is the audio mashup, but the act of mashing is not restricted to sound, and includes the separation and recombination of individual elements of books, movies, games, music videos, cinema advertising posters, costumes, fashions, even software and other digital and non-digital media forms. The idea of the mashup is not to steal, plagiarize or subsume the primary material in creating a new work, but to engage in an art practice whose acknowledgment has been a 'long time coming' (Bruns, 2009: 24).

The origins of remix are as old as the idea of creativity and the bringing together of disparate strands of ideas, repurposed materials and technical practices to create and perform art (Lessig, 2006). The specific act of cutting up samples and repurposing them while openly preserving, manipulating, disclosing and re-rendering the raw materials involved is typically traced to the prehistory of Dadaism in the early twentieth century. More recently, the mixtape of the 70s and 80s enabled by portable home-recording devices and compact magnetic audiotape technologies established a new type of personal relationship to the musical corpus later evidenced by the mashup. The functional limitations of the physical recording processes of the mixtape led to the development of creative and interpersonal expression through productive and personalized responses to the presentation of music in the album format.

Other notable mashup prototypes include The Grateful Dead compilations celebrated by Plasketes (2010: 210) as a contemporary example of the use of quodlibets to produce a composite song out of multiple different melodies. One of the more dominant mashup formulas in the early formations of the subgenre and its DJ club culture is the 'vs' or the A+B binary mashup, a mode in which David Bowie stands out as one of the more highly mashed artists: including notable tracks like Misstarretje's (2011) 'Katy Perry and David Bowie mashup of "Teenage Dream ft. Rebel Rebel" ', Fissunix's (2012) 'Santana vs David Bowie – Let's Oye Como Dance', and 'Let's Lose Ourselves to Dance (Bowie Vs. Daft Punk MC Squared Mashup)' by Marshall Conn (2013).

The song 'Under Pressure', which appears on Queen's *Hot Space* (1982) and the *Best of Bowie* (2002) compilation, is nominally a duet, but it can also be considered as a proto-mashup of the two 'figures' of Bowie and Mercury and the song's original 'ground', the demo version of 'Feel Like' by Queen drummer Roger Taylor. The 'Under Pressure' (1981) music video by David Mallet is also a mashup of found and archive footage, stock demolition scenes and a range of samples from black and white films of the 1920s silent era including Eisenstein's (1925) *Battleship Potemkin* and Mernau's (1922) *Nosferatu*. The famous opening riff by John Deacon, sampled without permission on Vanilla Ice's 'Ice Ice Baby' (1989), is now found in any number of unauthorized mashups including the infamous mashup of the Bowie and Queen collaboration with Michael Jackson's (1979) 'Rock with You', by DJ Mark Vidler. Released online only days after Jackson was detained by police and questioned regarding allegations of child molestation, Vidler's criticism of Jackson is unmistakable in the use of the pejorative nickname in the track's title 'Jacko Under Pressure' (2004). The mashup opens with news reports detailing Jackson's arrest and concludes with one commentator speculating that the next record he makes will be a criminal one. Vidler underscores this commentary by positioning Jackson's *a capella* vocal samples from 'Rock with You' as the mashup's main figure, but has Bowie's and Mercury's vocals emerging as a single figure at the song's close:

On his Web site, Vidler describes how he was inspired by the caption 'Under Pressure – Michael Jackson' from a story in the *London Evening Standard* documenting Jackson's 2003 arrest for child molestation. Vidler is able to capture this sentiment by taking a well-known love song from Jackson and then blending it with a song whose chorus intones that people are 'under pressure'. Vidler's combination of these two songs manages to create a dialogue about Jackson's legal issues while still allowing the hearer to listen, enjoy, and even dance to his mix.

Rennett, 2012: 391

Ayers (2005: 129) regards the release of Vidler's mashup as a contemporary and creative response to current events within a wider political frame, highlighting the political role of the unauthorized use of these works as copyright protected materials. Sinnreich (2010) goes further to frame remix practices at the core of mashup culture as evidence of the broader role that such resistance to musical regulation plays in the historical machine of aesthetic change. This suggests that beyond the political content and representational qualities, the technical form of the mashup is a significant dialectical process of opposing forces incorporated within a mode of perpetual resistance.

The mashup as an act of resistance has two overlapping interests, first as a direct threat to the dominant paradigms of an intellectual property regime designed on behalf of the legacy broadcast media content industries that do not adequately address the rapidly changing conditions of creativity and curation in digital and network cultures. Second, and more broadly, the mashup functions as a site of debate as to the democratizing potential of remix cultures enabled by those same technologies and structures of organization. The implied challenges to established models of creativity, authorship and ownership (Serazio, 2008) are lost in the focus on the mashup DJ as a creative artist and the revolutionary appeal of remix practices:

The mashup, an intertextual collage that unearths new repetitions at a historical distance from the texts that it signifies, is celebrated from within the media discourses as the next revolutionary spectacle that challenges the property system that has been symbolically linked to such technologies of storage and dissemination.

Vallee, 2013: 80

A key example of this celebration of the revolutionary discourse of remix culture is attention to DJ Danger Mouse's *The Grey Album* (2003) as a kind of mythological and heroic remix text, in which the instrumental tracks from The Beatles' *White Album* (1968) are mashed to the vocals tracks from Jay Z's *Black Album* (2003) to produce *The Grey Album*:

> It is one of the most important sampling experiments, along with MARR's "Pump up the Volume" which can still be considered an early mashup relying on the concept of a unifying groove as first experimented on the turntables by Grandmaster Flash.
>
> Navas, 2010: 67

The date 24 February 2004 became historically linked to mashup culture as the first 'Grey Tuesday', an online protest against EMI's and Sony's attempts to censor remix communities using Digital Millennium Copyright Act (DMCA) notices to 'take down' *The Grey Album* from the internet (Rimmer, 2005). The critical and popular success of *The Grey Album* drew the cultural industries' attention, which responded in line with the key domains of devaluation of the mashup by pursuing legal action against the potential copyright-infringing activity involved in the production of the album. The copyright case against the DJ was dropped, however, before he went to work for EMI as the producer for the second studio album by the Gorillaz, *Demon Days* in 2005, which involves the third key domain of the devaluation of the mashup, recasting *The Grey Album* as a derivative work whose primary value is self-promotional.

The postmodernism of remix cultures offers another clear intersection between Bowie and the mashup, as both have been drivers of experimentation in the deconstruction and intertextual reassembly of cultural production. Mashup and remix culture has been identified as part of a long lineage of postmodernist and deconstructionist methods (McLeod, 2005) through which meaning is siphoned away from the idea of the intention of the author. Mashups and other remix practices have been politicized as postmodern resistant strategies, an art practice in which consumers reject the cultural industries' policing of authorial ownership. Bricolage, as a precursor to the mashup, further contributes to the postmodern understanding of remix cultures, which Johnson (2012: 359–60) argues have a 'fractal geometry' connected to the qualities of the digital and the network that continue to ensure the notion of a 'finished' work remains a fiction. Vallee's (2013) and Gunkel's (2012) Žižekian critique of the mashup, however, considers the format of the subgenre to undermine its own radical potential. They argue that the register of cultural expression encapsulated by the mashup is founded on the perpetuation of the philosophy of the hierarchical differentiation of professional artists pursuing isolated acts of creativity and therefore any claim to a political potential of the mashup as a form of media power is the equivalent of a postmodern empowerment fantasy (Vallee, 2013: 85). Postmodernist accounts of the mashup might consider the displacement of meaning through ironic juxtaposition but are then chasing the patterns of consumption involved in remix as a means of production, which inevitably reinforces the cultural hierarchies of class and privilege. The mashup DJ, as an agent of bricolage, is similarly constrained by the 'historical density of the elements' (Johnson, 2012: 362) and the privilege of that position, and finds new possibilities of practice already restricted by the closed system of the dialogue between the producer and their tools. David Bowie provided a case study to explore the counterpoint to the idealism of *Grey Tuesday* and other digital utopianism accounts of remix culture, when he became the first celebrity performer to actively encourage the use of his music for a mashup (Buckley, 2005). Bowie's relationship to the mashup subculture has its foundations in an earlier stage of his career that can be observed first in his sartorial presentation of the public self as a mod, and the later construction of the Ziggy Stardust persona, both characteristic entry points in a trajectory of a lifelong bricoleur.

Bricoleur/bricolage

The bricoleur attends to the completion of a task with the resources at hand; their methods are unpredictable but not unreliable. The bricoleur makes do, but has plans nested within preparations; the bricoleur is distinctive and regenerates by finding new uses from existing means (Hatton, 1989: 76). The bricoleur is a collector of objects, skills, technologies, tools and techniques, should their potential be called on in the completion of various works of bricolage (Weinstein and Weinstein, 1991: 162). Claude Lévi-Strauss (1966) considered the French term to imply a technical proficiency, a skill, but it also suggests a capacity for invention and cunning, bordering on deviousness (Kincheloe, 2005). In *Life on the Screen* (1995: 57), Sherry Turkle frames bricolage as a problem-solving approach to innovation in programming as an alternative to more structured styles of coding. In this model both the programmer and the DJ can be seen to operate as bricoleurs within an incremental process of constant reiteration, problem-solving and personal and peer-based re-evaluation. From these definitions, we can consider bricolage as the confrontation between innovation and the finite set of resources available to be deployed in its resolution; for the DJ, bricolage applies to the delivery of a technical solution (Turkle, 1995), such as the organization of an experience that involves the individual or communal consumption and transformation of music within the networks of available technologies, samples, technical skills, legal restrictions, peer networks, community standards, audience capacities and the physical spaces of club culture.

Dick Hebdige (1979) noted that acts of identity formation accompany the bricoleur in the processes of appropriation, including the subcultural repurposing of symbolic commodities. Bowie's early bricolage is demonstrated by the presentation of himself in the fashion and style of mod subculture (Doggett, 2012: 35). Hebdige (1979: 227) via Ernst (1948) described the mod subculture as functioning bricoleurs, reshaping symbolic ensembles by appropriating commodities, especially the suit and tie and other 'figurative' accoutrements of the business world (Ernst 1948 in Hebdige 1979: 227):

> The subcultural *bricoleur*, like the 'author' of a surrealist collage, typically 'juxtaposes two apparently incompatible realities [i.e. "flag": "jacket": "hole": "tee-shirt": comb: weapon] on an apparently unsuitable scale . . . it is there that the explosive junction occurs'.

Hebdige considered practices of cultural subversion to alter meaning in the everyday sense through the identity formations associated with them and suggested the bricoleur can be identified by the appropriation of a range of commodities by placing them in a symbolic ensemble with subversive intent. Both the skills of the bricoleur and the product of the bricolage itself encouraged and then became a means for further creative self-expression and identity formation that Hebdige observed amongst working-class youth in the UK in the 60s. Bowie's mod persona was less occupied with class than it was with gender and, later producing within the confines of 'Big Music' and the recording industry of the 70s, Bowie's early personae formations attempted to force permeable delineations between aesthetics, genre, identity and gender resulting in the arrival of Ziggy Stardust. These strategies of uncertainty, subversion and appropriation are echoed by the attempts of mashup DJs to gain an audience while openly undermining the restrictions of intellectual property and the music industry's policing of notions of authorship and originality.

Chris Rojek (2001) considers Ziggy to be more than a character; he calls Ziggy a 'persona', whose careful remix of the sexual identities of Mick Jagger and Jim Morrison, and others, attracted a remarkably broad public interest; partly because of the availability of this identity for appropriation within the audience's own identity formations. Remixing the normalization of gender, sexuality and alienation with Japanese theatre and the mythology of the 'rock star', Ziggy, like the mashup, offers a 'low-budget science-fiction exuberance' (Critchley, 2014). Producing the self in the material world through the performative expression of a public identity, Bowie extended his bricolage with the creation of Ziggy Stardust, sampling from multiple archetypal rock 'figures' including Jimi Hendrix, Lou Reed, Marc Bolan, Bob Dylan and others. Included in the performance of Ziggy are the personal responses to these influences at the time, which would later became part of the production of the cultural 'ground' of elemental rock and roll, celebrity and stardom, from which other such 'figures' would arise in the future. Bowie was not the first artist to embrace such honest and transparent appropriation as a stage performance, but Ziggy was role-played with a simultaneously integrated sense of unity and separation, an explosion of meaning and experience, not dissimilar to what the mashup incurs on its audience (Nicholson, 2011).

David Bowie as a celebrity, and Ziggy as a persona, simultaneously maintain a timeless pedagogical function organized around their revolutionary aesthetic and the strength of their sexual power, argues Rojek (2001: 117–34), who saw the construction of Ziggy as a bricolage of style, androgyny, flamboyance and bisexuality, providing a new iconography of generational change. Lévi-Strauss used art history and modern art theory to explain bricolage as a process of tinkering and as a metaphor for the transmission of crucial information, the carrying of ancient teachings and methods for inquiry into the present day. The construction of Ziggy as a persona, rather than a fully rendered 'character' from a novel or film, then serves as a metaphor for the composition and generation of mythical discourse (Johnson, 2012: 358) which demonstrates Bowie's command over multiple levels of bricolage, from the semiotic to the technical. This practice continues beyond the death of Ziggy on stage in 1973, and the later lyrics in 'D.J' from *Lodger* (1979) 'I am a D.J. I am what I play', could be considered as the bricoleur's response to the perceived mediocrity in commercial radio of the late 70s; at the same time the lyrics can also be taken more literally, pointing directly to his capacity for remix. Bowie and the mashup DJ both operate within the constraints of pragmatism generated by the material considerations of production, the industrial regulation of the content and its distribution and the literacies of others in their reception. As the remix bricoleur, Bowie's multiple personae have been divergent operations, each examining different restrictions and boundaries of technologies, genres, fashions, markets, practices, values and obsessions, and the associated capacities of his audience in different ways.

Bowie's command of style and experimentation with fashion, demonstrated in his visual performance as a mod and later with Ziggy, argues Peraino (2012: 155), is useful for re-examining some of the assumptions the law makes about concepts such as 'original', 'authorship', 'ownership' and 'copy'. Drawing on Judith Butler's theory of gender, Peraino's (2012: 157) approach is to consider the deeply rooted performance of gender in Ziggy as a communication platform, from which to deploy localized strategies of resistance to the author function – for example, where Bowie combines his experience in theatre and mime to remix and recreate: 'the exaggerated strutting of Mick Jagger, the ecstatic shudders and head shaking of Robert Plant, and the fist-pumping and microphone swinging of Roger Daltrey'. Peraino considers Bowie and Ronson's onstage straddling as a revision of Jimi Hendrix's performance of 'stylized cunnilingus' with his guitar. Other visual forms of remix and mashup appear in this period of Bowie's career, including the LP cover of *Pin Ups* (RCA, 1973), Bowie's 'covers' album, which itself has an album cover image that physically 'mashes' Ziggy and Twiggy's heads together in the frame: 'Or is it Bowie/Ziggy who is made to look nearly like Twiggy? Who is covering whom? Or as Judith Butler might ask rhetorically, which is the original and which is the copy?' (Peraino, 2012: 152). Cover songs, argues Peraino, were prevalent in the early years of rock and roll as politically, socially and culturally significant in their reformist agendas and grew in popularity as the audiences and the industry diversified. Bowie as bricoleur invites us to consider the ground as well as the figure of the work in terms of the tools, resources, collaborations, skills and strategies involved in its production and reception. Martin (2013) does this when he highlights guitarist Mick Ronson's production skills as only recently being recognized as an essential component of the sound of Ziggy and the Spiders from Mars and Bowie's success in the role.

David Bowie's technical bricolage further foregrounded the potential of digital remix and mashups in the 1970s with the 'cut-up' lyrical process, where textual sources are physically dissembled, torn or sliced apart with scissors and randomly recombined to provoke affective interpretations and further writing. Cut-ups for Bowie are autobiographic and autoethnographic; the lyrics of *Diamond Dogs* (1974) were physically torn and cut from diaries, reflections and writings to break apart the obvious surface meanings and narratives and reassemble them to reveal new associations and relationships between previously unanticipated connections, and reintroduce spontaneity and accidental discovery. Bowie describes the process as a tool for reflecting on his past and driving a personal future as a: '. . . a very Western tarot' (Yentob, 1975). Burroughs and the cut-up co-progenitor, Brion Gysin, took inspiration from visual collage techniques and influenced Bowie with their generative and iterative creative processes, but also had a profound impact on other popular cultural innovators including The Rolling Stones, The Beatles, Andy Warhol and The Velvet Underground. Each saw the potential for using the cut-up approach to reframe perception as the driving force for experience over meaning. Critchley (2014: 16) suggests that Gysin's cut-up technique 'get's so much closer to reality than any version of naturalism' by drawing on David Hume's observation that inner life is made up of disconnected bundles of perceptions that is not far from the description of an encounter with a mashup.

2004

In the wake of 2013's surprise offering, *The Next Day*, 2004 might eventually be forgiven as the year that nearly ended Bowie. The shadow hanging over the 'A Reality Tour' was a blocked artery, powerful enough to undo the conclusion to the worldwide concert schedule. The massive commercial venture was in the top ten grossing tours for 2004 (Billboard, 2004) before being abruptly halted by the angioplasty procedure that followed the Hurricane Festival in Scheeßel, Germany on 25 June 2004. Schiller (2008) reflects on this 'time of crisis', suggesting the events would have been enough to cause an individual's psychological collapse or send them headlong into a creative fervour, but Bowie seemed somewhere and someone in the middle. The early 2000s had seen Bowie's star image shift again, and the persona which emerged appeared to be as close and as consistent to the idea of 'David Bowie' as was possible for the 'celebrated shapeshifter' (Schiller, 2008: np). Between the abrupt end to the tour, and until *The Next Day* (2013) nearly a decade later, Bowie was an absent figure to be marked by a symbolic moment in time, which preceded a gradual withdrawal from the world. The 2000s was an uncertain decade for Bowie, *Reality* (2003), his twenty-third studio release, was a commercial success but its reception was mixed. One critic reflected on hearing a lingering proximity to the events of 11 September 2001 and its relationship to 'ground zero' (Decurtis, 2003). Other reviewers were left underwhelmed by the interpretive 'originality' of the album's covers, including versions of George Harrison's (1971), 'Try Some, Buy Some', and Morrissey's (1992) 'I Know It's Gonna Happen Someday', that were read as symptomatic of a career in its twilight (Carr, 2003).

In April 2004 as part of the marketing campaign for the car manufacturer Audi, the sponsor of the North American component of the 'A Reality Tour', subscribers to Bowie's website BowieNet were offered the chance to create copyright-friendly Bowie mashups and enter the 'Never Follow' competition to win an Audi TT coupe, Sony VAIO laptop and licenced copies of industry recognized digital audio software. The competition accompanied the 2004 Audi television campaign featuring a mashup of 'Rebel Rebel' from *Diamond Dogs* (1974) and 'Never Get Old' from *Reality* (2003), titled 'Rebel Never Gets Old' (2004) by DJ Mark Vidler's Go Home Productions. Although perhaps only a minor moment in Bowie's astronomical career, he created mashup history by legitimizing and enclosing the mashup as a form of industrially acceptable remix with the song's first release as a promotion single via iTunes and later as a rare CD and 12-inch vinyl single. BowieNet itself was already a historical accomplishment, a major signifier of Bowie's business bricolage, as he was the first celebrity to offer personalized internet service provision in 1998, providing for his online fans long before others in the music industry had thoroughly recognized the potential of the web. Barely registering outside its role as a promotional and peripheral text, 'Rebel Never Gets Old' takes its place in mashup history but does little to reverse the devaluation of the media form by the mainstream industry.

Bowie was a fêted source in the 'bastard pop/rock' DJ and club scenes in the US and across Europe in the late 1990s and early 2000s, and he remains one of the most highly mashed artists. In part, this is because Bowie's incredible and prodigious career is a prominent feature of the everyday sonic experience that is replicated in the format of the mashup itself. According to Hellweg (2014: np):

> . . . in the end, for listeners, the mashup is a guided sonic tour – an extension of what many of us hear on any given day in an urban environment, where we're treated to a procession of Dopplerized sounds from passing car stereos, mixed to the yelps of dogs, pothole beats, and our own inner rhythms. Perhaps one of the reasons mashups are so popular is that they're a common acoustic experience many of us already know. They surprise us, and yet feel completely familiar.

Bowie said himself he was 'very comfortable with the idea and had been the subject of quite a few pretty good mashups' and that 'mashups were a great appropriation idea just waiting to happen' (Bowie cited in Thompson 2006: 281–2). A three-month subscription to BowieNet was packaged in every *Reality* CD and included in concert ticket purchases. Competition participants could download the specially formatted samples of songs from *Reality* and a selection of tracks from the Bowie back catalogue, as well as a 'demo' version of the music editing and mixing software Acid PRO. With just six weeks to submit a mashup to be judged by David Bowie and Mark Vidler, the competition offered a way in for those looking to make the transition to commercial DJ culture. However, claims that the Bowie/Audi mashup competition was a cynical marketing exercise were common on the mashup forums populated by the contest participants. Rimmer (2005) reports that DJs were suspicious of the over-commercialized nature of the contest, and aired concerns that the selection of the 'winning' entrants would disregard community aspirations to quality driving innovation in the subgenre in favour of commercially friendly advertising material for the car manufacturer. DJs suspected that the corporate Bowie had registered the 'cool' factor of a good mashup, but was not looking into the further potential of the mashup and remix in general as a creative media practice (Rimmer, 2005). Some of these fears bore out, as the lack of pure *a capella* vocals available on BowieNet meant the mashups produced were limited in their ability to transform the 'Bowie' sound. Although not strictly a form of DRM, the restricted access to the Bowie oeuvre and the limited range of high quality instrumental and vocal samples available to the DJs complicates but ultimately reinforces the music industry's primary domain of devaluation of the mashup through the technical enforcement of copyright restrictions and limitations to access.

David Choi's winning song, 'Big Shaken Car', brought together 'She'll Drive the Big Car' from *Reality* (2003) with 'Shake It' from *Let's Dance* (1983). Choi, at the time a seventeen-year-old Californian highschool graduate, is now a singer/songwriter/YouTuber with close to a million subscribers, clear evidence of Bowie's power to launch another's career in this new media environment with an almost casual ease. As senior paragon of the recording industry in 2004, the result of Bowie's commercial power is a centralizing force over a loosely aligned subcultural movement of digital bricolage that has been contingent on a range of ethical and moral perspectives regarding the treatment of intellectual property and the notions of authorship. Bowie's mashup competition both admonishes and reinforces this critique, encouraging the idea of independent creativity that makes use of the 'ground' and 'figure' of his work, but the standardized legal contract for entrants to the mashup contest prescribed that each entrant signed away all their rights, including copyrights and any other music publishing rights connected to the work (Rimmer, 2007). By retaining all copyrights the competition discouraged parasitical connections to the works produced and reaffirmed Bowie's original authorial expression and the second domain of devaluation typically deployed to discourage unauthorised remix practices. While the provision of the digital software enabled DJs to experiment with the materials and the tools of remix culture for the first time, the terms of entry of the competition reinforced the cultural industries' tactics of intellectual property enforcement to devalue mashup cultures. The release of Vidler's mashup for the Audi commercial as a promotional single but not Choi's, further expands the third domain of devaluation of remix culture, focusing on the mashup as an interesting, but aberrant, product.

The 'A Reality Tour', or rather its promotional strategies, represents the attempt to recapture the content creation value of the mashup, but Vidler's role and Bowie's history both suggest an awareness of the political as well as the commercial potential of this device. The competition effectively enclosed a musical subculture whose power and utility derives from the subversion of intellectual property rights systems, and whose colonization was achieved through the re-articulation of copyrights in the terms and conditions of entry.

Far from posing a radical challenge to the dominant regulatory forces within the cultural industries and modern media institutions (Sinnreich, 2010), Bowie demonstrated that like other remix practices, the mashup is perfectly suited to its incorporation within the mainstream industrial paradigm. This doubled nature, which for others would be paralysing, atypically works to reduce the tensions associated between idealized notions of authentic creative expression and the actual cost of producing that experience, which for Bowie has been a reality in the separation of his business and his art persona in 1976 and the formation of his independent business bricoleur persona. As Bowie (cited in Hilburn, 1976) himself has said: 'Over the last year I've become a businessman. I used to think an artist had to separate himself from business matters, but now I realise you have more artistic freedom if you also keep an eye on business.' Bowie's relationship to remix subculture predates the digital as a bricoleur and with the mashup competition comes characteristic complexity as Bowie's bricolage extends behind his art to his business persona and legal relationships. Bowie's business persona, suggests Rowe (1985), includes a strategic variation of Malcolm McLaren's recognition that any subcultural play with style and meaning must remain coherent enough to capture the audience's attention, and that staying ahead in the 'game' of the recording industry also meant being at one step distanced from its centre. Bowie is able to provide the mashup community with the opportunity to remix his work, but *only* his work, a legal requirement designed to eliminate copyright infringement, but goes further to ensure an exclusive copyright licensing arrangement in the conditions of entry to the competition. The effect of this legal restriction on the mashups themselves is the concentration of the teleological proximity between the two Bowies brought together in the mix, as there is little room for subtlety or ironic juxtaposition. Bowie is always both 'figure' and 'ground' and we hear his young, more schizophrenic selves talking back to the older star bricoleur which creates an interesting, but overly insular, dynamic. Bowie's direct involvement in the mashup subculture, bringing the remix DJ community into the 'official' if peripheral modes of music production within the industry, complicates the cultural register of the conflict involved in the broader operations of remix culture in which ideological battles over copyright resemble a 'war' between social classes (Sinnreich, 2010); a war in which Bowie, in this case, appears to be arming both sides.

Conclusion

David Bowie's bricolage and bricoleur persona signpost his accomplishments requiring a specific arrangement of industrial conditions and talented contributors, but also the right social, intellectual and political provocations in order to assemble the audio and visual experiences that are now the raw materials for the next generations of bricoleurs to play with and subvert. As bricoleur, Bowie moves on the wing, remediating, recycling and recreating; his path has been entrepreneurial and required the gambler's resolve in the application of his own skills and resources, and those of others, to move an idea from inception to its material availability. This history has been maintained through regions of distance and clear spaces of interaction, including BowieNet and the mashup competition, creating his own online domain, a space of intimacy between himself and his fans. The 'Never Follow' competition can be seen as the provision of a legitimizing opportunity by a distant bricoleur looking to play with mashup subculture on their own terms. Danger Mouse's *The Grey Album* is the reworking of the history of both Jay Z and The Beatles, as much as their sound it is the offering of a new site of political polysemic value (Vallee, 2013: 81), while the Bowie mashup competition inevitably reduces the polysemy to a conversation between two Bowie figures. *The Grey Album* quickly became symbolic of the utopian fantasy of endless hybridization (Knobel and Lankshear, 2008; Martin, 2013), while the 'Never Follow' mashups remain largely obscure and unavailable oddities even to the Bowie fandom. DJ Danger Mouse might have achieved notoriety from the success of the *Grey Album* as a mashup aesthetic, but it was Bowie who first provided a direct entryway into that territory for others, a move ultimately less renown, but perhaps an idea equally revolutionary. If remix is a political act – speaking back to the text, regardless of its audience's reach – then providing access to the tools of production is a calculated risk, regardless of how legally constrained the conditions, which fits within the Bowie business bricoleur persona. The mashup competition results may include attempts at the expression of authorial inscription or arrangement over the originals, like a sonic graffiti tag, but they can also be considered as interventions in the assemblages of their prior connections, with copyright forever acting as the hovering paternal figure, ensuring the rights of author in protecting his/her progeny from misuse and potential (Gunkel, 2008: 495). The competition gave limited permission to participants to put Bowie's material to work, but this strategy was designed to effectively prevent exposing the material to the full deconstruction associated with the subcultural practice (Gunkel, 2012). Ultimately, the competition launched one career, and introduced hundreds of new producers to digital tools and the materials to assemble their own expressions with them, but did so by replicating the domains of devaluation typically associated with the mashup as a peripheral media product.

Note

1 Listen to these examples from the playlist available at https://soundcloud.
com/christopher-moore-28/sets/bowie-mashups.

References

Ayers, Michael. 2005. *Cybersounds: Essays on Virtual Music Culture*. Oxford:
  Peter Lang.
Billboard. 2004. *Madonna Heads List of Year's Top Tours*, Billboard, 13 December,
  www.billboard.com/articles/news/65316/madonna-heads-list-of-years-top-
  tours, accessed 2 February 2014.
Bruns, Axel. 2009. 'Distributed creativity: filesharing and produsage.' In *Mashup
  Cultures* edited by Stefan Sonvilla-Weiss. New York: Springer, 24–37.
Buckley, David. 2005. *Strange Fascination: David Bowie, the Definitive Story*.
  New York: Random House.
Carr, Eric. 2003. 'David Bowie Reality'. *Pitchfork*, 16 September, http://pitchfork.
  com/reviews/albums/880-reality/16, accessed 2 February 2014.
Critchley, Simon. 2014. *Bowie*. New York: Or Books.
Decurtis, Anthony. 2003. 'David Bowie Reality'. *Rolling Stone*, 10 September,
  www.rollingstone.com/music/albumreviews/reality-20030910 10, accessed
  11 May 2014.
Doggett, Peter. 2011. *The Man Who Sold the World: David Bowie and the 1970s*.
  London: Vintage.
Gunkel, David. 2008. 'Rethinking the digital remix: mash-ups and the
  metaphysics of sound recording'. *Popular Music and Society*, 31 (4),
  489–510.
Gunkel, David. 2012. 'Recombinant thought: Slavoj Žižek and the art and science
  of the mashup'. *International Journal of Žižek Studies*, 6 (3), 1–21.
Hatton, Elizabeth. 1989. 'Levi-Strauss's bricolage and theorizing teacher's work'.
  Anthropology and Education Quarterly, 20 (2), 74–96.
Hebdige, Dick. 1979. *Subculture: The Meaning of Style*. London: Routledge.
Hellweg, Eric. 2014. 'Mix and mash: the mashup is born from a blend of two
  songs'. *Edutopia*, 13 April, http://www.edutopia.org/mix-mash-mashup-born-
  blend-two-songs.
Hilburn, Robert. 1976. 'Bowie: now I'm a businessman'. *Melody Maker*,
  28 February.
Johnson, Christopher. 2012. 'Bricoleur and bricolage: from metaphor to universal
  concept'. *Paragraph*, 35 (3), 355–72.
Kincheloe Joel, L. 2005. 'On to the next level: continuing the conceptualization of
  the bricolage'. *Qualitative Inquiry*, 11 (3), 323–50.
Knobel, Michele and Colin Lankshear. 2008. 'Remix: the art and craft of endless
  hybridization'. *Journal of Adolescent & Adult Literacy*, 52 (1), 22–33.
Lessig, Lawrence. 2006. *Code: version 2.0*. New York: Basic Books,
  http://codev2.cc/download+remix/Lessig-Codev2.pdf.

Lévi-Strauss, Claude. 1966. *The Savage Mind*. Chicago: University of Chicago Press.

Martin, M. 2013. 'Ch-ch-ch-ch-changes: David Bowie is and the stream of warm impermanence'. *Postmodern Culture*, 23 (2), np, web edition.

McLeod, Kembrew. 2005. 'Confessions of an intellectual (property): Danger Mouse, Mickey Mouse, Sonny Bono, and my long and winding path as a copyright activist-academic'. *Popular Music and Society*, 28 (1): 79–93.

Navas, Eduardo. 2010. 'Regressive and reflective mashups in sampling culture'. In *Mashup Cultures*, edited by Stefan Sonvilla-Weiss. New York: SpringerWien, 157–77.

Nicholson, Susan. 2011. 'The urban underground: the rise of the diy dandy, urban popcultures'. Paper presented to 1st Global Conference, Czech Republic, www.inter-disciplinary.net/wp-content/uploads/2011/02/nicholsonupaper.pdf, accessed 28 September 2014.

Peraino, Judith. 2012. 'Plumbing the surface of sound and vision: David Bowie, Andy Warhol, and the art of posing'. *Qui Parle*, 21 (1), 151–84.

Plasketes, George. 2010. *Play it Again: Cover Songs in Popular Music*. London: Ashgate.

Rennett, Michael. 2012. 'Quentin Tarantino and the director as DJ'. *The Journal of Popular Culture*, 45 (2), 391–409.

Rimmer, Matthew. 2005. 'The Grey Album: copyright law and digital sampling'. *Media International Australia, Incorporating Culture & Policy*, 114, 40–53.

Rimmer, Matthew. 2007. *Digital Copyright and the Consumer Revolution: Hands off My iPod*. Northampton: Edward Elgar.

Rojek, Chris. 2001. *Celebrity*. London: Reaktion.

Rowe, David. 1985. 'Rock culture and the dialectics of life and death'. *Australian Journal of Cultural Studies*, 3 (2), 127–37.

Schiller, Mike. 2008. 'David Bowie and the Crisis Pentalogy'. *Popmatters*, 3 January, www.popmatters.com/feature/david-bowie-and-the-crisis-pentalogy, accessed 28 September 2014.

Serazio, Michael. 2008. 'The apolitical irony of generation mash-up: a cultural case study in popular music'. *Popular Music and Society*, 31 (1), 79–94.

Sinnreich, Aram. 2010. *Mashed Up: Music, Technology, and the Rise of Configurable Culture*. Amherst: University of Massachusetts Press.

Thompson, Dave. 2006. *Hallo Spaceboy: The Rebirth of David Bowie*. Toronto: ECW Press.

Turkle, Sherry. 1995. *Life on the Screen: Identity in the Age of the Internet*. New York: Simon & Schuster.

Vallee, Mickey. 2013. 'The media contingencies of generation Mashup: A Žižekian critique'. *Popular Music and Society*, 36 (1), 76–97.

Weinstein, Deena and Michael A. Weinstein. 1991. 'George Simmel: sociological flaneur, bricoleur'. *Theory, Culture Society*, 8 (3), 151–68.

Yentob, Anton. 1975. *Cracked Actor, Omnibus*. London: BBC.

SECTION THREE

Body

Introduction

Eyes, scars, milk, and jacket

I'm not a prophet or a stone age man, just a mortal with potential of a superman. I'm living on.

In this section we consider Bowie through the carnal cartography of star embodiment. Bowie's charged and challenging body emerges in biography and auto-ethnography; song lyrics and music videos; film, theatre and television roles; in publicity and promotions; and in and across the threads and binds of his chameleon-coloured star trajectory. Bowie's body is its own meaty, sonic metronome; its movement and metric beat casting a glamorous shadow over many of the trends and fashions of contemporary rock and pop music. There are few others in the pantheon of higher-order iconicity that have done so much with their bodies to challenge the normative and bordered ways in which we are asked to survey and regulate ourselves.

Bowie's star body crosses thresholds and boundaries: it is or has been androgynous, polymorphous, transsexual, camp and queer. It is a body also haunted by imperfection, seemingly on the verge of breaking down, nearly always in the grip of addiction and mental illness. Bowie's anisocoria and heterochromia seemingly confirm his essential strangeness and difference to everyone else.

It is a body also easily resurrected, god-like in its ability to be reborn and remade, a new character emerging from its transcendental canvas. It is a body that is decidedly white and royal, and that has championed the *Übermensch* over the unwashed and slightly dazed masses. Bowie's body has become an art piece, and has been readily and regularly taken up by fans that imitate its fine features, painted faces and languid skin. Bowie's body is impeccably dressed, sensationally fashioned, covering his skin in shocking and revelatory threads. This is a body that is spectacularly covered.

Bowie's star body is closely connected to the vexing politics of identity formation, subculture identification and the ideologies of class, gender and sexuality. It is a body that has been key to the way young people have resisted normative roles and taken up the flesh of resistance. Bowie's strange and alien body has affectively connected with the dispossessed, the marginal, the neo-tribes lost in the watery wastelands of liquid modernity. It is a body that speaks liminality and marginality, even if ultimately it also becomes a commodity fetish, used up and abused by the operations of neoliberalism. Bowie has of course been actively complicit in the commodification of his numerous bodies. He is the star who sold us the world.

In **Kevin Hunt**'s 'The Eyes of David Bowie', Bowie's mismatched pupils are argued to have a prevalent role in his various identities as a performer, and of his 'presentation of self'. Hunt explores Bowie's eyes as a key element in his 'otherworldly' and 'alien' star(man) persona'. As Hunt notes, numerous iconic images of Bowie capitalize meaningfully upon the irregularity of his mismatched pupils, including Brian Duffy's *Aladdin Sane* (1973) photoshoot; Masayoshi Sukita's portrait for the cover of *"Heroes"* (1977); and Bowie's portrayal of Thomas Jerome Newton in *The Man Who Fell To Earth* (1976). Informed by the concept of parallax view referenced by Slajov Žižek, Hunt also focuses upon issues of vision, depth and perception to consider how – in addition to 'looking' different/uncanny – Bowie appears to 'see' the world differently. We asked Kevin what drew him to the eyes of David Bowie:

> Bowie is frequently discussed as having a changeling identity so it was interesting to focus upon an aspect of his body that appears not to change but nevertheless makes up a significant part of his artistic presence and persona. From a personal point of view, my thinking has been influenced by my grandmother who had a rare eye condition called cornea dystrophy, as well as suffering from cataracts, which changed both her vision and the appearance of her eyes over time. Unusual, damaged, or 'abnormal' eyes are often used in western culture (notably films, books and television) to symbolically convey negative connotations, sometimes working as a shorthand for psychological illness or an implied inherent evil or negativity: the 'evil eye' (which itself leads back to religious interpretations and moral judgements associated with the body). Part of my motivation was to counter this form of representation by looking at how Bowie's mismatched pupils have become a positive identifier of his individuality and his alternate, creative, way of seeing.

In **Toija Cinque**'s 'Semantic shock: David Bowie', Bowie is understood to be someone who embodies certain identity positions that are alien, alternative and transgressive. Cinque suggests that Bowie engenders transgression through the use of metaphor and metonym which has largely freed him from the constraints of merely describing the world; his use of metaphor and metonym have afforded possible re-evaluations of the world by breaking the association between language and things. Drawing upon Sara Ahmed's social philosophies of trauma and scarring, Cinque argues that what David Bowie's work frequently does is 'reopen wounds', reminding us of the scars that lie beneath the skin; asking us to notice their existence, while then offering a means to negotiate their healing. Toija's own personal journey to the chapter was described as:

> That David Bowie might afford one with a certain 'semantic shock' is, for me, bound both to his bodily form, his arresting presence and strangeness, as well as his articles of belief sonically and visually made manifest. Key moments in my life have been scaffolded frequently by Bowie's various songs and their oft-obtuse meanings that would jar me into critical contemplation over what they might mean, why, what is a life (or death) and what options are there for the path in between the two. Thus, mine is an academic endeavour, imbued by, and indebted to, Bowie's challenging ruminations about the world and its accepted associations between language, action and things.

In his chapter, 'The Whiteness of David Bowie', **Sean Redmond** argues that during the 1980s, in particular, Bowie embodied particular versions of white masculinity that were on the one hand supportive of its idealized hegemony and, on the other, subverted its normative power. Taking 1983 as the 'event' year, Redmond undertakes a textual and contextual analysis of three of the most popular and well-received texts and performances of that year: Bowie as the simmering vampire, John Blaylock, from *The Hunger* (Scott, 1983); the enigmatic character of Major Jack 'Strafer' Celliers from *Merry Christmas Mr Lawrence* (Oshima, 1983); and the blond orchestrator/ improvisator from the music video, *Let's Dance*. According to Redmond, Bowie has constantly operated along a white continuum, self-consciously embodying it, granting it carnal and ideological power, while drawing attention to its death-like instinct, its anti-reproductive progeny, its implicit queerness. We asked Sean what drew him to the whiteness of David Bowie.

His milky skin always seemed impossibly sweet and yet poisonous to drink. I wanted to dance with the Duke but white men can't dance. He had royal blue blood, and was vampiric, while mine was blue-collar and Irish – a pollutant in comparison. He would never drink me up and yet his poison and my pollutant seemed to exist along the same continuum of holy unholiness. His whiteness was aspirational, borderless, beyond earthly signification. I wanted to fuck him, fuck his whiteness. I wanted to be that special. I wanted to dance with The Thin White Duke . . .

In **Helene Thian**'s objective materialist analysis, 'David Bowie is . . . Customizing', a single-button green corduroy jacket, customized with blue printers' ink in the late 1960s by David Bowie, is analysed utilizing Jules Prown's methodology. Thian takes us through the four distinct phases to understand the significance of this jacket. First, there is an objective examination of the physical characteristics of the jacket. Second, there is intellectual analysis, or factual knowledge relevant to understanding this material culture object. Third, there is the emotional reaction of the analyst while interacting with the garment. Finally, there is speculation regarding possible sources of influence on Bowie's customization in this era. Speculation on the jacket's influences include traditional boating blazers of British sporting clubs; mod fashion, which incorporated stripes and the RAF Roundel and the practice of customization; the op art movement, particularly the striped artworks of Michael Kidner and Bridget Riley in the era; and the Peacock Revolution as spearheaded by gay style trendsetter John Stephen in London. For Helene:

Seeing the threads in the underarm area of Bowie's jacket pulling loose from the seams and the worn and misshapen elbow areas due to his wearing it while playing saxophone and singing in bands in the 1960s, I strongly felt that this was not merely a material culture object related to a rock icon, but rather, symbolic evidence of the artist stretching himself, literally and figuratively, in his formative period to find his artistic voice.

9

The Eyes of David Bowie

Kevin J. Hunt

Introduction: David Bowie is . . . watching you

During the display period of 'David Bowie is' at the Victoria and Albert Museum (23 March – 11 August 2013) a common sight around London was the 'David Bowie is here' poster, announcing the arrival of the exhibition and a return, of sorts, to public view by the (more recently) recondite rock star. Following Bowie's step back from the media spotlight for much of the previous decade, the V&A's tagline (one of many variants suggesting the scope of what Bowie 'is') playfully acknowledged the opening and ongoing presence of the show – a curated array of objects, sounds and visions exploring Bowie's creative output and mercurial public persona spanning six decades. Appropriately, the image chosen for the marketing campaign consciously revisited the past whilst also offering something new (Barnbrook 2014, interview): an outtake from Brian Duffy's photo shoot for the iconic *Aladdin Sane* (1973) cover, unpublished until 2011, capturing Bowie as he stares intently forward from beneath the famous lightning-flash make-up with his eyes wide open.[1] The result is quite startling (especially in contrast to the passive 'eyes-shut' version familiar from the album), picturing Bowie with a suitably arresting gaze – made mesmeric by his discordant eyes – easily capable of capturing the attention of casual passers-by. As one variation of the poster declared, with a sly nod towards George Orwell's influence upon *Diamond Dogs* (1974): 'David Bowie is watching you'.[2]

In his review for *The Guardian* of 'David Bowie is', which charts Bowie's 'journey' from Brixton to Manhattan by way of 'druggy Soho', 'grim, walled Berlin', and various embodiments of outer space, Peter Conrad briefly mentions Bowie growing up in the London suburbs, suggesting that, as a boy, he was probably overlooked despite his 'eerie, mismatched eyes' (2013). Bowie's stardom owes much to his polymorphic creation of engaging characters, theatrically portrayed and convincingly embodied, before being cast off even at the height of their (and his) success – most notably the onstage termination of Ziggy Stardust in July 1973, which surprised some of the Spiders from Mars as much as it shocked their fans.[3] And yet, for all the postmodern variation and his changeling identity, one curious aspect of Bowie's multiple personas and 'looks' that by definition remains constant is his permanently dilated left pupil. One key purpose of this chapter is therefore to look at an aspect of Bowie's body – his damaged left eye – which appears not to change but nevertheless plays a significant role in his artistic presence and persona.

Anecdotally, the cause of Bowie's anisocoria (the condition of having unequally-sized pupils) is attributed to the fallout from a lusty scrap in the spring of 1962, which saw Bowie come to blows with a friend, George Underwood, over a girl. Both were just fifteen at the time and the friendship seemingly remained intact – the two performed together as teenagers in various bands before Underwood turned from music to painting and graphics, being involved in the cover designs for *Hunky Dory* (1971) and *The Rise and Fall of Ziggy Stardust and the Spiders from Mars* (1972) – but Bowie's left eye was seriously damaged. An impulsive punch accidentally scratched the eyeball, resulting in paralysis of the muscles that contract the iris. From that day Bowie's left pupil has remained in a fixed open position, sometimes creating the appearance of heterochromia (a difference in colour) of his irises. In addition to developing anisocoria, Bowie's depth perception was also affected, which he touched upon with the remark: 'It left me with a wonky sense of perspective . . . When I'm driving for instance, cars don't come towards me, they just get bigger' (Bowie in Trynka, 2011: 24). Over time Bowie apparently thanked his friend for his notorious eye injury, telling Underwood that it gave him 'a kind of mystique' (Underwood in Trynka, 2011, 24). Bowie and his creative collaborators consciously use this mystique, generated by the 'abnormal'/unusual appearance of his eyes, to help define his creative 'outsider' identity (Barnbrook in V&A Museum, 2013, film). As one of his most recent collaborators, Jonathan Barnbrook,[4] has suggested: 'as a pop/rock star, one of the best things you can do [to generate visual presence and intrigue] is to have, or appear to have, different coloured or unusual eyes' (Barnbrook 2014, interview).

As an analysis of selected iconic and key images of Bowie will show, the irregularity of his mismatched pupils is frequently capitalized upon in a meaningful and creative – although sometimes quite abstruse – way. Unusual, damaged, or 'abnormal' eyes are often used in western culture (notably films, books and television) to symbolically convey negative connotations, sometimes working as a shorthand for psychological illness or an implied inherent evil or negativity: the 'evil eye' (which itself leads back to religious interpretations and moral judgements associated with the body). Running counter to this broad but prevalent representation of damaged eyes, Bowie's mismatched pupils have become a positive identifier of his individuality and his alternate, creative, way of seeing. With this in mind I am fascinated by how significant a role anisocoria plays in Bowie's various identities as a performer and his 'presentation of self' (Goffman 1961), and I will explore Bowie's eyes as a key element in his 'otherworldly' and 'alien' star(man) persona, drawing upon Richard Dyer's work in *Stars* (1979) and *Heavenly Bodies* (1986) and Chris Rojek's *Celebrity* (2001). I will argue that the mystique of Bowie's eyes tallies with ideas of 'the uncanny', based upon the theory of 'familiar turned unfamiliar' expounded by Sigmund Freud in his 1919 essay, and touches upon the magical aura discussed by Walter Benjamin in 'The Work of Art in the Age of Mechanical Reproduction' (1936). In addition, the suggestion that Bowie suffers from a visual disability, in the form of damaged depth perception, is intriguing. In the conclusion to this chapter, the concept of 'parallax' (seeing differently dependent upon one's perspective) provides a useful metaphor for exploring issues of vision, depth and perception in relation to Bowie's position as one of the predominant visual and visionary performers of the twentieth and twenty-first centuries.

The uncanny David Bowie

Aladdin Sane – Eyes Open is more than a promotional shot from 1973 re-appropriated from the Duffy Archives to become the lead photograph for the 'David Bowie is' exhibition. The emphasis upon Bowie's eyes, in 2013, provides an indexical image reaching beyond the Aladdin Sane character. As an identity for the exhibition, it suggests that 'David Bowie is' offers more than a simple retrospective of the past because it depicts an artist (with his eyes open) who is actively engaging with the viewer, with his audience, and with the environment that informs his work (Barnbrook 2014, interview).[5] As an identity for Bowie, *Aladdin Sane – Eyes Open* directly references the uncanny and otherworldly persona that broadly defines Bowie's career as an artist, performer and celebrity; by focusing upon how and why Bowie's eyes embody 'the uncanny' we can connect his aniscoria with these otherworldly, outsider, qualities that inform his public identity.

In an immediate sense, Bowie's 'freaky' and disconcerting appearance as Aladdin Sane (with eyes open) is enhanced by the disparity in the size of his pupils. His dilated left pupil is clearly visible, in contrast to his 'normal' (light-responsively) sized right pupil, and it has taken on a distinctly red tinge. The photograph effectively makes a virtue of 'red eye', where the light of the flash has reflected off the fundus (the back of the eye) through the open pupil and has returned a red colouration in the image of the eye by picking up tonality from the blood in the choroid lining of the eyeball. The impact of Bowie's single red pupil is amplified by the orange/red lighting-flash across his right eye and cherry-red coloured hair, contrasting with the cool blue accent of the make-up and gray-blue/green of his irises. The bold white of his sclera draws further attention to the eyes while the fixed stare into middle distance looks through and beyond the viewer, completing the intended connotation of an alien-type being who is familiarly humanoid but who possesses some unfamiliar – and therefore eerie – characteristics.

In a prosaic sense, *Aladdin Sane – Eyes Open* is an unfamiliar version of a familiar album cover. Metaphorically, in addition to spanning time and space between the 1970s and 2010s in a slightly unsettling (familiar turned unfamiliar) way, this image demonstrates Richard Dyer's well-known configuration of the star as someone both ordinary and extraordinary (1979, 1986). Bowie is human and flawed (visibly so with a damaged eye) as well as extraordinary in appearance, demeanour and projected self-belief. The ethereal aspect central to Bowie's star persona and epitomized in many of his characterizations – Major Tom, Ziggy Stardust, Aladdin Sane and so on – overtly embraces the 'otherness' of the outsider. The 'adoption and embodiment of alien and/or futuristic personas' represents one of the most powerful articulations of the socially disenfranchised (McLeod, 2003: 339); this affiliates Bowie with Dyer's notion of the individualistic qualities of the star when defined through their alienation from social norms and the values of the ruling class (1986: 8). The original UK album cover for *The Man Who Sold the World* (1970), for example, features Bowie in repose on a chaise longue wearing a man-dress designed by Mr Fish. While Bowie's exploration of gender, androgyny and sexuality is well documented, most recently (at the time of writing) by Camille Paglia in her 'Theatre of gender: David Bowie at the climax of the sexual revolution' (2013), it is useful to connect such bold statements of an alternate, subcultural or 'other' identity to the tradition of rock stars consistently identifying themselves with alienated elements of society. In Bowie's case his rise to stardom, as a more androgynous alternative to the heterosexual bravado of other white male rock stars, should be understood within the context of the early 70s, when the Gay Liberation Front formed in the US and the UK following the 1969 Stonewall riots:

> Rock begins when white, more or less middle-class kids embrace the music of blacks and rural, working-class whites in an effort to rebel against their parents and prescribed expectations. Next, as early as Little Richard, the feminine is adopted, as women represent another subaltern group. With Bowie, homosexuality is added to the mix.
>
> Shumway and Arnet 2007: 136

Within this tradition of unfamiliar, overlooked and underappreciated elements of society being brought into the mainstream, Bowie's 'presentation of self' (Goffman 1961) and public perception as a performer is tied in with Freudian notions of the uncanny. The brief and selective overview of star persona offered above is intended to set up the expanded meaning of Bowie's uncanniness, which is embodied by his eyes but is representative of his larger social and cultural significance as an artist. Because the physical qualities of Bowie's eyes have become a metonym, in his case, for the individuality of '"the self", "the soul", "the subject" and so on' (Dyer, 1986: 8), this approach combines socially constructivist views with foundationalist awareness of the body as a material, physical and biological phenomenon.

Freud's essay on 'The Uncanny' focuses upon the particular version of fear and unease generated by the aesthetic condition of experiencing the *unheimlich*. The nearest semantic equivalent to the *unheimlich* in English is the 'uncanny' or 'eerie'; etymologically it corresponds to the 'unhomely'. In Freud's words, 'the uncanny . . . goes back to what was once well known and has long been familiar [but has] become uncanny and frightening [because it has become] unknown and unfamiliar' (2003: 124–5). A comprehensive search across a range of languages, undertaken by Freud for the etymological roots of the *unheimlich*, provides a rich taxonomy of synonymous or comparable terms, many of which are instructive when analysing visuals of Bowie, his eyes and his persona as an artist:

LATIN: *locus suspectus* 'ein unheimlicher ort' ['an eerie place'];
             intempesta nocte 'in unheimlicher Nachtzeit' ['in the eerie
             night hours']
GREEK: *xénos* ['foreign, alien']
ENGLISH: *uncomfortable, uneasy, gloomy, dismal, uncanny, ghastly*; (of a
             house) *haunted*; (of a person) *a repulsive fellow*
FRENCH: *inquiétant* ['disturbing'], *sinistre* ['sinister'], *lugubre* ['gloomy'],
             mal à son aise ['ill at ease']
SPANISH: *sospechoso* ['suspect'], *de mal agüero* ['ominous'], *lúgubre*
             ['lugubrious'], *siniestro* ['sinister']

In Arabic and Hebrew the 'uncanny' merges with the 'demonic' and the 'gruesome'
             Freud 2003: 125 paraphrased with some added translation of words

Freud builds his analysis with noticeable emphasis upon looking, seeing and eyes; in particular, addressing what is visibly (although often unconsciously) communicated and how eyes – as organs of sight that can be retained or lost/

taken – are used by E.T.A. Hoffman in his short story 'The Sand-Man' (1817) to construct an uncanny narrative: the dominant motif of the mysterious Sand-Man is his inclination to tear out children's eyes. There are numerous implications of these associations with the visual that are worth considering. For example, one of the various shades of meaning identified in relation to the *heimlich*, referring to the comfortable and familiar home, merges with its formal antonym, *unheimlich*, in a secondary meaning relating to 'that which is kept hidden or secret [and therefore unseen]' within the home (2003, 132): 'Starting from the homely and the domestic, there is a further development towards the notion of something removed from the eyes of strangers, hidden, secret' (*German Dictionary of Jacob and Wilhelm Grimm*, 1877, in Freud 2003: 133). As a performer determined to embrace definitions of masculinity and sexuality previously kept secret or largely hidden from public view, it is comparatively easy to map Bowie's androgynous and pan-sexual flirtations as part of his star persona. Biographers, such as Paul Trynka, reference the significant shock impact within the UK of Bowie's July 1972 gender-bending performance of 'Starman', on the BBC's *Top of the Pops*, as an early career-defining moment (Bowie, 1972). Languidly draping his arm around Mick Ronson, Bowie pulls the guitarist towards him as he sings 'starman' for the second time but this time the octave leap 'doesn't [just] suggest escaping the bounds of earth; it symbolises escaping the bounds of sexuality' (Trynka, 2011: 2), bringing a homoerotic frisson (that was ordinarily kept hidden from public view) into the homes and living rooms of anyone who happened to be watching.

More specifically in relation to eyes, the iconic album cover of *Heroes* (1977) – featuring a photograph by Masayoshi Sukita – uses the eerie quality of Bowie's anisocoria to enhance the expressionistic style of the image. The black and white photograph forgoes the opportunity to create character and evoke otherworldliness through bold and unusual colour and make-up. Instead, Bowie's mannered position and the use of light compose a sense of the extraordinary. The grey background, black leather jacket and comparatively dark hair juxtapose with the bold lighting on Bowie's hand and especially his face. His jet-black pupils stare intently into an offset middle distance, avoiding any direct eye contact with the viewer, and their clearly defined darkness is thrown into sharp contrast by the strong light that partially bleaches out other details of his face. As with *Aladdin Sane – Eyes Open*, the spots of light reflected from the surface of Bowie's eyes draw attention and, in addition to the natural human response to look into or towards the eyes of another person (which in this case is a gaze never to be returned), the viewer is invited to register the disparity between the size of his pupils. In a compositional sense, Bowie's distended left pupil is (more or less) the central point of the image, adding to its significance as a focal point for the portrait from which a confidently sinister or alien quality emanates. As I have already suggested, Freud's list of synonyms for the *unheimlich* and their extended associations – such as alienation, otherness and disenfranchisement – are being utilized as evidence of the uncanny or, at least, as potential indicators of its presence.

With our focus on bodiliness in mind, Bowie's enlarged pupil also approximates the central hole of the vinyl record that the sleeve would have housed when originally printed in 1977, indirectly relating his expanded pupil (itself a hole created by a ring of muscle) to his music contained within. The tension in Bowie's fingers and rigid mannequin-like pose were apparently inspired by Erich Heckel's 1917 painting *Roquairol*, which references the aesthete from Jean Paul's novel *Titan* (1800–3) and is a portrait of Ernst Ludwig Kirchner (Trynka, 2011: 277). While the reference to Heckel and, by association, the connection between expressionism and the 'imaging' of mentally ill patients championed by Jean-Martin Charcot[6] will be returned to later, Freud's commentary on automata, dolls and manifestations of insanity provides further illustration of Bowie as uncanny. Following the work of Ernst Jentsch,[7] Freud considers how the uncanny is evoked by 'doubt as to whether an apparently animate object really is alive and, conversely, whether a lifeless object might not be animate' (Jentsch in Freud, 2003: 135). Reference is made to waxwork figures, ingeniously constructed dolls and automata, as well as the notion of how mechanical processes appear to take over a person suffering an epileptic fit or seizure of some kind; the idea being that automatic bodily responses remain hidden within a familiar person until an affliction reveals them. Contextualized by these observations, the conspicuously sinister or alien quality of the *"Heroes"* cover presents Bowie as an unemotional, doll-like figure made (additionally) uncanny through the blank stare of his irregular eyes – perhaps evoking sentiments of a doll with a darkly magical life of its own that is hinted at, even when rigidly inanimate, due to the flawed construction of its eyes.

Freud pursues the idea of uncanny narratives (following Jentsch) through close analysis of Hoffman's 'The Sand-Man', emphasizing the significance of the eponymous character's capacity for mutilating children's eyes. Alongside the macabre threat to vision and personage, Freud considers the uncanny element of narrative forms that deliberately confuse the ability to distinguish between reality and fantasy – a blur that Bowie has often deliberately embraced, such as performing under the guise of a character like Ziggy whilst simultaneously singing about that same character in the third person, thereby knowingly exposing the pretences of being a rock star. As Ken McLeod points out, 'Bowie's conscious construction of an alien rock star was certainly meant to shed light on the artificiality of rock in general' (2003, 341). While underplaying the relevance of this particular strategy in relation to 'The Sand-Man', Freud acknowledges the importance of seeing through the eyes of the narrator or taking on the vision of the author. In Hoffman's tale, this involves an extension of the eye motif that circulates around eye-related objects, as well as foregrounding different ways of seeing and interpreting information: a recurrent feature of the story is the presence of false eyes (for a doll); real eyes (under threat in metaphorical and literal ways); spectacles; weatherglasses; and spyglasses/telescopes.

A similar range of ocular devices and thematic concerns are symbolically deployed in Nicholas Roeg's film version of *The Man Who Fell To Earth* (1976), which self-consciously capitalizes upon Bowie's uncanny star persona by casting him as an extraterrestrial being. Perhaps unsurprisingly, *The Man Who Fell To Earth* uses a number of poignant close-ups to capture the alien 'otherness' suggested by Bowie's eyes. There is a meaningful link to be made between the filmic close-up and its photographic equivalent used on Bowie's album covers, because the closeness and subsequent detail is often interpreted as providing insight into the 'soul' of the star. The key features central to this method of building mythology are the eyes, which Martin Jay describes as one of our most expressive sensory organs – the only competitor being touch – because they are so effective at emitting emotions and messages as well as receiving them (1993: 10). Jay goes on to point out that even the dilation of the pupil 'can unintentionally betray an inner state, subtly conveying interest or aversion to the beholder' (10). Part of the uncanniness transmitted by Bowie's eyes is due to the simultaneously mixed messages they appear to impart: dilation of one pupil potentially signifies attraction, whilst contraction of the other more likely shows recoil of interest. Bowie's anisocoria therefore contains within it the possibility of contrariness, capable of registering suspicion in the onlooker (a feeling synonymous with the uncanny) as a response to an unfamilar gaze. With this in mind it is purposeful to quote from Dyer's reappraisal of Bela Balazs' philosophical consideration of the close-up, which acknowledges the widely-held view that: 'the close-up reveals the unmediated personality of the individual, and this belief in the "capturing" of the "unique" "person" of a performer is probably central to the star phenomenon' (1979: 17).

Roeg's lugubrious cult film (for which the intended score composed by Bowie instead became the basis of his 1977 album *Low*) is worth returning to shortly, after teasing out a few final points about eyes highlighted by Freud's analysis of 'The Sand-Man'. Freud connects the Sand-Man's stealing of eyes to the threat of castration, which has its own symbolic precursor in relation to eyes by way of the Oedipal complex.[8] This correlation between eyes and male genitalia ties in with the anxieties of the male protagonist in Hoffman's tale. Although Freud's psychoanalytic interpretation may feel like a stretched metaphor, it bears some similarities to Georges Bataille's sexually-charged novella *The Story of the Eye* (1928), which Roland Barthes analysed in 'Metaphor of the Eye' (1962), finding semiotic correlations between eyes, eggs, bulls' testicles and other ovular objects. Most importantly, the connection between eyes and castration is interpreted as a repressed childhood fear relating concern for the eyes to issues of power and identity. This is significant because Freud reveals a key aspect of the uncanny to be the return of the repressed, whereby the experience of the uncanny is triggered when a once-familiar fear that has been repressed is reactivated. The trigger can be an unrelated but symbolically potent reminder of this repressed fear, making the experience of something unfamiliar connect to an unconsciously familiar fear; hence the feeling of something distantly familiar and eerily unnerving.

The animistic and the shamanistic

While the return of the repressed underpins Freud's theory it is important to note that not every doll, mannequin, waxwork, horror story, image of Bowie's eyes, and so on, evokes the uncanny. As Freud points out, context is important. When the viewer is empowered by the right kind of knowledge, giving them reasonable control over an experience, something otherwise unnerving or alien can be rendered banal, unoriginal or even comedic. However, one area that is consistently uncanny is fear of the 'evil eye' and its close association with an envious glare. In relation to the evil eye, Jacques Lacan recognizes vision as a 'conflictual field in which the looker is always a body to be observed' (Jay, 1993: 368), so an envious look towards your personage evokes fear of a 'covert intention to harm' (Freud, 2003: 147). Such a look is not in itself the cause of an uncanny experience; instead, that experience is caused by the return of a repressed belief that the envious look might invoke harmful spirits or forces to act against us. As Freud explains, nearly all experiences of the uncanny lead back to:

> the old *animistic* view of the universe, a view characterized by the idea that the world was peopled with human spirits, by the narcissistic overrating of one's own mental processes, by the omnipotence of thoughts and the technique of magic that relied on it, by the attribution of carefully graded magical powers (*mana*) to alien persons and things . . .
>
> Freud 2003: 147

In other words, residual traces of our primary beliefs in gods, aliens, the supernatural and the magical – all areas of the fundamentally unknowable – are tapped into whenever we experience the uncanny. Bowie's myriad persona as the starman, the alien, the outsider, is constructed around an animistic mythology. Such associations are given an aura of authenticity by the physical discordance of his eyes because their otherworldly appearance is a biologically 'real' part of his body, not part of a show or act, even though they are frequently highlighted within his performance of a character.

In *Celebrity* (2001), Chris Rojek touches upon the idea of the animistic in his consideration of shamanism. Earthly order is disrupted as part of a shamanic seance through magical feats, consumption of drugs and the relaxation of conventional modes of dress. The wearing of a mask (or perhaps make-up or an equivalent form of face paint) often announces the incarnation of a spirit, such as a god, ancestor or other mythological/alien being. Given Bowie's penchant for masks, make-up and characterization, it is interesting to note that masks are historically dualistic: a traditional mask is 'a soul portrait' revealing an image of the wearer's 'essential nature' (Tseëlon, 2001: 26) and is used to identify a character as much as to conceal an identity, thereby adding to the already hazy line between fantasy/reality and the authentic/inauthentic. The shamanic spectacle focuses upon the lead figure, the shaman, as someone who possesses the capacity for social transgression and the ability to 'conjure different intensities of being that, through the metaphor and experience of the ecstatic journey, admit transcendence' (Rojek, 2001: 56). The capability to transport an audience away from earthly cares is subsequently associated with magic and possession. It also reinforces links between shamanism and the devil; we might recall here that the Arabic and Hebrew etymology for the uncanny merges with the 'demonic' and 'gruesome'. In the 1960s, rock music began twinning the shamanic persona with certain types of charismatic musical personality. Rojek includes Bowie as one of a list of performers – alongside Jimi Hendrix, Jim Morrison, Mick Jagger, Lou Reed, Mark Bolan and Iggy Pop – who 'consciously presented themselves as shamanic figures'; but what Bowie invented through Ziggy Stardust to set his shamanic identity apart was the persona of being an 'alien rock messiah' (2001: 68). It can be surmised that Bowie's alien persona does not just tap into residual animistic beliefs, it also uses those associations to augment fading religious or sacred convictions – albeit where it is 'never exactly clear what . . . sacred mission [is] involved' (68) – in favour of a secular, pop cultural, 'messiah'.

Seeing David Bowie: the 'aura' and the punctum

In keeping with his uncanny persona, the roles Bowie has played on film frequently trade on his affiliation with the supernatural, magical and surreal: as the vampire John Blaylock in *The Hunger* (1983), adapted from Whitney Strieber's novel; as Jack Celliers in *Merry Christmas Mr Lawrence* (1983), in which Bowie's 'ethereal air is perfect for a character who, as his initials indicate, is a Christ-like figure, human but other-worldly' (Trynka, 2011: 313); as Jareth the Goblin King in the fantastical world of *Labyrinth* (1986); as Pontius Pilate, arguably the ultimate outsider from the canonical Gospels, in *The Last Temptation of Christ* (1988); as sinister FBI agent Phillip Jeffries in David Lynch's surreal *Twin Peaks: Fire Walk with Me* (1992); as the automaton-like Warhol in *Basquiat* (1996) and the visionary electrical/mechanical engineer Nikola Tesla in the magic-centred thriller *The Prestige* (2006).

Science fiction and fantasy clearly inspires a large part of the Bowie mystique. While considering Bowie for the role of alien-on-Earth, Thomas Jerome Newton, in *The Man Who Fell To Earth* the director, Roeg, and producer, Si Litvinoff, were 'smuggled' an illicit copy of Alan Yentob's 1975 documentary about Bowie, *Cracked Actor*, which allegedly sealed the deal after they saw Bowie being driven around America in the back of a limousine: 'The pair . . . were struck by how, as Bowie gazed out of the back of the car window, he seemed totally isolated, disconnected from the world – alien' (Trynka, 2011: 229). As mentioned earlier, the film includes a thematic preoccupation with exosomatic organs mostly related to sight and vision – some of which are familiar tools and devices enhanced by extraterrestrial technology. Newton (Bowie) frequently wears dark glasses with photochromic lenses to shield his alien eyes; the scientist, Nathan Bryce (Rip Torn), uses cameras, microscopes, a telescope, an X-ray camera and different types of film; the patent lawyer, Oliver Farnsworth (Buck Henry), wears thick glasses with bifocal lenses that magnify his eyes; and both the narrative and *mise-en-scène* consistently employ glasses, a range of different mirrors, windows, televisions, film and other reflective/transparent surfaces or visual effects to emphasize the concept of seeing 'differently'. Newton, as the chief protagonist, is frequently seen to be looking at and through things. There are numerous shots of his face and gaze, some of which lead into visions across time and space through his mind's eye; such scenes provide a reminder of Freud's observation that to experience the uncanny sometimes relies upon seeing from a particular narrative or authorial perspective. The spaceman can also be seen pulling at the skin around his eyes and, in a key sequence about his identity, we see a series of close-ups intended to highlight his mismatched pupils. The most symbolically loaded moment shows Bowie's uncanny eyes clearly reflected in a convex shaving mirror that distorts the shape of his face. The naked alien, exploring his bodiliness, then peels lenses from the surface of his eyes with a pair of tweezers to reveal reptilian pupils beneath.

The multiple significance of the eyes in this sequence plays with a range of meanings. Bowie's star persona as an otherworldly outsider clearly informs his characterization of Newton, drawing upon his 'real world' identity as a performer known to personify an 'alien rock messiah'. Diagetically speaking, Bowie's biological eyes are presented as concealing alien eyes with the suggestion that the visible anisocoria is caused by the spaceman failing to create lenses that consistently replicate a standard human eye. When the reptilian eyes of Newton are revealed, the repressed secret of his true nature – hinted at by Bowie's uncanny eyes – is brought into view along with the unnerving notion that the animistic world of the extraordinary and alien is a reality.

In relation to eyes, close-ups, photographic portraits, authenticity and 'aura' – particularly with Bowie's shamanistic and animistic star persona in mind – it is instructive to consider Walter Benjamin's influential 1936 essay about photography and film in which he considers the impact of mechanical reproduction upon the ritualistic aura and cult value of art (Benjamin, 1968: 219–53). Benjamin suggests the ability to reproduce images withers the connection between an original artwork and its authentic connection to a historically specific time and place: reproducibility liquidates the relationship between art and tradition by mobilizing the image to appear in endless copies, potentially without context. As a result, Benjamin acknowledges the 'artificial build-up' of star personas within mass culture as a response to 'the shrivelling of the aura' (Benjamin, 1968: 233), recognizing the replacement (or what Freud would term the repression) of the ritualistic and magical by its secular and commodified equivalent; this cultural shift in meaning and value could at least partially account for the emergence of 'alien rock star' messiahs and pop cultural shamans. However, in the change from cult value (an artwork produced for the worth of its existence) to exhibition value (an artwork produced to be displayed regardless of context) Benjamin offers a curious 'caveat' to the dissolution of the aura in the form of the portrait photograph; more specifically, he seems to suggest that 'the gaze or the eyes are the vehicle for this connection [to an authentic aura]' (Sherlock, 2013: 167).

Stating that 'cult value does not give way without resistance', Benjamin proposes that the authentic aura instead 'retires into an ultimate retrenchment: the human countenance' (1968: 227–8). He sees this defensive strategy in the portrait as a focal point of early photography where the 'cult of remembrance of loved ones ... offers a last refuge for the cult value of the picture' (228). Benjamin swiftly moves on to discuss Eugene Atget as the photographer who pinpoints the historical shift from 'ritual value' to 'exhibition value', photographing empty Parisian streets as 'man withdraws from the photographic image' (228). Although Benjamin does not expand upon his reasoning, Barthes' explains in *Camera Lucida* (1980, 1993: 5) that '[a] specific photograph, in effect, is never distinguished from its referent'. A photograph, generally speaking, embodies the immediacy of a specific moment that cannot existentially be repeated: what Lacan calls 'the Tuché, the Occasion, the Encounter, the Real, in its indefatigable expression' (4). So, where photographic reproductions of people are concerned, 'an element of authenticity and connection to the original appears to remain, despite the numerous copies that might be available' (Sherlock, 2013: 167). Benjamin indicates this interpretation with the line: 'the aura emanates from the early photographs in the fleeting expression of a human face' (1968: 228).

While it would be a mistake to position Bowie as a representative of authenticity, due to his established position as a postmodern explorer of otherworldly – and by definition unknowable – identities (McLeod, 2003: 339), his eyes provide a fascinating meeting point between his socially constructed 'alien rock messiah' mythology and the physical/foundational reality of his person. In other words, for all the interpretive associations of the uncanny, Bowie's anisocoria is a real and authentic part of his biology. It seems reasonable to suggest that in many of Bowie's iconic images (beyond the limited handful discussed in this chapter) it is the muscle damage to his left iris sphincter that draws attention, makes Bowie distinctive, and provides what Barthes terms a *punctum*: a punctuating highlight or detail that jumps out at the viewer, disturbing an otherwise general study of the image (1993: 26). The etymology of punctum also gives us the meaning of a 'sting, speck, cut, *little hole*' (26, my italics), literally connecting the hole created by the muscles of Bowie's left pupil with its punctuating impact in certain images of him. One of the values of Bowie's anisocoria comes from turning an authentic (physically real) bodily defect into a magically charged element of his uncanny star persona. As a result, Bowie's eyes effectively confound certain theoretical approaches to the aura, advanced by Benjamin's essay, by simultaneously enhancing his artificial personality as a commodity (a commercially successful, primarily mainstream, performer) whilst also leading us back to the authentic reality of Bowie's human countenance.

The parallax view: seeing 'differently'

Aside from having uncanny qualities that affect how Bowie is seen, Bowie's eyes are also part of how *he* sees. In 2004 a lollipop briefly lodged in his left eye socket during a concert in Oslo after being thrown by an overexcited fan, eventually causing Bowie to playfully comment: 'I've only got one good eye, you know' (Bowie in Trynka, 2011: 385). Thinking about how Bowie sees is where the notion of a visual disability, in the form of damaged depth perception, becomes intriguing and the concept of parallax provides a useful metaphor for exploring issues of vision, depth and perception.

Drawing upon the Japanese philosopher and literary critic Kojin Karatani, Slajov Žižek plays with the idea of parallax and the concept of 'the parallax view' (2006). As he notes, the standard definition of parallax is: 'the apparent displacement of an object (the shift of its position against a background), caused by a change in observational position that provides a new line of sight' (17). The added 'philosophical twist' is that this observed difference is not simply subjective: the viewer's change in perspective reflects 'an "ontological" shift in the object itself' (17). Following Lacan, Žižek suggests the subjective gaze of the viewer is always-already inscribed into the object being perceived so that there is a point from which 'the object itself returns the gaze' (17), which leads him to quote Lacan directly: 'Sure, the picture is in my eye, but I, I am also in the picture' (Lacan, 1979: 63). To connect this concept to Bowie we can offer another play on the V&A's variable taglines by suggesting that, as a performer, Bowie is (for want of a better term) an 'object' on view. As Žižek suggests via Lacan, the 'object' itself returns the gaze: so Bowie on stage is seen from an array of perspectives but, in addition to presenting himself objectively, he is also looking back subjectively at his perceived audience.

Within this combination and exchange of the objective and the subjective, Bowie must be understood as the primary mediating source of his own assumed characters and guises. Major Tom, Ziggy Stardust, Aladdin Sane, The Thin White Duke, and so on, are visualized in his mind's eye and then made 'real' through meticulous design and picturesque portrayal. In other words, Bowie saw or sought these figures within himself – mining his range of cultural and creative references – before performing them, on stage and in the studio, in as rounded and three-dimensional a manner as necessary. The audience only ever experiences a percentage of the whole character, informed by the surface vision of what is visible. So how profoundly an audience might relate to any given version of Bowie – and how successful a character is – depends upon each beholder's perspective and perception of depth.

Speaking in the 1975 BBC documentary *Cracked Actor*, Bowie discusses finding characters within himself and how the roles he plays 'are all facets of me'. His creative process (at least in the 70s) is informed by Brion Gysin and William S. Burroughs' 'cut-up' technique. In keeping with Bowie's affiliation with the animistic, he refers to the cut-up process as 'a very western form of Tarot': an instinctive process of unpredictable cultural association, appropriation and fusion. The internal logic of Bowie's selection and combination of ideas seems to be ad hoc and fundamental, with its own hints of psychoanalysis: 'I had to take everything out and explore it.' Within twentieth-century art the roots of the cut-up trace back at least as far as Dadaism and Surrealism, both of which embraced the use of collaged forms and parataxis (a structured form where the connecting relationship between elements is omitted). What makes

Bowie stand out from the crowd, compared to his early 'invisibility' in the London suburbs (Conrad, 2013), is that he sees things 'differently', both literally (due to limited depth perception) and metaphorically, often in a way that could be regarded as off-kilter, original and strange. More importantly, he sees things differently and has found a way to visualize what he sees so that his unique vision is meaningfully communicated to an audience.

Bowie has spoken about the illustrative and vivid nature of his performances, the act of portraying a song rather than just singing it (*Cracked Actor*, 1975). A psychoanalytic interpretation, developed from the threat suffered by Bowie's left eye and subsequent damage to its function (as a metaphorical attempt at castration), might suggest that his seemingly quite obsessive need for depth and added dimension could be a response to flawed depth perception. Put another way, Bowie's immersion in character and his creative fecundity are a means of compensating for any sense of lost/threatened manhood or perceived 'flatness' in his vision. Whilst this analysis is not wholly convincing, it is interesting to probe the idea that Bowie literally seeing differently might affect his processes of visualization and self-presentation. Seeing differently potentially means engaging and communicating differently with the world. If you see differently enough, philosophically or biologically, you have a different perception of your environment, and (with the parallax metaphor in mind) your environment, in turn, might also perceive you differently. When someone moves too far beyond familiar and known philosophies, they are given the label of being 'insane' because they exist (at that moment in time) beyond the mythos of common knowledge and shared understanding (Pirsig, 1989). Bringing together aspects of the uncanny with insanity, which has concomitant associations with surreal visions and the predominance of 'strangeness', the common phrase '[m]adness is a foreign country' (Porter, 1987: 9) parallels some of the qualities affiliated with the uncanny, such as a sense of alienation and unfamiliarity.

Madness and modernity

Conscious of how significant strangeness is to his artistic persona, Bowie has flirted with ideas of madness throughout his career. His half-brother, Terry Burns, suffered from schizophrenia and has sometimes been alluded to in lyrics, interviews and through visual associations (Heylin, 2012; Trynka, 2011). Within this context, the historical connection between eyes and madness is also worth considering. In *Downcast Eyes* (1993), Jay explores the presumed ocularcentricity of Western culture and the historical ties between sight and knowledge, vision and identity: common clichés privilege the eye with being both 'a window on the world' and 'a mirror to the soul' (10). Partly due to this link between eyes and mind, which is neurological as well as cultural, our organs of sight have traditionally been regarded as an indicator of mental wellbeing. As mentioned earlier, Charcot's 'imaging' of the mentally ill – whereby the 'diagnostic value of the image of the patient went hand in hand with [the medical] belief that the gaze of the doctor has to be fused with the gaze of the artist' (Blackshaw and Topp, 2009: 29) – forged a link between expressionistic artworks and the romantic myth of the creative genius being tied to madness.

Charcot would invite artists to produce sketches and photographs of individuals entrusted to his care, ostensibly to aid the process of categorizing and examining neurological disease. Such images were widely available in Vienna during the establishment of modern psychiatry and psychoanalysis, causing expressionist artists such as Egon Schiele and Oscar Kokoschka to be influenced by, or to produce their own, studies of mentally ill people. Awkward, mechanistic, bodily poses were a common feature, which directly correlates with Freud's connection between the uncanny and its experience in response to seeing someone struck by an epileptic seizure. Such poses are visible in the work of Schiele and Heckel, both artists whom Bowie spent time admiring by 'leafing through monographs' of their work with Iggy Pop whilst producing *The Idiot* (1977) – hence the resulting cover of "*Heroes*" and Pop's equally strange pose on the cover of his album (Trynka, 2011: 257).

Within expressionistic paintings of people depicted as suffering from mental illness, reviews would frequently comment upon the eyes and act of looking. Kokoschka's 1911 show in Vienna prompted critics to write about 'those portrayed whose physiognomies leer, gawp and caper out from the sullied canvases with all the signs of quiet or raving madness' (Blackshaw and Topp, 2009: 47); other commentary asked viewers to '[t]ry to defy the horror which calls out from the lackluster gaze of a ruined intellect' (54) or to face 'the despairing expression of a soul in harrowing disintegration which looks at the world through calcified eyes' (55). Because the medical 'imaging' gaze would reduce the patient to an 'object without agency', modernist artists – who themselves often felt misunderstood and alienated from society – identified with the imaging process, contributing to a rhetoric within modernist art of anguish and alienation (19). It is no coincidence that this particular affiliation of modernity and madness emanated from Vienna as artistic expression and medical practice overlapped, or that both the medical gaze and the artistic gaze often imbue the eye with the ability to clarify particular insights about the body or society.

However, while the links between sight and the imaging of madness provide further suggestions about why eyes might so effectively convey a sense of the uncanny, Bowie has clearly never been reduced to an object in the manner of one of Charcot's patients. Returning to the concept of parallax explored by Žižek that places the shifting object in relative awareness of the beholder, and vice versa, Bowie is very distinct from a visual artist like a painter or photographer because he is both the subject and object of his own creations. In a sense – and this is the concept that seems to underpin the V&A's 2013 show – the focal point of David Bowie is David Bowie. Bowie once stated that when looking at himself and the environment he is in, he sees 'with the eyes of someone who is not involved in any particular line of the arts' (*David Bowie: Rare and Unseen*, 2010). Picking and choosing ideas without explicit commitment to anything apart from himself, Bowie is (conceptually, at least) free from external limitations. This is perhaps why, in addition to 'looking' uncanny and different, Bowie has so successfully envisioned his alternate, or parallax, perceptions of the world.

Conclusion: the visual and the visionary David Bowie

Bowie's eyes help us to see him in a way that defies convention – as a person who embraces the uncanny, the outsider and the alien, and who gives those identities a platform within mainstream culture. Looking at the design work by Barnbrook Studios for Bowie's most recent studio albums, *Heathen* (2002), *Reality* (2003) and *The Next Day* (2013), as well as the V&A exhibition catalogue and graphics, shows how significant a part Bowie's uncanny eyes continue to play in the imagery that represents him.

The cover of *Heathen* plays on the album title to depict Bowie with white 'demonic' eyes (another etymological variation on the 'uncanny') to represent a heathen who is 'human but in a way where you couldn't actually see there was a soul behind his eyes' (Barnbrook, 2014, interview). *Heathen* depicts a man unhappy with the world and what he is seeing and it was Bowie's idea to adapt Markus Klinko's photograph by 'doing something' with the eyes on the album cover (Barnbrook, 2014, interview). Thematically, the destructive and challenging nature of the heathen – as someone who destroys something civilization holds precious – continues in the (constructed) images of slashed and vandalized portraits used for the record sleeve and CD booklet. As Jonathan Barnbrook explained, his research for *Heathen* suggested that people seeking to desecrate an image frequently do so by attacking or destroying the eyes (Barnbrook, 2014, interview), so the interior artwork for the album reproduced the perverse beauty of damaged masterpieces including the slashed eyes of what appears to be the Virgin Mary.

Reality hosts a graphically illustrated version of Bowie on the cover, designed by Rex Ray, walking through a surreal landscape of expressionistic markings within which a series of stars near his head suggest a magical aura. Bowie's caricature stares intently forward. His obviously oversized blue eyes draw the viewer's attention and reflect triangular shafts of light. Bowie's distinctively enlarged left pupil is clearly visible, and the disparity between his pupils combined with the already expanded size of his eyes gives the resultant stare a hypnotic and unnerving quality.

The contentious removal of Bowie's visage from *The Next Day*, by covering over the iconic cover from "*Heroes*" with a blank white square, was intended as a play on 'sacrilege' (Barnbrook, in V&A 2013, film). The album cover acknowledges the past even while using it as a palimpsest for something new: the shock value of defacing or obliterating Bowie's face and eyes inverts any familiar expectations of identity. The process of 'blocking out' that is a characteristic of Barnbrook Studios' design plays with the expectations of the audience. A pop/rock star projects a set of images and generates certain expectations but this is part of a dialogue, whereby an audience is also capable of fitting their own symbolism, desires and associations onto the star (Barnbrook 2014, interview). The blank white square acknowledges this interpretive space, in part by covering over the most expressive and visually communicative part of the human body: the eyes.

The cover of *David Bowie is Inside* (2013) takes us back to where we started with the *Aladdin Sane – Eyes Open* photograph, but this time the photograph is reproduced with a vibrant orange tone throughout. The bold orange was selected because the colour emerged as being 'unconsciously associated' with Bowie, particularly throughout his iconic looks of the 70s, providing a strong key tone for the graphics of the V&A show (Barnbrook, 2014, interview). The single coloration enhances the importance of the eyes as the focal point of the portrait (especially so when there are no variations in colour to distract attention), allowing Bowie to stare out and beyond the viewer from the cover of the exhibition catalogue.

As this chapter has argued, Bowie's eyes have long been central to his identity as an artist and how his eyes are seen has evolved to function metonymically as an index for his otherworldly persona. Our understanding of Bowie's iconic imagery can be advanced by considering the punctuating effect of his anisocoria and how the uncanny qualities of his eyes opens up a connection with the animistic, providing a context through which to connect one key element of his body – the eyes – with his public persona as a creative outsider. Bowie's anisocoria has become a key feature of his unique character as a performer and he has turned the physical defect of a paralysed pupil into a positive marker of his highly inventive ability to see and be seen differently. As a final concluding point this chapter proposes that the apparent weakness or flaw of Bowie's traumatized left pupil is actually a curious strength that is often overlooked in discussion of his enigmatic identity. So, despite Bowie's assured status as a highly innovative performer who is profoundly defined by his understanding of the visual and the visionary, we can still learn a lot by looking into his eyes.

Notes

1   The thirtieth anniversary 2CD edition of *Aladdin Sane* contains a somewhat similar 'eyes open' image but this is less engaging because Bowie is not looking directly out at the viewer; his eyes are instead directed slightly downwards. The image is also contained within the booklet format of the anniversary edition, which is CD-sized, and it therefore lacks the impact and scale of the V&A poster.

2   Bowie appears quite confrontational, with the words providing a knowing parody of Orwell's famous phrase 'Big Brother is watching you' from *Nineteen Eighty-Four* (1949). Bowie's use of Orwell's dystopian novel as an inspiration for sections of *Diamond Dogs* is clearly evident in the second half of the album through the titles and lyrics of the tracks, including: 'We Are the Dead', '1984' and 'Big Brother'. Bowie had intended to produce a stage musical inspired by *Nineteen Eighty-Four* but the project was never realized, ostensibly due to issues over securing the rights.

3   The moment is captured on film in D.A. Pennebaker's recording of the concert on 3 July 1973 at the Hammersmith Odeon, London – *Ziggy Stardust and the Spiders from Mars* (1973). Before performing the final song, Bowie announces: 'Not only is it the last show of the tour, but it's the last show that we'll ever do. Thank you.'

4   Barnbrook Studios designed the album art for *Heathen* (2002), *Reality* (2003) and *The Next Day* (2013) as well as designing the exhibition catalogue, posters and graphics/typography used for the 'David Bowie is' exhibition whilst at the V&A – http://barnbrook.net.

5   Barnbrook has suggested that the use of the *Aladdin Sane – Eyes Open* image in the fortieth anniversary year of the album was largely coincidental. The image was chosen primarily for its variation from the original, its iconic status and the directness with which it engages the potential audience (2014, interview).

6   Jean-Martin Charcot (1825–93) was the most influential neurologist of the 1800s and spent his career in Paris. His approach to patients treated them as though they were pathological specimens to be observed and measured with an expert's objective eye. As a neurologist as well as a pioneer in the art and science of medical photography he produced a body of work that was highly influential as well as controversial. Freud studied under Charcot in Paris and although he rejected some of Charcot's theories he always acknowledged his influence and diagnostic eye (Science Museum 2014).

7   Ernst Jentsch was the first to explore the uncanny in a psychological sense in his 1906 essay 'On the psychology of the uncanny'. Jentsch put forward the idea that the uncanny relates to 'intellectual uncertainty' and he identified Hoffmann's story 'The Sand-Man', later used in Freud's analysis, as an example of how a writer can employ uncanny effects within a narrative – notably because of the lifelike doll, Olympia, that features in the story.

8   In the well-known Greek myth, the tragic hero Oedipus was a king of Thebes who blinded himself after discovering he had unwittingly fulfilled a prophecy predicting he would murder his father and marry his mother.

Bibliography

Barnbrook, Jonathan. 2014. Telephone interview/discussion with the author. 4 September.

Barthes, Roland. 1962, 2001. 'Metaphor of the eye'. Translated by J.A. Underwood. In *Story of the Eye*, by Georges Bataille. Translated by Joachim Neugroschal. London: Penguin, 119–27.

Barthes, Roland. 1980, 1993. *Camera Lucida: Reflections on Photography*. Translated by Richard Howard. London: Vintage.

Bataille, Georges. 2001. *Story of the Eye*. Translated by Joachim Neugroschal. London: Penguin.

Benjamin, Walter. 1968. *Illuminations*. Edited by Hannah Arendt, translated by Harry Zohn. London: Fontana.

Blackshaw, Gemma and Leslie Topp. 2009. *Madness and Modernity: Mental Illness and the Visual Arts in Vienna 1900*. London: Lund Humphries.

Conrad, Peter. 2013. 'David Bowie is, V&A, London – review'. *The Observer*, Sunday 24 March, www.guardian.co.uk/music/2013/mar/24/david-bowie-is -exhibition-review, accessed 24 March 2013.

David Bowie is Inside. 2013. London: V&A Publishing.

Dyer, Richard. 1979. *Stars*. London: BFI.

Dyer, Richard. 1986. *Heavenly Bodies: Film Stars and Society*. London: Macmillan.

Freud, Sigmund. 2003. 'The uncanny'. Translated by David McLintock. London: Penguin.

Goffman, Erving. 1961. *The Presentation of Self in Everyday Life*. Michigan: Doubleday.

Heylin, Clinton. 2012. *All the Madmen: Barrett, Bowie, Drake, Pink Floyd, The Kinks, The Who and a Journey to the Dark Side of British Rock*. London: Constable.

Jay, Martin. 1993. *Downcast Eyes: The Denigration of Vision in Twentieth-Century French Thought*. Berkeley: University of California Press.

Lacan, Jacques. 1979. *The Four Fundamental Concepts of Psycho-Analysis*. New York: Norton.

McLeod, Ken. 2003. 'Space oddities: aliens, futurism and meaning in popular music'. *Popular Music*, 22 (3) (October), 337–55.

Orwell, George. 2013. *Nineteen Eighty-Four*. London: Penguin.

Paglia, Camille. 2013. 'Theatre of gender: David Bowie at the climax of the sexual revolution'. In *David Bowie is Inside*. London: V&A Publishing, 69–97.

Pirsig, Robert. 1989. *Zen and the Art of Motorcycle Maintenance*. London: Vintage.

Porter, Roy. 1987. *A Social History of Madness: Stories of the Insane*. London: Weidenfeld & Nicolson.

Rojek, Chris. 2001. *Celebrity*. London: Reaktion Books.

Science Museum. 2014. *Brought to Life: Exploring the History of Medicine*, www.sciencemuseum.org.uk/broughttolife.aspx, accessed 21 September 2014.

Sherlock, Alexandra. 2013. 'Larger than life: digital resurrection and the re-enchantment of society'. *The Information Society: An International Journal*, 29 (3), 164–76.

Shumway, David and Heather Arnet. 2007. 'Playing dress up: David Bowie and the roots of goth'. In Lauren M.E. Goodlad and Michael Bibby (eds), *Goth: Undead Subculture*. Durham: Duke University Press, 129–42.

Trynka, Paul. 2011. *Starman: David Bowie, The Definitive Biography*. London: Sphere.

Tseëlon, Efrat. 2001. *Masquerade and Identities: Essays on Gender, Sexuality and Marginality*. London: Routledge.

V&A Museum. 2013. *David Bowie is*. www.vam.ac.uk/content/exhibitions/david-bowie-is/, accessed 26 March.

Žižek, Slajov. 2006. *The Parallax View*. Cambridge: MIT Press.

Filmography

Basquiat. 1996. Directed by Julian Schnabel. USA, Eleventh Street Productions, Jon Kilik, and Miramax Films.

Bowie, David. 1972. 'Starman'. *Top of the Pops*, 6 July. London: BBC, https://www.youtube.com/watch?v=v342TST9tFw.

Cracked Actor. 1975. Directed by Alan Yentob. London: BBC.

David Bowie: Rare and Unseen. 2010. Directed by Paul Clark, UK, Wienerworld.

Labyrinth. 1986. Directed by Jim Henson. UK/USA, Henson Associates, Lucasfilm, The Jim Henson Company, Delphi V Productions, and TriStar Pictures.

The Hunger. 1983. Directed by Tony Scott. UK, MGM and Peerford Ltd.

The Man Who Fell To Earth. 1976. Directed by Nicholas Roeg, UK. British Lion Film Corporation and Cinema 5.

The Prestige. 2006. Directed by Christopher Nolan. USA/UK, Touchstone Pictures, Warner Bros, Newmarket Productions and Syncopy.

Twin Peaks: Fire Walk with Me. 1992. Directed by David Lynch. France/USA, New Line Cinema and CiBy 2000.

Ziggy Stardust and the Spiders from Mars. 1973. Directed by D.A. Pennebaker. UK, Mainman, Pennebaker Productions, Bewlay Bros, Miramax Films and RZO Music.

10

Semantic Shock:

David Bowie!

Toija Cinque

On to that blank canvas, countless dreams have been written and re-written.

THOMSON and GUTMAN, 1996: xxvii

The mystic, as understood as sacred and obscure in many religions and reflected by numerous artists, is frequently manifest as a 'presence' that transcends our reality. The *métier* of David Bowie signals his introspective exploration of the philosophical, often within, but also beyond, his spiritual tradition. In his recent musical work 'The Next Day' (*The Next Day*, 2013), Bowie focused specifically on Roman Catholic tradition and ritual – dressed in sackcloth for the accompanying music-clip, he subverted and critically analysed messianism through the lenses of hypocrisy (a priest punches a homeless man and people kiss a cardinal's ring as he gives them cash), and Christian symbolic expressions (flagellation, the scarlet colouring of the cardinal's robes, drinking of blood, the stigmata and Bowie's own seeming ascension at the song's end). In this task, metaphor is both the means by which he explores and articulates notions of the sacred and its elusive presence and absence. For David Bowie, the operations of his music, intentionally or not, speak from and impel the listening body toward a source of introspection – a wellspring of ideas which confronts one with the temporality of one's existence and the incompleteness of being. Important thematic examples of such have included:

alienation and technology through folk music (*Space Oddity*), sexualized mysticism through heavy metal (*The Man Who Sold the World*), messianism and apocalypticism through blues-based rock-and-roll (*Ziggy Stardust, Diamond Dogs*), the American Dream and totalitarianism through soul and disco (*Young Americans, Station to Station*), solipsism in tension with global consciousness through avant-garde expressionism (*Low, Heroes, Lodger*) – and [from the 1980s] has signaled a return to rock-and roll and R & B in order to confront modernity (*Scary Monsters, Let's Dance*).

Finn, 1983: 467

His visual and sonic navigation has been a journey by which this artist has long questioned obstacles of the inherited established metaphors that bind many to a version of reality, handicapping a potentially sincerely lived experience. As the images that are all around us in the media we consume bear down on us all, so too does language, driving us to use words that are not principally our own with the effect of restricting us to pre-constructed and therefore assumed methods of speaking and perceiving the world.

Emerging as an artist in the 1960s, a time of intense ideological contestation that witnessed the birth of a 'new society' of change and contradiction, Bowie challenged the existing state of affairs with an approach that frequently cut through accepted verities. Choosing the name 'Bowie' was a metaphor for 'a truism about cutting through the lies' (Bowie in Copetas, 1974: 17). But as American author, William S. Burroughs, insightfully pointed out to Bowie in the same conversation, the 'cutting of the knife' (metaphorically) goes both ways and in the process of such synectic investigation and contemplation he might himself become damaged. Much comment and commentary engendered by Bowie's lyrics, his musical constructs, creative outpouring and his corporeity present a depiction that his existence has indeed been haunted by multiple overlapping modes of becoming that converged to constitute a haunted materialization of being. Here it is useful to think about Bowie's art/work in terms of Ahmed's (2004) social philosophies of trauma and scarring, with the understanding in this context that the exposure of the private emotional life is necessary to developing a connection with the listener-viewer. What Bowie's work frequently does is 'reopen wounds' and remind us of the scars; asking us to notice their existence, to become more aware, in the first instance. The action here traces Nietzsche's prototypical philosopher's aesthetic contemplation, whereby humankind is assisted in the 'vivisections on our own souls'; for

how little the 'salvation of the soul' matters to us now! We heal ourselves afterwards; we have no doubt that being ill is instructive, even more instructive than being well – *those who make us sick* seem to us today even more necessary than medicine-men or 'saviours'.

Bowie's work then, asks us to be 'nutcrackers' of our own soul, making us question and questionable and thus *'more deserving* [appreciative?] – of life? . . .' (Nietzsche, 1887, 2013: 99).

The purpose of this chapter is to question the extent to which David Bowie has used a kind of metonym of emotion in order to mobilize reaction and channel affect into political action via his visual and sonic creativity. I argue here that the power of Bowie's star image rests largely upon his private emotional life taking precedence (for the listening-body) over his private life. Bowie's private emotional life provides an interpretative framework for inner contemplation; raising questions of the value of stars and their art for the individual and collective weal. Bowie will be explored here through the way he embodies certain identity positions that are alien, alternative, and transgressive via metaphor and alter-egos that render him essentially strange.

Metaphor, metonym and neoteric art

While a very old assessment (Aristotle, 384–22 BC), contemporary linguistic theory also affords an understanding that metaphor is a fundamental tool in one's interpretation of what might be regarded as reality, the making of ourselves and the world in which we live. Studies by George Lakoff and Mark Johnson (1981: 287) revealed the pervasiveness of metaphor in everyday life, specifically through one's language, thought and action. For metaphors are the mediators of how we think and act and are the roads that map the terrain of our ordinary conceptual systems. Hermeneutic phenomenologist, Paul Ricoeur, asserted metaphor's power and pervasiveness in one's understanding and interpretation of the world, but the author placed emphasis upon metaphor's unique ability to create and re-constellate ways of seeing and being in the world. It is through the 'productive imagination', able to grasp similarities in differences, that metaphors are afforded the capacity to make new connections between things and produce a 'semantic shock' that 'draws out a new semantic pertinence from the ruins of literal meaning' (Muldoon, 2002: 60). Metaphor and the homologous metonym are able to simultaneously describe what 'is' and what 'is not', therefore giving rise to a tension in what might be perceived as real. Metaphors and metonym, consequently, amplify our comprehension of reality. It is through producing and maintaining multiple tensions that metaphor and metonym are able to articulate that which is inexpressible. Ricoeur has argued that metaphor has the capacity to 'make sense with nonsense, to transform a self-contradictory statement into a significant self-contradiction', whereby metaphor might give the impression that it is 'the solution of an enigma' (Ricoeur, 1991: 78).

Bowie makes sense despite the seemingly contradictory nonsense. Self-described as a 'faker' (in 'Changes', *Hunky Dory*, 1971), of being a liar and his actions as 'pure clown', Bowie has asserted that: 'I'm Pierrot. I'm Everyman. What I'm doing is theatre, and only theatre . . . I'm using myself as a canvas and trying to paint the truth of our time on it' (Bowie, 1976 in Rook, 1976: 6). He has also drawn upon the colourful plastic brick toy 'Lego' to describe what he 'is' artistically (Bowie, 1976, cited in Buckley, 2005: 1): 'Bowie was never meant to be. He's like a Lego kit. I'm convinced I wouldn't like him, because he's too vacuous and undisciplined. There is no definitive David Bowie.' It is precisely because there is 'no definitive David Bowie' that multiple interpretations are rendered possible. Lego is indeed a terrific metaphor for Bowie's creative approach to his work. So here, what might appear to be a cursory comment actually demonstrates acuity. In parallel to his select use of this particular metaphor is the current work in identity studies by sociologist and media theorist, David Gauntlet, who, in looking to determine a new way to explore self-identities via visual methods established an innovative method via Lego Serious Play that uses Lego as a problem-solving tool in which the individual or group make(s) models of their experiences to then be explored further (Gauntlet, 2008: 259). Not that Bowie was doing *this* one assumes, but that he chose the metaphor is interesting and typical Bowie whimsy – to express something significant via the obscure. The dean of teaching and learning from the London College of Fashion, Allison James, recently outlined the functionality of Lego Serious Play which:

> uses a process of metaphorical modelling, or building three-dimensional representations of thoughts and ideas, and it's a methodology that originated with the Lego group about 15 years ago. It was particularly important because they were looking for an alternative to the kind of processes that were at work in business meetings, where lots of people in suits would turn up and brainstorm with flipcharts and pens, and they felt they needed to find a different way of operating which would be more productive.

With striking similarity to Bowie's private emotional life, addressed through his art and his own choice of metaphorical comparison, James (2013: 8) describes the role of metaphor for the 'outsider':

> They also talked about something called 'The problem of the lonely guy', meaning that in meetings you get hierarchies, you get dominant players, and there's always somebody sitting quietly in the room, who doesn't feel

like they want to make a contribution, or is too shy to make a contribution, but probably has something really worthwhile to share. So they started exploring with literal builds using Lego bricks, but felt that it didn't really add anything to the process, and then it occurred to them that if they worked metaphorically they'd be able to loosen up their thinking and start coming at issues from leftfield (apologies for the metaphor) and end up with more creative, richer and more memorable solutions.

Using Ricoeur's interpretation of metaphor as a mechanism for examining the creative capacity of language to reveal reality, in the context of this chapter, it becomes reasonable to make the extended claim that creative acts such as painting or music, just like '[l]anguage in the making', can also acclaim 'reality in the making' (Ricoeur in Muldoon, 2002: 57). For creative artists, the ambition to communicate the otherwise inexpressible is unquestionably an enduring concern. The manifestation of the ineffable by metaphor or metonym is precisely artistic method. For metaphor and metonym have the capacity to open 'The Doors' to expression and speculation that other aspects of language, even creative language, are unable to retrieve. And Bowie's work acts as this conduit toward understanding; a full 'body without organs' to use Deleuze and Guattari's term; a catalyst for healthy change (Deleuze and Guattari, 1980, 1987). For a young Marc Spitz, author of *Bowie: A Biography* (2009: 23–4):

> I would look up at the sky and wonder what it would be like to be Major Tom, trapped way up there in outer space, floating in a tin can forever. Was it technically living? Do you age? . . . Bowie made me consider existentialism before I even knew what it meant to be alive (and before I ever really thought about my death) . . . but I already knew even then that Bowie's music had permanently changed me.

The work of feminist and cultural theorist, Sara Ahmed (2004), suggests that emotion for its part can also function metonymically, wherein emotions are cultural practices rather than psychological states. For Ahmed, the influence of emotions on the body is mobilized or directed toward a specific instance that can then be read as an emotional response to whatever that example is made to represent, through the ways that bodies interact. For instance, an affective response to the plight of individual (confusion, sadness, anger) can be read and mobilized as an affective response to that which caused the plight of the individual. Ahmed (2004: 196) argues that emotions are effects rather than origins and 'are not only about the "impressions" left by others, but that they involve investments in social norms'. Emotions demonstrate how certain histories subsist despite not always being consciously remembered. And, it is through emotions that the past persists in the surface of bodies. Ahmed (202) reasons for the usefulness of (metaphoric) scars of trauma and injustice as reminders of the injury:

> It's not that the wound is exposed or that the skin is bleeding. But the scar is a sign of the injury: a good scar allows healing, it even covers over, *but the covering always exposes the injury, reminding us of how it shapes the body.*

To cover over the injury completely (or hide certain narratives for fear of some kind of retribution) is, she argues, a kind of injustice that effaces the injury and, in doing so, reinjures. Ahmed's theory regarding the circulation emotion and how this can become weighted down with affect is relevant to the circulation of Bowie's affect-producing music, visual work and creative performances. One can see that Bowie's work over time has used a kind of metonym of emotion in order to mobilize the emotion of listening and viewing bodies and channelled affect into critical contemplation and political action. Reflecting Ahmed's philosophies of trauma and scarring, Bowie's work has had a tendency to open wounds and remind us of our own scars but also, importantly, offer a means to negotiate their healing. Redmond's (2013: 380–1) personal memory of Bowie's 'intimate' star image and music finds them fervently bound to his own identity formation as a teenager, whereby Bowie's music 'created the space for an embodied, transgressive sense of the self to emerge':

> My first fully intimate, meaningful engagement with Bowie occurred when I was aged 12. I had again been in trouble at school, and had crashed on my bed, alone and lonely. It was in this mood of melancholy and introspective alienation that I put *Diamond Dogs* (1974) on . . . I felt immobilised, enraptured, cut free from the physical and psychological limitations of place, space, and body, and I was exhilarated as a consequence. Bowie's music – the alien figure that created it – provided an escape from the limiting confines and regulatory conditions of my life, into a world that recognised the former while creating a space for the difference within me to be celebrated, extended, made into hopeful selfhood.

Nick Stevenson's (2009) study of fandom, emotionality and identity formation similarly plays Ahmed's theory out. Via interviews, Bowie fans clarify that:

Lee: There is an emotional attachment, an appreciation of art (84);
Guy: People tend to go back to it [Bowie's music] when they're having problems, they deal with it by secluding themselves through Bowie and turning to him for, like a guide, inspiration . . . or just to cope . . . (84);

Mickey: He has the sort of image that says, 'Come on, stand up for yourself. Be yourself.' He gave me confidence (92).

Stevenson (2009: 92) has argued that there is validity, in that Bowie's music and videos enable people to explore 'imaginative alternatives to a world of rules and regulations and cultural norms' and afford reflexive resources as they attempt to sustain a coherent identity.

David Bowie is mercurial. And, while this chapter refers to the musician, recording artist, public performer, actor, artist as 'Bowie', it is clear that on another level David Jones has never changed; he has just used different metaphors and metonyms at various times for different purposes. By that I mean that through the overarching 'Bowie' (the actor's actor), the creative work becomes a metathesis for life's grit. Jones uses Bowie to move on stardom's stage. In a 1973 interview for the BBC One news programme, *Nationwide* (5 June), he explained that: 'I am very much a character when I'm onstage . . . that's what "Bowie" is supposed to be about.' Indeed, he employs the trope of artist in the mould of Giacomo Puccini's Rodolfo in the opera *La Bohème*. Rudolfo is a starving poet (but Bowie's thin body is admirable in the context of a western society where *achieved* thinness is valued)[1] who lives in a sparsely furnished single-room garret along with his friends: the painter, the philosopher and the musician – an interesting parallel to be drawn here is that Bowie is all of these characters in one – imaginatively complementary. For the performances of Bowie, David Jones has drawn explicitly on the imagery of the (mad) artist. He used impressions of the artist's garret for the video-clip for 'Look Back in Anger' from *Lodger* (1979), but over a decade earlier was himself cast as 'art come to life' in the 1967 film *The Image*, written and directed by Michael Armstrong, who described it as 'a study of the illusionary reality world within the schizophrenic mind of the artist at his [sic] point of creativity' (Armstrong cited in Lindbergs, 2008).

Madness for its part is a theme in many of Bowie's compositions – the original album cover for *The Man Who Sold the World* (1971),[2] which depicts an asylum and includes the song 'All the Madmen' and *Aladdin Sane* (1973) – a lad insane – are but two examples. His metaphors and metonyms add to the mythology of the artist whereby brilliance and a certain mental state go hand-in-hand, but this is no 'surface' madness. The 'schizophrenic madman' here is by contrast an explorer of 'depths', one who flaunts conventions and rejects completely the surface, the shifting realm of socially accepted appearances and nonsense words, to return instead to the body. For the schizophrenic, words collapse, not into nonsense, but into the bodies that produce and hear them. Deleuze (1969, 1990: 88) proffers:

For the schizophrenic, then, it is less a question of recovering meaning than of destroying the word, of conjuring up the affect, and of transforming the painful passion of the body into triumphant action, obedience into command, always in this depth beneath the fissured surface . . .

Rejecting the surface of artistic conventions, Bowie has shown up his own plagiarism. One occasion in the early 70s sent Elton John fleeing a concert protesting Bowie's provocative statement when, during the midst of the song 'Starman', Bowie sang intentionally instead 'Somewhere, over the Rainbow', thus signalling his 'gross inauthenticity' but also his own theft (Buckley, 2005: 138). While Bowie has sonically demonstrated his enthusiasm for the world of fine art in such works as 'Unwashed and Somewhat Slightly Dazed' (*Space Oddity*, 1969) and found in 'Joe the Lion' is a reference to the artist Chris Burden ("*Heroes*", 1977), the much later album *1. Outside* (1995) for its part, (a conceptual work via a detective story) presents the listener-viewer with the conundrum of whether some crimes can be considered an art form. Within the work are references to the Venice Biennale, the artists of Viennese Actionism between 1960–71 (Günter Brus, Otto Mühl, Hermann Nitsch, and Rudolf Schwarzkogler), the mythological Greek Minotaur, and again, performance artist and sculptor, Chris Burden. Significantly, reference is made to Thomas De Quincey's (1827) essay 'On Murder Considered as One of the Fine Arts' in which a fictional, satirical argument is made concerning the aesthetic appreciation of murder. Moreover, in the videos and on tour for the album, Bowie is presented as a fervent artist with an aesthetic inspired by Viennese Actionism, specifically in 'Art's Filthy Lesson' and its accompanying video that sees 'art' as an event on a stage. Still working metaphorically, we might consider that if life is a 'stage' and we the 'actors' upon it (Goffman, 1959), then art is the comment upon life. Drawing again on the atmosphere of 'madness' (including the sense of that which is not society's norm) for the album title *1. Outside* is the understanding of Outsider Art (or rough art) put forward by French artist, Jean Dubuffet, to describe art that had been created by those on the outside of the boundaries of official culture and specifically, on art made by those on the outside of the established art scene, such as insane-asylum inmates and children (Cardinal, 1972). Bowie has said that the 'fragmentation of society' is an enduring interest that he has never moved away from and that, in his view, art 'shouldn't be institutionalised or put in galleries' because it is 'for the public to use . . . sustenance to life' (Bowie, 1995).

Bowie paints, sculpts and exhibits his works and in 1994 become a member of, and interviewer for, *Modern Painter*. Away from music, he has commented critically upon established precepts embedded in the 'high' arts through his controversial art works (his 1994 commissioned design for Laura Ashley wallpaper ironically depicted the naked body of British figurative painter, Lucian Freud[3] that was part of his original series entitled 'British Conflicts Series No. 2 – Art and Conflict') and a cheeky hoax played on respected London galleries, as Pegg (2011: 645) recounts:

April 1998 saw one of the more eccentric episodes in David's relationship with the art world when he was revealed as one of the perpetrators of an elaborate hoax: William Boyd's monograph on the life of Nat Tate, an obscure artist who had committed suicide in 1960, was published by 21 [Bowie's own fine arts publishing company from 1997] in a handsome edition with forewords by noted names in modern art. At an official launch several respected art critics made fools of themselves by sounding off about Nat Tate's life and work, but it didn't take long for someone to notice that the artist's name was blatantly concocted from 'National' and 'Tate', London's two biggest art galleries. Nat Tate was not merely an April Fool joke but a cutting exposure of the fragile web of reputation and credibility that holds the art world together.

To many he possesses the fire of genius; for others his 'pop' is hebetudinous. For Bowie has used William S. Burroughs' cut-up and random assemblage technique (Savage, 1980), itself inspired by Dadaists of the early twentieth century who rejected reason and logic in favour of irrationality and intuition, to assemble song lyrics that (seemingly) render any 'real' narrative obsolete. Bowie has revealed that his own process of writing is informed by words being ambiguously juxtaposed to facilitate polysemic interpretation while elevating the place of emotion. In the 90s, Bowie worked with a colleague to develop a software program called the 'Verbasizer' to achieve a similar goal. Bowie explained his process in the 1997 documentary *Inspirations*:

It will take the sentence and I will divide it up [into columns in the program] and then when I've got 3 or 4 or 5, sometimes I'll go as much as 20, 25 different sentences . . . and then I'll set it to randomise. And, it will take those 20 sentences and cut in between them all, all the time, picking-out, choosing different words from different columns and from different rows of sentences so what you end up with is a real kaleidoscope of meanings and topics and nouns and verbs all sort of slamming into each other. The choices I now make from this form I can then re-imbue it with a different quality if I want *or* take it as it writes itself.

In Bowie's compositions, a song's emotional intent being linked to the sonic and the visual has been imperative. The personae he has created standing central to his temporal musical style, linking the visual with the music; crucial to bringing forth an affective response in his audiences. For Bowie, 'the wrong words make you listen' ('Fantastic Voyage', *Lodger*, 1979). Assistant film director, Rory MacLean, on the film *Just a Gigolo* (1978), starring Bowie, came to know him well as they were two of only four English speakers on the project in West Berlin. He recalls from his time in a recording studio with Bowie that: '[w]ords never came before music, hence sound never simply echoed its meaning' (MacLean, 2014). This is 'language without articulation' (Deleuze, 1990: 89) and has more to do with the primal act of making sound and conveying emotion than it does with communicating specific words. Bowie uses his body as a metaphorical canvas; a sensorial 'canvas of flesh'.

Channelling affect into commodity consumption

The narrative of Bowie's physical body is predominantly one of androgyny but also that he is 'cyborg' and characterized by a sense of otherworldliness. For feminist author and professor of humanities and media studies, Camille Paglia (1990: 368), David Bowie in the 70s was the 'classic modern android' when his 'skull-like face seemed coldly artificial'. The affect of his controlled and haughty mask-like mannequin style for many Bowie-boys and Bowie-girls was sexually and/or fashionably desirable. For Nicholas Roeg's character of Thomas Jerome Newton in the film *The Man Who Fell To Earth*, his performative 'look' made the perfect alien outer-body. And, like Ziggy Stardust before him, the perfect metaphor for 'the outsider'.

While observing the inherent contradictions in the notion, aesthetic and cultural performances researcher, Philip Auslander (1998: 10) has argued that a romantic understanding of authenticity (with reference to the ideology of rock music broadly defined) necessitates the music be as sincere and genuine as the artist's expression. Arising in the 60s, a time that can be regarded as 'an individual and collective experiment in new forms of lifestyle and self-expression', this principle of authenticity signifies 'the inward turn and search for personal forms of liberation that connect the concerns of authenticity and personal expression', and naturalness and spontaneity were valued (Stevenson, 1996: 28). The problem for artists at this time was, however, that they also needed to promote their creative work via commercial means, thus becoming part of 'the system' they opposed. For some, this had an impact upon their perceived 'sincerity'. Stevenson (1996: 29–30) has reasoned that:

> This ambivalence has given rise to some of the most powerful myths of contemporary music. The distinction between popular music and rock

music has arisen from these contradictions. Rock is defined through the rejection of music that is characterized as soft, trivial, overly commercial and worthless. These features are seen as being characteristic of pop; whereas rock is concerned with authentic forms of rebellion, freedom, technical musicianship and uniqueness . . . that rock music uses similar means of promotion, selling techniques and commodification to popular music is of course obscured by this logic.

In similarly evaluating critically the concept of rock authenticity, Auslander (1999: 970) considers the generation of the effect of authenticity in rock music and performance as a matter of culturally determined convention, not an expression of essence. Moreover, 'semiotic markers of authenticity' vary between musical genre (jazz, soul, dance) as well as amongst subgenres (e.g., rock subgenres include art-rock, progressive rock, alternative rock etc.) and these interpretations are ascribed and can change over time. Auslander (1999: 70) provides the example of how '[t]ightly choreographed unison dance steps may be necessary for a soul vocal group to establish itself as authentic but would be a sign of inauthenticity in a rock group because they belie the effect of spontaneity rock audiences value'. The creation of the effect of authenticity is also 'a result of industrial practice: the music industry specifically sets out to endow its products with the necessary signs of authenticity'.

Recent research by Nunn and Biressi (2010: 49–50) finds that the economies of affect and intimacy now structure public life and authenticity in the public sphere, demanding and compelling performances of emotion and intimacy, or 'emotion work'. The authors have proposed that celebrities are emotional labourers, whereby the tensions and dilemmas at the heart of celebrity emotional labour, critically foreground the affective terrain which all individuals are forced to negotiate in the public realm in order to be regarded as socially successful. Useful to this understanding is the definition of 'emotion work' as proposed by sociologist Arlie Hochschild (1979, 2003) which is work requiring the artist to perform the 'right' feeling and ultimately even 'feel' the right feeling according to the rules of the setting and often in the service of commerce (Nunn and Biressi, 2010: 50). The ideology of intimacy and the primacy of emotion in performing authentic and normative subjecthood means that frequently the celebrity figure performing emotion is at the high (visible) end of a spectrum of emotional conduct (Nunn and Biressi, 2010). In other words, 'ideology of intimacy' have formed the conditions in which the celebrity now labours as an emotional subject in the public realm. This ideology operates via the conviction that social relationships are considered to be 'authentic' or 'real' mainly by virtue of their commitment to the 'inner psychological concerns of each person' (Sennett, 1974: 259).

As noted above, research into rock music performance and audience response reveals that the production of affect is of critical importance in negotiating the seeming authority and legitimacy of the music. Certainly during the 60s, David Bowie did present his own authenticity by positioning himself as a singer-songwriter so as to establish his sincerity with the audience (Stevenson, 2006: 30). Inspired by the Pop Art movement of the 1950s and 1960s, and principally the prime provocateur, Andy Warhol, Bowie's work came to challenge the theory of 'authenticity'. Pop Art simultaneously expanded upon and negated the ideals of Dadaism (1915–20s) while employing aspects of mass culture, including advertising, and everyday cultural objects and images (such as road signs, comic books, product packaging or company logos) with an agenda to collapse the distinctions between elite and mass cultural realms (Harrison, 2001). What Warhol suggested through the subject matter he chose and the way 'he' made 'his' art was that commercial and replicable art (as a commodity) was acceptable – and that good art sells. Stevenson (2006: 50) has highlighted the significance of such thinking for Bowie's own work:

> The idea was that art was inevitably caught up in a commercial setting, implying that cultural producers should seek to develop an aesthetic of mass consumption. This meant that artists could both draw aesthetic lessons from mass culture while seeking to work within commercial media.

Hence, it is equally the case that Bowie has been disingenuous frequently and his lyrics ironic if not ostensibly absurd. Moreover, Bowie's live performances are tightly choreographed and professionally controlled experiences, as Mackay (1984 in Thomson and Gutman, 1996: 195) recounts:

> Carefully timing the removal of his jacket. Selecting the right moment to casually roll up the sleeves of his shirt. Nonchalantly loosening his tie. In earlier rock eras, these movements might have been in the heat of the moment. But not now. Not for Bowie. He's in control.

In the context of contemporary challenges to 'authentic' productions of affect, it becomes reasonable to consider that the listening-body/viewer comes to experience authenticity of *intent*. In a recent study of repetition and authenticity in the performances of the touring musician, McKinna (2014: 68) concluded that:

> Each night or event within a performance is a simulacrum, not in the negative sense of an imitation, but in that they are the 'superior', hyperreal forms. Contained within these forms, or events, is an internal disparity that

allows for difference within itself. Considering each night's performance in this way allows for difference in repetition, whether small or large, and for each to contain at least the possibility of the sublime . . . Whether there is a desire to put on a good show, to get lost in the music or connect with the audience, the sincerity of intensions is what appears to be important.

While interpretations of authenticity remain layered, coupling the debate with consideration given to the machinations of affect adds much to understanding, as Thompson and Biddle (2013:17) suggest:

> paying attention to affect in this context represents a way of getting beyond the true/false binarism that has haunted scholarly attempts to understand the kinds of attachment invariably made in the name of communitarian authenticity: we can begin, that is, to understand authenticity and its cognates (the affective processes of attaching, feeling at home, feeling invested) as a kind of delicate cluster or node in the broader field, and as vulnerable but stubborn.

Multiple personae, Bowie's metaphors for conveying the didactic, are as much the result as they are the essence of his work. This is the fusion of art forms, vision and sound, that Bowie has creatively and performatively employed but for some, the question of the extent to which these sorts of guises are simply and precisely the effect of the popular music industry remains. In his chapter on popular music celebrity and affect, Marshall (1997) argued that the music industry is organized and structured by affect and he examined how cultural conditions evolved in the music industry that allowed for the development of music celebrity and of affective relationships with the star persona. Marshall (167) writes that:

> . . . in its perpetual construction of new phenomena, is an apparatus that tries to organize and focus the crowd's intensity into recognizable forms and products of consumption. The industry is an apparatus for the congealing of emotions and sentiments into recognizable sounds, images, and personalities that work to maintain the intensity of emotion. When the emotional intensity dissipates, the industry works to construct new forms of intense sentiments around new images, sounds, and personalities. In many senses, the popular music industry works to manage the contemporary crowd and, in fact, to organize its irrationality.

For Stevenson (2006: 13), the mass production of culture, lifestyle choices and leisure industries has led to the commodification of everyday life in western nations. The author emaphsizes that such cultural and lifestyle options are contingent upon the operation of a dominant capitalist economic system:

> The development of a commodity culture is as much about the ways in which subcultures and lifestyle groupings make culture as it is about capitalistic concerns seeking to manufacture dreams and forms of identification. For a form of popular music, star image or product to become successful, it will need to be marketed, constructed and consumed.

The studies of Ter Bogt *et al.* (2011), creating a typology of music listeners based on listening habits, demographics and emotional uses of music uncovered concrete and quantifiable links between affect-production in consumers and music. In essence, individuals who are highly involved in music are also the most moved by it. Such a correlation, when considered within the context of fan consumption practices is interesting, because one finds in this research that fans are far more likely to respond with high levels of affect to the preferred music and perhaps be primed to have high levels of affective responses to other, related music products, across cultural forms. Highly involved or committed fans are, therefore, 'primed' to respond emotionally to other cultural products issued by the celebrity (Ter Bogt *et al.*, 2011). Situated in this context, that Bowie recycles his 'poses' makes economic and 'pop artistic' sense (to the derision of some). He has promoted ice cream; alcohol via Crystal Jun Rock Japan (1979); Prima brand fruit drinks (within the clip for 'China Girl', 1983); and the fashionable Louis Vuitton (2013). Examples from his visual art include Major Tom (*Space Oddity*, 1969) resurging in his video clip for 'Ashes to Ashes' (*Scary Monsters . . . and Super Creeps*, 1980); Aladdin Sane (1973) is manifest in *Little Wonder* (1997); an impression of The Thin White Duke (*Station to Station*, 1976, *Low*, 1977) makes an appearance in 'The Stars (Are Out Tonight)' (*The Next Day*, 2013). And, years after 'Pierrot in Turquoise' (1967) and the clown of 'Ashes to Ashes', Bowie's Halloween version of 'Love is Lost' (*The Next Day*, 2013) sees life-size wooden puppet-bodies, one dressed as The Thin White Duke, cradling Scary's 'blue clown' in its arms as Bowie sings 'say hello to the lunatic men' over the self-referential melody from 'Ashes to Ashes' – but in this recent song. Bowie's work is frequently simultaneously artistically luminous (numerous collaborations attest to this including: dancer, choreographer and actor Linday Kemp; German countertenor, Klaus Nomi; musicians Carlos Alomar, Luther Vandross, Brian Eno, Nile Rodgers among many others; costume designer Kansai Yamamoto; director Floria Sigismondi; video/performance artist Tony Oursler) and an economically sound recycling strategy, and this reinforces his metaphors and adds to his (artist's) myth. In the process, he might just be invoking Deleuze's

1968 linear sense of time in which his performances can be appreciated as him trying to authentically (re)express thoughts and emotions that have been worked through in the past (Deleuze, 2004), but with a new interpretation and unapologetically in a commercial setting.

Despite any alleged commercial agenda, good art sells and David Bowie, as singer-songwriter, embodied performer and artist, escapes the perspective given him by language, by music and by image. His artistic concern has been to transform his words, music and visions into a thoughtfulness that might expand others' perspicacity. By using metaphor and metonym throughout his visual and sonic creations, he has been largely freed from the constraints of merely describing the world; metaphor and metonym have been able to re-evaluate it in new ways by breaking the association between language and things. Borrowing from the Dadaists (via William S. Burroughs), his own sonic and visual assemblage meant that fissures were created; new and multiple meanings rendered possible and valid, going beyond both the creator and viewing/listening-body. Such sensations of incongruence are of course essential to the effect of his creative execution. Bowie presents us with the insidious nature of the temporality of existence and the incompleteness of being, he helps us plumb 'the depths' by critically questioning accepted conventions to confidently reject the surface of socially constructed truths, subtly taking control of our breathing, offering us pause. His jarring of metaphoric rhythms imparts a challenge to the patterns of our own engagement so that we might be forced to confront the vehicle for our discomfort. *E'sporca lezione del cuore. Cade su orecchie sorde.*

Notes

1 Through a critical review of research on the medical, political and cultural meaning of weight in the USA, law Professor, Paul Campos (2004: 95–6) revealed that:

> What American Culture considers appropriate is a body that signals its owner is in control of that body's desires. This, fundamentally, is the metaphorical significance of thinness in America today. In other words, [what] Americans – and especially American elites – . . . consider most desirable is a body whose appearance signals a triumph of the will over desire itself. Thus bodily virtue is not so much indicated by thinness per se, but rather by an *achieved* thinness.

2 The original 1970 US release of *The Man Who Sold the World* saw a colourful cartoon-like cover drawing by Michael J. Weller that featured a cowboy in front of the Cane Hill mental asylum located in Coulsdon in the London Borough of Croydon, England (as of February 2013 it is no longer there). This was the

asylum where Terry Jones, Bowie's older half-brother, was periodically admitted. In the original image, the cowboy has his mouth open as if saying something but only an empty dialogue balloon appears – calling to mind the blank space on *The Next Day* (2013) album and perhaps inviting viewers to insert their own tag.

3   The segment of Laura Ashley wallpaper features a repeat print of Bowie's portrait of artist Lucian Freud, OM (1922–2011). Freud's artistic task was not to flatter. Indeed, his images, many of them highly detailed nudes, were frank if not stark, with few precedents in the art of the human form. Bowie's impression of Freud was originally included in a limited edition box made available at the War Child fashion event Pagan Fun Wear, held at London's Saatchi Gallery, on Midsummer's Eve 1995.

References

Ahmed, Sara. 2004 *The Cultural Politics of Emotion*. Edinburgh: Edinburgh University Press.

Auslander, Philip. 1998. 'Seeing is believing: live performance and the discourse of authenticity in rock culture'. *Literature and Psychology*, 44 (4): 1–26, http://lmc.gatech.edu/~auslander/publications/seeing.pdf, accessed 11 May 2013.

Auslander, Philip. 1999. *Liveness: Performance in a Mediatized Culture*. New York: Routledge.

Bowie, David. 1995. *Inside Outside*, documentary shown on German ZDF TV, 30 September.

Buckley, David. 2005. *Strange Fascination: David Bowie, The Definitive Story*. London: Virgin Books.

Campos, Paul. 2004. *The Obesity Myth: Why America's Obsession with Weight is Hazardous to Your Health*. New York: Gotham Books.

Cardinal, Roger. 1972. *Outsider Art*. London: Studio Vista.

Copetas, Craig. 1974. 'Beat godfather meets glitter Mainman'. *Rolling Stone*, 28 February, 14–17.

De Quincey, Thomas. 1827. 'On murder considered as one of the fine arts'. First paper, *Blackwood's Magazine*, February.

Deleuze, Gilles. 1969, 1990. *The Logic of Sense*. Translated by Mark Lester with Charles Stivale, edited by Constantin V. Boundas (1990). New York: Columbia University Press.

Deleuze, Gilles and Félix Guattari. 1980, 1987. *A Thousand Plateaus: Capitalism and Schizophrenia*. Translated by Brian Massumi (1987). Minneapolis: University of Minnesota Press.

Deleuze, Gilles. 2004. *Difference and Repetition*. Translated from the original French by Paul Patton. London: Bloomsbury.

Finn, Deborah Elizabeth. 1983. 'Moon and gloom: David Bowie's frustrated messianism'. *Commonweal*, 110 (9), September, 467–8.

Gauntlet, David. 2008. *Media, Gender and Identity: An Introduction*, 2nd edition. New York: Routledge.

Goffman, Erving. 1959. *The Presentation of Self in Everyday Life*. New York: Doubleday.

Harrison, Sylvia. 2001. *Pop Art and the Origins of Post-Modernism*. Cambridge: Cambridge University Press.

Hochschild, Arlie Russell. 1979. 'Emotion work, feeling rules, and social structure'. *American Journal of Sociology*, 85 (3), November, 551–74.

Hochschild, Arlie Russell. 2003. *The Commercialization of Intimate Life: Notes from Home and Work*. Berkeley: University of California Press.

James, Alison. 2013. 'Creative reflection and employability'. Transcript of a talk given at the Historians Reflect Event, University of Wolverhampton, 6 February, www2.wlv.ac.uk/celt/Projects/historians_reflect/Alison_James_Presentation_Transcript.pdf, accessed 1 May 2014.

Lakoff, George and Mark Johnson. 1981. 'Conceptual metaphor in everyday language'. In Mark Johnson (ed.) *Philosophical Perspectives on Metaphor*. Minneapolis: University of Minnesota Press, 286–328.

Lindbergs, Kimberly. 2008. 'David Bowie is the image (1967)'. *Cinebeats*, 28 October, http://cinebeats.wordpress.com/2008/10/27/david-bowie-is-the-image–1967/, accessed 21 May 2014.

MacLean, Rory. 2014. 'The Berlin landmarks that inspired Bowie'. In 'European Destinations' section of *The Financial Times*, January, www.ft.com/intl/cms/s/2/b20113b0–8753–11e3–9c5c–00144feab7de.html#axzz32shJNb8u, accessed 20 May 2014.

Marshall, David P. 1997. 'The meanings of the popular music celebrity: the construction of distinctive authenticity'. In *Celebrity and Power: Fame in Contemporary Culture*. Minneapolis: University of Minnesota Press, 150–84.

McKinna, Daniel Robert. 2014. 'The touring musician: repetition and authenticity in performance'. *Journal of the International Association for the Study of Popular Music*, 4 (1), 56–72.

Muldoon, Mark. 2002. *On Ricoeur*. London: Wadsworth/Thomson Learning.

Nietzsche, Friedrich. 1887, 2013. *On the Geneology of Morality: A Polemic*. Translated into English by Michael A. Scaarppitti (2013). London: Penguin Books.

Nunn, Heather and Anita Biressi. 2010. ' "A trust betrayed": celebrity and the work of emotion'. *Celebrity Studies*, 1 (1), 49–64.

Paglia, Camille. 1990. *Sexual Personae: Art and Decadence from Nefertiti to Emily Dickinson*. London: Yale University Press.

Pegg, Nicholas. 2011. *The Complete David Bowie*, 6th edition. London: Titan Books.

Redmond, Sean. 2013. 'Who am I now? Remembering the enchanted dogs of David Bowie'. *Celebrity Studies Journal*, 4 (3), 380–3.

Ricoeur, Paul. 1991. 'Word, polysemy, metaphor: creativity in language'. In Mario J. Valdés (ed.) *A Ricoeur Reader: Reflection and Imagination*. Toronto: University of Toronto Press, 65–85.

Rook, Jean. 1976. 'Waiting for Bowie – and finding a genius who insists he's really a clown'. In Elizabeth Thomson and David Gutman (eds) *The Bowie Companion* (1996). Cambridge: Da Capo Press, 133–5.

Savage, Jon. 1980. 'The gender bender'. *The Face*, November, 16–20.

Sennett, Richard. 1974. *The Fall of Public Man*. New York: Norton.

Spitz, Marc. 2009. *Bowie: A Biography*. New York: Crown Publishers.

Stevenson, Nick. 2006. *David Bowie, Fame, Sound and Vision*. Cambridge: Polity Press.

Stevenson, Nick. 2009. 'Talking to Bowie fans: masculinity, ambivalence and cultural citizenship'. *European Journal of Cultural Studies*, 12 (1), 79–98.

Ter Bogt, Tom F.M., Juul Mulder, Quinten, A.W. Raaijmakers and Saoirse Nic Gabhainn. 2011. 'Moved by music: a typology of music listeners'. *Psychology of Music*, 39 (2), April, 147–63.

Thompson, Marie and Ian Biddle. 2013. 'Introduction: somewhere between the signifying and the sublime'. In Marie Thompson and Ian Biddle (eds) *Sound, Music, Affect: Theorizing Sonic Experience*. New York: Bloomsbury, 1–24.

Thomson, Elizabeth and David Gutman. 1996. *The Bowie Companion*. Cambridge: Da Capo Press.

11

The Whiteness of David Bowie

Sean Redmond

Introduction

David Bowie has been a figure that has readily drawn attention to both the empowering symbolic markers of whiteness, and to the contradictory ways in which it is embodied. On the one hand, Bowie's 'hyper whiteness' (Bonnett, 2000) is the epitome of elite cool and a rarefied, higher-order form of upper class masculinity – he embodies a translucent aristocratic sensibility that sits at the apex of identity power relations. On the other hand, his whiteness is also the material out of which an alien androgyny and an unstable sexuality emerge. Bowie's star image draws attention to the cloak of invisibility that whiteness usually travels under, uncovering whiteness in the process, while creating the very conditions for its representational and cultural power to be sustained.

In this chapter, through the lens of one year, 1983, I will examine the contradictory ways in which Bowie embodies whiteness. The analysis will concentrate on three of the most popular and well-received texts and performances of that year: Bowie as the simmering vampire, John Blaylock, from *The Hunger* (Scott, 1983); the enigmatic character of Major Jack 'Strafer' Celliers from *Merry Christmas Mr Lawrence* (Oshima, 1983); and the blond orchestrator/improvisator from the music video, *Let's Dance*.

I have chosen to read Bowie's whiteness through this shortened window of temporality to enable me to draw into the analysis the historical and cultural issues of the period in question. The year 1983 registers as that in which whiteness is acutely imagined to be under threat from the 'Asian tiger' and transforming geopolitical realities, its own languid anti-corporeality, the AIDS 'epidemic' and the rise of racism in Europe and elsewhere – realities which require it to reposition its power relations with the sexual and ethnic Other.

The whiteness in/of David Bowie speaks particularly eloquently to this historical moment.

Structurally, I will first set out to define whiteness as a type of representational construction. I will then explore Bowie's particularized version of whiteness through the three case studies listed above, taking each in turn. I will also look at the key historical contexts as I explore each case study, as well as in a conclusion that draws textual analysis and history together in order to 'place' Bowie's hyper-whiteness in the context of the fiery year of 1983.

Whiteness matters

Like the colour itself, whiteness is a screen for projecting the political phantoms of the past on the unfilled surfaces of the present; but at the same time it resembles what house painters call a primer, a base colour that regulates all others.

BHAHA, 1998: 22

In representational terms one can argue that whiteness is imagined as an identity that has 'the power not to be named', and where to-be-white is *just to be human* (Gabriel, 1998: 13). In this understanding, whiteness can be conceived as an invisible meta-identity that sits above all else in the spectrum of subjectivities and where it is very often given an *a priori*, logocentric status that raises it above and beyond all other social relations. As Richard Dyer (1997: 9) notes:

> The equation of being white with being human secures a position of power. White people have power and believe that they think, feel and act like and for all people; white people, unable to see their particularity, cannot take account of other people's; white people create the dominant images of the world and don't quite see that they construct the world in their own image; white people set standards of humanity by which they are bound to succeed and others bound to fail.

Nonetheless, whiteness is also constituted through a set of contradictions, or what Elizabeth Ellsworth (1997: 226) calls its 'double binds'. When whiteness is explicitly brought into representation – when it is made textually visible through symbolism and metaphor – it is understood to be an unstable and contradictory identity. The representation of whiteness becomes one that actually involves a *life* and *death* struggle.

On the one hand, when whiteness is made symbolically visible it is essentially connected to the highest ideals of human civilization: to purity, innocence, rationalism, naturalism, and to the 'higher' motifs of Christianity, such as ascending angels and the concept of 'spirit'.

On the other hand, this purity in spirit and thought is also considered to be death-like because it necessarily brings white people closer to, or in touch with, the lack of life, corporeality and sex drive that such higher ideals bring to bear on them as white subjects. When one reaches the highest ideals of whiteness one literally disappears into the ether. In fact, one is already dead, since 'the very things that make us white endanger the reproduction of whiteness' (Dyer, 1997: 27).

Idealized white masculinity embodies this contradiction in particular ways. Perfected white masculinity sits at the apex of what constitutes appropriate civil and civilized behaviour. These types of white *gentle*men are upper-class, well-educated and refined, a subjectivity that both Frantz Fanon (1986) and Richard Dyer (1997) have argued has been used to differentiate them from 'other' races, and from the lower classes. Idealized white masculinity is marked by rationalism and advanced thinking, and by a series of dress and behavioural codes that define hyper-white males as enlightened beings. As Richard Dyer (1997: 120) illustrates, eighteenth- and nineteenth-century (self-commissioned) portraiture evidenced this synthesis between civility, superiority and white embodiment:

> The dark clothing of men, especially respectable men, and the upturned face combined with overhead lighting, became the standard way to produce an image of (ideal, privileged) white masculinity that showed it to be touched with a spark of light.

In paintings such as James Northcote's portrait of Henry Fuseli (1778), what might be termed 'hyper-white' men display their civility through their body postures and projected gaze/vision. They are represented as refined, cultured, expansive in outlook and demeanour; and in terms of the painting's hue, of course, spiritually white. In effect, whiteness/lightness is doubly encoded in the painting through the way white skin is lit so that it looks as if it literally lights up the world.

This civil empowerment grants white men privileged access to, and agency in, making the world in their own image. White male privilege acts like 'an invisible weightless knapsack of special provisions, assurances, tools, maps, guides, codebooks, passports, visas, clothes, compass, emergency gear and blank cheques' (McIntosh, 1988: 1–2).

On the other hand, perfected white masculinity is imagined not to be particularly sexual or reproductive, in part because what is being delineated and denied is the carnality of the pure male body. The idealized white male body often lacks a sex drive because of this over-investment in the cerebral; it is as if one cannot be ideally white and have a (hard) cock and a brain at the same time.

Idealized white masculinity can in fact become an almost literal form of death for those who embody it. It is represented through ghost-like imagery and metaphors and exists within a tradition of representing white people as zombies or the epitome of the walking dead. As Richard Dyer (1997: 211) writes in relation to *Night of the Living Dead* (Romero, 1969): 'There is no difference between whites, living or dead; all whites bring death and, by implication, all whites are dead (in terms of human feeling) . . . Whites are dead, bring death and cannot stand that others live.' Death is often visualized in paintings, horror and folk stories as ghostly white: one only has to think of the ash-white vampire as the epitome of this, one who is 'ghastly white, disgustingly cadaverous, without the blood of life that would give colour' (Dyer, 1997: 210). The figure of the vampire is important here because 'just as the vampires' whiteness conveys their own deadness, so too their bringing of death is signalled by whiteness – their victims grow pale, the colour leaves their cheeks, life ebbs away' (Dyer, 1997: 210).

Connected to this is the theme where illness or ill health is often represented in health and beauty adverts through pale skin, as if white embodiment is actually a form of corporeal disappearance or wasting away (Williamson, 1986). In short, death seems to be much in evidence when it comes to 'thinking' idealized white masculinity. Nonetheless, this double bind of whiteness can be considered to be one of its ontological strengths since (while) it is an:

> Impossible identity, a fiction, something never fully achieved or achievable. It is never pure or real. And yet . . . despite such instability, individuals or groups cannot, at this present historical moment, destabilize whiteness enough to escape it, make it collapse under the weight of its own paradoxes, or ever speak or act outside of it.
>
> Ellsworth, 1997: 266

This instability in the way whiteness is represented and embodied helps secure its position as the dominant form of cultural identity, one that is imbued with real social power. The loosely defined borders of what it means to be white, the absence effect (Dyer, 1997) at the core of white identity, allows white people to move more freely in, out and through other non-white identities. This 'travel pass' awards them a subjectivity that cannot be fixed, rooted or pinned down, and as such allows them to try on and play with 'Other' identities through 'passing' games and performativity (hooks). It creates for whiteness, as Richard Dyer observes, 'the sense of a border that might be crossed and a hierarchy that might be climbed . . . a dynamic that has enthralled people who have had any chance of participating in it' (1997: 20).

These are a set of definitions, positions and provocations that I would now like to employ to begin to read the whiteness of David Bowie.

The matter of Bowie's whiteness

Bowie's star image is one built out of the contradictorily embodied and performative signifiers of idealized male whiteness. He has carried these markers of hyper-whiteness through various characters, roles and performances, including the figure of the wan (alien) messiah in *The Man Who Fell To Earth* (Roeg, 1976), the coke-addled Thin White Duke on the album *Station to Station* (1976), the reborn, heroic *Übermensch* on the album *"Heroes"* (1977), the deathly vampire in *The Hunger* and the enigmatic English major in *Merry Christmas Mr Lawrence*. In all these incarnations Bowie is physically hyper-white: pale, thin, ethereal, often blond, while his mannerisms speak of an elite educated background (even if the star's truth is different). Bowie's idealized whiteness emerges more generally through his brilliance as a musical innovator and thinker, taking on the tropes of the over-cerebral inventor, to cement his position as (a) head of all other subjectivities.

And yet Bowie's higher-order whiteness is at same time marked by crisis and disintegration. The whitely otherness of Bowie removes him from 'normal' human relations, his star image appears as anti-reproductive and immaculate. Bowie appears untouchable, marked by higher-order values and abilities, a living white messiah amongst the unwashed masses or inferior Others.

But Bowie is also sexual, decidedly transgressive, moving freely between gender and sexual identities and relations – a position granted him by his privileged position as a super-white male icon. Bowie's idealized whiteness allows him to travel into other subjective dimensions. His own musings, song lyrics and interviews have explicitly placed him within this fractured discourse of hyper-whiteness. As Doggett (2012) writes:

When he described The Thin White Duke of 'Station To Station', he was effectively condemning himself: 'A very Aryan, fascist-type; a would-be romantic with absolutely no emotion at all but who spouted a lot of neo-romance.' Michael Lippman, Bowie's manager during 1975, said his client 'can be very charming and friendly, and at the same time he can be very cold and self-centred'. Bowie, he added, wanted to rule the world.

Bowie encapsulates the double binds of whiteness, then, but in a way that is seemingly self-reflective and critical of its power. And yet, his power as a star rests on his idealized whiteness, and he maintains this power through the way he negotiates its operations and processes. Bowie threatens whiteness and yet ensures its survival.

This is particularly true of 1983, his 'comeback' year, which is marked by the release of the internationally best-selling album *Let's Dance*, the 'Serious Moonlight' stadium tour, and two aforementioned major movie releases (*The Hunger* and *Merry Christmas Mr Lawrence*). One can read into his output and performances that year a complex embodiment of whiteness that not only speaks to his star image but the cultural conditions of the age; a time when whiteness and various forms of Otherness were in open play and contestation. Let me now take in turn the three examples from Bowie's oeuvre that I mentioned would be under analysis in the introduction to this chapter.

The hunger of whiteness

In *The Hunger*, Bowie plays John Blaylock, a vampire first 'turned' by Miriam (Catherine Deneuve) in the eighteenth century, with the promise of eternal life. Set in contemporary New York, John and Miriam take on the personae of a wealthy couple, teaching classical music at their opulent New York townhouse. However, they only have one student, the androgynous tomboy violinist, Alice Cavender (Beth Ehlers). At the date John turns 300 years of age he begins to age rapidly. It is then revealed that Miriam has lied to him: John has been given immortality but not ever-lasting youth. John's decrepit body is eventually placed in a coffin in the house's attic where all of Miriam's aged vampiric lovers are left to anguish and misery. She then takes Dr Sarah Roberts (Susan Sarandon) as her next lover but is usurped by her, and the army of near-dead vampires who rise to take their revenge. The film ends in London, with an aged Miriam now entombed, and a triumphant Sarah grooming her next would-be-immortal lovers.

I would like to suggest that *The Hunger* is centrally a film about the double binds of whiteness and that Bowie is key to the way this is materialized. It is also a film that eternalizes and damns whiteness, and one that places it under the threat of its own extinction, driven by a wanton consumption logic in which its border crossings lead to contamination. The reality of AIDS, the incidence of which was rapidly rising at the time, haunts the film, but here it is a plague that whiteness itself produces because of its need to destroy the Other, and yet at the same time the Other is the force that must be expelled. Whiteness is under threat from its own subjectivity and the sexual and racial Other in the film. Bowie embodies this dual threat while also acting as a recuperative sign of these troubled times.

The opening scene is essential to the way this paradoxical dichotomy is established. Set in an underground nightclub, and then the Blaylock's townhouse, and juxtaposed with what are perceived to be disconnected parallel cuts to a laboratory where one primate is eating another, we witness hedonism, sex and death wrapped in one another. John and Miriam visit the club to select and then drain and kill their latest victims. Dressed in 30s fashion suits and dark shades, they embody the cool excesses of the 80s in which the film is set. In the background the gothic band Bauhaus are playing the track 'Bela Lugosi's Dead', an ironic and pretentious take on what will eventuate in the film.

Bowie and Deneuve carry into the film star images honed out of idealized whiteness and the contradictions it brings. Deneuve's Miriam carries the presence of an ice-maiden, cool and detached, as well as a sexual experimenter and temptress, to the scene; while Bowie's John is illuminated in ways that suggest he carries the 'spark' of whiteness in his genes. The Bauhaus modernism reflected in the clothes they wear and the design of their townhouse suggests a sterile functionality that epitomizes one of the binds of whiteness. However, they are also signified as up-market swingers, bisexual and promiscuous, as they 'hunt' the scene for their next sexual prey. As Deborah Michel (2007) suggests:

They reflect a spectator position of perversely polymorphous sexuality. Here, the spectator's gaze might well be that of a heterosexual male, but it might also be a gay or bisexual male – or female – gaze which appreciates the images of both Miriam and John. This slippage of gender in the assumed spectatorial gaze and on the screen represents only the first in a series of border transgressions to come; masculine and feminine, sex and violence, animal and human, love and death, all shift uneasily like quicksand in this narrative.

What is central to these border crossings is the ontology of whiteness and the star images brought to the text by Bowie and Deneuve. The hunger that whiteness has for the Other has led to it being contaminated. The cross-cutting to the image of the primate cannibalizing its mate acts as a metaphor for the consumption logic of whiteness; an unconscious reference to the simian primitivism of the ethnic Other; and to the mythic birth of AIDS in a laboratory run and controlled by white scientists. The Other is also living in whiteness' neighbourhood, and whiteness employs its travel pass to cruise the forbidden areas outside of its subjectivity.

Bowie's polymorphous and transgressive star image is central here: he brings the animal to the scene, but this is an animal without emotion or empathy. He is a fusion figure: suave and playful, and deadly dangerous. This is the 'Bowie' from Chicago and Berlin, a thin white duke who believes in his own superiority, hell-bent on destroying those around him. He wants sex but sex that destroys – this isn't reproductive sex in the traditional sense, but only selflessly regenerative. It is Bowie/John's sexual conquests and violent overcoming that attempts to secure his future and the eternal future of whiteness.

Whiteness is immortalized in the film and yet it is always close to negation and termination. The vampire myth of eternal life naturalizes the power of whiteness while simultaneously making it invisible. As Michel (2007) argues:

> When Sarah is stricken with the unnatural disease of vampirism and lays feverish and wasting, Miriam sits at her bedside with implacable poise; she remains fresh and beautiful, a carrier of the plague who does not sicken or die of the disease, and can be perceived as a pariah, an AIDs-infected 'Typhoid Mary'.

However, for whiteness to remain eternal it has to live off the flesh of Others and this brings it into mortal danger. In these zones of contagion and contamination we also witness the possibility of its demise.

The ageing of John is central here because it provides an image of whiteness that is fragile and paper-thin. It suggests that whiteness is close to expiration and has to find constant ways to remain a dominant subjectivity. At the end of the film, when the army of vampire-zombies rise up to take revenge on Miriam we glimpse its double binds: the immortal gentlemen who refuse to be silenced or usurped even as they disintegrate into dust.

Richard Dyer suggests that the theme of white people belonging to an endangered species is increasingly found across a range of contemporary cultural texts which, 'may suggest that the suspicion of nothingness and the death of whiteness is, as far as white identity goes, the cultural dominant of our times, that we really do feel we're played out' (Dyer, 1997: 217). In particular, according to Dyer, the threat of extinction haunts the representation of white men who are shown to suffer a terrifying identity crisis over their place within the social and economic order. Such white men struggle to hold down a 'regular' job, or to protect their family, and the white community, from those racial Others who threaten its stability, their racial purity.

One can read Bowie's star image in this respect, albeit with a particular inflection. The image of a thin white duke is at the point of expiration in the film, as it is in Bowie's performativity. It no longer fits with the mood of the 1980s. That John ages and descends to dust allows another version of whiteness to emerge, one that sits more easily with contemporary times. His death also gives birth to another Bowie identity, one that is taken up in the *Let's Dance* album. Before that though, I would like to examine his role in *Merry Christmas Mr Lawrence* in terms of how his whiteness functions as a complex, if ultimately empowering form of spirit.

White spirit

In *Merry Christmas Mr Lawrence*, a Japanese-British film that also came out in 1983, Bowie's character Major Jack Celliers is defined by idealized whiteness in terms of an 'inner spirit that is indestructible', and a number of biblical and Christian religious motifs that assign him the qualities of the Messiah. At the level of characterization, Celliers' blond hair and Etonian background places him at the apex of white social hierarchy, although his nickname, Strafer (soldier's soldier), renders him ordinary, one of the boys. In the film he is both extraordinary and ordinary, capturing the qualities of its star, and of whiteness in microcosm.

There is another dimension to Celliers' characterization that centres on his idealized beauty and empowered sexuality: Captain Yonoi (Ryuichi Sakamoto), the young camp commandant, is attracted to him and this undermines and problematizes the binary oppositions between straight and gay, West and East. Bowie's feminized Celliers is Yoni's masculine Other, and yet Yoni is also feminized and therefore part of the Orientalist tradition in which, 'the man is depicted as feminine, weak' (Said, 1978: 2). Yoni adores Celliers' spirit, his idealized whiteness no less, and is enthralled by it, ultimately confirming an unequal Orientalist power set of relations between them.

The white messiah motif is presented through various scenes and allusions: Jack Celliers' initials are JC while one of the first scenes in the movie has Celliers prepare to be executed in Christ-like fashion in a classic crucifix pose. However, this is a mock/mocking execution – there are no real bullets in the execution guns – and so Celliers undergoes a kind of resurrection in the film. Later Celliers gives out food from a woven basket to feed his fellow prisoner soldiers after Yoni has ordered a fast – reminiscent of the way Jesus gave out fish and loaves of bread – while Celliers is repeatedly shown sacrificing himself for others, including a fellow officer who is about to be slain by Yoni. He has only once let someone take a beating, his young brother, and the dreams that haunt him are like visions. Reflecting this Christ-like persona, the Japanese soldiers are in awe of Celliers, as if he possess a magic that they cannot control or see – this in effect is again the ontological power of idealized whiteness over the Other.

Bowie is a perfect star fit for this role; he has been a white alien messiah figure not only in and through stage performances, fan adoration, but in the character of Newton in *The Man Who Fell To Earth*. Bowie's star image authenticates the role he is playing, cementing the relationship between idealized whiteness, spiritual power and worship.

There is one key scene I would like to focus on from the film: the forbidden kissing scene. In this scene, Celliers intervenes in an execution. He nonchalantly strides through the camp to stand in the way of Yoni and the would-be victim. Yoni pushes him to ground, using Celliers' face to force the separation. The contact is violently sexual; a confused mixture of love and hate. Celliers then proceeds to hold, and kiss, Yoni on each cheek, which is captured in quick edits, and slow-motion cuts. Yoni's eyes are full of tears, while Celliers appears detached and aloof – a man-god before the worshipping Yoni. This is a scene that powerfully distils the ontology of idealized whiteness and of Bowie's star progeny. Bowie's Celliers carries the weight of the knapsack of white history and religion to bear, while the kiss itself has echoes of turning the other cheek. There is an aggressive and passive dynamic at play, with Yoni weak Oriental flesh, and Celliers spirit and transcendental light.

Celliers in effect consumes the exotic Other in a process of exchange that Sara Ahmed (2000) refers to as 'stranger fetishism'. Ahmed argues that through consuming the Other one is both making the 'strange' familiar and subordinate to the Western subject: since such consumption confirms the 'subject's ability to "be oneself" by getting closer to, and incorporating the stranger (a form of proximity which produces the stranger as *that which can be taken in*)' (2000: 133).

In the context of 1983 this is particularly telling as the first wave of the economic Asian tiger took ascendancy, and where Japanese companies such as Sony were making global acquisitions and entering the cultural market through their entertainment streams. In this light, *Merry Christmas Mr Lawrence* becomes a vehicle for a postcolonial global exchange where what takes place is the reinforcement of racial difference, and the re-centring of white culture in a master/slave relationship with the Other.

David Bowie has a long history with Japonisme, particularly in terms of fashion and costumes for his stage shows. For example, Kansai Yamamoto designed a range of outfits for the 1973 *Aladdin Sane* tour, including a cloak decorated with kanji characters. This association or appropriation of the Other can be argued to be part of the commodification of the Orient that takes place in a global marketplace. Jackie Stacey suggests that: 'By consuming global products, the Western subject and the exotic other are thus reaffirmed even as such a dichotomy is apparently transcended by the appeal to a universal global culture' (2000: 104).

Bowie's 'Let's Dance' video arguable plays out this consuming the Other in a very particular way, utilizing Aboriginal culture to, on the one hand, critique whiteness, and, on the other, essentialize racial difference.

Bowie's dancing dirt

The video to 'Let's Dance' narrates the unequal relationship between two young indigenous Australians and the white power structures that operate on them. The video sets up a binarized division between the 'authenticity' of Aboriginal culture and its rural or outback origins, and the exploitative modernity and urbanism of white Australian culture. Bowie is the omnipresent narrator – a figure who seems to transcend both realities while investing in Aboriginal myths and contexts. It is his starry and luminescent whiteness that carries his authority in the video, however, reinforcing the subjectivity that is supposedly being undermined.

We first meet Bowie in the Carinda Hotel, a one-room pub in rural New South Wales, Australia, where parts of the video are shot. He is dressed in creamy white trousers, white shoes, lightly striped white shirt, green tie, and his hands are sheathed in immaculate, rolled white gloves. The rest of the patrons in the bar are marked by their blue-collar backgrounds – sweat, muscle, physicality – or by their Aboriginal identity which allows them to 'naturally' dance to the rhythm emerging from Bowie's fiery red Stratocaster. This is the first time we are introduced to Joelene King and Terry Richards (both cast from Sydney's Aboriginal-Islanders Dance Theatre), who dance with ease and perfect timing. The only one securely white in the scene is Bowie himself.

The spotless gloves are a powerful signifier in this respect. They protect or shield the hands from dirt, reinforcing the notion that Bowie is separate from the unclean environs he finds himself in. He is 'matter out of place' (Douglas, 1966, 2002), even as he attempts to create a condition in which Aboriginal Otherness is set free. Dirt pollutes and sullies all the pure things that it touches – it metaphorically brings sin to innocence, sex to Madonna. But dirt and the pure signifiers of whiteness need one another to come into being; without dirt, there would be no clean; without dark there would be no light; and without black there would be no white. Ultimately, dirt/clean, sin/purity, dark/light, black/white 'are the products of cultural systems of classification which create order' (Woodward, 1997: 34).

The red high-heeled shoes are employed to seemingly produce and undermine these classifications of difference. When Joelene King puts on the red shoes for the first time she becomes possessed by the modernist dance steps they offer her, losing her own ethnic identity in the process. The scene is set in the Blue Mountains and moments after she puts the red shoes on a nuclear explosion engulfs the skyline, a surreal metaphor between cultural appropriation and annihilation. However, what is interesting here is the way Bowie plays the role of the songmaster and seductive magician – it is his calling to 'put on the red shoes and dance the blues' that entreats Joelene to try the shoes on. Bowie appears, then, as a postcolonial figure, offering guidance at the same time as he criticizes the position from which he enunciates. It is a position which undermines his whiteness while cleverly situating it as prophetic.

The next time we see the red shoes worn they are on the feet of a suited female secretary as she traverses the floor of a machine shop in downtown Sydney. Bowie accompanies her, now in the guise of a flash factory owner. The clash or difference between clean and dirty is again established in this scene: Terry Roberts is seen sweating over a huge lathe, exploited and far removed from the rural background where the video ultimately suggests he belongs. Bowie has again been given the travel pass that allows white people of power to move through different identities and to comment on them.

The red shoes become the object that seems to have drawn them to the city to work. In striking metaphoric terms, we see Terry pulling the lathe up a hill, and Joelene scrub and wash the road that he advances up. Scenes where they adopt or pass as a white couple – walking along a golden beach, having dinner out at an expensive restaurant, going to an art gallery and shopping for fine clothes, follow this. In the latter two instances, however, we can begin to see the facade crumble: they create their own Aboriginal artwork on the wall of the art gallery, and mysteriously buy the pair of red shoes that brought them here in the first place. The video is taking a dig at cultural exploitation, and at the absent heart of white consumption. We next see Joelene, Terry and extended family returned to the outback, the red shoes trampled upon and left behind, as they return to their ancestral home, barefoot and supposedly free.

There is of course an issue with such a positioning: it frames Aboriginal culture as naturally authentic, rural, reproducing an essentialized myth at the same time the video seeks to criticize the cold modernity of whiteness. Idealized whiteness ultimately holds the video together through Bowie's white-gloved orchestration. At the end of the video three images dominate:

Joelene and Terry are framed looking back at Sydney harbour as an ominous helicopter flies overhead; Bowie is captured in the bush, a blazing sun setting beside him, playing with passionate intensity the riff to the song; and then we finally see Joelene and Terry dancing to it at the top of a mountain. In the video this creates a favourable binary between the rural and the urban, Aboriginal culture and whiteness, and yet undermines this through the way Bowie literally calls the tune. And yet, out in the outback, Bowie seems to be set free; it is as if the Aboriginal Other is making its mark on his spotless white body.

The 80s was a key period in which white people began embracing racialized Otherness in fundamentally profound ways. Alastair Bonnett suggests that this is because, 'to be outside whiteness is to be outside the cold and instrumental realm of modernity' and 'the forging of non-whiteness as an identity that is *not* alienated and *not* dominated by instrumental logic' is both liberating and life confirming for the whites who yearn for some sort of human authenticity denied to them in and through their 'mechanical' whiteness (Bonnett, 2000: 78). The purchasing of ethnic products, the travel to exotic 'far away' destinations and the 'wholesale introjection of Eastern beliefs and practices (such as religions) into the West' (Stacey, 2000: 123) suggest a modern world where whiteness is being left behind if never ultimately rejected.

Alistair Bonnett has examined the mythopoeic men's movement that emerged in North America in the 80s and 90s as a concrete example of white people's flight into the arms of primitivism. Bonnett argues that 'mythopoeic men are creatively reworking colonialist fantasies of non-western societies and landscapes' (2000: 95), and, moreover, that mythopoeticism represents an attempt to reaffirm and reinstate white male power in response to an increasing feeling of powerlessness in the modern world. Mythopoeic men venture into wilderness regions not only because of the way they 'may experience freedom from social constraint, and a sense of liberation' (2000: 103) but because of the 'cult of the primitive' who they imagine they can find there and can become like.

This incarnation of Bowie seems finally caught in this flight from (his) idealized whiteness. He is not only commenting on racism in Australia, negotiating its form, but is ingesting the authenticity of the Other as he does so. This is also true of the video to *China Girl* where the love of the exotic Orient is played out through sexual desire, drug addiction and a cryptic critique of hyper-whiteness in terms of its historical imperialism.

One can argue that at the core of a white longing for primitivism and easternizaton is a 'dissatisfaction with and alienation from the limitations of the white bourgeois self – a white self-loathing – and a romanticization of the racial other' (Vera and Gordon, 2003: 117). Play and performance is key here. In fact, Celia Lury suggests that the 'making of races' or the creation of racial identities is central to consumer culture and the way that in contemporary representations, 'all races are represented, not as a biological category, but as a question of style, as a choice' (1996: 168). Of course, the play with race may be argued to be a hegemonic tactic for ensuring that whiteness maintains its racial superiority, particularly when it comes to white people taking on/in racial Otherness. As Hernan Vera and Andrew M. Gordon suggest, 'white privilege includes the privilege to temporarily change one's colour, to masquerade as non-white' (2003: 120).

Nonetheless, one can also argue that there is potentially a transgressive and subversive quality to white masquerade and the desire for the racial Other. In terms of primitivism, Bonnett argues that there must be some attempt to 'cross the boundaries of cultural and racial purity' (2000: 117). Similarly, Gina Marchetti concludes that racial masquerade films 'implicitly critique the racial hierarchy of mainstream American culture, since they feature the conscious and deliberate impersonisation of another race, putting aside a supposed racial superiority so as to become part of a supposedly inferior other' (quoted in Vera and Gordon, 2003: 119). Through impersonation, passing, performing, masquerading, racial identity shifts, moves, floats, so that the borders and boundaries in and between white and non-white people begin to melt into air.

Conclusion

Bowie's idealized white image very often melts into air. He is a figure that is able to travel in and through various identity positions, while always securing his whiteness as he does so. In the examples under discussion in this chapter we see that he embodies the bouble binds of whiteness if only ultimately to secure its ontolgical power. The year that has been focused upon – 1983 – is considered pivotal in not only Bowie's ouevre but in the changing and challenging cultural conditions which were under way. Whiteness was under threat from a range of Othering forces and its own pale subjectivity, and a super-iconic white star such as Bowie was able to both express these tensions and to resolve them, returning idealized whiteness to its invisible home.

This desire for the Other, for the 'strange' in 1983, radiated out from a cultural centre that was white, and stemmed from a 'white' need that was about both owning the exotic Other, and devouring or ingesting them. Jackie Stacey defines this as the desire to (be able to) get closer to the Other: to 'literally ingest otherness . . .' (2000: 104). The 'strange' is imagined to give whiteness a more intense life experience, an experience that is hard to match within white culture, and symbolic power over the Other – bell hooks argues that this is why the 'commodification of otherness' has been so successful: 'it is offered as a new delight, more intense, more satisfying than normal ways of doing and feeling. Within commodity culture, ethnicity becomes spice, seasoning that can liven up the dull dish that is mainstream white culture' (1992: 21).

And yet Bowie was already Other, and carried the complexities of otherness and difference within his star trajectory, particularly in terms of his sexuality. This is what makes him such a fascinating figure for carrying idealized whiteness forward. Bowie is not only able to deal with the double binds of whiteness, but the politics of the difference of the Other. Put on your red shoes and dance the blues.

Bibliography

Ahmed, Sara. 2000. *Strange Encounters: Embodied Others in Post-Coloniality*. London: Routledge.

Bell, Mary. 1985. *Holy Anorexia*. Chicago: University of Chicago Press.

Bhabha, Homi K. 1993. 'The postcolonial and the postmodern: the question of agency'. In Simon During (ed.), *The Cultural Studies Reader*. London: Routledge, 189–208.

Bhabha, Homi K. 1998. 'The white stuff'. *Artforum*, May, 36 (9), 21–3.

Bonnett, Alistair. 1993. 'Forever "white"? Challenges and alternatives to a "racial monolith" '. *New Community*, 20 (1), 173–80.

Bonnett, Alistair. 1998. 'How the British working class became white: the symbolic (re)formation of racialized capitalism'. *Journal of Historical Sociology*, 11 (3), 316.

Bonnett, Alistair. 2000. *White Identities: Historical and International Perspectives*. Harlow: Prentice Hall.

Doggett, Peter. 2012. *The Man Who Sold the World: David Bowie and The 1970s*. London: Vintage, http://thequietus.com/articles/07233-david-bowie-cocaine-low.

Douglas, Mary. 1966, 2002. *Purity and Danger: An Analysis of Pollution and Taboo*. London: Routledge.

Dyer, Richard. 1987. *Heavenly Bodies: Film Stars and Society*. London: Palgrave.

Dyer, Richard. 1993. 'White' in *The Matter of Images: Essays on Representations*. London. Routledge.

Dyer, Richard. 1997. *White*. London: Routledge.

Dyer, Richard. 1998. *Stars*, new edition. London: BFI.

Ellsworth, E. 1997. 'Double binds of whiteness'. In M. Fine, L. Weis, L. Powell and M. Wong (eds), *Off White: Readings on Race, Power, and Society*. London: Routledge, 259–69.

Fanon, Frantz. 1986. *Black Skin, White Masks*. London, Pluto Press (first published 1952).

Gabriel, John. 1988. *Whitewash: Racialized Politics and the Media*. London: Routledge.

hooks, bell. 1992. *Black Looks: Race and Representation*. Boston: South End Press.

Lury, Celia. 1996. *Consumer Culture*. Cambridge: Polity.

Lury, Celia. 1998. *Prosthetic Culture*. London: Routledge.

McIntosh, Peggy. 1988. 'White privilege and male privilege: a personal account of coming to see correspondences through work in women's studies'. In Margaret Andersen and Patricia Hill Collins (eds), *Race, Class and Gender: An Anthology*. Belmont: Wadsworth, 70–81.

Mercer, Kobener (ed.). 1994. *Welcome To The Jungle*. London: Routledge.

Michel, Deborah. 2007. 'The Proprietary Cinematic Gaze in Tony Scott's *The Hunger*'. *ACIDEMIC Journal of Film and Media*, available at: www.acidemic. com/id97.html, accessed 23 May 2014.

Said, Edward. 1978. *Orientalism*. Harmondsworth: Penguin.

Stacey, Jackie. 1994. *Star Gazing: Hollywood Cinema and Female Spectatorship*. London: Routledge.

Stacey, Jackie. 2000. 'The global within: consuming nature, embodying health'. In Sarah Franklin, Celia Lury and Jackie Stacey (eds), *Global Nature, Global Culture*. London: Sage, 97–145.

Vera, Hernan and Andrew M. Gordon. 2003. *Screen Saviors: Hollywood Fictions of Whiteness*. Oxford: Rowman & Littlefield.

Williamson, Judith. 1986. 'Woman is an island: femininity and colonization'. In Tania Modleski (ed.), *Studies in Entertainment: Critical Approaches to Mass Culture*. Bloomington: Indiana University Press.

Woodward, Kath. 1997. *Identity and Difference*. London: Sage.

12

David Bowie is . . . Customizing

Helene Marie Thian

Utilizing Jules Prown's methodology as outlined in *Interpreting Objects and Collections* (Pearce, 1994), this chapter undertakes a materialist analysis of David Bowie's jacket first worn as stage attire around the age of fifteen while in a band known as The Kon-rads (1962–3). The jacket is currently in the collection of the Bromley Museum in Orpington, near London. The three major stages of garment analysis are: (1) description of the jacket in objective detail; (2) deductive reasoning on the garment's attributes based on the descriptive details; and lastly, (3) speculation on the possible sources of influence on its style as well as customization of the jacket as undertaken by Bowie. This type of concentrated analysis of a single item of clothing will allow me to see Bowie's performative body emerge and to explore the contexts in which his star image began to materialize. Many of the facets that we associate with Bowie can be read back into this well-worn green jacket.

Description

The jacket, as pictured in front view in Figure 12.1, though at first glance appearing boxy, is sewn to slightly taper at the waist – it is 16 inches across at its narrowest point – and is of unknown manufacture and without any label. The jacket is, according to Bromley Museum records, 'approximately 600 millimeters wide and 710 millimeters in length' (LDBMP: 2006.8: 1). The length from the edge of the jacket to near the lapel is 27 inches. The sleeve width at the widest point is 6½ inches across; cuff width is 5½ inches; the widest area of the lapel is 2 inches; and the arm length is 22¾ inches, shoulder to cuff end.

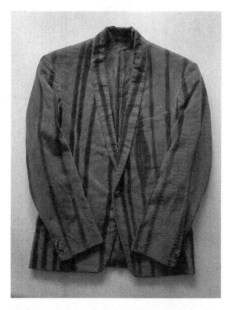

FIGURE 12.1 *The front of Bowie's jacket (photo courtesy of Bromley Museum)*

It is a single-breasted corduroy jacket with one button closure, which is ¾ inch wide, and featuring three buttons at each cuff, each being ½ inch wide. There is a black and white mottled, or marbled, appearance to the buttons, and the stitching on them is dark grey.

There are navy blue lines on the emerald green jacket, running vertically, with two large, irregular blue stripes on the front left side. One of these bulging areas of blue is noticeable due to the irregularity of the shape in comparison to the stripes but is also quite strong in colour. Lines are faded at the top of the jacket and in some areas, but other lines are not faded.

Figure 12.2 shows the back of the jacket. There is a design in addition to the stripes. Asymmetrical lines feature on the back whereby the right side has a line drawn to under the arm but the left side does not.

There is noticeable wearing on the upper body across the back shoulders and darkened areas on the elbows where the material is puffed out. Wear on the corduroy on the left lapel is most noticeable. The jacket is a murky green colour on the arms but bright green on the lower back, and there are darker areas of green on the front of the jacket.

The jacket has one outer pocket on the left breast, which has an opening of 4 inches across and a stitch on the pocket hem about 1 inch from the top of the pocket opening. This is in comparison to the slit, or hidden, pockets on the left

FIGURE 12.2 *The back of Bowie's jacket (photo courtesy of Bromley Museum)*

and right sides on the front of the jacket with openings stitched down around the edges for a double-lip effect. The inner pocket lining in the pockets on the front of the jacket is a grey, slightly textured, material with green stitching.

The inside of the jacket features a dark grey, nearly gunmetal colour lining with a sheen and is quite wrinkled. There is a tab for hanging the jacket on a peg which is attached to the inner collar lining and made of the same gunmetal-coloured, shiny fabric. The jacket's inner pockets have a grey, dull lining, and the one on the right, upper side has an opening which is 6 inches across, and a pocket on the lower, left side has an opening of 4¼ inches across. The inner sleeve lining is a beige fabric, also with a sheen, and the stitches around the armholes are pulled and coming loose and are of beige thread.

As for noticeable damage and defects, there is a hole on the right lapel; two brown stains or spots on the left arm about 3 inches from the top cuff button; brown stains on the cuffs; white specks on the right jacket arm; and a pinkish splotch on the lower back on a stripe.

Deduction

Sensory engagement

The jacket is heavy in relation to its size. Although wearing gloves while handling the jacket, I could feel the ribbed texture of the corduroy and see the differences in texture in the inner lining and sleeves, and the lining of the pockets, the first two linings resembling a shiny, synthetic material such as a polyester blend, and the latter with the non-shiny, rough and grainy texture of linen, cotton or a blend of these. In touching and holding this jacket one experiences the traces of Bowie's corporeality; his DNA and fingerprints are a part of the historical fabric of the piece. As a fan, I engage with it as if it is memorial, charged with Bowie's biography and my own investment in his star image.

Obviously well worn, the jacket has changed shape and colour accordingly. Splotches and stains on various parts and wear on the corduroy ribbing, particularly on the lapel, are markedly apparent. The jacket has changed shape most noticeably at the elbows and around the inner armholes, obviously due to the body movements of the wearer, the wear and discolouration of the material on the outer surface evidence of change. One can imagine, then, how these stains and splotches got there; the jacket becomes the object through which to imagine a living history and for events to take place that produces this bare life. Star memorabilia hold a particular affective currency for fans (Redmond, 2014).

Intellectual engagement

Based on the documentation for the provenance of the jacket as held by the Bromley Museum, a young David Jones, who in 1965 changed his name to David Bowie (Kinder, 2001), owned and wore this jacket *sans* stripes and design while a member of his first band known as The Kon-rads in 1962–3, playing saxophone and contributing vocals. He later wore the jacket, which he customized with blue printers' ink, for about twenty shows on a springtime tour of the UK in 1967 while in a band called The Riot Squad, performing as lead vocalist and playing mouth-harp and guitar. Bowie himself has confirmed the authenticity of the jacket (Mead, 2006a), the garment is categorized in Bromley Museum records, and is confirmed by its curator, Marie-Louise Kerr, as having been produced in the time period of 1960–3. According to a document in the Museum records, an individual named J. Deacon attested on 29 August 1991 that he came into possession of the jacket in the mid-1960s and that it had been owned and decorated by Bowie.

The jacket and its stripes became a lightning-rod for a debate on sartorial transformation as a former backup singer in The Kon-rads contested Bowie's memory regarding the time frame for the addition of the stripes, maintaining that the jacket for The Kon-rads was originally '. . . just plain green so [Bowie] might have put the lines on afterwards' (Mead, 2006b).

Bowie's addition of the stripes to the jacket around 1967 can be defined as a 'transformation':

Transformation refers to the alteration of a figure, form or structure into something different without loss of substance. The aim of transformation is to tap fresh energies (in a creative-artistic sense as well), stimulate new processes and achieve new aims.

Loschek, 2009: 66

Taylor has noted the importance of learning about the personal cultural biographies of things, a process that 'can make salient what might otherwise remain obscure' (2002: 15, in Kopytoff, 1986: 100). As noted above, Bowie decorated the green corduroy material with blue stripes by using cartridge printers' ink, dovetailing with the mid-1960s trends initiated by the mods of wearing striped blazers and customizing clothing. Questions surrounding the time frame and motivation for adding the stripes to the surface material of the jacket demonstrate the importance of learning about the personal cultural biography of a garment as a means of fully and accurately comprehending its cultural history. Due to the response of a former band member to a newspaper article on the jacket after acquisition by the Bromley Museum, confirmation of the jacket's transformation by Bowie and clarification of the time period was obtained, resulting in making salient what otherwise might have remained obscured.

The former curator of the Bromley Museum responsible for the acquisition of the jacket in a Christie's auction stated that the style and colour are right for the period, and that the size was noteworthy. '[The size was] . . . really quite small, so it would have fit the build he [Bowie] was at the time, probably when he was under the age of 18 . . . It actually looks a bit like a schoolboy's jacket!' (Mead, 2006a). The jacket became, by the late 50s, the symbol of personal identity for teenage boys, an identity separate and apart from pre-teen boys and, importantly, older men, 'marking the passage from growth to maturity' (Cole, 2012), symbolizing the initiation ritual (Winer, 2007) for the archetypal *puer aeternus*, or eternal youth (von Franz, 2000). It is a sign for a process of psychic transformation on an individual level, as well as evidence that a distinct social group situated midway between childhood and adulthood exists. The customized jacket by Bowie bears a striking resemblance to Australian

Aboriginal artwork by Don Tjungarrayi (b. 1938) titled *Men Initiation Ceremony* (2002), consisting entirely of lines and a target-like design or mandala with a focal point at its centre (see, for example, www.galeriaaniela.com.au/Don%20 Tjungurrayi.htm).

Emotional engagement

Examining the jacket for the purpose of material culture analysis – and in line with the Prown's methodology stage entitled 'emotional engagement' – I monitored my feelings during the curation process. I observed that I entered a state of excitement overlaid with awe and wonder, which alternated with an intense curiosity. Seeing and touching, for a period of two hours, a significant item of fashion-and-music history that was once worn by a cultural icon and personal hero evoked a range of emotions. Holding the jacket awakened a whole set of affecting memories, so that my own biography became part of the engagement. The jacket, with its faded colour, stains, worn elbows, strained seams and frayed stitching survives fifty years after Bowie first sported it on stage in 1963, and that fact alone elicited excitement and awe. As I fingered the garment, an intense curiosity arose as to the particulars of its customization, which provide the basis for categorization as a Bowie artwork. I felt thrilled by the thought that this small, customized jacket embodies that singular fusion of art, fashion and music for which Bowie is known and reveals his status as a 'genius'.

> The term *genius* can be traced back to the Latin word ingenium: a natural-born talent. The essence of this talent is seen as original productivity, which employs confident intuition to access new areas of creativity. The person has genius – that is, a brilliant creative power – is also known as a genius.
>
> Loschek, 2009: 37

While the concept of the genius is often understood to be a cultural construction, set within a discourse of hyper-individualism, for a fan it becomes the portal through which identification and pleasure emerges. I read into the jacket his authorship and delighted in doing so.

Speculation

After examination of the jacket, four areas of possible investigation come to mind. These are: (1) the historical influences in British men's dress leading to the popularity of striped men's jackets in the 1960s in London; (2) mod fashion with its emphasis on customization of men's apparel; (3) the Op Art movement, particularly the striped paintings of British artists Bridget Riley and Michael Kidner, and; (4) gay style and the Peacock Revolution.

Striped men's jackets in 1960s London

The ascendance of the UK subculture group known as the mods, and their fashion propositions, spanned roughly three periods, 1958–61, 1961–3, and 1963–6 (Chenoune, 1993: 253). These middle-class adolescents and working-class youths were music and fashion connoisseurs, preferring modern jazz – thus the name 'modernists' shortened to 'mods' – as opposed to traditional New Orleans jazz then popular in London, and were fans of 'custom-made clothes' (Chenoune, 1993: 253). Mods, classified as working-class dandies (Hebdige, 1974a, 1974b; Goldman, 1974) were devoted to the fitted, elegant Italian way with suit styling (Melly 1972; Waters 2014).

From the early 60s, mods wore brightly-striped boating blazers, sports jackets and suits (Braggs 2012). This attire was associated with the leisured lifestyle of the British upper class, particularly the sports jackets and men's blazers worn at the Henley Royal Regatta. 'The striped flannel jackets, under the familiar name "blazer", brilliant in colouring, created for the river and the cricket field are worn on nearly all occasions now by girls and boys . . .' (*Lady's World*, 1887 in Sims, 2011: 125).

Boating club members of Oxford and Cambridge dress in striped boating blazers based on a sailor's reefer-style jacket reportedly created by a Captain Wilmott of the British Navy ship HMS *Blazer* to make his sailors more fashionable for presentation to Queen Victoria in 1837 (Gunn *et al.*, 2012). The striped blazer came to symbolize a high level of achievement in academia and sport, awarded to those worthy to wear the garment, thereby associating it with the elite class, which held appeal for the mods (Sims, 2011). Figure 12.3 shows a photo of an Oxford University club's striped blazer.

The colour blue is key for the boating blazer as an 'Oxford Blue' was the term for an undergraduate student awarded the right to wear such a jacket for his excellence at sports (Gunn *et al.*, 2012). Bowie's utilization of blue printers' ink to customize his green corduroy jacket with stripes can be observed as being directly connected to the historical 'Oxford Blue' by way of colour and pattern as well as garment style, and echoes the 1964 mod-style, striped cotton, single-breasted blazer with narrow lapels and flap pockets rendered by a costume historian as daywear for the 1960–4 period (Peacock, 1996). According to Breward, 'A nostalgic preference for the louder elements of the

FIGURE 12.3 *Oxford University old style half-blue blazer (grateful thanks to Walters & Co)*

nineteenth-century dressing-up box, as embodied by striped flannel boating blazers . . . generally prevailed in the wider realm of 1960s pop and fashion culture' (2011: 13).

One can see why such mod attire held a fascination for Bowie since it involved a performative and narcissistic style of dress, and clothes that openly challenged normative class categories.

Customization of clothing by mods

Roger Daltrey, former lead singer of The Who, related in a video on Carnaby Street and 1960s dress in London that he and the band used felt-tip pens to make designs on their clothes during the mod era (Oeser and Ben-Moshe, 2011). Mods began making shirts and jackets into personal statements, sewing on initials or patterns as in Daltrey's notable creations for The Who (Rawlings, 2000).

This nostalgia for loudness in men's dress by way of the striped blazer in vivid colours became de rigueur for mod musicians, such as The Who, The Animals, The Yardbirds, as well as The Kinks (Sims, 2011), whose lead singer, Ray Davies, authored a song in 1966 ('Dedicated Follower of Fashion') specifically mentioning stripes.

Bowie customized his jacket in or around 1967 at the tail end of the mod era in keeping with the then current interest in self-decorated fashion, resulting in the making of an individualistic sartorial statement due to the freeform, irregular nature of the stripes and abstract design on the back of the garment, but with distinct reference to the traditional blue-striped boating blazer of British sartorial history.

In 1967 or so, roughly at the end of the third wave of the mod movement, Bowie customized his one-button closure, single-breasted, green corduroy band jacket into an artistic take on the traditional British club blazer, and in so doing effectively changed his image into that of a mod, albeit with an avant-garde slant due to the abstracted bull's eye on the back of the jacket. The customization of the jacket signalled a change in style which in turn signalled a definitive change in identity for Bowie, affiliating him with mod fashion culture.

The design on the back of the jacket as drawn by Bowie is as significant as the striped club blazer effect he created with the printers' ink. It linked him with the mods and the customization of clothing with 'existing styles, symbols and artefacts', such as the Union flag and the Royal Air Force roundel symbol. This self-fashioning not only birthed a personal style for Bowie, but promoted a proactive stance in the pursuit of self-adornment, a major preoccupation of his, and of the mods (Jobling and Crowley, 1996: 213).

Bowie's creation of the hard-edged design on the back of the jacket evidences his inclusion in the mod subculture due to the extremely individualized customization of what can be interpreted as a form of target or roundel. The freeform, biomorphic effects of the irregular stripes on the front left portion of the jacket are direct examples of Daltrey's words regarding freeform customization of mod-wear with felt-tip pens. As such, Bowie's singular artistic, and personal, identity statement is visible in this small-sized yet significant jacket. It is also a statement rooted in the subculture movement of the mods and their customization of clothing for the purpose of bonding as a social group to expand the boundaries of acceptable limits of self-presentation for working-class men in Britain in the 60s. As Bengry (2010: 57) notes,

While studies of fashion and gender identities have tended toward women's experiences, scholars also agree that men's fashion choices have long-held resonance beyond utilitarian necessity. They have been identity choices . . . [as] self-presentations and definitions have been aided, according to sociologist Diana Crane, by fashion's capacity to redefine identities by 'continually attributing new meanings to artifacts'.

Prown's methodology, which encompasses assertions regarding classification of a garment in comparison with other objects, raises questions such as whether the artefact is typical or unusual (McClung Fleming, in Steele, 1998). In the case of Bowie's jacket, one can conjecture that the artefact is both typical and unusual.

The jacket is typical of mod-wear such as striped jackets, suits and shirts, which paid homage to historical British boating and club blazers, and was also fitted rather than boxy in the manner of the preferred mod look of tailored Italian suits with a body-defining silhouette. 'Mods . . . wore suits or sports jackets that were sometimes boxy, but more often had a nipped-in waist with square shoulders . . .' (Ross, 2011: 33). Tailored apparel, the opposite of a casual aesthetic, appealed to mods eager to create a persona with a sophisticated patina in order not to end up 'watering down the whole emphasis of what Mod was about' (Rawlings, 2000: 63).

The jacket can also be classified as unusual in comparison with other mods' jackets as it is customized entirely, arguably making the garment a piece of modern art in the form of an abstract painting on corduroy 'canvas' which 'reveals a striving for innovation and progress' (Loschek, 2009: 179–80). While the iconic Union Jack jacket of The Who's Pete Townshend featured a bold print of the flag, for example, the Bowie jacket is a comprehensive customization, as the entire original green corduroy surface was painted, in a manner of speaking, freehand with printers' ink.

Mods in the early 60s did not customize and in fact adopted standard City dress for a carefully contrived, 'overall cosmetic air' (Chenoune, 1993: 254). Thus customization of an entire jacket is not typical of the original sartorial code of the mods but instead reveals more about Bowie's personal artistic orientation (as a student he had achieved a GCE O level in Art), and his own unusual take on the design motifs beloved by the later wave of mod culture in the mid-60s.

Influence of op art

The customization of the jacket by Bowie occurred at the time of the emergence of several seminal modern art movements and an admixture of the elements of op art, hard-edge painting and colour field painting can in some sense be glimpsed in the jacket. Furthermore, as mod style underwent a continuous process of integration and modification of styles, such as Italian suiting (Waters, 2014), it has been characterized as akin to pop art, which emerged in the 50s, with its 'visual eclecticism' (Jobling and Crowley, 1996: 213). A late 50s to 60s American art movement, hard-edge painting emphasized non-figurative, precise lines and flat colours, such as the wide blue and green bands sharply highlighted by Kenneth Noland in *Trans Shift* (1964) (Guggenheim Foundation, 2014), putting the emphasis on form, colour, precision and impersonal execution (Wolf, 2014). Although Bowie's customization is anything but impersonal or sharply precise in execution, the painterly coloration and emphasis on formal lines reveal a touch of the hard-edge painting style. Associated with colour field painting as well, in 2001, Noland created *Mysteries: Excavate the Past*, a direct rendering of an RAF roundel, thus incorporating mod fashion iconography in its abstracted form in the customized Bowie jacket, and coincidentally, primarily featuring blue and green hues. An exhibition 'The Sixties Art and Fashion' in 2003 at the National Museums of Ireland affirms the connection between Noland's work and fashion design in the era, featuring a striped, bright-pink dress bodice and its obvious connections to a Kenneth Noland painting in the gallery (Stewart and McCrum, 2003). Another colour field painter, Morris Louis, poured his paints 'directly onto unprimed canvas' (Stewart and McCrum, 2003) in order to create paintings of lines in the same way that Bowie applied blue printers' ink directly to the green jacket.

But possibly the most directly influential art movement, if only unconsciously, on Bowie's creativity in or around 1967, was op art, a movement dating from 1964, as it was preoccupied with optical illusions, colour play, lines and 'the effect of dazzle' (Popper, 2009). Bowie's striped customization can be linked in its essential details of stripe motif and appearance of movement to a painting by Russian constructivist Olga Rozanova called *Untitled (Green Stripe)* (1917–18), proclaimed as the first striped painting of the twentieth century by the Guggenheim Museum (Robinson, 1996). But it is the op art offerings of British artists Bridget Riley (1931–) and Michael Kidner (1917–2009) with more than a passing resemblance to the thematic treatment of Bowie's jacket customization that provide good evidence for some form of parallel invention type of relationship between the Bowie jacket customization and this particular art movement.

Kidner painted stripes (McNay, 2009) (see Figure 12.4) focusing eventually on chaos theory and the idea of an underlying order to things, utilizing colour to explore afterimages and the rational, scientific approach to understanding colour and form (*Telegraph*, 2009). Despite his interest in systemic ordering, his emphasis ultimately lay in an emotional, visceral response to art. 'Unless you read a painting as a feeling, then you don't get anything at all' (Kidner at Flowers Gallery, 2014). In Kidner's work, *Blue, Green and White Wave* (1964),

FIGURE 12.4 *Michael Kidner* Blue, Green
and White Wave, *1964. Oil on linen, 223.5
× 131.5 cm. Neues Museum Nuremberg,
acquired in 2002/3 through the association
of friends (Museumsinitiative Freunde und
Förderer des Neuen Museums e.V.) Photo
courtesy of Neues Museum Nuremberg
(Birgit Suk)*

stripes, and two of the colours of the outer surface of the Bowie customized
jacket, blue and green, feature prominently as if foreshadowing the Bowie
artwear. Bowie's customized jacket with its irregularly coloured lines, eccentric
bulge on the front left panel and irregular placement of the stripes on the right
back and front panels, along with the asymmetrical geometric design on the
back, seem a *Gestalt* echoing Kidner's discourse on chaos theory by shifting
between the desire for the rational and ordered and the irrational and
disordered. Just as Kidner sought to render in concrete, artistic form the
underlying, balanced order of things, akin to Carl Jung's theory of the natural
ordering principle of the psyche (Eisendrath and Hall, 1991: 5), Bowie's jacket
customization documents the push-pull between the tension of the opposites

(Jung, 1970) of order and disorder. The freeform rendering of the irregularly placed and colour-saturated stripes, in tandem with the off-kilter mandala-like design on the back, a modified square within a variation of an open octagonal and wide line at centre, depict the process of shifting toward wholeness. Rather than a fixed point, or focused 'Self' (Jung, 1925: 120), as seen in a target or mandala, however, the wide line reveals a man in the process of making his mark on the world.

One of the principal British op artists of the early 60s, Bridget Riley, brought the stripe into prominence as an art form in and of itself. In 1967, she began to explore the phenomenon of colour by way of the vertical stripe in the work *Late Morning*. In the same year Bowie likely customized his jacket with vertical stripes, in order to maximize the play of colour in the image due to the long edges allowing for a play between colours which created distinct optical effects (Moorhouse, 2003). 'The line has direction and length, it lends itself to simple repetition and by its regularity it simultaneously supports and counteracts the fugitive, fleeting character of colour' (Riley, in Bracewell and Riley, 2009: 17). Although created by Riley in a later era, *Blues and Greens 2001* explores the effects of juxtaposing shades of green and blue, colours seen in the Bowie customized jacket, the format appearing in 'Colour and Sequence Study' works dating from 1967 used to create *Late Morning*. The stripe paintings of Riley provided a 'fluctuating colour field' (Riley, in Moorhouse, 2003: 210) in order to reveal the way colours change when juxtaposed.

Riley's colour and composition in *Late Morning* can be defined as musical (Bracewell and Riley, 2009), as repetition and interplay of the same sorts of tones produce particularized effects in a layered manner, yet with alternating tones of regularity and irregularity at the core of the composition. This observation applies to the 'musically' customized Bowie jacket with its series of repetitive stripes making for a musical-like theme communicated by way of free interpretation of the individualized 'notes' or components of the overall musical score due to the irregularity of the undulating stripes. The bulges and irregular saturations of colour in the stripes on the jacket can be likened to improvisations in the thematic composition. Bowie's customization appears to be a musical work as well as a visual artwork influenced by op art's interest in the assemblage of patterns and simulation of movement imitating musical effects, thereby creating a synesthetic experience.

Perhaps the example of music, another abstract art, might help. On the simplest level, it appears to be made up of sounds which are assembled according to certain sensations: high-low, long-short, loud-soft, etc. These differences are put together, or composed, in a highly abstract, conceptualized manner. Repetition and variation, assembling and dispersing, reversal, mirroring and development are part of a method which, far from inhibiting the sensual pleasure in sound, actually provides for and enhances it.

Riley in Kudielka, 2009: 162

'Fashion shop windows are [in 1965] full of "Op" imitations of her [Bridget Riley's] work' (Bracewell and Riley, 2009: 80), with Mary Quant's blue striped dress designed in 1964 (Casburn, nd) and Johnson's black and white op art print cotton shirt and wool suit for men from 1965 (Stewart and McCrum, 2003) providing proof of the effect of Riley's op art work on fashion designers for both sexes in the period. The appropriation of Riley's artwork for usage as fashion motif, once described as '. . . shop front dummies of swinging London's West End decorated in bastardised versions of Bridget Riley's art' (Bunker, 2012), did not sit well with the artist who took umbrage at the usage of her painting motifs for fashion offerings in New York during the time of her 'The Responsive Eye' exhibition in 1965 at the Museum of Modern Art (Reed, 2012: 38). That Riley was a major influence on the fashion world in the 60s is not disputed, such that her stripe paintings may have resonated with Bowie, even if on an unconscious level, due primarily to the works' optical illusions, with colour and line expressive of the fluctuations of life energy and the relationship to the psychological realm of the unconscious (Popper, 2009). Bowie's energetic transformation of his persona from schoolboy saxophonist and vocalist in The Kon-rads in 1962–3 to lead vocalist, mouth harpist and guitarist in a rhythm and blues band with visual pizzazz reflected in its name, The Riot Squad, is mirrored in the jacket's transformation from sedately conservative green corduroy to striped and emblematically decorated artwear by way of Bowie's customization. The jacket, like Bowie, was earning its stripes.

Influence of gay style and the Peacock Revolution

Bowie likely customized his jacket in a bold, artistic way in 1967 while in the band The Riot Squad because the group was noted for 'its flamboyant use of stage paint and theatrical show' (Kinder, 2001–15), and that flamboyancy can be traced back to the origins of 'gay style' and the Peacock Revolution in 60s London. There was 'a hedonism in masculine apparel' in the 60s in London, with its locus on Carnaby Street, which ushered in an era known as the Peacock Revolution (Chenoune, 1993: 254). Colourful, flamboyant clothing in sensual fabrics designed to make young men appear more Adonis-like debuted in Carnaby Street shops owned by homosexual entrepreneurs such as John Stephen and Bill Green, and mods patronized the stores and partook actively in the Peacock Revolution. Velvet and corduroy suits, for example, created a romantic effect for Peacocks (Ross, 2011).

Although mod style was not exclusively, or even predominately, gay, mods began wearing clothing that gay men had been wearing for years (Cole, 1999). The change in men's dress from drab to debonair in London in the 60s during the Peacock Revolution constituted in effect the adoption of gay men's dress style by the non-gay, male population: 'Throughout the 1960s, commentators noted the "hermaphroditic" styles coming out of West Soho, and identified the ambiguous sexuality of the mods who wore Stephen's styles as part of this concern' (Bengry, 2010: 64).

David Bowie's later dalliance with sexual ambiguity as highlighted in his 1974 song 'Rebel, Rebel', with the lyrics, 'You're not sure if you're a boy or a girl', and interest in androgynous, gender-bending stage presentations, were perhaps foreshadowed, if only in a diluted and indirect way, by his customization of a simple corduroy jacket into a bold statement along the lines of Peacock Revolution dress. Mod style likewise featured bold colours and bright patterns not seen in traditional British menswear (Steele, 2000). Bowie customized his jacket around 1967 with flamboyant patterning on colourful corduroy as if miraculously capturing the spirit of gay sartorial style emerging from the shadows boldly into the public arena, as in that year the British government decriminalized homosexuality.

It is noteworthy that Bowie reportedly had a strong affinity for John Stephen's clothing, even appearing in a *Fabulous 208* magazine advertisement modelling the gay designer's clothes on Kingly Street in 1965 (Gorman, 2010), further proof for the theory that Bowie's androgynous stage costuming in the Ziggy Stardust era was first inspired by the gay dress styles he had seen in the mid-60s in Carnaby Street shops during the Peacock Revolution. It is also further proof that his customization of the jacket for his theatrical The Riot Squad stagewear had more to do with the theatricality of John Stephen's clothing than the tailored look of Italian suit jackets of the early mods or even the customized shirts and jackets of mid-60s mods such as The Who: 'Personalities and pop stars were keen to be associated with Stephen. . . . David Bowie (then David Jones) even boasted in an interview that he was supplying designs for Stephen' (Gorman, 2001: 54).

The colour blue continues as a theme in the evolution of the Bowie style as Bowie's blue-tinged printed man-dress by Mr Fish (Pegg, 2000) worn on the cover of *The Man Who Sold the World* album (1970) 'touched on Peacock notions of vanity – "look at me"' (Ross, 2011: 108). Deep royal-blue printers' ink customization of the green The Kon-rads jacket can even be speculated as demonstrating a linkage with royal-blue men's bikini briefs produced in 1961 in the early years of the Peacock Revolution by Montford Knitting Mills in the UK (Cole, 2012). Bowie's customized jacket is, ultimately, classifiable as Peacock Dress in the vein of John Stephen's sartorial prescriptions as mod-wear and was actually also clearly influenced by Stephen's and Green's 'gay style' propositions.

Conclusion

The customized green corduroy jacket of David Bowie in the collection of the Bromley Museum illustrates the transformation of an individual performer's style from suburban generic sartorial dress code for a boys' band member, the transformation of men's dress in 1960s London during the Peacock Revolution and the rise of the mods enamoured of traditional British boating blazers. Additionally, the jacket is illustrative of Bowie's budding artistic talent at the tender age of twenty or so as the striped customization happens to dovetail with the 60s op art movement and its preoccupation with stripes. The initiative to take delight in dressing the male body as precipitated by the Peacock Revolution and the mods ran counter to the '. . . pathologising [of] a dissonant and "unseemly" personal interest in appearances as evidence of inversion and unmanliness' (Breward, 1999: 53). David Bowie customized his green corduroy jacket with blue stripes and bold abstract design around 1967 for the ostensible purpose of creating flamboyant stage attire for The Riot Squad performances, but made a modern art statement in a gay-inflected subculture context as a resounding riposte to any such pathologizing.

Acknowledgement

The author wishes to sincerely thank Marie-Louise Kerr, curator at the Bromley Museum, for her most kind cooperation in providing access to the garment, photographs and extensive documentation related to its provenance.

Bibliography

Bengry, Justin. 2010. 'Peacock Revolution: mainstreaming queer styles in post-war Britain, 1945–1967'. *Socialist History*, 36, 55–68, www.academia .edu/204080/Peacock_Revolution, accessed 30 March 2014.
Bracewell, Michael and Bridget Riley. 2009. *Bridget Riley Flashback*. London: Hayward Publishing.

Braggs, Steven. 2012. *Retrowow 60s Mods*, www.retrowow.co.uk/retro_style/
60s/60s_mods.html, accessed 30 March 2014.

Breward, Christopher. 1999. 'Renouncing consumption: men, fashion and luxury,
1870–1914.' In *Defining Dress: Dress as Object, Meaning and Identity,* edited
by Amy de la Haye and Elizabeth Wilson. Manchester and New York:
Manchester University Press.

Breward, Christopher. 2004. *Fashioning London*. Oxford and New York: Berg.

Breward, Christopher. 2011. *Introduction to Mr. Fish . . . The Day of the Peacock
Style for Men 1963–1973*. London: V&A Publishing, 8–13.

Bunker, John. 2012. 'Michael Kidner: dreams of the world order: early paintings'.
Abstract Critical, 5 October, http://abstractcritical.com/article/michael-kidner-,
accessed 30 April 2014.

Casburn, Melissa. nd. *A Concise History of the British Mod Movement*.
www.gbacg.org/costume-resources/original/articles/mods.pdf, accessed
27 January 2015.

Chenoune, Farid. 1993. *A History of Men's Fashion*. Paris: Flammarion.

Cole, Shaun. 1999. 'Invisible men: gay men's dress in Britain, 1950–70.' In Amy
de la Haye and Elizabeth Wilson (eds) *Defining Dress: Dress as Object,
Meaning and Identity*. Manchester and New York: Manchester University
Press.

Cole, Shaun. 2012. *The Story of Men's Underwear*. New York: Parkstone
International.

Crane, Diana. 2000. *Fashion and its Social Agendas: Class, Gender and Identity
in Clothing*. Chicago: University of Chicago Press.

Eisendrath, Polly and James A. Hall. 1991. *Jung's Self Psychology*. New York: The
Guilford Press.

Guardian Film Blog. 2012. www.guardian.co.uk/film/filmblog/2011/aug/18/
reel-history-quadrophenia-riot, accessed 30 March 2014.

Goldman, Albert. 1974. *Ladies and Gentlemen, Lenny Bruce*. London: Panther.

Gorman, Paul. 2001. *The Look*. London: Sanctuary Publishing.

Gorman, Paul. 2010. *The Look blog*. http://rockpopfashion.com/blog/?p=616,
accessed 4 May 2014.

Guggenheim Foundation. 2014. *Trans Shift*. www.guggenheim.org/new-york/
collections/collection-online/artwork/3247, accessed 27 January 2015.

Gunn, Douglas, Roy Luckett and Josh Sims. 2012. *VINTAGE MENSWEAR: A
Collection from the Vintage Showroom*. London: Laurence King Publishing.

Hebdige, Dick. 1974a. *Subculture: The Meaning of Style*. London: Routledge.

Hebdige, Dick. 1974b. *The Style of the Mods*. Birmingham: University of
Birmingham Centre for Contemporary Cultural Studies.

Jobling, P. and David Crowley. 1996. *Graphic Design Reproduction &
Representation Since 1800*. Manchester: Manchester University Press.

Jung, Carl Gustav. 1925. *Analytical Psychology: Seminar Given in 1925*. In
'History and development of Jung's psychology: the early years, 1900–1935',
Gary V. Hartman, *The Jung Page*, 27 October 2013, http://www.cgjungpage.
org/learn/articles/analytical-psychology/161-history-and-development-of-jungs-
psychology-the-early-years–1900-to–1935, accessed 24 April 2013.

Jung, Carl Gustav. 1970. 'On psychic energy.' In *The Structure and Dynamics of
the Psyche, Collected Works*, Vol. 8, para. 49. New York: New York Association

for Analytical Psychology, http://www.nyaap.org/jung-lexicon/o, accessed 24 April 2014.

Kidner, Michael. 2014. Flowers gallery. www.flowersgallery.com/artists/michael-kidner/, accessed 24 April 2014.

Kinder, Paul. 2001. *Bowieworld*. http://www.bowiewonderworld.com/faq.htm, accessed 30 March 2014.

Kopytoff, Ira. 1986. 'The cultural biography of things: commodization as process'. In Arjun Appadurai (ed.), *The Social Life of Things: Commodities in Cultural Perspective*. Cambridge: Cambridge University Press.

Kudielka, Robert (ed.). 2009. *The Eye's Mind: Bridget Riley, Collected Writings 1965–2009*. London: Ridinghouse.

Loschek, Ingrid. 2009. *When Clothes Become Fashion: Design and Innovation Systems*. Oxford and New York: Berg.

McNay, Michael. 2009. 'Michael Kidner obituary.' *Guardian*, 13 December, www.theguardian.com/artanddesign/2009/dec/13/michael-kidner-obituary, accessed 24 April 2014.

Mead, Kate. 2006a. 'Museum finds space for rock style oddity'. *Kentish Times*, 20 July.

Mead, Kate. 2006b 'Will Starman call the Riot Squad in jacket clash?' *Bromley Times*, 3 August.

Melly, George. 1972. *Revolt into Style*. London: Penguin Books.

Moorhouse, Paul (ed.). 2003. *Bridget Riley*. London: Tate Publishing.

Peacock, John. 1996. *Men's Fashion The Complete Sourcebook*. London: Thames & Hudson.

Pearce, Susan (ed.) 1994. *Interpreting Objects and Collections*. London and New York: Routledge.

Pegg, Nicolas. 2000. *The Complete David Bowie*. London: Titan Books.

Popper, Frank. 2009. *Op Art* (Grove Art Online). Oxford: Oxford University Press, www.moma.org/collection/theme.php?theme_id=10139, accessed 22 April 2014.

Rawlings, Terry. 2000. *MOD A Very British Phenomenon*. London: Omnibus Press.

Redmond, Sean. 2014. *Celebrity and the Media*. Basingstoke: Palgrave Macmillan.

Reed, Paula. 2012. *Fifty Fashion Looks that Changed the 1960s*. London: Conran.

Robinson, Walter. 1996. 'Complaining about abstraction: abstraction in the 20th century: total risk, freedom, discipline'. Guggenheim Museum, *artnet*, http://www.artnet.com/magazine_pre2000/features/abstraction/abstraction2.asp, accessed 13 April 2014.

Ross, Geoffrey Aquillina. 2011. *Mr. Fish . . . The Day of the Peacock Style for Men 1963–1973*. London: V&A Publishing.

Sims, Josh. 2011. *Icons of Men's Style*. London: Laurence King Publishing.

Steele, Valerie. 1998. 'A museum of fashion is more than a clothes-bag'. *Fashion Theory*, 2 (4), 327–36.

Steele, Valerie. 2000. *Fifty Years of Fashion: New Look to Now*. New Haven: Yale University Press.

Stewart, Anne and Elizabeth McCrum. 2003. 'The Sixties Art & Fashion' (exhibition factsheet). https://img3.nmni.com/Documents/UM/Applied-Art/The_Sixties_Art-(1), accessed 21 April 2014.

Taylor, Lou. 2002. *The Study of Dress History*. Manchester and New York: Manchester University Press.

Telegraph. 2009. 'Michael Kidner'. www.telegraph.co.uk/news/obituaries/culture-obituaries/art-obituaries/6886325/Michael-Kidner.html, accessed 27 January 2015.

Victoria and Albert Museum. 2014. 'History of 1960s Fashion and Textiles'. www.vam.ac.uk/vastatic/microsites/1211_sixties/history_page.htm, accessed 30 March 2014.

Victoria and Albert Museum. 2014. 'Mr Fish'. www.vam.ac.uk/content/people-pages/mr-fish/, accessed 30 March 2014.

von Franz, Marie-Louise. 2000. *The Problem of the Puer Aeternus*. Toronto: Inner City Books.

Waters, John Leo. 2014. 'Mods and mohair suits.' In *The Mod Generation*, www.themodgeneration.co.uk/2010/11/mods-and-mohair.html, accessed 7 April 2014.

Winer, Robert (2007) 'Developing markers for initiation.' *Psychological Perspectives: A Quarterly Journal for Jungian Thought*, 50 (1), 52–78, www.academia.edu/1489656/Developing_Markers_for_Initiation, accessed 30 March 2014.

Wolf, J. (2014) '*Hard-Edge Painting* at The Art Story.org'. www.theartstory.org/movement-hard-edge-painting.htm, accessed 13 April 2014.

Other sources

Images

Blues and Greens 2001 by Bridget Riley in Paul Moorhouse (ed.), 2003. *Bridget Riley*. London: Tate Publishing.

Blue, Green and White, 1964, by Michael Kidner. www.mi-nuernberg.de/de/photo/sammlung/galerie/1.22.42.html, accessed 4 May 2014.

David Bowie in his The Kon-rads jacket. Photo by Roy Ainsworth. Courtesy of the David Bowie Archive and © V&A Images, www.vam.ac.uk/users/node?page=198, accessed 24 April 2014.

David Bowie's customized jacket, Images 1 and 2. Courtesy of the Bromley Museum, UK.

Late Morning, 1967, by Bridget Riley. *Bridget Riley Flashback*. London: Hayward Publishing.

Mary Quant blue striped dress, 1964. www.gbacg.org/costume-resources/original/articles/mods.pdf, accessed 7 April 2014.

Men Initiation Ritual, 2002, by Don Tjungayarri, www.galeriaaniela.com.au/Don%20Tjungurrayi.htm, accessed 7 April 2014.

Mod-style cotton striped jacket in 'Daywear, 1960–64, p. 161.' Peacock, John. 1996. *Men's Fashion The Complete Sourcebook*. London: Thames & Hudson.

Oxford University old style half blue blazer for all clubs. Courtesy of Walters of Oxford, www.walters-oxford.co.uk/oxford-university-full-and-half-blue-for-all-clubs/half-blue-blazer, accessed 24 April 2014.

RAF roundel. www.raf.mod.uk/history/theroyalairforceroundel.cfm, accessed 30 March 2014.

Suit by Mr Fish, 1968. www.vam.ac.uk/content/articles/m/mr-fish/, accessed 24 April 2014.

Trans Shift, 1964, by Kenneth Noland. Guggenheim Online, www.guggenheim.org/new-york/collections/collection-online/movements/195217, accessed 13 April 2014.

Untitled (Green Stripe),1917–18 by Olga Rozanova. www.artnet.com/magazine_pre2000/features/abstraction/abstraction2.asp, accessed 13 April 2014.

Interview

Smith, Donald. 2012. Director at CHELSEA space, London, 23 February, approx. 90 mins.

Lecture

Cole, Shaun. 2012. Lecture at London College of Fashion, 13 February.

Lyrics

Bowie, David. 1974. 'Rebel, Rebel'. 15 February, RCA.

Davies, Ray. 1966. 'Dedicated Follower of Fashion'. February 25. Pye Records UK, Davray Music/Carlin Music Corporation.

Video

Oeser, Kym and Ben-Moshe, Danny. 2011. *Carnaby Street Undressed*. Orangeleaf productions and Identity Films, DVD, 92 mins at about 17 mins: Roger Daltrey comment.

SECTION FOUR

Memory

Introduction

Specter, sense-flow, wall, video

Introduction

A commercial failure at the time, *Labyrinth* (1986) is now remembered by a strong cult following of fans who continue to celebrate Jim Henson's dark fantasy world with its beguiling soundtrack from Trevor Jones and David Bowie, and Bowie's overtly sexualized performance as the Goblin King, Jareth. A recent round of Hollywood rumours hinted at a sequel, sending fans and bloggers into premature and simultaneous celebrations and proclamations of disaster, while the Facebook page dedicated to 'David Bowie's Crotch in Labyrinth' ticked over its 14,000th like. Social media platforms are the most recent sites for public memorializing, working as repositories for the sharing of reports of close proximity, interaction or fascination, all carrying on well-established tropes and traditions of celebrity fandom. The *Labyrinth FanFiction Archive* has a library of more than 8,000 stories, with regular contributors updating their epic narratives daily. Bowie personally encouraged his fans to take up this model of online community with Bowienet email addresses and online chat rooms. The service diminished as the internet quickly changed around it and eventually DavidBowie.com became the official 'home' of Bowie online. Bowienet is occasionally found referred to in the dead links haunting the web, pointing to the former experience and archive whose memory has proven as reliable as its human contributors.

This section offers a series of connections between the memories haunting Bowie's past and present, his listeners' and viewers' senses of audial and visual flow, and the physical and metaphorical divides in his incredible career. In 'He's not there: *Velvet Goldmine* and the Spectres of David Bowie', **Glenn D'Cruz** views Todd Haynes' film as haunted by the Derridean phantoms of Bowie and his Ziggy Stardust persona. Impossibly, Bowie is both entirely absent from, and fully present in, the fictional account of Brian Slade and his space alien alter ego Maxwell Demon. Bowie and Ziggy are conspicuous in their (non)presence in the paradoxical fairy tale that demythologizes glam rock's emancipatory appeal and rediscovers a sometimes shady and electrically seductive period. D'Cruz considers how Bowie, and the nineteenth-entury aesthete Oscar Wilde, act as ghostly figures in a cast of spectres both outside and figuratively inside the frame; including Iggy Pop, Lou Reed and Kurt Cobain. D'Cruz proposes the Derridean phantom and the hauntological approach as a new way to view the disruption of identity in Haynes' film.

> I've been enchanted and haunted by David Bowie for more years than I care to remember. Bowie, along with Marc Bolan, opened my ears to pop music as a child. So, I grew up with Bowie, and always felt his albums were cinematic, immersive – the sort of records you could listen to all the way through, in the dark. He made me want to dance, think and write, and you could never pin the guy down. Bowie continues to open doors into other worlds for me. In all likelihood I probably would have encountered the works of Andy Warhol, Bob Dylan, William S. Burroughs and the Velvet Underground without Bowie's prompting, but the fact is I came to these artists through Bowie's work. He always seemed prepared to let other artists speak through him, which is one of the reasons I responded to the call put out by the editors of this collection, and decided to write about *Velvet Goldmine*, a film that is and isn't about the evasive, elusive, mysterious David Bowie.

In 'Between Sound and Vision: *Low* and Sense', **Dene October** remembers a modernity and popular culture under assault from the direct challenge to the accessibility of 'pop' music and the politics of taste, gender, fashion and consumption by the post-Ziggy Bowie in Berlin. October seeks to complicate readings of the digestion of popular music in order to reject the detached objectivity of criticism and to recognize a deep ongoing immersion in sound that organizes the understanding of how we experience *Low* and how the sense that emerges complicates the haunting of a triptych of figures which territorialize music and predetermine the responses to it: the composer, the performer and the listener. October considers how *Low* collapses the top-down relations of this hierarchy and subverts these figures, uprooting their essentialist representational qualities. The Deleuzian and counter-Deleuzian turn of the analysis works to establish an understanding of the album as a 'sense-flow', connecting and confusing the experience of the listener, with a renewed interest in agency.

I've been a Bowie fan forever. I am drawn in particular to *Low* and clearly recall my first experience listening to it, the day it came out: I played it at night, mesmerised by the green light on the 'music centre' console. I continue to be hypnotized by Thomas Jerome Newton's ear, which I tend to float into, losing focus in those long blurry stares where vision is augmented by fantasy. It struck me one day that *Low* stimulated an inter-sensory collaboration where the edges of sound and vision blur into and influence one another. Listening to *Low* also reminded me of sensory 'disturbances' I'd had growing up, where sound and touch felt heightened, experiences that no one else seemed to have and which I probably socialized myself out of. This isn't peculiar to *Low* of course, it just seems that way. After all, Bowie sings about 'Sound and Vision' and asks don't you wa[o]nder sometimes.

In **Tiffany Naiman**'s 'When Are We Now? Walls and Memory in David Bowie's Berlins', memory is the principal means of understanding the affective melancholy of 'Where Are We Now?' as a critique of neoliberal capitalism and a signalling of loss in postmodern life. Naiman considers the physical walls dividing Bowie's time, spaces and recording practices in Berlin, including the Berlin Wall, the former anti-fascist protection rampart turned tourist marker and physical remainder. Other more metaphorical walls are examined amongst a network of memorial traces that Naiman considers as a 'performative poetics of walls'.

When the call for papers for the *Celebrity Studies* journal special issue on David Bowie landed in my inbox, I had already begun to wade through the sonic layers of the skilled and nuanced self-referencing that Bowie performed across his latest record, *The Next Day*. It was impossible to miss the roadway signs directing us towards *Heroes* and Berlin as the historical landscape for the album's first single, 'Where Are We Now?'. I worked the year prior on another piece on Bowie that had primed me to think about David Bowie's career as one long sonic and performative staging of his own narrative of decline regarding the West, its art, politics, landscapes, etc. Additionally, I saw a relation to Bowie's own personal narrative of decline, as an ageing being and a celebrity, within the context of *The Next Day*. I came to realize what an intriguing and rich area of inquiry memory and its relationship to music is, especially through the lens of an extended career such as Bowie's. Music can serve as both a time stamp and a yardstick grounding memories in a moment and measuring our own growth. In regards to Berlin, I knew that it held a special place in both Bowie's career and his personal life, and that Berlin had been a place where

Bowie was afforded the freedom to roam and experience the city because his celebrity did not overtake his day-to-day life in the way it did in places like England or the United States. Along with that, the Berlin that David Bowie traversed was a very different place than the Berlin of 2013 when his latest record was released. As I researched for this particular project, I became interested in how celebrity changes a subject's relationship to memory. I considered how for celebrities memories can be both personal and public constructions, and the ways these memories and experiences are then configured for public consumption in order to create a narrative that impacts the public persona, the way an artist is marketed, and audience reception of the artist's output. Through a person's celebrity and the public story attached, the audience is engaged with the artist in memory and the construction of meaning from it becomes publicly accessible, making one of the most personal processes we do into a shared activity.

In ' "You never knew that, that I could do that": Bowie, Video Art and the Search for Potsdamer Platz', **Daryl Perrins** analyses two videos from *The Next Day* (2013), the unannounced birthday surprise 'Where Are We Now?' and the 'The Stars (Are Out Tonight)'. Bowie's role as a video artist, argues Perrins, facilitates an ongoing search for sincerity, and the approach in the chapter is to draw on the music video genre to examine Bowie's engagement with the video format and his expression of self and experience through a multiplicity of intertextual points of reference between his visual performance on video and in cinema.

I'm writing this as a middle-aged man who has grown up and grown 'old' with Bowie's music and the attendant media around him. Just like those awfully clichéd TV docs on the 70s where celebrities with 'photographic memories' recall exactly what they were doing during the power cuts and strikes of the 70s, I remember the impact of seeing Bowie performing 'Starman' as a child in 1972. Of course I don't remember that actual transmission, what I visually recall comes from the dozen or so times I've seen it since in re-runs. What I remember from that day is how uncomfortable it made my father, who was an ex-miner, feel. It was inexplicably dangerous and that feeling has stayed with me to this day. Without reverting directly to Sontag I guess what I witnessed that day was the ideology of style. When I saw the video for 'Where Are We Now?' in 2013 with Bowie as a conjoined puppet looking out over an artist's studio, while scenes of Berlin where back-projected behind him, I felt a similar sense of ambiguity again. Both performances, while very different, were ventures into 'making the familiar strange'. The album *The Next Day* and the accompanying videos for

'The Stars (Are Out Tonight)' and 'Where Are We Now?' seemed to me to bring a process of peeling back personas, which was begun with the 1980 video *Ashes to Ashes*, to a head. The film and song 'Where are we Now?' stood out however and seemed to be a rare direct address beyond generic parameters. To write about it I had to apply readings from literature: Bowie as a *flâneur* and ex-dandy who drifts dreamily through the city to reveal its marvels, and film studies. I approached the video as if it were an art house movie and compared extensively with *Wings of Desire* to consider Bowie's invocation of lost youth alongside the idea of freedom that the nostalgic monochrome-framed West Berlin presented to viewers.

13

He's not there:

Velvet Goldmine and the Spectres of David Bowie

Glenn D'Cruz

Introduction

Named after a relatively obscure David Bowie outtake, *Velvet Goldmine* is an audacious film, which divided critics and audiences alike. Inspired by David Bowie's Ziggy Stardust period, the film, on a literal level, provides a complex account of glam rock as a cultural phenomenon, identifying its major motifs with specific reference to questions of history, memory and identity. The film tells the story of a group of characters in the social, sexual and professional orbit of Brian Slade – a rock star who shoots to fame by creating a space alien alter ego – Maxwell Demon. Sound familiar? The parallels between Bowie and Brian Slade abound in *Velvet Goldmine*, but Bowie is not there, he does not literally appear in a single frame of the film, which, while avowedly a work of fiction, tells us a lot about Bowie's contribution to popular culture and what we might call an aesthetics of the self. This chapter will argue three things: first, *Velvet Goldmine*, a film about the *memory* of glam rock, functions as an archive. That is, it provides us with a rich account of a somewhat neglected period in pop culture history by acting as a repository for a wide range of images, sounds, fashions and historical details. Second, Haynes adopts what I will call, with Carolyn D'Cruz, a 'hauntological' approach to the celebrity biopic by providing a space for the spectres of Bowie to appear and confound any simple notion of Bowie as a self-sufficient identity (Darby, 2013; D'Cruz and D'Cruz, 2013). Finally, the chapter will contend that *Velvet*

Goldmine explores contradictions within glam rock's emancipatory promise by exposing the dark side of its liberatory dream.

The memory of glam

In many ways, *Velvet Goldmine* inaugurated a renewed popular and scholarly interest in the glam rock phenomenon. While researching his film, Haynes became aware that there was a paucity of serious criticism on glam rock. The commentaries that existed before 1998 were written for fans, and tended to focus on music trivia and gossip without any sense of historical context or critical self-reflection. Haynes sought to fill this lacuna in knowledge by making *Velvet Goldmine*, and commissioning the rock journalist Barney Hoskyns to write a history of the genre, which appeared with the film's release. According to Hoskyns' book, *Glam! Bowie, Bolan and the Glitter Rock Revolution* (1998) the glam era was in danger of being forgotten: 'with a few exceptions, glam would ultimately fall through the cracks of pop-cultural memory, dispersed and absorbed by gay disco and straight heavy metal, and punctuated by Bowie and Lou Reed's apparent disavowal of their homosexual pasts' (Hoskyns 1998: ix). Hoskyns' slim volume provides a cogent account of glam, and echoes many of the ideas expressed in *Velvet Goldmine*. In general terms he argues that the movement was subversive, primarily because it unsettled common assumptions about sexual identity. He writes,

> For a brief time pop culture would proclaim that identities and sexualities were not stable things but quivery and costumed, and rock and roll would paint its face and turn the mirror around, inverting in the process everything in sight.
>
> Hoskyns, 1998: xi

Of course, popular music since the advent of early rock and roll in the 1950s had always implicitly questioned hetero-normative identities. Both Elvis Presley and Little Richard wore make-up and adopted flamboyant, theatrical stage personas. In the 60s, the 'flower power' wing of the counterculture superficially disturbed secure gender identities through unisex hairstyles and fashions, but failed to dislodge the dominant machismo attitudes that characterized the pop music culture of the era. Glam rock was a seismic event, for Haynes and Hoskyns, because it shook the heterosexual foundations of society in general by, paradoxically, appealing to heterosexual boys: 'All over Britain, in public schools and comprehensives alike, young males were seduced by glam's androgyny and excess. For thousands of primarily straight adolescents, the Bowie of Ziggy Stardust was a transgressive revelation: an incitement to nonconformity' (Hoskyns, 1998: 6).

Bowie was the key figure in this movement for a variety of reasons: his music, sense of personal style and apparent bisexuality, which he publicly flaunted, marked him as a singular figure. Hoskyns' book reinforces the common view of Bowie as a chameleon, a transformer, a 'subversive' artist, but tempers an unequivocally celebratory account of the superstar's glam period by drawing attention to Bowie's disenchantment with the trappings of success that he achieved by creating his Ziggy Stardust persona. Haynes uses Bowie's career as a very loose template for his film, but does not follow the factual arc of Bowie's biography. For example, Slade/Demon (the Bowie proxy in *Velvet Goldmine*) fakes his own death at the height of his fame (instead of retiring his alter-ego as Bowie did on 3 July 1973 at London's Hammersmith Odeon). Moreover, Haynes gives equal weight to the story of Arthur Stuart, a journalist and fan of Slade's, who is given the task of investigating the mysterious demise of the space alien rock star. Stuart, as we shall see, plays an important role in the film, especially in terms of providing a fan's perspective on the glam phenomenon.

Hoskyns' book makes a convincing argument for paying close critical attention to glam rock's place in the cultural history of the 70s without actually conveying the movement's impact on fans. In contrast, *Velvet Goldmine* evokes the era's 'structure of feeling' (Williams, 1977: 130), which makes it a rich resource for those seeking to understand the era, and Bowie's place in history. This is not a view shared by many of the film's critics. Robert Ebert gave the film a two-star rating on its release, claiming that it 'is a movie made up of beginnings, endings and fresh starts'. He went on to declare that 'there isn't enough in between [the beginnings, endings and fresh starts]. It wants to be a movie in search of a truth, but it's more like a movie in search of itself' (Ebert, 1998). A more recent assessment of the film by Emanuel Levy characterizes it as a 'postmodern musical' that 'never allowed viewers entry into the characters' milieus – or the director's POV' (Levy, 2012). The film's 56 per cent rating on the Rotten Tomatoes website reflects this critical antipathy.

Most of the film's negative reviews focus on the opaque nature of its complex narrative structure, and its lack of fidelity to the truth about Bowie and the glam rock scene in the early 70s, while its advocates revel in its dizzying array of intertextual references and surreal, labyrinthine structure. In my view, neither Ebert's or Levy's account of the film is convincing, for its dense, multi-layered text does not attempt to reveal the 'truth' about glam rock, nor does it attempt to provide a singular directorial point of view. It does, if you listen to its spectres, something far more interesting, for it is not a movie that is, as Ebert would have it, 'in search of a truth', but a film that unsettles any simple understanding of 'truth'.

Ebert is correct, though, in identifying *Velvet Goldmine* as a film made up of 'beginnings, endings and fresh starts' – the film plays like a dream, or a fairy tale, which requires the spectator to suspend disbelief, and undertake a certain amount of work in order to grasp its logic. Moreover, it is precisely what is in between these haltering beginnings, endings and fresh starts that enables us to think about Bowie, glam rock, celebrity, life, death, mortality and a variety of other themes and issues differently, or, perhaps more correctly, to think about these themes under the sign of *différance*. Tellingly, the film contains a pink inter-title with a quote from the psychoanalyst Norman O. Brown – 'Meaning is not in things but between things'. Indeed, it is the space between things and the relationships between things that provide the conditions of possibility for anything to 'mean' at all, if one accepts Derrida's account of *différance*. *Velvet Goldmine* revels in the space between, revels in contradictions – it is a film about Bowie, but not about Bowie. And, paradoxically, it is a film that tells us a lot about the cultural and political significance of Bowie by using Bowie as an enabling absence. He's not there. Not there, as literal figure, or proper name, yet he is present in every frame of the film. In short, Haynes lets the ghosts speak about the possibility of Bowie. So, who are these spectres of Bowie that Haynes summons in his film?

The spectres of Bowie

If you accept David Bowie's invitation to listen to *The Rise and Fall of Ziggy Stardust and the Spiders from Mars* at maximum volume, you may hear a plethora of ghosts – spectres who shake, rattle and roll their way through a glorious 38 minutes and 37 seconds of sublime, rowdy, extraordinary music. If you listen very carefully to 'Star' you might hear the eerie jungle rhythms of barrelhouse blues, hammered out on the piano with double-time triads in the manner of Fats Domino or Jerry Lee Lewis. The song's aggressive use of the keyboard also holds traces of the Velvet Underground's percussive pounding on 'Waiting for the Man'. You may also hear, scattered throughout the record, faint traces of such disparate singers as Noel Coward, Iggy Pop, Jacques Brel and Anthony Newly in Bowie's vocal style and phrasing, and you can certainly hear a lonesome blues howl on the album's only cover version – 'It Ain't Easy'. And it is impossible to miss Bowie's acoustic guitar, a ubiquitous element of the LP's sound, and a sign of its connection with a much older folk tradition. Look at images of Bowie as Ziggy, and you may see even more ghosts in the cut of his clothes, his gait, his demeanour, the make-up on his face and his raw, animal grace. On stage, Bowie's space alien rock star channels even more spirits from the outer limits of theatre history – mime, pantomime, *commedia dell'arte* and *kabuki* theatre mix it up with the aforementioned ghosts of old time rock and roll.

But, then again, you might not hear or see any of these apparitions, for it is always a possibility that you may not be attuned to Bowie's music and musings, which, for a plethora of reasons, may never arrive on your turntable, CD player, iPod or whatever future technology you might use to listen to music. Sometimes we need a little help to apprehend ghosts – and *Velvet Goldmine* provides us with such assistance. If you accept Todd Haynes' invitation to play *Velvet Goldmine* at maximum volume, you will hear, at the outset, a melange of ghostly sounds: children's voices, gunfire, strains of distant voices singing, whispering, jostling, competing for attention and space. This opening gambit – an aural tapestry of overlapping spectres – is 'the sound of time itself passing'. At least that's what Haynes' screenplay tells us. So, on one level, *Velvet Goldmine* is about the complexities of time, and, as I will argue, a community of spirits – spectres that speak through David Bowie, perhaps, and a myriad of other figures that precede him, and will succeed him. Furthermore, the spirits that manifest in *Velvet Goldmine* are best apprehended, I will argue, with reference to Jacques Derrida's neologism, 'hauntology'.

Before explicating this term, it is worth remembering that the recurrent and fundamental idea in Derrida's philosophy concerns what he calls the metaphysics of presence. That is, the endemic practice of prioritizing and privileging presence over absence. For Derrida, the western tradition is invariably concerned with what 'is' and this has consequences for what we presume to be 'real', 'pure', 'truthful' and 'authentic'. These metaphysical concepts also shape how we think about *everything*, so the metaphysics of presence conditions the way we think about identity, subjectivity and pop idols like David Bowie. What 'is' is never self-sufficient if we follow Derrida's logic, for the play of signification, *différance*, ensures that every referent refers to an inexhaustible number other referents. In short, nothing can be fully present in and of itself because of the play of signification (Derrida, 1981: 38–9). This is not to say that Derrida is anti-metaphysical or *opposed* to what 'is' present. Rather, he is drawing our attention to the necessary operation of metaphysics while demonstrating that presence, the 'is-ness' of Being, always deconstructs itself. For Derrida, the cinema is a tele-technology – a medium that produces virtual images – and also an art that, 'when it is not boring', allows 'ghosts to come back' (*Ghost Dance*, 1983). The cinema also points to the spectral nature of identity itself since everything and everyone within the cinematic frame is both present and absent, here and not here, there and not there. According to Louis Burchill cinema is:

> spectral not simply by virtue of its technical apparatus – the operation of the camera, the projected image, the celluloid and the screen all marking in advance the presence of their absence – but by its equally engaging a modality of 'belief', which, in an unprecedented way, suspends the distinction between imagination and the real, hallucination and perception, indeed, life and death, such that, by believing in the apparition on the screen, all while not believing, the spectator undergoes a vacillation of her/ his own sense of identity.
>
> Burchill, 2009: 4–5

While it is difficult to affirm Burchill's claims about cinema's *effect* on the spectator's sense of identity, I think she provides an astute description of cinema's spectral dimension, its flickering vacillation between presence and absence that enables the dead to return.

Derrida's resolute and rigorous logic unsettles binarism, and proposes, if one follows his lead, a way to make the cinema reckon with ghosts, entities that are there on the screen, yet not there on the screen, elusive figures that disavow monolithic conceptions of self and sexuality. The phantom is always present and absent, always more than one. As previously mentioned, I will argue that Derrida's neologism 'hauntology' enables us to apprehend how Todd Haynes' film, *Velvet Goldmine*, reckons with spirits, spectres and questions of temporal dis-adjustment and inheritance, but before proceeding to offer a reading of *Velvet Goldmine* in the wake of Derrida's remarks on the science of ghosts, I need to say a little more about hauntology.

Hauntology is a pun, a play on the word ontology, the study of what 'is'. Derrida deploys this neologism to unsettle any simple understanding of Marxism as a spent force, something that existed once, and 'is' no more. It also disturbs the notion of pure Marxism – one composed of essential, monolithic doctrines and principles. Derrida wants to keep the spirit of Marxism in play, and tempt out the phantoms that are part of its heritage, for the sake of those who have come before and those who are yet to come (D'Cruz and D'Cruz, 2013). So, I say again, the logic of hauntology involves a reckoning with ghosts – figures that are simultaneously present and absent, dead and alive, here and not here, material and immaterial – figures that do not belong to past, present or future, but roam between indeterminate temporal categories. So much for spectres of Marx – it is time to turn our attention to spectres of Bowie, and one especially powerful phantom in particular.

Oscar Wilde and the aestheticization of the self

Velvet Goldmine plays like a dream. Its temporal schema is 'out of joint' – it wanders restlessly between the nineteenth century (Dublin), the early 70s (London) and the 80s (New York) – the nominal 'present' of its diagetical world. It certainly does not follow the casual narrative logic of the biopic, although it uses other films, primarily the structure of *Citizen Kane* (1941), to organize its melange of ghosts. Moreover, historical personages like Bowie, Iggy Pop, Lou Reed and Kurt Cobain do not have direct analogues in the film's parallel universe. Rather, aspects of their public images are condensed into composite characters. For example, Ewan McGregor's Curt Wilde is a composite of Lou Reed, Iggy Pop and 90s grunge icon Kurt Cobain. While Cobain was almost the antithesis of a dandy, he was known to take to the stage in a dress in order to unsettle preconceptions about his image and sexuality. Cobain doesn't obviously belong to the world of glam, and Haynes did not actually intend to make reference to the singer (who was better known for his penchant for cardigans rather than glitter). Nonetheless, McGregor's resemblance to Cobain is striking, and further complicates the film's temporal structure by summoning Cobain's spirit. David Bowie is not 'present,' yet *Velvet Goldmine* is suffused with traces of Bowie's world and career – from the 70s fonts used for the titles and credits, to the grain of the film stock, Haynes produces an uncanny world that evokes the 'structure of feeling' of the 70s, for those who lived through the period. *Velvet Goldmine* also blurs the distinctions between fantasy and reality, fact and fiction, past, present and future. In short, it creates a fabulous, phantasmagoric parallel universe for the spectres of Bowie to inhabit. In the interview that prefaces the film's published screenplay, Haynes observes that many of the artists associated with the glam movement:

> were both looking backward into history – into Hollywood references, nostalgia, Valentino, etc – and looking forward into Kubrickesque futurism. That's what David Bowie did at the time – he was becoming a human Xerox machine, pulling constant references and recompiling them, condensing them, distilling them down into his own narrative diagram which became Ziggy Stardust . . . Obviously in this process of recombining and reconstructing the notion of truth [and] authenticity gets lost.
>
> Haynes, 1998: xiii

As intimated earlier, *Velvet Goldmine* begins with an epigraph: 'Although what you are about to see is a work of fiction, it should nevertheless be played at maximum volume.' As any self-respecting Bowie fan knows, this is a playful reference to the quotation inscribed on Bowie's *Ziggy Stardust* album. The epigraph signals the film's fictional status while making an explicit connection with Bowie and his Ziggy Stardust persona. The epigraph is followed by an image of the night sky saturated with stars. We see what looks like a shooting star move across the screen while a female narrator speaks the following words: 'Histories, like ancient ruins, are the fictions of empires. While everything forgotten hangs in dark dreams of the past, ever threatening to return.' These auspicious words signal Todd Haynes' scepticism towards the authority of official history and, paradoxically, his intent to produce a forgotten history of sorts, one that recalls the spirits of glam rock's non-musical forebears who inhabit the realms of myth, mysticism and science fiction. So, the film offers a genealogical and historical analysis that reveals the conditions of possibility for the formation of Bowie as a cultural icon by identifying the spectral antecedents masked by the proper name, Bowie.

Even those critics who celebrate Bowie's shape-shifting, chameleon-like identity assume the integrity of a singular Bowie – they count him as One, and occlude the ghosts that haunt his art by reinforcing the idea that Bowie's shifting identity is merely a question of aesthetic choice, or an expression of some kind of postmodern cultural logic, instead of making sense of Bowie's art in terms of cultural inheritance. At this point, I need to acknowledge that Haynes invokes the spirits of a multitude of figures, some obscure, others prominent. Within the first ten minutes of the film it is possible to identify the traces of Oscar Wilde, Marc Bolan, Roxy Music, Norman O. Brown and D.A. Pennebaker, to name a few of the spectres who haunt *Velvet Goldmine*. All of these ghosts clamour for attention and all are worthy of critical comment, but the word-length limitations of this chapter make it impossible to give each spectre of Bowie its due, so I will focus on a singular figure, the one, who is also many, that speaks most eloquently about questions of ambiguous sexual identity – Oscar Wilde.

Let us return to the beginning of the film. After the voiceover narration sounds for the first time, the shooting star explodes in a series of sparks (presumably descending to earth as stardust). The next shot shows a spaceship leaving earth having just deposited an infant at the doorstep of a Georgian townhouse in Dublin in the year 1854 – the year of Oscar Wilde's birth. The camera shows the surprised servants of the grand house who gather around the child. The next shot is a close-up on the child who is wrapped in a blanket. A luminous emerald green pin is attached to the infant's pinafore, and this image dissolves into a sequence that shows a series of schoolchildren in an Irish classroom in 1862. The camera tracks past a series of young faces, and lingers long enough for us to see and hear them talk about their future ambitions. Most of the children proclaim their desire for conventional occupations with phrases like 'I want to be a farmer' or 'I want to be a barrister'. The last child is the young Oscar Wilde who states that when he grows up he 'wants to be a pop idol'. The film immediately cuts to an English schoolyard in 1955 and we see a group of young boys beating up one of their peers, the effete Jack Fairy. After taking his beating, Jack lies face down in the dirt. He notices a small object partially covered by the soil. It turns out to be the baby Oscar's emerald pin. While inspecting his wounded mouth, the young boy notices he has a cut lip. He carefully smears the blood over his injured lips as though he were applying lipstick, and smiles at his reflection in the mirror – this is an important epiphany. For the young Jack Fairy sees the possibility of making style an act of rebellious and celebratory self-fashioning.

So, *Velvet Goldmine* is a fairy tale about 'fairies', and the pin is a recurring motif in the film, which symbolically connects Wilde with *Velvet Goldmine*'s other 'pop idol' characters, even though they are separated in time by more than seventy years. Let us pause here, and unpack the significance of the scene I have just described. Haynes uses the iconography of science fiction, or what we might call the genre's 'alien futurity' – the glowing flying saucer, the twinkling stars – to introduce the film's loudest spectre – Oscar Wilde. Wilde is renowned for his wit, whimsy, flamboyance, glamour and unique sense of style. An unapologetic dandy, he was both a celebrity feted by London's literary elite, and a rebel, marginalized by his Irish ethnicity and homosexuality. Today, Wilde is remembered, according to S.I. Salamensky, 'as both the wittiest talker in all history and the most iconic martyr for queer rights. These two Wildes, while not opposed per se, are rarely fitted together. Yet they are inextricably, complexly tied' (Salamensky, 2011: 3). *Velvet Goldmine* presents both of these figures.

Wilde not only functions as a spectre of Bowie, but his work resonates with the scholarly spectres that haunt this chapter. In the preface to his play, *Saint Oscar*, Terry Eagleton argues that Wilde's creative work prefigures the 'insights of contemporary theory' (Eagleton, 1997: 3). Wilde, for Eagleton, is some kind of proto-poststructuralist who sees 'language as self-referential, truth as a convenient fiction, human identity as an enabling myth, criticism as a form of creative writing, the body and its pleasures pitted against a pharisaical ideology' (1997: 3). If glam needed a patron saint, it need not need to look further than Oscar Wilde, which is why his ghost features so prominently in Haynes' film – a work that embodies many of the qualities Eagleton identifies with Wilde's creative output.

In presenting Wilde as an alien, Haynes is not merely acknowledging the ways Wilde's ghost haunts Bowie's Ziggy Stardust, but underscoring Wilde's pivotal place in the genealogy of glam. It is, in fact, tempting to see Wilde as the first of a new (alien) species, but the logic of hauntology teaches us to be wary of identifying origins. Nevertheless, Bowie's ambiguous sexuality is perhaps the most memorable thing about his Ziggy Stardust period, and the gender-bending practices associated with glam suffuse *Velvet Goldmine*'s narrative. This requires us to pause here, and consider Wilde's 'alien' status, for Wilde, Bowie and Haynes ask us, in different ways, to rethink common-sense assumptions about sexual identity, sexual practices, and connections between sexuality and society by disturbing the distinction between heterosexual and homosexual, and reminding us that such classifications also have a history. This unsettling of the categories of normative sexual identity is captured in Nick Davis' description of the film, which suggests that '*Velvet Goldmine* plays out as an unresolved inquiry into whether Brian [the Bowie surrogate in the film] is bi-, inter-, trans- or pansexual, and whether after the controversial "shooting" incident, he is alive, dead or "trans-alivedead" ' (Davis, 2007: 91).

Michel Foucault famously declared that the homosexual as a distinct category of identity, or personality type, did not appear until the nineteenth century. In a much-quoted passage from *The History of Sexuality, Volume One*, Foucault argues,

> Homosexuality appeared as one of the forms of sexuality when it was transposed from the practice of sodomy onto a kind of interior androgyny, a hermaphrodism of the soul. The sodomite had been a temporary aberration; the homosexual was now a species.
>
> Foucault, 1978: 43

Obviously, this is not to say that people did not engage in homosexual acts before the nineteenth century – sodomy was a criminal charge that could be levelled at anyone. The nineteenth century saw the act of sodomy associated with a particular personality type, 'the homosexual'. So, if Foucault is correct, it was not possible to identify oneself or others as homosexual, bisexual or polymorphously perverse before the nineteenth century.

Oscar Wilde as glam's alien progenitor is a brilliant artistic conceit that resonates with Foucault's argument about the emergence of homosexual identity. However, many scholars do not accept Foucault's thesis. Ann Stoler and John Boswell, for example, contest Foucault's chronology and provide compelling evidence to suggest that a distinct homosexual identity predates the nineteenth century (Boswell, 1980). Stoler also suggests that 'an implicit racial grammar underwrote the sexual regimes of bourgeois culture in more ways than Foucault explored and at an earlier date' (1995: 7). So, the status of Wilde as an exemplar of a new category of homosexual identity is not uncontested. In many ways, though, questions of chronology are beside the point since the film is more concerned with the politics of style and disturbing linear conceptions of genealogy. The salient point is that Wilde brings together a series of elements that we will later identify as key aspects of Bowie's Ziggy Stardust persona, a persona that presents the self as a work of art. Indeed, it is Wilde's unique blend of glamour, wit, celebrity and 'decadent' sexuality that marks him as a quintessential gay rock star, albeit one that predates the rock era. It is the connection between wit celebrity and decadent sexuality that marks Wilde as a distinctive personality – the first 'Starman', perhaps, a man of the theatre, undoubtedly, and a figure that boldly explored the transformative possibilities of style.

The logic of deconstruction teaches us to be wary of origins, so it is important to acknowledge that Wilde, like Bowie, like Haynes, and all subjects, nominal and famous, are more than one. In fact the proper name, Wilde, often functions as a metonym for a more diffuse, widespread social phenomenon in the nineteenth century, a phenomenon connected to the literary movements of aestheticism and decadence, which are commonly associated with the figure of the dandy. Most of the film's spectres are associated with these rebellious aesthetic movements, which deserve closer inspection. In his book, *The British Pop Dandy*, Stan Hawkins sees this figure as 'a creature of alluring elegance, vanity and irony, who plays with conventions to his own end. At the same time he is someone whose transient tastes never shirk from excess, protest or rebellion' (2009: 15). Hawkins sees the dandy as an outsider obsessed with a revolt through personal style. Here Hawkins echoes Albert Camus' characterization of the dandy as rebel – 'the dandy is, by occupation, always in opposition. He can only exist by defiance' (1991: 51). The dandy, in his account, self-consciously adopts poses and embraces artificiality and theatricality as key markers of identity – Charles Baudelaire, one of the major French proponents of dandyism, remarked that 'the dandy must aspire to be sublime without interruption; he must live and sleep before a mirror' (Seigel, 1986: 98–9). This interest in aesthetic style is also manifest in the writings of Walter Pater, the most prominent exponent of British aestheticism in the nineteenth century and a former teacher of Wilde (Pater taught Wilde at Oxford University). Pater saw all forms of beauty, in nature, art and human personality, 'as powers and forces producing pleasurable sensations, each of a more or less peculiar kind' (2005: 2).

There is another reason why Wilde's spirit haunts *Velvet Goldmine*. The film explores the emancipatory possibilities of glam, but also shows how the excesses of the glam 'lifestyle' are inseparably connected to the aesthetics of self. As we know, Oscar Wilde's wit and celebrity did not save him from an ignoble fate. In fact, Wilde's own artistic work was proffered as evidence of his 'aberrant' character during his famous court appearances, which resulted in his conviction for sodomy. The prosecution used Wilde's novel, *The Picture of Dorian Gray* (1891), to indict its author by arguing that it described 'the relations, intimacies, and passions of certain persons of sodomitical and unnatural habits, tastes, and practices' (Hyde, 1973: 326). Ironically, the book is a cautionary tale about the devastating consequences of living and sleeping before a mirror, since its protagonist, Dorian Gray, destroys everyone he loves through his vanity. The rise and fall of Oscar Wilde haunts *Velvet Goldmine* as the subversive frivolity of Maxwell Demon turns, towards the end of the film, into the mercenary greed of Brian Slade's subsequent alter ego – Tommy Stone (who bears a striking resemblance to the Bowie of the 80s, the 'sellout' Bowie of *Let's Dance*). The self-obsessed Slade/Demon character destroys the lives of those people close to him (his manager, wife, and friends). Despite Wilde's belief in the 'art for art's sake' principle, art cannot be self-sufficient and exist in a rarefied realm. Art, as Edward Said reminds us, is worldly, and always contaminated by the conditions of the world (Said, 1975).

The character of Arthur Stuart anchors *Velvet Goldmine*, and embodies the contradictions between glam's promise of personal liberation and its, dark, narcissistic underbelly. Stuart is a fan of Brian Slade/Maxwell Demon. We learn during the course of the film that Stuart is haunted by the memories of his glam idols – Slade, but also Kurt Wilde. Music gives Stuart a glimpse of an alternative lifestyle to the one he leads as a sexually confused, suburban teenager. As an adult in 1984, a decade after Slade's fake assassination on stage, Stuart is given the task of investigating Slade's demise, and solving the mystery that continues to surround the incident. Stuart tracks down the key players in Slade's life, and gets them to reminisce about their relationships with the glamorous Bowie surrogate (this narrative structure owes a lot to Citizen Kane – Stuart is searching for Slade's 'rosebud'). The film also keeps flashing back to key moments from Stuart's own life to reinforce the centrality of popular music in the lives of ordinary people. Arthur Stuart literally reinvents his sense of personal identity by consuming Slade's music and adopting his sense of style. He also fulfils the ultimate fan fantasy by having sex with one of his heroes – Kurt Wilde. Tellingly, and in keeping with *Velvet Goldmine*'s contamination of binaries, the following dialogue between Kurt Wilde and Arthur Stuart provides a pithy summation of the contradiction within the aesthetics of the self.

Kurt: We set out to change the world, and ended up changing ourselves.
Stuart: What's wrong with that?
Kurt: Nothing. (Silence) If you don't look at the world.

Haynes, 1998: 130

Velvet Goldmine and the emancipatory promise of Bowie

So, if you accept the invitation of this chapter to pay attention to the spectres of Bowie, you might detect an emancipatory promise within the sounds and images of *Velvet Goldmine*. The characters and spectres that inhabit the fantasy world of Haynes' film – Maxwell Demon/Brian Slade, Curt Wilde, Jack Fairy, Arthur Stuart – and its ghosts – Oscar Wilde, Walter Pater, Iggy Pop, Lou Reed, Arthur Rimbaud, Charles Baudelaire to name a few of the most prominent ghosts – cannot be easily categorized since each, in their own way, dislocates the binary logic that sustains normative, static conceptions of sexual identity, and each of these rebels sings a freedom song of sorts. But, if you look closely, you will also find a darker side to *Velvet Goldmine*, one that doesn't assume that any space alien is inherently subversive. The space of experimentation and play opened up by the spectres of Bowie are exorcised from the Orwellian world that constitutes the 'present' of the film's complex temporal scheme. Arthur Stuart, the journalist charged with investigating the mystery of Maxwell Demon, lives in a bleak, sinister analogue of New York City in 1984. The transformative possibilities of the previous decade, in the film as in our world, have been extinguished by the drab imperative to survive in the era of Reagonomics. To put this ambivalence differently, the film roams between the promise of Ziggy Stardust's subversion of normative sexuality and the menace of the Orwellian world – 'wrecked up and paralysed, Diamond Dogs are stabilized'. Will they come? This is a question that the film cannot answer, and its ambivalence about sexual identity, politics and the transformative potential of popular culture is perhaps its greatest contribution to our understanding of the cultural significance of David Bowie.

Finally, I am not sure whether the sober tone of academic discourse can do justice to the plethora of ghostly voices that speak through the medium of Haynes' film, and, in any case, this chapter will have been necessarily unjust in prioritizing one spectre – Oscar Wilde – above others. Nonetheless, I think we can learn something important about the cultural and political significance of Bowie by attending to, and conversing with, Bowie's spectres – the spectres that return and remind us that the present is never what we think it is. I'd like to conclude by summoning one final spectre.

Like all fans, I am haunted by the spectre of David Bowie – that is, David Bowie from 1972, to be more precise. I can summon this ghost with a few taps on my computer's keyboard, and a click of the mouse. Courtesy of YouTube, I can turn Ziggy Stardust and the Spiders from Mars into *revenants*, such is the power of tele-technology. A *revenant* is a particular kind of ghost – one that returns after a long absence. I saw David Bowie for the first time on *Top of the Pops* in 1972. I failed to remember much about this initial encounter beyond a general sense of wonder. I didn't find Bowie weird or strange. I just liked the song he sang, I think. Looking at the clip again on YouTube, I notice that Bowie strums a blue twelve-string guitar, he is impossibly lithe, his skinny frame enveloped in a multi-coloured jumpsuit. His spiky hair is coloured a reddish shade of orange. It doesn't look especially unnatural or futuristic to me now. Mick Ronson, Bowie's equally lithe and charismatic guitar player, joins Bowie at the microphone to sing the song's chorus. Bowie puts his arm around Ronson's shoulders. It's a tender gesture, affectionate, playful and more than a little sexual. Bowie and Ronson sing joyously. They look and sound fabulous, which is more than can be said for the unfortunate teenagers in the audience. These suburban kids don't really 'boogie' – they shuffle awkwardly from side to side. Some move with a hint of grace, but most of them look mildly bored. They look drab. One young man wears an especially garish 1970s' tank top. His lank brown hair is styled more in the manner of Donny Osmond than David Bowie – his dancing is especially lumbering. I can't help noticing the contrast between Bowie and his audience. His flamboyance, charm and wit radiates from the screen while the teenagers look inhibited. I wonder how many of these suburban kids transformed themselves with glitter and make-up after witnessing Bowie's performance? I wonder how many of them broke the shackles of their conformist, consumer society to find new ways of being? I wonder how many of them became pop idols? I wonder, where are they now?

Bibliography

Boswell, John. 1980. *Christianity, Social Tolerance, and Homosexuality*. Chicago: University of Chicago Press.

Burchill, Louise. 2009. 'Derrida and the (Spectral) Scene of Cinema'. In *Film, Theory and Philosophy: The Key Thinkers*. London: Acumen Press, 164–78.

Camus, Albert. 1991. *The Rebel: An Essay on Man in Revolt* (1951). Translated by Anthony Bower. New York: Vintage.

Darby, Helen. 2013. 'I'm Glad I'm Not Me: Subjective dissolution, schizoanalysis and post-structuralist ethics in the films of Todd Haynes'. *Film-Philosophy*, 17 (1), 330–47.

Davis, Nick. 2007. '"The invention of a people": *Velvet Goldmine* and the unburying of queer desire'. In James Morrison (ed.) *The Cinema of Todd Haynes: All that Heaven Allows*. London: Wallflower Press.

D'Cruz, Carolyn and Glenn D'Cruz. 2013. '"Even the ghost was more than one person": hauntology and authenticity in Todd Haynes' *I'm Not There*'. *Film-Philosophy*, 17 (1), 315–30.

Derrida, Jacques. 1981. *Positions*. Translated by Alan Bass. Chicago: University of Chicago Press.

Derrida, Jacques. 1994. *Specters of Marx: The State of the Debt, the Work of Mourning and the New International*. Translated by Peggy Kamuf. New York and London: Routledge.

Derrida, Jacques. 2001. 'Le cinéma et ses fantômes'. *Les Cahiers du cinéma*, 556.

Eagleton, Terry. 1997. *Saint Oscar and Other Plays*. Oxford: Blackwell.

Eagleton, Terry. 1990. *The Ideology of the Aesthetic*. Oxford: Blackwell.

Ebert, Robert. 1998. 'Review of *Velvet Goldmine*'. http://www.rogerebert.com/reviews/velvet-goldmine–1998, accessed 4 May 2014.

Foucault, Michel. 1978. *The History of Sexuality: An Introduction, Volume One*. Translated by Robert Hurley. New York: Random House.

Hawkins, Stan. 2009. *The British Pop Dandy: Masculinity, Popular Music and Culture*. London: Ashgate.

Haynes, Todd. 1998. *Velvet Goldmine*. Screenplay. London: Faber & Faber.

Hoskyns, Barney. 1998. *Glam!: Bowie, Bolan and the Glitter Rock Revolution*. London: Faber & Faber.

Hyde, Montgomery, H. 1973. *The Trials of Oscar Wilde*. London: Dover Publications.

Levy, Emanuel. 2012. '*Velvet Goldmine* (1998): postmodern musical'. http://emanuellevy.com/review/velvet-goldmine–1998/, accessed 4 May 2014.

McCleod, Ken. 2003. 'Space oddities: aliens, futurism and meaning in popular music'. *Popular Music*, 22, 337–55.

Pater, Walter. 2005. *The Renaissance: Studies in Art and Poetry* (1873). New York: Dover Publications.

Said, Edward W. 1975. 'The world, the text, the critic'. *The Bulletin of the Midwest Modern Language Association*, 8 (2), 1–23.

Salamensky, S.I. 2011. *The Modern Art of Influence and the Spectacle of Oscar Wilde*. New York: Palgrave Macmillan.

Seigel, Jerrold. 1986. *Bohemian Paris: Culture, Politics, and the Boundaries of Bourgeois Life, 1830–1930*. Baltimore: Johns Hopkins University Press.

Stoler, Ann Laura. 1995. *Race and the Education of Desire*. Durham and London: Duke University Press.

White, Rob. 2013. *Todd Haynes*. Urbana, Chicago and Springfield: University of Illinois Press.

Wilde, Oscar. 1913. 'The critic as artist'. In *Intentions*. London: Methuen.

Wilde, Oscar. 2013. *The Picture of Dorian Gray*. London: Spear Press.

Williams, Raymond. 1977. *Marxism and Literature*. Oxford and New York: Oxford University Press.

14

Between Sound and Vision: *Low* and Sense

Dene October

Introduction: 'Don't you w[o]ander sometimes'

On his *Low* (1977) profile, where the celluloid Bowie has been flattened out by George Underwood's cover art, only his ear seems to have corporeal depth, alert and cocked to one side, an emblem of the *hinge-sense*[1] connecting sound and vision. Here the ear is the material centre of a solipsistic, synaesthetic sonic-space, the door to interior flâneurism. Framed by licks of amber hair and a volcanic alien sky, it is the interstice between materiality and virtuality, as if exhorting us to occupy that space between sense-worlds.

This chapter considers how we experience *Low* and how the sense we make of it is haunted by the historical tripartition of composer / performer / listener, figures which territorialize and marshal music. In the artwork to *Low*, this hierarchy has collapsed into the virtual figure of Bowie-Newton,[2] a superimposed spectre which threatens both to materialize each discreet monadic position and dissolve them into a nomadic force,[3] one that's visuality confounds the 'listening ear', that legacy of music training and writing.[4] To subvert these figures and uproot the essentialist representational doxa on which they depend, I turn to Deleuze,[5] and concepts amenable to experiencing the album as a sense-flow, one that connects and confuses sense and through which Bowie's ear becomes a shell from a strange beach: we place it to our ears to be invited inside-out, to *become* as a sound-body assemblage.

Deleuzean concepts[6] are useful in terrorising the hierarchies that territorialise music. Although not strictly related to music, concepts such as the *rhizome*,[7] the minortarian,[8] and the *body without organs*[9] lend themselves to thinking of music as a limitless force, while *sense*[10] seeks a deterritorialization of the signifying doxa of European classical thought. Such concepts may help to reconfigure *Low* as an assault on the *empire* of the author,[11] one ushering in the birth of the listener. For Deleuze, both music and philosophy must be rethought since each produces recognition as 'common sense' and 'good sense',[12] principles that block *difference*[13] as a creative force. Rather than seeing *Low* as a container with something of signifying value inside, sense asks you to treat it as a 'non-signifying machine',[14] to relate to its surface as body to event, 'one *flow* among others', asking not what it is but 'Does it work, and how does it work?' How does it work for you?'.

In order to make *Low* work for the listener, it is necessary to understand how the tripartite of figures encourages specific ways of reading the work, ways that are by turns Deleuzean and counter-Deleuzean. Taking each of these figures in turn, I argue that Bowie assumes the privileged position of author only to subvert it, and creates an identarian focus as performer only to surrender identity. By abandoning predictive sense, Bowie enables a more amenable account of listening agency, one which must nevertheless acknowledge the ghosts of the tripartite as they form rhizomic connections at the hinge between senses.

The artist: 'waiting for the gift'

David Bowie's tenth studio album *Station to Station* (RCA, 1976) foregrounds another sound-image on its cover art, but one in striking contrast to *Low*'s depiction of synaesthetic metaphysical [f]*Low*. The focus is on the black conical shapes of an anechoic chamber, a room that organizes and arrests sound and which, in the film *The Man Who Fell To Earth* (Roeg, 1976), marks Thomas Jerome Newton's alien-sense as well as the eventual compromise of his Otherness. The Bowie-Newton figure[15] is dressed in a formal black suit, his top collar fastidiously buttoned. The stripped-back modernism is echoed by the *striated* rational space of his ship as well as the graphic design, a black and white photograph[16] cropped onto a grid of white breathing space with the album title rendered in a red sans-serif upper case type. All seem to herald the avant-garde direction and the critical construction of Bowie as a composer of merit, a 'poet, possibly a modern-day genius'.[17]

The *composer* is the principal figure of Western music as art, one around whom cultural notions of authenticity and creativity coalesce and who embodies the discursive and historical values which give meaning to 'Music' as commodity and concept. This figure is both the product and benefactor of the contracted knowledge of the *being*-man.[18] We imagine him as his delegate, the formally-suited conductor whose jurisdiction over time is formalized by his wand of office and the laborious task of reproducing *the* singular-work from the *becoming*-flow.[19] For his others, the figures of *performer* and *listener*, the latter of which is hardly even a figure, he is the tyrannical director of mimesis and reception. Music books tend to celebrate *him* rather than evaluate his music, daunted perhaps by translating the abstract-flow into words.

For the 'creative genius' is a popular tyrant, one whose 'natural' energies compel him to the very edge of sociality and lift him above the musical zeitgeist.[20] Such figures as Van Gogh and Beethoven are enduring fictions precisely because we turn deaf ears against the critical deconstruction[21] of those whose own ears are so essential to their construction. Bowie is only recently the subject of sustained critical inquiry and so it is not surprising that the biographical picture tells us less about him than the culture of mythology. Previously critically positioned as the *theatrical* artist,[22] he is reimagined in the period covering *Station to Station* to *Lodger* (RCA, 1979) as the creative genius – his record company RCA even promoting *Heroes* with the catchy phrase 'There's Old Wave. There's New Wave. And there's David Bowie.'[23] Indeed, Bowie embodies the outsider who suffers for his art. His prolific drug use, mental health concerns and *autistic* communications[24] are all self-actualizing discourses of the isolated genius. Bowie's 'Berlin period' was his retreat[25] from where he evolved 'a new musical language',[26] one addressed to 'the European canon' (*Station to Station*) of German expressionism and modernism.[27] This minimalist-sounding project, *New Music Night and Day*, was one his own record company expressed indifference to and which Bowie admitted was 'indulgent',[28] unaffordable[29] and had no audience. Bowie's response to the possibility of alienating his audience is typical of the trickle-down elitism of the avant-garde earlier in the century.[30] Answering a journalist's questions about *Low*'s immediate failure to sell, Bowie tellingly remarks, 'It's rather pleasing in a perverse kind of way.'[31] His affectation that, 'I really get so embarrassed that my records do so well in discos' narrates his switch from the situated pop culture of *Young Americans* (RCA, 1975) to the transcendent figure of the artist.

If Bowie had partly identified with the artist construction, he nevertheless approached the writing of *Low* as a 'studio authorship'. The album begins *in medias res*, an *untimely* move that the listener scrambles to keep up with. Wilcken describes it as opening the door on a band in mid-session,[32] a useful analogy since not only is the entire cast present on the track, but the experience of the *untimely* perists. 'Speed of Life' is about movement, but not specifically forward movement, its structure cyclical with major and minor themes repeating, the *all-at-once-ness* of each instrument speeding desirously across each other and in all directions: the Eno/Bowie synthesizer collisions, George

Murray's bass line rising while other instruments descend, the unhalting scream of Carlos Alomar's guitar and the crashing echo of Dennis Davis' drums. It is an unruly orchestra of furiously independent players whose virtuosity by chance coalesces into the brief melody line, before speeding away again, each attempting to find its own sense. In contrast to the occult conceit of the 'Tree of Life' on *Station to Station*,[33] 'Speed of Life' does not proffer itself as the totalizing despotic signifier but seems to doubt its own right to actualize, ever flowing into rhizomic connections.

Deleuze's vegetal model of *rhizome* is an opposition to the branch structure of trees since unlike the 'hierarchical modes of communication and preestablished paths, the rhizome is an acentred, nonhierarchical, nonsignifying system'.[34] Rhizomes are processes rather than structures, have no beginning or end, so shoot off from the middle, making connections through any node to any point on any other.[35] They are not reducible to a plan but pertain to one that is 'connectable, reversible, modifiable, and [which] has multiple entryways and exits and its own lines of flight'.[36] An account of music that has at its centre the figure of the composer however is one which communicates ideas from a privileged and despotic root signifier; it is also one that disdains the creative energies of those who surround and support the composer,[37] energies that he shares with others in the social and studio matrix through which the *bricoleur*[38] gathers tools exactly where they lay.

A rhizomic account of *Low* shifts the attention from the composer figure to the non-hierarchal collaborative and connective intensities that inspire the sense-[f]*Low*. For Deleuze, sense-making is created through the inbetweenness of series-combinations, for example, of the Deleuze-series and Guattari-series, since these collaborations inspire the sense-flow beyond the 'two-series'. This force, say Deleuze and Guattari, describing the *rhizome*, opens a new series and new flows as the 'principle of rhizomatic multiplicity . . . Puppet strings . . . tied not to the supposed will of an artist or puppeteer but to a multiplicity of nerve fibers, which form another puppet in other dimensions connected to the first'.[39] The Bowie-series and the Eno-series are intensified by a working disdain for the transcending position of composer. Brian Eno, like Deleuze, insists he is not a musician. Despite his interest in connecting music and concept, 'Deleuze was never a musician'[40] while 'Eno styled himself as a "non-musician" '.[41] Bowie saw himself as 'a 'generalist', not a musician',[42] nevertheless an *artist* (and painter) who experimented, with Burroughsian cut-up techniques for example, to bring about deviation and digression.

The rhizomic connections had already started when Bowie collaborated with Iggy Pop on *The Idiot* (RCA, 1977), 'a dry run for *Low*'[43] and which flowed into it[44] as material Bowie had previously toured with, like 'Sister Midnight', flowed into *The Idiot*. This slippage between one discrete project-series and another also connects *Low* with *The Man Who Fell To Earth* which Bowie made an aborted attempt to score, carrying material such as 'Subterraneans' forward[45] as he (non-consciously, perhaps) carried forward the *identarian* affects of the film.[46] All the same, *Low* was mainly written in the studio[47] where collaborative energies of the cast came together in a controlled chaos.[48] The process began with musicians jamming, with little direction from Bowie,[49] igniting further writing connections and studio treatments, laying the seed-bed for overdubs and guitar work and finally the lyrics.

Unlike the *striated* and hierarchical system of notation-based composition, writing in the studio offers the *smooth* unformed surface over which intensities take flight. This is not space as such, nor even really in space, but more the *ganzfeld* view[50] of the studio as a *becoming*-space, the 'matrix of intensity' for the intensities produced.[51] The *studio process* dissolves hierarchies and, here, brought out many of Tony Visconti's various skills as writer and instrumentalist, in addition to his more conventional studio roles as technician and producer. The *studio process* draws from the situatedness of the musician rather than serves his mastery, a machine of assemblage enabled by the state-of-the-art recording tools at the Château d'Hérouville, which, for example, included an MCI–500 console and the first Westlake monitors in Europe. Visconti brought in a pitch-shifting Eventide Harmonizer which he boasted 'fucks with the fabric of time'[52] since it changed the pitch of instruments without slowing the tape, and could be played back to augment Davis' live percussion on 'Speed of Life'. Thus the writing felt liberatory. According to Visconti, 'we were freewheeling, making our own rules'.

For Bowie, writing in the studio meant breaking down walls and wandering about into 'new processes and new methods of writing', creating 'new information without even realising it . . . by not trying to write about anything we had written more about something'.[53] It was a philosophy he also embodied, one that imperilled him, keeping him awake at night, threatening his sense of self.[54] Bowie claimed he was being haunted by the ghost of the celebrated composer Chopin[55] – who was Polish, brought up in Warsaw – and reported 'some strange energy in that chateau.'[56] These psychic-social sensations, intensities crashing against investments, were sometimes met by efforts to shore up the defences. Eno's attempts at deconstructing conventional authorship, his 'Oblique Strategies' – cards with random instructions such as 'Mute and Continue' and 'Honour thy error as a hidden intention' – were intended to direct the musician to 'both discovery and enjoyment',[57] however Carlos Alomar found it impossible to surrender the designation of 'musician' and sought to block those intensities that threatened his psychic and physical investment: 'I totally, totally resisted it.'[58]

Meanwhile, Bowie's physical and mental health was causing concern. Recovering from the celebrity excesses of Doheny Drive,[59] he was also in the middle of an acrimonious breakup with his wife and had started legal proceedings against his ex-manager, Michael Lippman. It all came to a head in Bowie's nervous collapse, sensationally reported in the music press as a heart attack, a meme given considerable voracity by conflating it with a publicity still from *The Man Who Fell To Earth* which refers to Newton undergoing health tests. Bowie's *Low* profile may owe as much to a *Low* disposition as a *Low* authorial presence, wires which seem to cross in any case. His trips to attend court in Paris left Eno working alone at the Château d'Hérouville on the track that would eventually be entitled 'Warszawa'. Bowie simply requested it have a religious feel[60] and it dutifully opens with a bell, most likely tolling for the ghostly city dwellers Bowie once glimpsed as he wandered about the Polish capital, figures shocked from war and communism. Or perhaps it was the funeral dirge of the composer figure, the resident ghost Chopin or the existential angst of Bowie-the-author . . . for Bowie now found himself lost for words.

If his mutism was the symbolic death of the ego, it helped birth 'Warszawa' as an aural space, a city sensually reimagined. The 'words' – *sula vie delejo* – have the open vowel sounds of Japanese and the melodious thickness of Italian, sound objects that emanate from well inside the body and that crystalize in the vocals rather than on the written page, a language of intensity rather than intelligibility. The struggle to complete sentences also resulted in the fragmented 'Breaking Glass', the lyric-free 'Speed of Life' and 'A New Career in a New Town' (the intention was to write lyrics for both), the vibrating wordless chorus of 'Weeping Wall', the autistic private language of 'Subterraneans', the emotional interjections ('Ahhhh') of 'What in the World', the circularity of 'Always Crashing in the Same Car' and the repetitions of 'Be My Wife'.

But then there is 'Sound and Vision', a song about songwriting which openly worries that the author has 'nothing to say' and must wait for the divine spark. It is an authorial hiatus which gifts Bowie the opportunity to wander aimlessly, surrendering to the sense-[f]*Low* 'over my head'. Yet the ghost of the creator continues to haunt *Low*, his absence registering as a lack. Ghosts are crystal-figures, at once transparent and opaque; they can be deconstructed through the studio process and reconstructed as an absent presence, the almost-beings Bowie invokes in his masquerade of identities. It is to this Bowie I turn now, whose contraction into Bowie-Newton is what haunts *Low* in particular. For Bowie is clear in his evocation of the muse that he is 'waiting for the gift of sound . . . *and* vision.'

The performer: 'listen/don't look'

Bowie's performance of *Low*'s instrumental tracks at the Nippon Budokan in Tokyo on 12 December 1978[61] is strikingly dissimilar to the electric spectacle of 'outrage on stage'[62] and 'shiny costumes as they wove around the stage under the coloured lights',[63] the act fans had come to expect from him. Instead, the performance envisages the orchestral staging suggested by synthetic instruments and the temporal manipulation of Bowie's voice becoming several voices of a choir. Bowie's latest *act*, as it were, mimics the European classical tradition, foregrounding the (authentic) work, pushing the performers into the background and distancing itself from the audience altogether.[64] By Bowie standards it is an understated performance that has him standing in line with band members at the back of the stage, static and unsmiling behind his keyboard, studiously following the puppetry of the conductor – a role Carlos Alomar took up as leader of band rehearsals. In this instance, Bowie is of course both the puppeteer and the puppet, both the originator of the work and its performer. But what is striking about his *performativity* is the presentation of *Low* as a masterwork, a puppetry that cuts the strings to the performer's virtuosity, leaving the composer as the sole figure on stage.

This performer figure is a replication of the classical masterwork, the notation system, and music criticism, which are not simply archives or responses to the work, but the reproduction of its *sameness* as a standard.[65] For Voegelin music criticism mutes the sonic, *seeing* it through 'historical or cultural references' or 'relatable ideas from art history', replacing it with 'the quasi visual conventions of the score, the performance set up, the installation shot, the (visual) instrument, the headphones, the concept, etc.'.[66] The art reporter forgoes 'the *thinging* of its sensorial and physical encounter . . . in favour of understanding' while the hermeneutical tradition of criticism permits the reconstruction of the *thing* through the root metaphor which critical thinking clings to because 'it sees itself as uncovering something it claims was hidden'.[67]

It is the metaphor of Bowie-as-chameleon which has most identified him as performer figure, but just as his own spiritual search has been for the non-judging Gnostic 'God behind the God'[68] so music critics, journalists and lately cultural theorists have sought the man behind the masks. Buckley insists Bowie is the '*real* McCoy',[69] dismissing 'factional' accounts by those who 'try to create truths out of . . . Bowie's deceits',[70] an approach that exposes the biographer as a mediating figure between illusion and reality. While Matthew-Walker insists that his critical focus is on 'art' rather than 'salacious details'[71] he nevertheless sets about constructing a grand narrative of the artist, with its attention to biographical cause and consequence. For the Gillmans, Bowie controls the media having 'learned how to create and manipulate a succession of images of himself'.[72] Cultural theorists are perhaps better tooled up, with theories like *performativity*[73] to prize open Bowie's self-created identities. Waldrep[74] argues that through his performance Bowie becomes the designer of him-*self*, an Oscar Wilde figure, one who is nevertheless dressed in 'theatrical costume' which has nothing to do with who he *is*.[75] Chambers focuses on the cultural importance of Bowie's gender as performance[76] while Klevgaard points to the disappearance of the body in the glare of the spotlight: in the Mick Rock video for *Life on Mars* (1973) 'Bowie's pale skin is indistinguishable from the background . . . his body disappears.'[77] These are interesting lenses on Bowie, ones perhaps more appropriate to the re-imagining of *Low* as a musical essay on identity.

Bowie's '*Low* profile' is a metaphor about ducking the identarian – indeed Bowie insists he dropped all characters to free up his writing[78] – but one the self-referencing on the cover challenges. As Wilcken points out, the Berlin period itself becomes another character,[79] one fuelled by the romance of Berlin[80] while many journalists saw the totalitarian figure of The Thin White Duke in the music of *Low*.[81] Bowie also admits to centring 'strongly' in Newton,[82] the character congealing through performance into an identity that he experienced as authentic and *performatively* evoked,[83] the 'New Face of David Bowie'.[84] It is indeed difficult to escape the visual orbit of the film *The Man Who Fell To Earth* (Roeg, 1976) when listening to *Low* since each has that quality described by Gorbman as 'mutual implication'.[85] Elsewhere I have argued that the Newton character loses his innate *sense* over the course of the film.[86] Not a loss of identity; quite the opposite. His reliance on the various optical tools – the television sets, the microscope and telescope (gifts which he and Mary Lou exchange) – all offer a perspective on reality that merely repeats the sameness already anticipated in man's knowledge. These machines are the tyrant's toys, as apparent in the sequence where the X-ray machines that scientists use to reveal Newton's *true* identity instead eliminate his difference and actualize him as man's identity. Newton's problem is he looks human, and the tyranny of the sight-sense verifies the relationship between appearance and knowledge.

The intensities of performance no doubt inhere for, as Hasty points out, 'performance (*per-formare*) means to actually, really form (*per*-here is an intensive). What is not per-formed is thus not truly or fully formed'.[87] The academy's fear of the spectre of the performer is not misplaced since the latter represents a challenge to the principle of singularity expressed in the composer's will to power.[88] The performer is that necessary figure in the reproduction of *the* work who through the discharge of his 'duties' imperils this singularity even through his enslavement to it, exposing its sameness to *différance*.[89]

This danger may be most apparent at the *'encounter between a language and a voice'*,[90] where the wooden puppetry of *sameness* is performed as the body-in-movement. The instability of (Kant's) interplay between 'the mouth of one interlocutor with ear of the other'[91] begins in the body as a desiring flow that crashes against the organs shored up to organize it. For Barthes, the 'grain of the voice' (borrowed from Kristeva's *genosong*) is the 'materiality of the body speaking its mother tongue',[92] one that circumvents the law of linguistic representation. This grain is perhaps a revelation of the *body without organs*, the planar surface across which desire flows unchecked by the territorializing limits of signification.[93] Barthes compares the grain to the *pheno-song* that draws on a 'myth of respiration',[94] what we might call the masterly territorializing of the lung – 'a stupid organ' – which brings meaning into the *recognition* of performance as a feat of technical and expressive prowess. It is perhaps a stretch to describe all the vocal treatment on *Low* as *writerly* – as a deterritorializing and reterritorializing force – for there are times when the vocals are controlled, like the emotionless drone of 'What in the World' or the *identarian* Cockney angst of 'Be My Wife', but there are also tracks where the body is wired up as part of the studio matrix, surrendering its ego without surrendering its materiality. Bowie had been equally influenced by the electronic sounds of European bands like Neu and Kraftwerk as by Eno's ideas about West Indian music, where the vocals floated around 'coming into focus and disappearing again'.[95] These influences are evident at the end of 'Subterraneans' where the vocals hang in mid-tone while the synthesizer appears to get a *frog in its throat*. On 'Weeping Wall' there is a clearer fusion between voice and instrument, without the technical proficiency of Reich – whose 'Music for Mallet Instruments, Vocal and Organ' (1973) inspired Bowie – but retaining what Bowie may have interpreted as the 'humanity' of the voice, and which is certainly its corporeality, its *grain*. It is the genosong that 'must speak, must write'[96] but disobeys the rules of communication and expression (of feelings), articulating 'structures that are ephemeral . . . and non-signifying', multiplying *difference* rather than *sameness*.[97]

The performance takes place at the very scene of the agency of the body as a moving force, one that infects the sense of the pure work, what we see when we hear words sung. It is an intersensorial confession Bowie offers on 'Sound and Vision', a song about composing and pulling down the blinds on the distractions of performance, a message repeated in the later Buggles hit 'Video Killed the Radio Star' (Island, 1978): sight trumps sound.[98] The visual allusion on *Low* to *The Man Who Fell To Earth* is itself an imaginative reframing of the film, an image of burnt orange alien skies that is not present as an actual scene, and gives permission for further hallucinations of (lava) [f]*Low*, perhaps, or crystal grains, actualized memories of the historical modes of construction. These are productive *mis-sights* which befit the Deleuzean commitment to connections. The mis-sight is the work of the *hinge-sense* that reports on the *sense-flow*, those connections made *between* senses. The hinge-sense reminds us that we when we 'listen / Don't look' we must paradoxically 'see'.

The listener: 'I saw you peeping . . . so deep in your room'

The V&A 'David Bowie is . . .' exhibition (London, 23 March – 11 August 2013) mapped out a possible resolution to its rhetorically incomplete title with biographical rooms, citing Bowie as author, leading to a soundstage surrounded by costumed mannequins representing Bowie the performer. It also identified him as a reader – a 'voracious' one[99] as described by the winged-library of books caught mid-flight above the spectator. Historically, the reader is not only an unimportant figure, despite occupying 'the very space in which are inscribed . . . all the citations a writing consists of',[100] but the passive stooge[101] of consumerist discourses that safeguard his readership from the limitless 'space outside the book'.[102] It is to this figure I turn now, not specifically to promote the affective sonic dimension of *fanaticus* 'as the site of discursive power'[103] but to reposition the listener as one slipping between striated typed-lines into the sense-[f]*Low*.

Hearing, having received little philosophical attention,[104] follows sight's association with somatic detachment and rationalism in maintaining a critical distance between the auditory and the auditor. For Pasnau, sound and sight are '*locational* modalities'[105] not features 'of our sensory experiences'.[106] The disciplining of the senses is, according to Marx, 'a labour of the entire history of the world down to the present'[107] while for Adorno the senses each 'have a different history [and] end up poles apart'.[108] Western music students thus come to prioritize the visual-rational learning of scales and staff notation – language conventions which do not merely represent sound, but actualize it – and centralize the composer rather than the listener as the *maker* of music. This training means the dilettante has advantage over the scholar, the latter finding himself 'unable to experience the full extent of music's' (to recall Hegel's phrase) 'elemental might',[109] while the ear has advantage over the eye, its *passivity*.[110] Since it is lidless, the ear is vulnerable to sonic assault. It processes quicker than the eye,[111] thus opening an experiential gap between the sound event and the sound referent, a hiatus which, at the very least, reorders the conventional sense hierarchy and demands we re-evaluate the significance of the sonic.

The *identarian* Bowie of Ziggy Stardust meant fans and critics could both claim a high degree of agency in making sense of the music, projecting the fantasy onto the skin, *identifying*. A phenomenological experience of *Low* invites listeners to cast off these skins and go with the esoteric [f]*Low*, committing to a sonic immersion rather than a detached and rational 'observation'. Is this what Strick discovers in struggling to make sense of 'Warszawa'? 'Melodious harmonica moans . . . chorale scored dissonant symphonic . . .'. In the end the critic rightly passes the interpretative problem to the listener: 'These are the facts – now fill in the fancy.'[112] For Voegelin, a philosophy of sound art must be willing to share time and space with the sound object as sound 'sits in my ear'.[113] A sonic sensibility in criticism should highlight the notion of 'interpretative fantasies . . . not linked to the logic of . . . visual reality' whilst illuminating those 'unseen aspects of visuality'.[114] Such an encounter heightens perception rather than pretends that knowledge of the album is not offered *a priori*. Thus listening becomes generative of the audio-imaginary, an affective architecture desirous of new connections rather than 'confirming old listening habits'.[115]

Just as the listener is not a discrete agency but 'always-already interpellated'[116] as a listening subject, so to speak, the private listening space is always converging on the public.[117] The experience of space[118] is always *becoming* as place, contracting in *performative* interactions with cultural and historical mediations. Yet space *is* material, its experience meeting this mediation 'as contingencies of subjective experience'.[119] On *Low*, space is configured as rooms and imagined geographies, aural mirrors that hinge the virtual and the material, the psychic and the social. Just as, alone in his own room, the young David Jones envisaged being a 'fantastic artist' when he would 'see the colours, hear the music',[120] so the bedroom retreat of the teenager[121] is the one Bowie fans typically identify as where they first experience *Low*.[122] This space is 'dark,' 'intimate', 'cold', a place where they are 'on their own' going through 'teenage angst', and where *Low* inspires the further 'detachment from things around me', installing them in another space 'floating somewhere between reality and some other world'. This soundspace is also partially visual, augmented by the lights of the record player which fur luminescently in the dark, or the hypnotic 'orange colour of the cover' and the figure of Bowie-Newton, referencing another space since 'my head was already spinning with The Man Who Fell To Earth'.[123]

The sonic architecture of *Low* is imagined across various rooms and places, fantasy boundaries between the inner and outer that continue to work on each other and that do not limit their intensities to the mapping of the sense-organ. The side room, at the London V&A show, which covered the innovative 'Berlin-period' connects to rooms at Château d'Hérouville and the Berlin apartment at Hauptstraße 155 that had offered Bowie 'sanctuary'.[124] The album's isolation rooms are superimposed one upon another, 'Newton's vast interior landscapes'[125] augmenting the 'drifting into my solitude' and reconstructing the world as 'an outright fiction of the imagination'[126] through which the tripartite of figures 'w[o]ander sometimes'. At the Château d'Hérouville the iron-weight of history makes its presence felt in that most abject of forms, the ghost. At the Hansa by the wall, it is a different kind of spook that intrudes into psychic-social space, the forceful gaze of border guards – a 'provocative and stimulating and frightening'[127] intensity that collapses politics and geography into a force refracted 'through the gloom' and into the sonic.

Where are the walls to all these rooms? They are as porous as Newton's masculinity and Bowie's ego. When the gaps between walls becomes an anxiety it is the work of the rationalizing sense organ in marshalling boundaries between sight and sound, psychic and social, human and Other. To be surrounded by walls, to take that *identarian* approach, is to invite the *Mauerkrankheit* (wall sickness)[128] that brought Bowie low. Theweleit[129] has shown us how 'hard' fantasies breed a sickness of the soul. The firm body of the *freikorp* (renegade soldier), whose disciplined muscles steady his hand as he scrawls his melancholic biographies, is imperilled by the very figure that haunts his self-image as an absence, the feminine Other who floods the interstices between the materiality and what Foucault calls the 'materialism of the incorporeal'.[130]

The room is not the sanctity Bowie hoped for, not a rational space (the 'cold room with omnipotent blue on the walls')[131] but the very scene of self-imperilment.[132] 'I'll never touch you' he warns his image-other before crashing the looking glass in 'your room', the very sound of which crashes back into his. At the threshold, the incorporeal body greets his other in a handshake – a term used by Cramer[133] to account for untimely quantum transactions – and allows in a maniac who bludgeons the body senseless.[134] This is the masochistic bodily experience of Shaviro's[135] cinema-goer for whom the virtual images of film 'do not correspond to anything actually present, but *as* images, or *as* sensations, they affect me in a manner that does not leave room for any suspension of my response'. The body has already been touched and affected, before being given the opportunity to close the door to the event, or become conscious of the affective presence in the room.[136] As Blanchot says '[t]he ungraspable is what does not escape'.[137]

Was Freud wrong to assert that, through technology, man 'is perfecting his own organs'?[138] Sonic contact between the sound-object and listening subject is not a collision of agencies, the ear actively listening, since that initiative has been lost, leaving us, as Shaviro puts it, 'powerless not to see'.[139] For many naïve listeners to *Low*, the preferred listening point was the bedroom, with the lights off and the defences down. In this situational blindness of the *cathected* space – one already associated with privacy and identity, where intensities are 'stoked by listening' and 'auditors feel imperilled by what is heard'[140] – the sight organs struggle vainly to combat those visual intensities produced by listening. Similarly the *disturbances* of the synaesthetic experience occur at a liminal nonplace, that 'peri-personal' space 'at the border of what we think of as internal, personal space' and what we think of as the world.[141] Patients recovering from eye surgery may experience the 'vague dimensionality of the Ganzfeld' across which the formless 'chaos of color' flows.[142] Massumi speculates that a clinical synesthete retains perceptual abilities otherwise lost in the process of maturation. Not vision as such; 'more like other-sense operations at the hinge with vision, registered from its point of view'.[143]

The hinge-sense is not an active organizer of sense: synesthetic forms are 'not mirrored in thought; they are literal perceptions'.[144] Similarly, listening may absorb 'other sensory organs besides the ear'.[145] Although for Halliday there is an organizational aspect since the senses corroborate with listening to ensure they 'are not working at cross purposes', the *BwO* is 'the unformed, unorganized, nonstratified, or destratified body'.[146] While the optical equipment in *The Man Who Fell To Earth* contracts Newton's unbound alien desire, the sound-image flows through sense, carrying the listener towards a horizon that is always *becoming*, a Ganzfeld that is enriched by 'seizing hold of other forces and joining itself to them in a new ensemble: a becoming'.[147]

Perhaps this is what the original title of *Low* counselled. *New Music Night and Day* suggests the affective interplay of light and dark across the fast fragmented pop tracks of side one and the ambient movie music of side two, the otherwise differential experiences of sound and vision. And perhaps the tactile materiality of the original album format spoke more clearly than a download does of the transition from side to side, a reminder that our experience of *Low* lingers at the hinge between one and another, the gap between night and day, the f[*Low*] between senses.

Conclusion: 'I was always looking left and right'

One of the last tracks completed on *Low* is also its most clearly narratory, gesturing however to a completion it can never achieve. Critical response unhesitatingly links 'Always Crashing in the Same Car' to various biographical anecdotes of drug-crazed attacks on a dealer's car and suicidal speeding around the garage of a hotel.[148] These accounts may well have voracity but seem to miss the point. While even the most fragmented narrative of Bowie's identity-based songs finds resolution, here the crashing is cyclical, repeated across the track's imagined spaces, Gardiner's solo in the third verse extending the event-repetition the lyric has set up, as if reflecting on the event as eternal. Yet it is also one of just two tracks on *Low* to find its musical full stop, resting on a discordant E minor, which immediately repeats, underscoring the uncertainty of the conclusion and reverberating in the sonic space. Here 'those kilometres and the red lights' are the intensities and limits of our listening journey. For while it seems everyone on the track is sight-orientated 'looking left and right' or *seeing* others 'peeping' – and the only one listening is not mentioned, *overlooked* as it were – this is truly a track for the *hinge-sense*. What is 'the car' but the body across which the intensities of music crash in a reverberating relay between the corporeal and incorporeal?

The conventional use of sense is always *looking* for a cause rather than an affect, *looking* for reason and recognition rather than sensual entanglement, *looking* for identity in the verse rather than the transition that materialises in the encounter. As Voegelin says, '[l]istening is intersubjective in that it produces the work and the self in the interaction between the subject listening and the object heard'.[149] This does not stop us peeping. Like Bowie, we are always crashing, every chance that we take, materializing in *becoming-*collisions, 'going round and round' the small and uncanny space of the sonic, our body, its desires. As we wander away from the figures of composer and performer, traffic police of the sense-organ, we stop listening in that proscribed sense, surrendering instead to the *becoming-*collision of the hinge-sense, that *wall* between senses and sense.

Notes

1 This chapter tasks itself with exploring the album *Low* as *intersensorial*, engaging, that is, vision as well as hearing (indeed touch is also explored, if only a little as the focus here is on the hinge-relationships between sight and sound). This approach is enabled by the recent turn to the multisensory in both the humanities and the sciences (see for example Feld, 2006; Howes, 2006; Smith 2007). Schmidt criticizes the 'great divide' theory of the senses – McLuhan categorized the environment as producing either visual or acoustic space (McLuhan, 1989) – arguing that the 'modern sensorium remains more . . . diffuse and heterogenous, than the discourses of Western visuality and ocularcentrism allow' (see Smith, 2007: 19). The knowledge that senses are discrete is itself a fallacy of 'good sense' (see Deleuze, 1994: 136). Kant's corporeal demarcation of the senses (Kant, 1974: 33–7) creates an objective distance between the listener and the sound object, however the sense of touch means he cannot simply 'ignore that bodies are affected by while differentiated in their contiguous relations' (Vasseleu, 1998: 100). For Sathian and Lacey, touch is not unisensory but employs many of the 'visual' regions of the brain, meaning our perceptional experience is 'richly multimodal' (Levent and Pascual-Leone, 2014: xxi; see also, Lacey and Sathian, 2014).

The claim to sensual interrelationship is supported by Howes who argues that paintings 'need not be mediated by sight alone' (Howes, 2014: 297). Smith notes that historians are beginning to think about the 'interpretative value of examining how the senses worked together' (126). The relationship described is not one where senses corroborate the dominant sense of sight but is rather unpredictable, sometimes working in complementary fashion, sometimes in conflict (see Smith, 2007: 126 and Howes, 2006: 9), as 'one sense surfaces in the midst of another that recedes' (Feld, 2006: 180–1). The senses comingle synesthetically, causing a disorientation to recognized sense. Stindberg, for example, reports feeling 'roughed-up' by sensations associated with modernity, a derangement that 'enabled him to perceive new aesthetic arrangements' (Howes, 2006: 12). Indeed, focusing on the multisensory offers the opportunity to rethink the paradigm of embodiment with its insistence on mind-body integration to a theory of emplacement, one suggesting 'the sensuous interrelationship of body-mind-environment' (Howes, 2006: 7).

The concept of hinge-sense goes further than shifting the focus from the unisensory to the multisensory perspective, and onto the invisible *seams* between senses. As conventional meaning systems are challenged by intersensorality we enter what Howes calls 'the empire of the senses' (2006: 4) and move away from Barthes' empire of the author (Barthes, 1977: 145). There is therefore much new ground to cover in conceptualizing the multisensory and multimodal, particularly those concerned with tracking generative sonic experience. While Kant's folded corporeal schema (Kant, 1974), which manages the outer/inner distinctions between object and perception, is challenged by reconsidering the distance between the listener and sound object and the perceived distinctions between senses, his *fold* does at least point to a corporeal and unstable *hinge* between sense and sensation. Serres' knot (see Howes, 2006: 9) is more useful in envisaging a mechanism of sensual entanglement. Such models permit Bergson's insight that 'there is no perception which is not full of memories . . . With the immediate and present data of our senses, we mingle a thousand details out of our past experience' (Bergson 1908, 1988: 33 in Feld, 2006: 181). The concept of hinge-sense posited here thus attempts to describe the twisted and interwoven machine of perception, one amenable to a positive account of agency since our brain is not a passive receiver of sensory stimulus 'but rather an active source of expectations in hypothesis about the world and its objects – that we can then contrast and refine by experience' (Levent and Pascual-Leone, 2014: xx).

2   The album art to *Low* features the image of Bowie playing the alien Thomas Jerome Newton in the 1976 film *The Man Who Fell To Earth*, a configuration that conflates the singer with the fictional character.

3   Nomadic space opposes striated space, since '[o]ne can rise up at any point and move to any other' (Massumi, 2002: 6). Nomadic thought-space is rhizomic (one of difference), thus wandering is not achieved in a 'solid state, where molecules are not free to move about' (Deleuze, 2005: 86) – what Deleuze calls 'molar' – but 'gaseous' and 'molecular.' Bowie's wandering is a nomadic movement in thought, an interior wandering witnessed as a duration, one depicting 'the foundation of time, non-chronological time' (Deleuze, 1989: 79). Deleuze describes the cinematic process as collating and collaging things (Deleuze, 1989: 129–30). Here then, in this time-image, are the three untimely figures subsisting and persisting in the same space.

4   In *Listening to Noise and Silence* (2011) Vogelin seeks to dematerialize the distance between sound object and sound space, to account for the phenomenological response to sound. Sharing space with the sonic opposes the conventional teaching of music which disciplines the 'listening ear' and instructs what to *look* for in music. Adapting Shaviro's work on the cinematic gaze (Shaviro, 1993), I will argue that a successful immersion in sonic space is a masochistic one that surrenders to the tangle between body and sense.

5   Gilles Deleuze (1925–95) was such an influential philosopher that Michel Foucault claimed the twentieth century as 'Deleuzian' (Foucault, 1977: 165). In his 'encounters' with key philosophers he committed to *difference* and *becoming*, challenging the presuppositions of philosophy and thus opening up a 'radical gap' with the past (Žižek, 2004: xi). His work on painting, literature and film focuses on art as 'a bloc of sensation' (Deleuze and Guattari, 1994: 164), a tool for 'thinking otherwise' (Stivale, 2005: 1) and breaking apart the predictable pattern of identity (Deleuze, 1990: 75). His collaborations with psychoanalyst Felix Guattari work through the 'sense-flow' of *performative* writing that affirms their discrete *difference* in approach while opening up connective ideas that cannot be attributed to either: '[s]ince each of us was several, there was already quite a crowd.' (Deleuze and Guattari, 1987: 3).

6   Deleuze challenges the notion that the role of thought is to represent that which already exists in the world (recognition). The 'abstract image of thought' (Campbell, 2013: 7) is both the response to and the creation of something new. 'With the identical, we think with all our strength, but without producing the least thought: with the different, by contrast, do we not have the highest thought, but also that which cannot be thought?' (Deleuze and Guattari, 1994: 266). This image of thought is based on the concept of 'difference' (Deleuze, 1994). Since everything is simulacra, and repetition is no longer subject to sameness, but to heterogeneity, the primacy of the original is challenged (Deleuze, 1994: 128) in terms of identity of the object and the multiplicity of readings available (Deleuze, 1994: 69). Deleuze's 'image of thought' as difference has implications for how music configures the composer, performer and listener as engaged in dynamic and heterogeneous acts. The static image of thought is replaced by that of flows, connections and assemblages. The rhizome (Deleuze and Guattari, 1987: 15) thus opposes the hierarchical structure of the rooted 'tree system', allowing 'communication [to run] from any neighbour to any other' (Deleuze and Guattari, 1987: 17). Deleuze and Guattari give the example of music as 'a superlinear system' (1987: 95), one that is therefore not explainable by static knowledge (recognition) of music but by difference engendered in the reproduction of music (from composition, to performance to listening).

7 Deleuze and Guattari, 1987: 8.

8 Deleuze and Guattari's study of literature can also find a use as a music concept. Unlike majoritarian literature, 'minor, or revolutionary, literature begins by expressing itself and doesn't conceptualize until afterward' thus encouraging 'ruptures and new spoutings' (see Gilles Deleuze and Felix Guattari, *Kafka: Towards a Minor Literature* 1986, passage quoted in Campbell, 2013: 148–9).

9 The concepts suggested above, which are not specifically music-related, can be viewed as working to force a rethink of music as forming the 'body without organs', 'the unformed, unorganised, nonstratified, or destratified body' (quoted in Campbell, 2013: 147). 'The musical body without organs is one in which the familiar aspects and functions (organs) of recognizable systems (bodies) such as tonality, modality or serialism are no longer apparent, as we are confronted with new possibilities in situations where such functions (organs) are not already predetermined' (Campbell, 2013: 164). Although the BwO repels the organs of the organism (that which imposes on the organs a regime) it also attracts organs, appropriating them to use for itself in another regime (Deleuze and Guattari, 1983: 9–11). Also see Deleuze and Guattari (1987: 149–66).

10 Deleuze, 1990: 12.

11 Barthes, 1977: 145.

12 Deleuze's concept of *sense* contrasts with the Western philosophical tradition, which reduces knowledge to recognition, a 'common sense' (Deleuze, 1990: 89–90) that dismisses difference (Deleuze, 1994: 136–7). Deleuze critiques the universalism of 'good sense' as creating predictive order from the flow of time, affirming sense as difference (Deleuze, 1990: 76–8).

13 Deleuze dismisses 'the primacy of original over copy, of model over image' as a fallacy of identity-based thinking, proposing the concept of difference in its place. A world of difference is a world of intensities, 'built on the tomb of the unique God' (Gilles Deleuze discussion in Cahiers de Royaumont, quoted in Bidima, 2010: 147).

14 Deleuze, 1995: 7–8.

15 Bowie played Newton in the film *The Man Who Fell To Earth* and images from this are used on the covers of both *Low* and *Station to Station*.

16 The album art was rendered in black and white on its original release (later issues are in colour).

17 Rook, 1976.

18 Culture and history usher in the being-man as the standard against which all else is aberrant (Deleuze and Guattari, 1987: 167–9).

19 For Deleuze, becomings are created by the *body without organs*, the plane across which life-flows take flight, desirous of freedom but interrupted into contractions of constitution (Deleuze and Guattari, 1987: 150).

20 For more on this argument about the social construction of the artist, see Parker and Pollock, 1981: 82–113.

21 Even critical theory has *turned deaf ears* while 'musicology has enjoyed [immunity] from outside scrutiny, primarily, we imagine, because "outsiders" simply can't understand the language music scholars speak, especially when it comes to technical descriptions or analysis of music' (Hulse and Nesbitt, 2010: xvi).

22 Bowie has cast himself both as an artist and theatrical artist, showing a clear interest in other modes, such as sculpture and painting (he was on the editorial board of *Modern Painters* and uses his own work to illustrate some cover art, e.g. *Outside 1*, 1995) as well as spending a great deal of time in the preparation of himself as a canvas for album covers and tours. Although in his preface he goes out of his way to retreat from the subtitle, in *David Bowie: Theatre of Music* biographer Robert Matthew-Walker (1985) charts Bowie's rise as one from art school through 'charismatic' performance through to legitimate theatre.

23 Carr and Charles Shaar Murray (2013: 165) consider Bowie a 'second wave' absorber rather than an innovator, one who digests the experiential and transforms it into something modish.

24 These are well documented, for example by Thomas Jerome Seabrook (2008: 32–56); Christopher Sandford (1997: 141); David Buckley (1999: 259); and Hugo Wilcken (2011: 45).

25 Various sources. See Seabrook, 2008: 84; Buckley, 1999: 311.

26 Wilcken, 2011: 14.

27 'The new modernist music of Germany has been a major force behind Pop's and Bowie's assimilation of cybernetic theories. Bands such as Can, Faust, Cluster, the early Kraftwerk, Neu! And Neu!'s offspring La Dusseldorf developed music which, although it was particularly "scenic" and evocative, used a meticulous construction. It shifted moods and layered changing textures around a repetitive, minimal rhythm pulse: it was stark and hypnotic yet responsive' (Rose, 1979).

28 Tobler, 1978.

29 'The three of us agreed to record with no promise that it would ever be released. David had asked me if I didn't mind wasting a month of my life on this experiment if it didn't go well. Hey, we were in a French chateau for the month of September and the weather was great!' (Tony Visconti quoted in Wilcken, 2011: 60).

30 A lack of audience acclaim was often seen as a confirmation of a work's credibility by the modernist tradition, a position which Schoenberg subscribed to, believing that if the audience 'was truly musically literate [it] could grasp music [and] truly appreciate the music of Schoenberg and his followers'. Instead, 'at a loss . . . the audience . . . does not know how to react' (Botstein, 1999: 19–54).

31 Watts, 1978.

32 Wilcken, 2011: 71.

33 The lyrics to 'Breaking Glass' – 'Don't look at the carpet / I drew something awful on it' (David Bowie, George Murray and Dennis Davis, 1976) – appear to reference the feverish period when *Station to Station* was being written and recorded, a time when Bowie apparently got little sleep, took copious amounts of cocaine and lived on a diet of milk and occult books, many of the latter by Aleister Crowley and his followers, one being *The Tree of Life*, written by Israel Regardie. The tree of life is a diagram connecting the *kether* godhead to the *melkuth* world, one Bowie was particularly obsessed with, drawing it on the floor as an act of metaphorical ascension (various sources including Wilcken, 2011: 4–15).

34 Deleuze and Guattari, 1987: 21.

35 Deleuze and Guattari, 1987: 7–8.

36 Deleuze and Guattari, 1987: 21.

37 Not only does the cultural production of art affect who is recognized as an artist, it plays down the importance of his cultural emplacement. It also 'enables' the apparently subjective 'judgements and evaluations of works' (Wolff, 1993: 40)

38 Levi-Strauss, 1962.

39 Deleuze and Guattari, 1987: 8.

40 Bidima, 2010: 145.

41 Wilcken, 2011: 31.

42 Buckley, 1999: 302.

43 Wilcken, 2011: 42.

44 Sound engineer Laurent Thibault explained that, 'There were even tracks that we recorded for Iggy that ended up on Low, such as "What in the World" which was originally called "Isolation" and which Pop's vocal appears on' (Wilcken, 2011: 42–3).

45 There is argument about how much material was brought over to *Low* from *The Man Who Fell To Earth* soundtrack sessions. According to Paul Buckmaster who worked with Bowie on the soundtrack, the only piece that has been heard in re-recorded form is 'Subterraneans' (Buckley, 1999: 278) although Eno believes that 'Weeping Wall' (Wilcken, 2011: 16) and 'Some Are' (Seabrook, 2008: 130) were also conceived there. Buckmaster reports that the pair worked on some 'rock instrumental pieces', with Bowie's rhythm section and J. Peter Robinson (thus explaining the credit to Peter and Paul on *Low*), along with 'slow and spacey cues' and 'a couple of weirder, atonal cues', a piece by Buckmaster using African thumb pianos and 'a [melancholy] song David wrote called Wheels' (Buckley, 2007: 57).

46 This is fully discussed in the next section, but it is worth recalling that the sensory impact of working on the film, and identifying with the character Newton, was an intense one for Bowie, who bought Newton's wardrobe when the film was finished and seemed, according to the director Roeg, to have become the character (Seabrook, 2008: 44).

47 According to Bowie, '[t]he music was spontaneous for the most part and created in the studio' (Roberts, 1999).

48 Eno says of the working methods on *Low*, '[t]he Interesting place is not chaos, and it's not total coherence. It's somewhere on the cusp of those two' (Wilcken, 2011: 68).

49 ' "I'd continually ask him if what we were playing was OK," recalled bass player Laurent Thibault in 2002. "He wouldn't reply. He'd just stare at me without saying a word. That was when I realised he was never going to reply" ' (Wilcken, 2011: 45).

50 The *ganzfeld* effect is a visual perception caused by loss of vision. In his study of perception, Wolfgang Metzger observed 'a mist of light which becomes more condensed at an indefinite distance' (Metzger, 1930: 6–29). Here and later in this chapter, I use *ganzfeld* as a metaphor for the series-combinations on perception inspired by the hinge-sense.

51 The studio becomes a metaphor for a way of writing that opens itself to connectivity without the pretence of sole authorship. In such an scenario, the studio is an example of Deleuze and Guattari's BwO which is 'not space, nor is it in space; it is matter that occupies space to a given degree – to the degree corresponding to the intensities produced. It is nonstratified, unformed, intense matter, the matrix of intensity, intensity = 0; but there is nothing negative about that zero, there are no negative or positive intensities' (Deleuze and Guattari, 1987: 153).

52 Tony Visconti interview (Roberts, 1999).

53 Tobler, 1978.

54 According to *Record Mirror* reporter, Jim Evans, 'There are two walls in Berlin . . . One divides the city. The other surrounds David Bowie' (Gillman and Gillman, 1986: 438).

55 The ghosts were reported to be of Frederic Chopin and his lover Georges Sand who had lived in the chateau. Brian Eno also claimed to have been haunted, and developed a cough he attributed to the presence of the composer, who died from consumption. Various sources including Trynka, 2104.

56 Tony Visconti interview (Roberts, 1999).

57 Rose, 1979.

58 Carlos Alomar explained to Bowie biographer David Buckley: 'Brian Eno had come in with all these cards that he had made and they were supposed to eliminate a block. Now, you've got to understand something. I'm a musician. I've studied music theory, I've studied counterpoint and I'm used to working with musicians who can read music. Here comes Brian Eno and he goes to a blackboard. He says: "Here's the beat, and when I point to a chord, you play the chord." So we get a random picking of chords. I finally had to say, "This is bullshit, this sucks, this sounds stupid." I totally, totally resisted it' (Wilcken, 2011: 67–8).

59 Bowie moved house to North Doheny Drive, Los Angeles in 1975, consumed copious amounts of alcohol and drugs, was sexually promiscuous and became fixated on black magic (several sources, including Sandford, 1997).

60 Seabrook, 2008: 128.

61 There was no promotional tour of *Low* but the later *Isolar II World Tour* shows how the instrumental tracks were visually rendered. This Tokyo show concluded the tour and is discussed here as it is publicly viewable on social media platforms.

62 Kemp, 1972.

63 MP, 1972: 6.

64 It is not strictly true that the conventional audience has no role, since it is disciplined to applaud only at the conclusion of the masterwork. Interestingly, there are reports from the tour that some of the audience subverted this by booing the instrumentals. Various sources.

65 The principle of originality has partly mediated the fan reception of Philip Glass' *'Low' Symphony* (Point Music, 1993) with some expressing disappointment in the way it deviated from the 'founding' work (October 2014b). Glass meanwhile focuses on his own 'compositional bent' (Philip Glass, 'Low Symphony', www.philipglass.com/music/recordings/low_symphony.php, 1 March 2014), thus framing the work as a new identity albeit one that extends difference as a result of being revisited: 'the darkness is gone' in his version since '[l]ife looks different when you're in your fifties' therefore 'it was bound to have a different emotional colour to it' (Gill, 1993).

66 Voegelin, 2011: 26–7.

67 It is a problem as much for critical thinking as for music thinking or any thinking that 'disavows its own inventiveness' (Massumi, 2002: 12). Metaphors are amenable to writing; they slip in so easily that they often need pointing out. Indeed, I shortly point out how the reimagining of *Low*'s cover art as lava flows and crystal grains has rhetorical significance. Like all metaphors, these threaten to materialize the objects they describe.

68 This in fact 'just pervades everything . . . when you're expressing oneself, you are also trying to express one's existence, so it's wrapped up in the same thing' – David Bowie interviewed (*Lola da musica*, 2010).

69 Buckley, 1999: 5, my italics.

70 Buckley, 1999: 10.

71 Matthew-Walker, 1985: npg.

72 Gillman and Gillman, 1986: 8.

73 Performativity refers to the discursive formation of identities and is thus interested in how identities are 'performed'.

74 Waldrep, 2004.

75 Moers, 1978: 298.

76 Chambers, 1996: 67.

77 Klevgaard, 2013.

78 According to Bowie, there could be no characters after the Duke if he was to continue writing a 'descriptive observation of any environment that I happened to be in' (White, 1978). This, admittedly, is a different kind of wandering, one inspired by the *flâneur*-artist who pursues real places to translate into art-spaces, rather than the desirous free wandering of the rhizome. It is also one that centralizes the author as opposed to the studio-process (at least) and listener.

79 Wilcken, 2011: 111.

80 Stevenson, 2006: 135.

81 For details about what the journalists wrote, see Gillman and Gillman, 1986: 439.

82 Bowie: 'I can centre very strongly in [Newton] because most of my characters have that feel' (Davidson Dalling Associates, 1976: 19).

83 Butler follows Althusser (1971) in arguing that identity is the result of an *a priori* ideological hailing stating that it 'congeals over time' through repeat acts 'to produce the appearance of substance, of a natural sort of being' (Butler, 1990: 33).

84 From the cover of *The Sunday Times Magazine* ('The New Face of David Bowie,' 20 July 1975).

85 Gorbman is referring to the relationship between a film and its soundtrack. Here the Bowie-Newton actualization persists across projects, giving identity to the untimely [f]Low, a burden on our listening bodies as we wander rhizomically through its soundscape (Gorbman, 1987: 15).

86 October, 2014a.

87 Hasty, 2010: 5.

88 For Nietzsche (1967), the will to power is a doctrine that describes the ambition to reach the highest social position.

89 According to Derrida, writing extends the reach of the speech act across time and space: the 'radical absence' of speaking and listening agents shows how the linguistic mark is repeatable without being anchored to any specific context. Since it must be citable, the mark exhibits sameness while it is simultaneously exposed to being taken up differently (Derrida, 1988: 12–17; see also Derrida, 1982: 5–27). By this explanation, the performer, through necessarily repeating the work, opens it to new ways of being heard and understood.

90 Barthes, 1977: 181, italics in original.

91 Halliday, 2013: 22.

92 Barthes, 1977: 182.

93 Discussing desire, incest and imperial representation, Deleuze and Guattari show how the despotic machine overcodes desiring flows and subordinates the voice: 'there occurs a crushing of the "magical triangle" [of the vocal, graphic and visual]: the voice no longer sings but dictates, decrees; the graphy no longer dances, it ceases to animate bodies, but is set into writing on tablets, stones, and books; the eye sets itself to reading' (Deleuze and Guattari, 1983: 200–5).

94 Barthes, 1977: 183.

95 Gillman and Gillman 1986: 432.

96 Barthes, 1977: 185.

97 Barthes, 1977: 179.

98 Bowie also admits: 'The music is the mask the message wears – music is the Pierrot and I, the performer, am the message' (an article from *Rolling Stone*, 1 April 1971 quoted in Mendelsohn, 1996: 46).

99 Several reviews picked up on this description of Bowie by V&A curator Geoffrey Marsh.

100 Barthes, 1977: 148.

101 Buckley, for example, refers to Bowie followers as a 'flock' (1999: 5).

102 'Normally, the function of most books, it must be said, is precisely to close down such a space, to make what the book attempts to think unliveable, to remove any oxygen from its atmosphere so one can no longer breathe. Sooner or later, perhaps naively, one quickly abandons the space of a book in order to go outside and get a little breath of air, not realizing that the air outside is not much better, and these days is becoming more asphyxiating. There are too few spaces that one can find to breathe these days especially in societies like ours, which Deleuze diagnosed shortly before his death as in the process of becoming a "controlling society".' (Lambert, 2006: 11–12).

103 Booth and Kelly, 2013: 56–72.

104 Metz, 1980.

105 Pasnau, 1999: 196, 313.

106 Pasnau, 1999: 309.

107 Marx, 1978: 88–9.

108 Adorno, 2005: 91.

109 Halliday, 2013: 31–2.

110 'One might say that to react with the ear, which is fundamentally a passive organ in contrast to the swiftly, actively selecting eye, is in a sense not in keeping with the present advanced industrial age and its cultural anthropology' (Adorno and Eisler, 1994: 20–1).

111 Chion, 1994.

112 Strick, 1977.

113 Voegelin, 2011: xi.

114 The problem with sound subsumed into the visual, without such an intervention, is it 'invites our bodies to meet the work after its mediation through language and documentation, rather than before' (Voegelin, 2011: 26). Quote in text: Voegelin, 2011: xiii–iv.

115 Campbell, 69.

116 Althusser, 1971: 175.

117 According to Lefebvre, space is fluid rather than fixed. Lefebvre identifies three levels of social space that are 'interwoven'. That is, public, private and mediating space all share elements, none are absolute as fixed public or private space, but act as 'passageways' between categories (see Lefebvre and Nicholson-Smith, 2007: 156–8).

118 See for example Merleau-Ponty, 1945, 2002.

119 October, 2013a.

120 Cann, 2010: 19.

121 Wilcken, 2011: 2.

122 I am indebted to those davidbowie.com members who shared their experiences. Fans were asked to recall their first experience of *Low*, to report on the space, their feelings, their imaginings as well as how any foreknowledge of the album, through the press for instance, informed their responses. Some of these responses are recorded in the main body of the text (October, 2014b).

123 The long quotes here are from the contributions of Valerie Le-Pottier-Mace, Canvey Island Baby, johnt and jimmy.haig (October, 2014b).

124 Bowie: 'For many years Berlin had appealed to me as a sort of sanctuary-like situation.' (Roberts, 1999).

125 Wilcken, 2011: 21.

126 Deleuze, 1991: 80.

127 Visconti quoted in Gillman and Gillman, 1986: 437.

128 *Mauerkrankheit* (wall sickness) is a psychic-somatic illness recognized as an epidemic by doctors when the Wall was erected around West Berlin.

129 Theweleit, 1996.

130 Foucault, 1981: 48.

131 Bowie in interview: 'That was an ultimate retreat song; actually, the first thing that I wrote with Brian in mind when we were working at the Chateau. It was just the idea of getting out of America, that depressing era I was going through. I was going through dreadful times. It was wanting to be put in a little cold room with omnipotent blue on the walls and blinds on the windows' (Watts, 1978).

132 'I'm absolutely and totally vulnerable by environment, and environment and circumstances affect my writing tremendously' (Bowie quoted in Jones 1977).

133 Cramer, 1986: 660.

134 McClary describes Beethoven's poundingly physical Ninth Symphony as an 'unparalleled fusion of murderous rage' (1991: 128).

135 Steven Shaviro's book *The Cinematic Body* (1993) argues that films are abject pleasures with intense unavoidable sensorial impact on the body. Just as Shaviro argues that visual spectatorship of film is a masochistic pleasure, so I am arguing that listening submits to the violence of sonic experience and that this may be the basis for the surrender of the *active* listener, that legacy of ear-training (quote: Shaviro, 1993: 59).

136 Massumi describes the body as always changed by the event, a 'successfully shot arrow' (Massumi, 2002: 7). For Massumi, the position of the body is 'an emergent quality of movement' (Massumi, 2002: 8).

137 Blanchot, 1981: 84.

138 Especially given, as Aristotle had already suggested, sense-objects cannot control the sense-excesses from destroying the sense-organs (Halliday, 2013: 29). (Quote: Freud, 1930: 90).

139 Shaviro, 1993: 61.

140 Halliday, 2013:174–5.

141 Massumi, 2002: 187.

142 Massumi, 2002: 156.

143 Massumi, 2002: 186.

144 Massumi, 2002: 186.

145 Halliday, 2013: 158–9.

146 Deleuze and Guattari, 1987: 43.

147 Deleuze, 1997: 132.

148 Various sources including Wilcken, 2011: 91–2 and Doggett, 2011: 264–5.

149 Voegelin, 2011: 28.

Bibliography

Adorno, Theodor. 2005. *In Search of Wagner*. London: Verso.

Adorno, Theodor and Hanns Eisler. 1994. *Composing for the Films*. London: Athlone Press.

Althusser, Louis. 1971. *Lenin and Philosophy and other Essays*. New York: Monthly Review Press.

Barthes, Roland. 1977. *Image Music Text*. London: Fontana Press.

Benjamin, Walter. 1992. *Illuminations*. London: Fontana.

Bidima, Jean-Godefroy. 2010. 'Intensity, music, and heterogenesis in Deleuze'. In Brian Hulse and Nick Nesbitt (eds), *Sounding the Virtual: Gilles Deleuze and the Theory and Philosophy of Music*. Farnham and Burlington: Ashgate.

Blanchot, Maurice. *The Gaze of Orpheus*. 1981. New York: Station Hill Press.

Booth, Paul and Peter Kelly. 2013. 'The changing faces of Doctor Who fandom: new fans, new technologies, old practices?' *Participations*, 10 (1) (May), 56–72.

Botstein, Leon. 1999. 'Schoenberg and the audience: modernism, music, and politics in the twentieth century'. In Walter Frisch (ed.), *Schoenberg and His World*. Princeton: Princeton University Press.

Buckley, David. 1999. *Strange Fascination: David Bowie – The Definitive Story*. London: Virgin.

Buckley, David. 2007. 'The lost Bowie album'. *MOJO Classic*, 2 (2).

Butler, Judith. 1990. *Gender Trouble: Feminism and the Subversion of Identity*. London and New York: Routledge.

Campbell, Edward. 2013. *Music After Deleuze*. London and New York: Bloomsbury.

Cann, Kevin. 2010. *Any Day Now. David Bowie, The London Years: 1947–1974*. London: Adelita.

Carr, Roy and Charles Shaar Murray. 1981. *Bowie: An Illustrated Record*, New York: Avon.

Chambers, Iain. 1996. 'Among the fragments'. In Elizabeth Thomson and David Gutman (eds), *The Bowie Companion*. Boston: Da Capo Press.

Chion, Michel. 1994. *Audio-Vision: Sound on Screen*. New York: Columbia University Press.

Cramer, John G. 1986. 'The transactional interpretation of quantum mechanics'. *Reviews of Modern Physics*, 58 (July), 647–88.

Davidson Dalling Associates. 1976. 'The Man Who Fell To Earth, Long Star biographies'. *Davidson Dalling Associates Information Folder*. London: Davidson Dalling Associates.

Deleuze, Gilles. 1989. *Cinema Two: The Time-Image*. London: Continuum.

Deleuze, Gilles. 1990. *The Logic of Sense*. Edited by Constantin V. Boundas. New York: Columbia University Press.

Deleuze, Gilles. 1991. *Empiricism and Subjectivity: An Essay on Hume's Theory of Human Nature*. New York: Columbia University Press.

Deleuze, Gilles. 1994. *Difference and Repetition*. New York: Columbia University Press.

Deleuze, Gilles. 1995. *Negotiations 1972–1990*. New York: Columbia University Press.

Deleuze, Gilles. 1997. *Essays Critical and Clinical*. Minneapolis: University of Minnesota Press.

Deleuze, Gilles. 2005. *Cinema 1: The Movement-image*. London and New York: Continuum.

Deleuze, Gilles and Felix Guattari. 1983. *Anti-Oedipus: Capitalism and Schizophrenia*. Minneapolis: University of Minnesota Press.

Deleuze, Gilles and Felix Guattari. 1987. *A Thousand Plateaus: Capitalism and Schizophrenia*. Minneapolis: University of Minnesota Press.

Deleuze, Gilles and Felix Guattari. 1994. *What is Philosophy?* London: Verso.

Deleuze, Gilles with Claire Parnet. 1977. *Dialogues*. New York: Columbia University Press.

Derrida, Jacques. 1982. '*Différance*'. In *Margins of Philosophy*. Chicago: University of Chicago Press.

Derrida, Jacques. 1988. *Limited Inc*. Chicago: Chicago University Press.

Doggett, Peter. 2011. *The Man Who Sold the World*. London: Bodley Head.

Donnelly, Kevin J. 2005. *The Spectre of Sound: Music in Film and Television*. London: British Film Institute.

Dyer, Richard. 1979. *Stars*. London: Educational Advisory Service, British Film Institute.

Feld, Steven. 2006. 'Places sensed, senses placed: toward a sensuous epistemology of environments'. In David Howes (ed.), *Empire of the Senses: The Sensual Culture Reader*. London: Berg.

Foucault, Michel. 1977. 'Theatrum philosophicum'. In D. Bouchard (ed.), *Language, Counter-memory, Practice: Selected Essays and Interviews*. Oxford: Basil Blackwell.

Foucault, Michel. 1981. 'The order of discourse'. In Ian McLeod and R. Young (eds), *Untying the Text: A Poststructuralist Reader*. Boston: Routledge & Kegan Paul.

Freud, Sigmund. 1930. *Civilisation and its Discontents*. In *The Standard Edition of the Complete Psychological Works of Sigmund Freud*, Vol 21. London: Hogarth Press.

Gill, Andy. 1993. 'Going about as low as it is possible to go: what did Philip Glass take from David Bowie? Andy Gill met the composer to find out'. *Independent*, 18 March.

Gillman, Peter and Leni Gillman. 1986. *Alias David Bowie*. London: Hodder & Stoughton.

Goodhall, Howard. 2013. 'Bowie music Lucky Old Sun is in My Sky'. In Victoria Broackes and Geoffrey Marsh (eds), *Bowie is Inside De Luxe Edition*. London: V&A.

Gorbman, Claudia. 1987. *Unheard Melodies: Narrative Film Music*. Bloomington and London: BFI & Indiana University Press.

Grosz, Elizabeth. 1994. *Volatile Bodies: Towards a Corporeal Feminism*. London: Routledge.

Halliday, Sam. 2013. *Sonic Modernity: Representing Sound in Literature, Culture and the Arts*. Edinburgh: Edinburgh University Press.

Hasty, Christopher. 2010. 'The image of thought and ideas of music'. In Brian Hulse and Nick Nesbitt (eds), *Sounding the Virtual: Gilles Deleuze and the Theory and Philosophy of Music*. Farnham and Burlington: Ashgate.

Howes, David (ed.). 2006. *Empire of the Senses: The Sensual Culture Reader*. Oxford and New York: Berg.

Howes, David. 2014. 'The secret of aesthetics lies in the conjugation of the senses: reimagining the museum as a sensory gymnasium'. In Nina Levent and Alvaro Pascual-Leone (eds), *The Multisensory Museum: Cross-Disciplinary Perspectives on Touch, Sound, Smell, Memory, and Space*. New York: Rowman & Littlefield.

Hulse, Brian and Nick Nesbitt (eds). 2010. *Sounding the Virtual: Gilles Deleuze and the Theory and Philosophy of Music*. Farnham: Ashgate.

Jones, Allan. 1977. 'Goodbye to Ziggy and all that'. *Melody Maker*, 29 October.

Kant, Immanuel. 1974. *Anthropology from a Pragmatic Point of View*. The Hague: Martinus Nijhoff.

Kemp, Al. 1972. 'David Bowie: Festival Hall'. *NME*, 15 July.

Klevgaard, Trond. 2013. 'David Bowie and notions of gender, truth and artifice in dress'. *fbi-spy*, October, www.fbi-spy.com/david-bowie-lady-sardust, accessed 5 May 2014.

Lacey, Simon and K. Sathian. 2014. 'Please DO touch the exhibits! Interactions between visual imagery and haptic perception'. In Nina Levent and Alvaro Pascual-Leone (eds), *The Multisensory Museum: Cross-Disciplinary Perspectives on Touch, Sound, Smell, Memory, and Space*. New York: Rowman & Littlefield.

Lambert, Gregg. 2006. *Who's Afraid of Deleuze and Guattari?* London: Continuum.

Lefebvre, Henri and Donald Nicholson-Smith. 2007. *The Production of Space*. Malden: Blackwell.

Levent, Nina and Alvaro Pascual-Leone (eds). 2014. *The Multisensory Museum: Cross-Disciplinary Perspectives on Touch, Sound, Smell, Memory, and Space.* New York: Rowman & Littlefield.

Levi-Strauss, Claude. 1962. *The Savage Mind.* Chicago: University of Chicago Press.

Lola da musica. 2010. 'David Bowie interview'. *Lola da musica,* VPRO (the Netherlands), 26 January, www.youtube.com/watch?v=TRkIvInTT0w, accessed 2 June 2014.

Marx, Karl. 1978. 'Economic and philosophic manuscripts of 1844'. In Robert C. Tucker (ed.), *The Marx Reader,* 2nd edition. New York: Norton.

Massumi, Brian. 2002. *Parables for the Virtual: Movement, Affect, Sensation.* Durham and London: Duke University Press.

Matthew-Walker, Robert. 1985. *David Bowie: Theatre of Music.* Buckinghamshire: Kensal Press.

McClary, Susan. 1991. *Feminine Endings: Music, Gender, and Sexuality.* Minnesota: University of Minnesota Press.

McLuhan, Marshall. 1989. *The Global Village: Transformations in World Life and Media in the 21st Century.* Oxford: Oxford University Press.

Mendelsohn, John. 1996. 'David Bowie pantomime rock'. In Elizabeth Thomson and David Gutman (eds), *The Bowie Companion.* Boston: Da Capo Press.

Merleau-Ponty, Maurice. 1945, 2002. *Phenomenology of Perception.* London: Routledge.

Metz, Christian. 1980. 'Aural objects'. *Yale French Studies,* 60 (1), 24–32.

Metzger, Wolfgang. 1930. 'Optische Untersuchungen am Ganzfeld II. Zur Phänomenologie des homogenen Ganzfelds'. *Psychologische Forschung,* 8, 6–29.

Moers, Ellen. 1978. *The Dandy – Brummell to Beerbohm.* Lincoln: University of Nebraska Press, 1978.

MP. 1972. 'Hundreds flock to Dave Bowie concert'. *The Bucks Herald,* 20 July.

Nietzsche, Friedrich. 1967. *The Will to Power.* New York: Random House.

October, Dene. 2013a. 'Adventures in English time and space: sound as experience in *Doctor Who,* "An Unearthly Child".' Paper presented at Mad Dogs & Englishness: Popular Music and English Identities, St Mary's University College, London, 20 June.

October, Dene. 2013b. 'David Bowie changed my life'. *fbi-spy,* October, www.fbi-spy.com/david-bowie-changed-my-life.

October, Dene. 2014a. 'The becoming (wo)man who fell to earth'. In Eoin Devereux, Aileen Dillane and Martin Power (eds), *David Bowie: Critical Perspectives.* London: Routledge.

October, Dene. 2014b. 'What was your first experience of *Low* like?' http://community.davidbowie.com/index.php?/topic/57415-what-was-your-first-experience-of-low-like/, accessed March 2014.

Parker, Rozsika and Griselda Pollock. 1981. *Old Mistresses: Women, Art and Ideology.* London: Routledge & Kegan Paul.

Pasnau, Robert. 1999. 'What is sound?' *The Philosophical Quarterly,* 49 (July), 196.

Poxon, Judith L. and Stivale, Charles J. 2005. 'Sense, series'. In Charles J. Stivale (ed.), *Gilles Deleuze: Key Concepts.* Durham: Acumen.

Roberts, Chris. 1999. 'Bowie – the man who changed the world'. *UNCUT*, October.

Rook, Jean. 1976. 'Waiting for Bowie and finding a genius who insists he's really a clown'. *Daily Express*, 5 May.

Rose, Cynthia. 1979. 'Oblique strategies'. *Harpers & Queen*.

Sandford, Christopher. 1997. *Bowie: Loving The Alien*. London: Warner.

Seabrook, Thomas Jerome. 2008. *Bowie in Berlin: A New Career in a New Town*. London: Jawbone.

Shaviro, Steven. 1993. *The Cinematic Body*. Minneapolis: University of Minnesota Press.

Smith, Mark M. 2007. *Sensory History*. Oxford and New York: Berg.

Stevenson, Nick. 2006. *David Bowie: Fame, Sound and Vision*. London: Polity Press.

Stivale Charles J. (ed.). 2005. *Gilles Deleuze Key Concepts*. Durham: Acumen.

Strick, Wesley. 1977. 'Bowie now, new songs for day and night'. *Circus*, 28 February.

Theweleit, Klaus. 1996. *Male Fantasies: Volume 1, Women Floods Bodies History*. Translated by Stephen Conway. Minneapolis: University of Minnesota Press.

Tobler, John. 1978. '12 minutes with David Bowie'. *Zigzag*, January.

Trynka, Paul. 2014. 'Safe European Home. How David Bowie rescued Iggy, found himself – and made Low'. www.trynka.net/archive/Low.html, accessed 1 May 2104.

Vasseleu, Cathryn. 1998. *Textures of Light: Vision and Touch in Irigaray, Levinas and Merleau Ponty*. London and New York: Routledge.

Voegelin, Salome. 2011. *Listening to Noise and Silence: Towards a Philosophy of Sound Art*. New York: Continuum.

Waldrep, Shelton. 2004. *The Aesthetics of Self-Invention – Oscar Wilde to David Bowie*. Minneapolis: University of Minnesota Press.

Watts, Michael. 1978. 'Confession of an elitist: for what is a man like David Bowie profited, if he shall sell the whole world and lose his own mind?' *Melody Maker*, February.

White, Timothy. 1978. 'Turn and face the strange.' *Crawdaddy*, February.

Wilcken, Hugo. 2011. *David Bowie's 'Low'* (33 1/3). London and New York: Continuum International Publishing.

Wolff, Janet. 1993. *The Social Production of Art, Communications & Culture*. Basingstoke: Palgrave Macmillan.

Žižek, Slavoj. 2004. *Organs without Bodies: On Deleuze and Consequences*. London: Routledge.

15

When Are We Now?

Walls and Memory in David Bowie's Berlins

Tiffany Naiman

On his sixty-sixth birthday, following ten years without a release, David Bowie re-emerged with a new song and music video, 'Where Are We Now?' (*The Next Day*, 2013), which appeared in cyberspace unannounced and without fanfare. Within minutes the video began rapidly circulating via the internet; that same day, the song rose to number one on the iTunes charts of nine countries. These unusual circumstances are noteworthy in themselves, but even more intriguing is the affective dimension of Bowie's birthday release as a memorial and expression of loss, evoking a special kind of melancholy. While most journalistic writing about 'Where Are We Now?' has treated the song as a solely personal narrative, another possible interpretation is to understand it as a rare moment of political commentary from David Bowie concerning post-Wall Berlin as a synecdoche for the melancholy of postmodern life under neoliberal capitalism.[1] Through analysis of the instrumentation and vocals in the song, in conjunction with the images of Berlin shown in the music video for 'Where Are We Now?', this chapter considers the work that the sonic and visual cues do to transmit through a collage of memorial traces[2] the ways that Bowie uses various types of memories tied both to temporal and spatial referents to create a political critique.

In *Unmarked: The Politics of Performance*, Peggy Phelan theorizes the radically ephemeral nature of performance, stressing that the 'document of a performance . . . is only a spur to memory, an encouragement of memory to become present' (Phelan, 1993: 146). In line with Phelan's assertion, Bowie's construction of the song and its release arguably activates a series of memories in the song's audience that are, on the one hand, personal and, on the other, very public, embedded in Western musical and historical culture. Listening to 'Where Are We Now?' utilizes the performative possibilities of traces, of memories. By performing partial memories and embedding sonic spectres, Bowie's song brings the past very much into the present – a present imbued with melancholy.

I propose that a performative poetics of walls is at play, with memory configuring the way they reappear in the present. I will examine the presence of two types of walls in Bowie's work, the physical Berlin Wall and the critical wall that divides Bowie's career. Analysing the album art of *The Next Day* (2013), and the video, music and lyrics to its first single, 'Where Are We Now?' I will attend to the legacies from Bowie's Berlin days as they appear in his birthday release, as well as what their interaction with images and sounds from other eras point to, and examine how the aforementioned combine to create the melancholic nature of the song. I intend to tease out, in this limited space, a number of public memories Bowie evokes around the Berlin Wall and his song and record *"Heroes"* (1977),[3] and then address the ways in which Bowie uses both the facts and the myths of his own time spent in Berlin to create a piece that is able to flow between the personal and the political as it moves through the world, expressing the absolute powerlessness of politics under neoliberal capitalism as melancholia.[4]

Melancholy and memory

This chapter is not a psychoanalytic reading of Bowie as melancholic, but instead proposes that his song is expressive of a postmodern melancholy linked, at least partially, to a life lived under neoliberal capitalism. The poignancy of the melancholy in 'Where Are We Now?' is that it arises not just as a mood brought about by the sound of the music or the words attached to the song; it is also an experience of loss conjured through multiple temporal layers. Bowie puts in motion an intertextual bricolage of media (audio, video and graphic design), invoking and alluding to collective and personal memory (Bowie's own memories of Berlin, his fans' memories of the era in which his record *"Heroes"* was released, and the collective memories of Berlin and the Wall, which trace a narrative of political struggle from the 60s to the present). Because this loss has multiple layers tied to different objects and moments, it makes the melancholy stronger and the object of its cause more difficult to pinpoint.

This multivalence is also how Freud differentiates mourning and melancholia, where mourning is a conscious response to the loss of a known object and melancholia is a function of the unconscious, stemming from a loss that cannot be physically perceived, such as an event in the past, youth or love (Freud, 1962: 243). Melancholia is a feeling that cannot be shaken because, whatever the loss, what is being mourned has been taken in and made part of the mourning subject and thus there is no longer a recognition of what was lost as a separate, lost object; rather the 'shadow of the object falls upon the ego' (Freud, 1962: 249), which is to say that the object becomes part of the self as consequence of the subject's inability to complete his/her mourning. It is an unconscious refusal to let go in which the object is made one's own. In the end, for Freud, a person who can be thought of as possessing a good memory is one that does an excellent job of forgetting. It is precisely when memories remain that the desire for what is lost continues, is reanimated and becomes the cause of melancholy. There is an unsettling reflective nature that resides in melancholy, in that the feeling is brought about through memories related to the absent object. Memories are the driving force of our desire and, ultimately, a constant push towards what we can never have again, that which is lost to the past, be it a time, place or momentary feeling. Memories are inherently temporal. Memory itself can be lost, or altered – memory is the future already past, memory indicates lost access to an experience – but memory can also perform in the present and shape new experiences. Though grounded in the past, memory is not confined there, but reaches forward to be performed in the present. It is this performance of the past through re-articulations and reverberations of it via memory expressed in song and image that animates David Bowie's 'Where Are We Now?'

One city, two walls

Wall one: the Berlin Wall – Bowie and proximity to it

Tony Visconti, the co-producer of both *Heroes* and *The Next Day*, recalls Berlin circa 1977 as a place where 'The impending danger of the divided military zones, the bizarre nightlife, the extremely traditional restaurants with aproned servers, [and] reminders of Hitler's not-too-distant presence' (Hughes and Dalton, 2001: 46) were all part of what seeped into the creative energy at work in the studio, just a few hundred yards from the Wall, where *Heroes* was conceived and recorded. This studio, which Bowie dubbed 'The Hall by the Wall' (Turner, 1991), had once been used as a Nazi social club. 'It was a Weimar ballroom,' Bowie said, 'utilized by Gestapo in the '30s for their own little musical "soirées"' (Hughes and Dalton, 2001: 56). The studio sat next to a guard tower where East German border guards stood, guns in hand, ready to stop anyone attempting to traverse the Wall. Bowie could gaze out from the studio onto the Wall while working on *Heroes*

> and as such it is the album on which the culture, the history and the very essence of Berlin come to bear most fully on Bowie's work. The fact that he and his fellow musicians were working directly in the shadows of the Wall, surrounded not just by echoes of wars past but by reminders of the contemporary conflicts between East and West, instilled a drive and seriousness into their work.
>
> Seabrook, 2008: 171

These words are not just those of a biographer hypothesizing. Bowie has also talked about the effect of his surroundings on his music when he stated, 'Whether it's fortunate or not I don't know, but I'm absolutely and totally vulnerable by environment, and environment and circumstances affect my writing tremendously' (Jones, 1977: 9).

Political walls are also epochal markers, which have significance not just for the histories of states but for personal histories touched by the temporality of walls. Though Berlin allowed for personal and artistic freedom for Bowie, his city was not the experience for many in 70s Berlin, and the oppression and divisiveness of the Wall is a far more present affect on *Heroes* than any expression of freedom might be. The wall that ran through Berlin becomes an aural expression of the very real tension that existed in the divided city, from the swirling flanged guitar threatening to swallow Bowie's voice in 'Sons of the Silent Age' to the rapid rhythm of 'Look Back in Anger', where Bowie's crooning vocals appear in juxtaposition with the frantic pace of the instrumentation. These musical moments, where vocal melody is completely split from the music's rhythm or tone, can be read as compositional and aesthetic choices that are in relationship to the environment Bowie was living and working in. All the songs on *Heroes* have reverberations of Berlin within them; however, it is 'Heroes', the title track, and the most beloved and remembered song on the album, that has the most obvious musical and lyrical connections to the city and the Wall.

The massive room in Hansa Studios, where the recording of *Heroes* took place, was large enough that it once easily held the 150-person orchestras that performed there during World War II. With all that space, the musicians that comprised Bowie's band were set far apart from one another, and Bowie was literally walled off from the rest of the performers by gobos, barriers that are put up to keep sounds from one instrument from bleeding into another's microphone rig (see Figure 15.1). In some ways, then, the studio recreated what was happening in the city at large, and this division, this separation, undoubtedly had an effect on the construction and sound of *Heroes*.

This effect is heard throughout the record and especially on the titular song, as evidenced by the choices made in the composition and the innovative use of instruments and overdubbing. The song's drummer, Denis Davis, with a mechanical precision, plays the almost unchanging rhythm, solely on the snare and hi-hat, with the kick drum (a steadfast marker of rock and roll rhythm) having been faded way back in the mix. The consistent drum beat, rather than being tiresome, allows the listener to find a sonic connection to cling to while Brian Eno's experimental use of his EMS Synthi (a synthesizer built in a

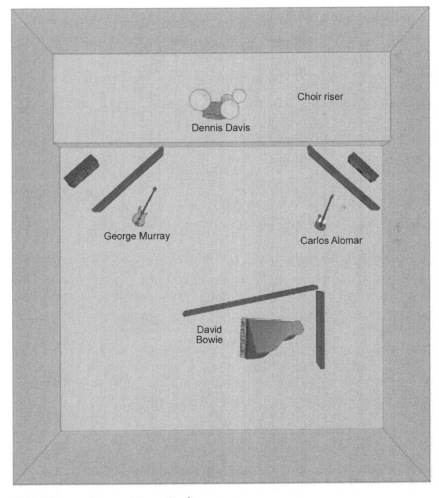

FIGURE 15.1 Heroes: *Hansa Studios set-up.*

briefcase) swooshes and chatters, becoming more and more clear as the track continues and develops in intensity.[5] Meanwhile, Robert Fripp's triple-tracked guitar soars over all the layers of the sound wall Tony Visconti constructed in the booth. Visconti remembers, 'He [Fripp] and Eno had already enjoyed a long partnership where Fripp would plug his guitar into the EMS Synthi and Brian would just play around with it, so Fripp did exactly that and he came up with that beautiful line which everyone thinks is an e-bow sound, but which is actually just Fripp standing in the right place with his volume up at the right level and getting feedback' (Buskin, 2004). Technology and the recording studio also played key roles in Bowie's vocal performance. In the traditional manner, Visconti placed one mic directly in front of Bowie. He also placed gated mics in separate areas of the chamber that would open when Bowie sang louder, thus creating an echo effect that was gained from the size of the room, which in turn lent drama to the song. Bowie's vocals start in a clear, low, almost spoken croon and build to what Bowie himself calls 'Bowie histrionics', a kind of overwrought hysterics in the timbre of Bowie's voice that appear when he pushes it to sing higher pitches (Buskin, 2004). The lyric 'we can/ could be heroes' is sung multiple times, but with varying emotive cues and radical shifts in timbre. There is a unique balance of difference and repetition happening in the song, aurally signifying the stasis of the Wall and the flurry of lives that are lived on both sides of it.[6]

Wall two: reception/perception wall – time and proximity to it

The effects of walls on personal psychology and experience of time is apropos to Bowie's album and career. The records that constitute the Berlin trilogy, *Low* (1977), *Heroes* (1977) and *Lodger* (1979), create a second wall, a wall dividing the way that Bowie is perceived and judged as an artist. Wendy Brown discusses the function walls serve in relation to understandings of the past, future, and temporality, writing, 'They produce not the future of an illusion, but the illusion of a future aligned with an idealized past' (2010: 133). Brown here is specifically talking about the way the walls of a nation-state relate to sovereignty and the construction of cultural identity, but I posit this relationship works equally well when it comes to the construction of an individual identity. Individuals create walls in their own histories in order to cordon off parts of their past into constructed chapters that can then be used to compose the narrative of their lives – a reshaping of memory that effects our present and allows us to project a future. In other words, the position of those boundaries determines the narrative and shapes the way we understand and perform our identities. When dealing with a public figure these walls are not purely personal because a narrative is established through journalism, musical output etc. and because of the larger group of participants the walls become less fluid.

If we consider the division of Bowie's career as a wall, then Brown's construct elucidates the way that critics and fans understand Bowie. This is shown in the way that Bowie's catalogue of work is often discussed as either 'pre' or 'post' Berlin; his time spent there has been mythologized and the Berlin trilogy held up as a moment of perfection, as an ideal piece of artistry, specifically *Heroes*. Listeners believe they have access to Bowie's memories, but, in fact, what exists in interviews, books and films are constructs; they are idealized versions of the origin story of these records. For example, in a 1979 television interview, Bowie said of living in Berlin that it was 'a very tight life there surrounded by a wall with machine guns'. He continued, 'The more you live there, the longer you live there, the more it comes in, and the Wall by the end feels as though it is right around the apartment or house you are staying in.'[7] However, twenty-two years later, in 2001, when he reminisced about his time in Berlin he said it 'was an irreplaceable, unmissable experience and probably the happiest time in my life up until that point'. He continued, 'I just can't express the feeling of freedom I felt there' (Hughes and Dalton, 2001: 66). While these are clearly not irreconcilable versions of his time there, as he could have experienced a great sense of personal happiness but also been aware of the political environment, his memories of his emotional life in Berlin changed as the years passed. The juxtaposition of these quotations illuminates the idealization that distance brings to our memories.

The Next Day and 'Where Are We Now?' are part of Bowie's post-Berlin output, but in this context we need to consider what 'post' really means. Wendy Brown defines 'post' in a way that is useful for thinking about David Bowie's relationship to Berlin in the post-Berlin era of his music making, writing that:

> 'post' signifies a formation that is temporally after but not over that to which it is affixed. 'Post' indicates a very particular condition of afterness in which what is past is not left behind, but, on the contrary, relentlessly conditions, even dominates a present that nevertheless also breaks in some way with this past. In other words, we use the term 'post' only for a present whose past continues to capture and structure it.
>
> Brown, 2010: 21

Although Bowie's time of living and creating in Berlin has ended, and he is in his post-Berlin era, his relationship with that period and that Wall persists in the present. However, the past that he refers to in his post-Berlin period, specifically in the first single on his latest record, is, I argue, not just his own past and a past not always quite as distant as 1977.

With the creation of *The Next Day*'s cover art and the song 'Where Are We Now?', Bowie made use of Western society's collective memory of historical moments: moments such as when the city of Berlin was divided physically and ideologically, which coincided with the time period when Bowie lived and worked in the city; the era shortly after the Wall came down on 9 November 1989, when neoliberal global capitalism began to gradually take hold from 1990 through to the present moment; and the release of his record *Heroes* in 1977. The album *Heroes* is not just an object (either physical or musical), but a catalyst for memory. The album's cover and the recorded songs are part of a narrative of Bowie and Berlin. This period of Bowie's time in Berlin has evolved into a myth, conjured in films, magazines and across the internet, told and retold as a period of pure artistic genius where he '. . . produce[d] the most courageous music of his life' (Rüther, 2008). For, critics and fans, it is a placeholder of a particular time, yet it shifts and moves with its audience and with Bowie. An album accumulates meaning with each listening; yet it can also, at the same turn, elicit memories of previous encounters with the work. Through the use of these common references, we get visual and sonic fragments performing back and forth, linking the personal, political and historical in performances of memory that in this instance create one new message out of 'Where Are We Now?', yet one still haunted by many ghosts.

Where are we now?

The heroes of Bowie's song 'could be' heroes, 'can be' heroes, and 'will be king', but they are not in the moment of the song, in the present of each listening – there is potential built into the song, but it is not realized. This unrealized potential adds to the melancholy in that it exemplifies what David Bowie had said was ingrained in the music he created in Berlin, 'a sense of yearning for a future that we all knew would never come to pass' (Hughes and Dalton, 2001: 66). There are so very many hopes, dreams and wishes laid out in the song (the desire to be royalty, to be one with nature, to be free), yet all this was tempered by Bowie's pessimism and forward-mindedness that, if it ever did come, it would last 'just for one day' (Bowie, 1977). Where are we now, the next day, after our dreams of being heroes didn't come true? Or, what would allow heroes to exist at all? These are just two of the many questions Bowie's surprise release entices audiences to ponder.

In the German version of 'Heroes', the lovers' narrative is diminished as the song starts on the fourth verse of the original English version; this move stops one for a moment to wonder about the 'Heroes' and who they really were for Bowie. In 1977, during an interview with Allan Jones of *Melody Maker*, Bowie stated that in Berlin 'the Turks are shackled in bad conditions', and, pointing to their circumstances, he went on to describe the title track of *Heroes* as being 'about facing that kind of reality and standing up to it' (Jones, 1977). If we take Bowie at his word, in this moment, so soon after the song's creation, this makes 'Heroes' an intriguing kind of memorial to aliens in a foreign land, mistreated and misunderstood, and, in the end, a memorial with political underpinnings, much in the way I am claiming 'Where Are We Now?' takes a political position for the self-proclaimed 'apolitical' Bowie.[8]

'Where Are We Now?' was released on David Bowie's birthday, a day that is often pregnant with personal remembrances and, often, a poignant longing to hold on to things past. The song evokes memories of Bowie's creative time in Berlin, both in the mix of overflowing synthesized sounds and the dramatic, longing vocal presence singing the lyrics. As Bowie looks back through 'Where Are We Now?', listeners are able to sense the sadness of his sonic premonition on 'Heroes' come true. The Wall was torn down, but little was built from its destruction; there is a failure, a lack of history, an erasure of many of the places illuminated by Bowie's lyrics, and, in many ways, we are living in a future with a disregard for the past.

There are multiple pasts referred to in the construction of the 'Where Are We Now?' video, music and artwork for the album that contains the song. I will detail each object's relationship to the different temporal moments Bowie connects and examine how these work as a whole. Bowie is using his personal memories in order to ignite a mass memory of the hopefulness of the moment when the Wall came down and contrast it with what has happened since: global capitalism moved in and radically altered the character and culture of the city. He is an artist creating with memories, structuring them into a dirge that laments the loss of the uniqueness of Berlin prior to the Wall coming down. Solemnly singing the question, 'Where are we now?' turns the dirge into art that can be read as a political critique, clearly questioning neoliberal capitalism and its ability to radically alter the architecture and culture of a city. How are these fragments of memory at work? The video refers to several different temporal moments by juxtaposing images with lyrics that do not share the same temporal referent, thus bringing to life a new piece of art that makes a statement about the present and what has been lost to it.

This is not a common function of popular music, which normally lives in its moment; most songs that do play with nostalgia and memory do so with one particular time or instance. This song doesn't take you back to the time of *Heroes*, it doesn't take you back to 90s Berlin (you need the video for that), but when the two are combined it reflects on a specific kind of postmodern anxiety. In some ways it is like a thaumatrope, the toy that utilizes optical illusion, often a paper with a bird on one side and a cage on the other, that causes the mind to perceive the image of a caged bird when one flips the paper fast enough. In other words, two separate things combine in our mind to make something new. 'Where Are We Now?' creates its message by having the audience continually experience separate epochs spliced with others, which blurs our sense of time, and allows for the creation of new meaning.

Our *Heroes* are still here

The album cover of *The Next Day*, the image of which was released along with the first single on 8 January 2013, is the image of David Bowie's 1977 record *Heroes*, partially eclipsed by a clean, white square containing the text *The Next Day*. There is also a line drawn through the original title text, *Heroes*. *Heroes* is the only album in what fans called his Berlin trilogy that was composed and recorded entirely in Berlin. Almost half of the *Low* (1976) sessions occurred at the Château d'Herouville in France, where Bowie confessed, 'I was at the end of my tether, physically and emotionally, and had serious doubts about my sanity' (Hughes and Dalton, 2001: 49). *Lodger* (1979) was recorded entirely at Mountain Studios, in Montreux, Switzerland; when Bowie reflects upon it, he concludes that he and Tony Visconti 'didn't take enough care mixing', and he continues 'This had a lot to do with my being distracted by personal events in my life.' *Heroes*, then, is the central album of a mythic Berlin trilogy, a trilogy that really never existed. However, *Heroes* is an album completely conceived and created in Berlin and it operates as a marking point for Bowie's career. Though in its initial release the album topped out at number thirty-five on the US charts, *Heroes* has stood the test of time and has become a favourite of critics and fans alike. So, to obscure this visual but let it still be seen simultaneously creates a rupture *with* and a bridge *to* the past. Jonathan Barbrook, the graphic designer who collaborated with Bowie on the cover, states:

> The '*Heroes*' cover obscured by the white square is about the spirit of great pop or rock music which is 'of the moment', forgetting or obliterating the past. However, we all know that this is never quite the case, no matter how much we try, we cannot break free from the past . . . It always looms large and people will judge you always in relation to your history, no matter how much you try to escape it. The obscuring of an image from the past is also about the wider human condition; we move on relentlessly in our lives to the next day, leaving the past because we have no choice but to.
>
> Barnbrook, 2013

Bowie is toying with a particular kind of collective memory of himself through the artwork for his latest album. He is saying, 'Remember my greatness? Here's some more of it.' He is playing with the second wall, the wall that divides his own career, clearly acknowledging it in a masterful marketing move. Bowie, even if he does question where global capitalism has led the world, is still making art under that capitalism and that art is up for sale.

Just as the Berlin Wall echoed through *Heroes*, the sounds of *Heroes* echo through 'Where Are We Now?' The song relies on Bowie's voice as the main emotive factor just as in 'Heroes', but the similarities do not stop there. For the first half of 'Where Are We Now?' we are once again confronted by an almost unchanging tempo, as in 'Heroes', which then shifts at 1:33 with the drums beginning to move forward in the soundscape, allowed to deviate from the original rhythm. Additionally, there is an echo in the drums on 'Where Are We Now?' that sounds reminiscent of the drum sound producer Tony Visconti got in that large room in Berlin in 1977. Sharing a similar drum sound and using minimal kick drum, the bass line is what beefs up the rhythm both in 'Heroes' and in 'Where Are We Now?'; its presence is felt as the instrument that bears down simultaneously with the kick, giving this song its dirge-like pacing. Then, with a minute and thirty seconds left in the song, the rhythm changes again, and a swirling guitar becomes audible, alluding at times to Fripp's lines in the opening of 'Heroes'. As the guitar builds the song to its crescendo, Bowie's voice becomes both more adamant and hopeful, akin to the dramatic development in 'Heroes', where Bowie takes his voice up an octave and the synth sounds and guitar line become louder and more spectacular. The decaying synths that appear in 'Where Are We Now?' are audibly less forceful than in 'Heroes' (just as Bowie's voice is), yet they remain and trigger our memory of Eno's EMS Synthi. As 'Heroes' ends it is Bowie's voice that leads us out, singing, 'ohh ohh ohhhh oh'. 'Where Are We Now?' has a solely instrumental fade out, a removal of Bowie from the sonic ending. However, both songs' conclusions are hopeful, though somewhat ambiguous. These similarities in style, use of instruments and affect, bind the songs together, tying 'Where Are We Now?' to 'Heroes', and juxtaposing past Berlin with the here and now.

The 'Where Are We Now?' video, with the lyrics tied to it, performs a relationship to a different collective memory than the artwork of *The Next Day* or the music itself.[9] The video is not nostalgic for Berlin of 1977, rather it is fixated on the moment of change in the 1990s when the Wall was demolished and global capitalism encroached upon a city that had been divided. Bowie's opening lines reveal the temporal moment he is marking as he sings, 'Had to get the train, from Potsdamer Platz, you never knew that, that I could do that' (Bowie, 2013). Taking the train from Potsdamer Platz became possible only in the 1990s when the Wall had been removed; until then it was nothing but a ghost station with a no-man's land surrounding it. The image that is shown is a view of the border of Potsdamer Platz where the Wall once was, driving home the idea that this song is, at least partially, a rumination on the Wall and what its destruction has meant to Berlin. As the video continues, Bowie explicitly shows buildings and locations that are not the ones he is naming in the song, except with the Nurnberger Strasse, which is represented visually in conjunction with the words. There is an interesting moment when he sings, 'KaDeWe', which is a large luxury department store like Barney's or Harrods, but shows the Berliner Dom. The Dom and its various incarnations on the same location has always been central to religious life in the Berlin area since 1465. The Dom was laid to ruin between 1940 and 1944 due to air raids and bombings. Yet time after time it has been rebuilt. The Dom is a major tourist attraction as well, a monument to the connection of tourism and profit. What could be inferred by aligning the Berliner Dom with KaDeWe is that Bowie is commenting on capitalism being the ideology that now has primacy in the city. In the simplest of terms, he is showing the modern turn in subjectivity, religion and power structures from one place of worship to the new one under capitalism, the temple of consumerism.

Furthermore, in the video for the song we are shown almost exclusively images of Berlin post-Wall and the shots of the Berlin Wall itself we see are also post-Wall images. At one point a portion of the wall is shown with graffiti writing that says 'Tacheles', which is the name of the experimental art squat in East Berlin that thrived in the years shortly after the Wall came down. This famous squat was a last bastion of a kind of unco-opted artistic freedom. Tacheles, after a long fight, was shut down by the property owners and is scheduled for demolition in order for a shopping centre to be erected. What is even more fascinating is that this piece of the Wall is really a tourist site, placed in the parking lot behind Tacheles: in other words, it's a piece of the original Wall but it has been relocated to a spot where the Wall never stood. The significance of this is around the Wall and memory and the obliteration of events – augmenting history with the goal of capital accumulation. One clearly modern shot we see of is of Hauptstraße 155, the apartment building Bowie resided in during his stay in Berlin. This shot is not of the building as it was in 1976 as revealed by signage of the Lotus Tattoo Shop. The shop did not open until at least the turn of the millennium in 2000.[10]

One final clue I'll point to in order to support my assertion that this song and video are making a statement about capitalism, rather than it being just a wistful reminiscence of Bowie's own past in Berlin, arrives at 3:05 into the song, when we see Bowie's full body for the first time, standing next to a large shopping bag stuffed full that reads 'thank you for shopping with us'.

At 3:30, when we come back to Bowie again the shot is tighter, the bag no longer in view, but we see a pensive Bowie, his mouth moving in a way that makes him look nervous about what might be coming from the direction he is looking, which is away from the camera. In these two shots, Bowie wears a navy blue t-shirt with white lettering that reads 'm/s *Song of Norway*'. There are layers of Bowie's personal memories that could be inferred by examining the shirt alone. Bowie, a man not fond of flying, often took ships to his destinations and the m/s *Song of Norway* was a ship that was the founding ship of the second largest cruise line in the world.[11] It was a ship that is part of the history of tourism, as is Berlin, and both are part of Bowie's narrative. The *Song of Norway* is also the title of a 1944 operetta and a film from 1970. The latter starred Hermione Farthingale, an early love of Bowie's. It was on the set of the film that Hermione found a new love and then ended her relationship with Bowie. She was the inspiration of Bowie's songs 'Letter to Hermione' and 'An Occasional Dream' found on *Space Oddity* (1969). Although there are clear ties to Bowie's past in Berlin, the video also operates as a nesting doll for layers of Bowie's past. This is one example of many where Bowie is alluding to his own past, asking his audience to reconnect through a Bowie undefined by the dividing wall of pre- or post-Berlin. Finally, the plot of the operetta *Song of Norway* is 'very loosely based on the art and life of Edvard Grieg, the patron saint of Norwegian music' (Henahan, 1981). The operetta rewrites history. Not surprisingly one could easily compare the story line to the relationship Bowie had with Farthingale and his own journey from Los Angeles to Berlin and the artistic shift that ensued.[12] My aim in this tracing of the shirt worn by Bowie is to highlight the way in which just one object (or lyric or image) can operate as a trace and spur to memory for multiple collectives, such as those who may have travelled on the cruise ship or patrons of the film, into which memories Bowie then inserts himself, creating a new one with his involvement.

The song's lyrics name specific Berlin locations important to Bowie's time in the city. Within the song, Bowie also repeatedly refers to 'walking the dead' through the German city's streets, a possible meditation on loss. There exists the personal meaning of his own loss regarding a particular time in his life, but there also remains the imagery that is evoked when the images of Berlin are tied to this lyric – those of mass violence and death. There are two things to consider within this lyric: walking is done in public, and the dead are dependent on their walker, so the act of walking the dead is at once communal and personal. Additionally, walking and waking the dead are sonorously quite close together. Thus, I would posit that Bowie is raising spirits . . . perhaps his own for his birthday, but also the ghost of the former self (selves) and the ghosts of those whose lives where lost (in so many different ways, not just death, but forms of living death, including the eradication of a space for artists to thrive) in Berlin. Loss, memory, and melancholy, which are all internal private experiences, are made public (collective) through Bowie's video for the song – a strolling visual and sonic display of the ghosts of a divided Berlin, a Berlin made almost unrecognizable by capitalism, and subtle allusions to his own previous musical works. This process combines his personal memories, which are publically owned, and public memories of transition and change, which are privately reconfigured. Then, these memories are doubly mediated by the production in the song and the filming of the music video.

'As long as there's me': in conclusion

As David Eng keenly points out,

> The ability of the melancholic object to express multiple losses at once speaks to its flexibility as a signifier, endowing it with not only a multifaceted but also a certain palimpsest-like quality. This condensation of meaning allows us to understand the lost object as continually shifting both spatially and temporally.
>
> Eng and Kazanjian, 2003: 5

Bowie sings that he is 'a man lost in time', and the song resonates with qualities of melancholic memory, saturated with a sense of time and place just out of reach, and laden with a wistful, personal nostalgia that runs side by side with the significant questions raised by and in coincidence with Berlin's history. 'Where Are We Now?' builds to a hopeful yet still ambiguous conclusion with the line, 'As long as there's me, as long as there's you', drawing both the listener and Bowie's persona back to the present and pointing towards a future with the past brought into the present. Much like Walter Benjamin's angel of history, whose 'face is turned toward the past' yet is being blown into the future by a great storm 'while the pile of debris before him grows skyward' (Benjamin, 1968: 257–8), Bowie is turning our heads, forcing us to look back at the remains of history, making us question the 'storm of progress' at both a personal and political level. Unlike mourning, 'in which the past is declared resolved, finished, and dead, in melancholy', which is the affect I am tying here to both Bowie and Benjamin, 'the past remains steadfastly alive in the present ... constituting an ongoing and open relationship with the past – bringing its ghosts and specters, its flaring and fleeting images [and sounds] into the present' (Eng and Kazanjian, 2003: 3–4). Bowie brings these elements from various pasts together into the present through his reflective song, causing us to evaluate our own position. Loss here is not an act of disappearance, rather it is a mechanism that allows for a shift in the narrative that creates an even greater awareness of a kind of absence of creativity that we are made more and more aware of as the song progresses. This loss leaves one to deal with the collective melancholy of postmodern life, with David Bowie as a soundtrack.

Notes

1   I use the term 'neoliberal capitalism' throughout this chapter, as it is the defining political and economic paradigm since the later part of the twentieth century. More specifically, it had a major impact on Berlin following the destruction of the Wall as the neoliberal strain of capitalism is characterized by practices and policies that favour multinational corporations, often at the expense of smaller businesses. The ubiquity of these global corporate entities diminishes a city's unique character in some ways.

2   Derrida writes of 'traces' in *Of Grammatology* (1997) in a similar way as I am with regard to memory, stating, 'It should be recognized that it is in the specific zone of this imprint and this trace, in the temporalization of a lived experience which is neither in the world nor in "another world," which is not more sonorous than luminous, not more in time than in space, that differences appear among the elements or rather produce them, make them emerge as such and constitute the texts, the chains, and the systems of traces' (65).

3   The title of the album includes quotation marks around it, however, from this point forward in order to distinguish the album from the song I will remove the quotations from the album title and only use them when speaking of the song.

4   My thinking around this owes a debt to Michael P. Steinberg's 'Music and Melancholy' (2014). Though his study does not look at popular music in the vein of an artist such as David Bowie and his examples focus primarily on the nineteenth century with some from the eighteenth, his hypothesis 'that melancholy is the condition of music – all music' (289) is an intriguing one. If this is the case, I would claim that Bowie's album expresses a melancholy different from the melancholy inherent in all music. Furthermore, he expands Freud's use of Hamlet as an exemplary melancholic, in order to show how 'Melancholia becomes the impotence of politics'.

5   In Tony Visconti's interview with *SOS* he articulated the unique style Eno had of using the Synthi in that he would forego the tiny keyboard as a tool and instead 'He used the joystick a lot, and the oscillator banks, and he would do live dialling'.

6   It would be interesting here to consider Gilles Deleuze's *Difference and Repetition*, relating it back to Bowie's career and the possibility of reading his performances and music through the Deleuzian concepts of difference: where sameness is a second-order derivative of difference, and duplicates

are always something new, and where existence is solely about constant change, and reality is a constant becoming, not a static mode of being. See Gilles Deleuze's, *Difference and Repetition*, translated by Paul Patton (New York: Columbia University Press, 1995).

7 Bowie, television interview *Afternoon Plus*, 1979, http://youtu.be/QJFcyp0bqvU, accessed December-2013.

8 In the same interview with Allan Jones of *Melody Maker*, Bowie, when asked about the accusations that ensued around a wave he gave in Victoria Station, London, in 1976 linking him to Nazism, emphatically answered, 'I'm not a fascist. I'm apolitical.'

9 The song's lyrics appear in the video as visual subtitles as well as being sung.

10 The Lotus Tattoo's website gives the bio of the owner and main tattoo artist Bruno, who also goes by 'Fabio'. It states that he was born into a family of artists in Apulia in Italy, and that his creative talent was early discovered and encouraged by his mother, a famous painter. After the successful completion of the Hotel Management School in 1983, he earned his living until 1990 as a professional diver and fisher of sea urchins. He arrived in Berlin and became a cook in a Berlin hotel in 1991. Later, however, he understood that this profession has suppressed his creativity and decided in 2000 for independence. The result was the Lotus . . .

11 The ship helped usher in the modern era of cruising. *Song of Norway* was in the end sold for scrap in November 2013. What was once a part of history was now essentially being put on the trash heap. Reminiscent of the building pile Benjamin's angel gazes upon.

12 A more in-depth description of the *Song of Norway* can be found on The Guide to Musical Theatre's website, www.guidetomusicaltheatre.com/shows_s/song_of_norway.htm.

Bibliography

Barnbrook, Jonathan. 2013. 'David Bowie: The Next Day. That album cover design.' Barnbrook Blog, 8 January, http://virusfonts.com/news/2013/01/david-bowie-the-next-day-that-album-cover-design/, accessed 2 October 2014.
Benjamin, Walter. 1968. *Illuminations*. Edited by Hannah Arendt. New York: Harcourt, Brace & World.
Brown, Wendy. 2010. *Walled States, Waning Sovereignty*. Brooklyn: Zone Books.
Buskin, Richard. 2004. 'Classic tracks: Heroes.' *Sound on Sound*, October, www.soundonsound.com/sos/Oct04/Aarticles/classictracks.htm#Top, accessed March 2014.
Deleuze, Gilles, 1995. *Difference and Repetition*. Translated by Paul Patton. New York: Columbia University Press.
Derrida, Jacques. 1997. *Of Grammatology*. Baltimore: Johns Hopkins University Press.

Eng, David and David Kazanjian (eds). 2003. *Loss: The Politics of Mourning*. Los Angeles, London: University of California Press.

Freud, Sigmund. 1962. 'Mourning and melancholia.' In *The Standard Edition of the Complete Psychological Works of Sigmund Freud*, translated by J. Strachey, Vol. 14. London: The Hogarth Press, 239–60.

Henahan, Donald. 1981. 'City opera: Song of Norway opens.' *New York Times*, 4 September, www.nytimes.com/1981/09/04/arts/city-opera-song-of-norway-opens.html, accessed 29 September 2014.

Hughes, Rob and Stephen Dalton. 2001. 'David Bowie.' *Uncut*, April.

Jones, Allan. 1977. 'Goodbye to Ziggy and all that.' *Melody Maker*, 29 October, 8–11.

McChesney, Robert W. 1999. 'Noam Chomsky and the struggle against neoliberalism.' *Monthly Review*, www.chomsky.info/onchomsky/19990401.htm, accessed 3 June 2014.

Nora, Pierre. 1989. 'Between memory and history: *Les Lieux de Mémoire*.' *Representations*, special issue, 'Memory and Counter-Memory' (spring), 26, 7–24.

Phelan, Peggy. 1993. *Unmarked: The Politics of Performance*. New York: Routledge.

Rüther, Tobais. 2008. 'A foreign affair: David Bowie in Berlin.' *Standing Point Magazine*, December, http://standpointmag.co.uk/node/713/full, accessed 13 April 2014.

Seabrook, Thomas Jerome. 2008. *Bowie in Berlin: A New Career in a New Town*. London: Jawbone Press.

Steinberg, Michael P. 2014. 'Music and melancholy.' *Critical Inquiry*, 40 (2) (winter), 288–310.

Turner, Steve. 1991. 'The great escape of The Thin White Duke: David Bowie in Berlin.' *Independent*, www.rocksbackpages.com/Library/Article/the-great-escape-of-the-thin-white-duke-david-bowie-in-berlin, accessed 13 June 2014.

Discography

Bowie, David. 1977. *"Heroes"*. RCA Records.
Bowie, David. 2013. *The Next Day*. ISO Records.

16

'You never knew that, that I could do that'

Bowie, Video Art and the Search for Potsdamer Platz

Daryl Perrins

Unannounced on his sixty-sixth birthday, 8 January 2013, David Bowie released *Where Are We Now?* via iTunes and on the same day the accompanying film by the multimedia and installation artist Tony Oursler appeared on Bowie's official website. It was Bowie's first new material since 2003's *Reality* and his first visual media appearance since his cameo in *Extras* (BBC2: 2005–07) in 2006. The commonly held fear was that Bowie had retired from music after his onstage heart attack in 2004; a friend and Bowie fan, who was caught out by the unexpected and melancholic nature of the song, the sight of the aged star, and the sound of an almost cracked voice in a sweet and unusual tone, could only come to the conclusion that 'he has broken the silence to tell us he is dying'. There was no hype, fanfare or tragic news however, and it soon emerged that Bowie had even made a new album, *The Next Day*, with long-time collaborator Tony Visconti.

This chapter brings together an examination of Bowie's use of video, the language of film and the Baudelairian *flâneur*'s mode of the stroller's 'remembrance' in order to closely examine two music videos for singles released from the 2013 album, and traces the series of connections, memories and associations which offer a review of the artist's search for cinematic sincerity. The musical and lyrical tones of the new album were of remembrances and acknowledged key influences that stretch from Elvis Presley to Scott

Walker. Often at odds with the downbeat nature of the first single, after a few airings the record creates its own hauntology whereby musical spectres begin to stalk the margins, as in the case of the heartbeat drumbeat in 'Five Years', the opening track from *The Rise and Fall of Ziggy Stardust and the Spiders from Mars* (1972), which reappears at the end of 'You Feel So Lonely You Could Die'. Bowie's mortality is underlined by the signposting of temporality in the title track in which Bowie grinds out the line: 'here I am not quite died, my body left to rot in a hollow tree'. A central trope throughout, this mood of reflection carries into the sixties stoner anti-war protest of 'I'd Rather Be High' where Bowie stumbles to his parents' graveyard to whisper 'just remember duckies everybody gets got'. In the school shooting confessional 'Valentine's Day' whose musical axis is the Spiders from Mars swagger of the glam-rock riff, wherein between its ragged licks, hand clapping and 'sha-la-la' harmonies we find residing the spirit of the quintessential Bowie sideman Mick Ronson. And in 'How Does the Grass Grow?', which despite selling us a lyrical dummy by setting itself in the Eastern Bloc, as in the Berlin trilogy, is actually an introspective meditation on the nature of adolescence in an urban setting according to the storytelling mode of fellow Londoner Ray Davies. While the above-mentioned musical tracks often straightforwardly acknowledge the past, the sparse video for 'Where Are We Now?' set in an artist's studio featuring Bowie and the unnamed woman as conjoined 'face in the hole' puppets with footage of Berlin running behind on a screen and out of sync with the lyrics, was far more oblique. This was partly due to problems of genre, as unlike much of the music on the album that followed it was difficult to place in any existing topology of music videos. And here I am using the tropes assigned to the form by Andrew Goodwin (1992: 106). It did not appear for example on first viewing to be a form of parody, or homage, or promotion, or social criticism, or even pastiche, given the furry puppet outfits both figures in the video inhabit. Rather I will argue the video for 'Where Are We Now?' is perhaps the last in a series of videos that searches often cinematically for sincerity in a form dominated by the above. For Bowie this started back in 1980 when he used the video 'Ashes to Ashes' to exorcise himself of the personae of the 70s. This he did by 'summoning up the archetypes, archetypes that had pervaded his writing in the past decade, in order to kill them off and lay to rest the ghost of impersonation' (Buckley, 2005: 317). Uncharacteristically we see Bowie in a mode of direct address when he calls out 'I want an axe to break the ice / I wanna come down right now'. Here of course he is referring to the detachment that had marked his stage persona from *Station to Station* on. In *Ashes to Ashes* we can see him in masquerade for the first time since *Diamond Dogs* in 1974, as a Pierrot clown leading the New Romantic mourners as they give the last rites to 70s Bowie in front of the oncoming bulldozer on the solarized beach at the edge of the decade. In this guise, he is conjuring up a composite of the pantomimic characters of the early 70s; Ziggy Stardust and Halloween Jack. The Pierrot clown then as narrator asks us to reconsider a close relation: 'Do you remember a guy that's been, in such an early song'. Then via each on screen persona holding up a mirror with the next persona performing in it, the video's point of view cuts between the clown, the astronaut hero of 'Space Oddity' Major Tom, who is revealed as 'a junky', and the asylum inmate in his padded cell whose admission that 'time after time I tell myself I'll stay clean tonight' clearly references the coke addicted 'Thin White Duke' character.

This video exorcism in 'Ashes to Ashes', complete with the release of white doves over water, allowed Bowie to enter the 80s, the decade of MTV, as a global pop star free of masquerade and, more importantly, sexual ambiguity (a commercial necessity). By 1983, and the album and single *Let's Dance*, Bowie was speaking in a universal funk idiom fashioned by Nile Rodgers with liberal universal values, replacing the high European philosophies of Nietzsche and the occult teachings of Aleister Crowley that had dominated the philosophical and mythological underpinnings of his 70s world view. And so we see The Thin White Duke recast in both the 'Let's Dance' and 'China Girl' videos as the colonial master, hereby re-imagining the *Übermensch* that he had previously flirted with as imperial oppressor: 'I'll give you television. I'll give you eyes of blue. I'll give you men who want to rule the world' ('China Girl', *Let's Dance*, 1983). These videos, largely free of the surrealism of 'Ashes to Ashes', fit perfectly into the subgenre of the pop video identified by Andrew Goodwin as 'social criticism' (Goodwin, 1992: 161), alongside such conscience-led MOR rock as Bruce Springsteen and U2. The 80s continued with Bowie using the form of the pop video in the service of a metanarrative of ongoing normalization. As Goodwin notes, this process of 'falling to earth' resulted in the development of 'an "ordinary" self, cumulating in an appearance at the 1985 Live Aid concert in which theatrical characterization was completely absent' (Goodwin, 1992: 111). This did not mean the removal of characterization for Bowie and he was obviously aware for example of the importance of social class as a signifier of 'realness' to a British audience, particularly during a period that was dominated by the divisive policies of neoliberal Thatcherism. Therefore, during this period, authenticity appeared to mean foregrounding his south London-ness over his former other-worldly-ness.

One of the keys to this new persona was the vernacular speech patterns mimicked by impersonators like Phil Cornwell on the Radio One show *Steve Wright in the Afternoon*, which emerged strongly during the period. These were foregrounded in spoken word sections of songs, as in the opening of the single from 1983, 'Modern Love' and in Bowie's film choices, most notably

Absolute Beginners (Julian Temple, 1986). Here he plays an advertising executive, Vendice Partners, who uses a false American accent despite in reality being a working-class Londoner. Perhaps the process of normalization went furthest however in the video for 1984's 'Blue Jean' which was also directed by Julian Temple. This was made into a short nineteen-minute film shown at cinemas essentially as a 'B movie' with Bowie playing two roles: Vic, a cheeky 'jack the lad', and Screaming Lord Byron, a drug addicted dandy rock star who only becomes animated on stage. By the end, as Shelton Waldrop notes, the rock star is seen to be a snob and a fake. Vic pretends to know Byron at one of his gigs to impress a girl 'out of his league'; however, she ends up leaving with the fading star, leaving Vic to shout after him, 'You conniving, randy, bogus, oriental old queen, your record sleeves are better than your songs. Car stops, girl gets out, hello Julian . . .' The camera then pulls back to an overhead position revealing the fiction and Bowie's pleading with the director to change the outcome in favour of his character. This has been interpreted as: 'Bowie's most sustained attempt at a commentary on the fusion of man and mask, the film ends with a shot through a window whose design suggests prison bars, or perhaps barbed wire' (Waldrop, 2004: 129).

The video for 'Blue Jean' (1984) continued a dialogue that Bowie had been having with the nature of celebrity since his Lennon collaboration – the hit single 'Fame', which asked 'what's your name?' back in 1975. His most recent statement on the topic 'The Stars (Are Out Tonight)', the second single from the album *The Next Day*, considers the subject within the framework of his own ageing process. It does this by positioning Bowie's everyman character in a domestic setting that reflects his own retreat from the limelight. His 'wife' is played by long-time Bowie simulacrum, the actor Tilda Swinton and the Bowie and Swinton personae are literally only semi-detached from earlier selves because younger versions are played by the female fashion models Andrej Pejic (as Swinton) and Sashiade Brauw (as Bowie) who both reside through the adjoining wall. The promotional video is constructed as a film, indicated by the opening establishing shots of the older couple's abode as the captions 'A Film by Floria Sigismondi' and then 'Starring Tilda Swinton' appear overlaid on the screen. Thus, pastiche is signalled non-diegetically before the narrative begins. The film is bookended by a freeze frame of the four characters over which the caption 'fin' is placed.

The temporal world the characters inhabit is constructed as a free-floating mid-twentieth century west coast Americana, a bricolage largely constructed from the memories of movies from the classical Hollywood period. Most notably the darkness beyond the picket fence of American suburbia is signalled through the open plan Californian villa styling of the couple's home and the prologue set in the supermarket. Both locations appear to be visual quotations from the film noir *Double Indemnity* (Wilder, 1946). Yet at the same time the video appears fiercely contemporary in its satirical theme. Contemporary objects within the *mise en scène* that would remove the conceit behind this fully furnished world are edited out, but a copy of *Parthenon*, a fictional celebrity magazine is allowed in. The Bowie character picks up a copy as he enters the store at the beginning of the video. The front page carries as its cover headline 'Celebrity Couples Twisted Antics' over the image of the younger 'neighbour' selves dodging flashing cameras; alongside is a still of Bowie as the alien Newton from *The Man Who Fell To Earth* (Roeg, 1975); next to the caption 'alien lives next door' are actual reprinted tabloid headlines from Swinton's appearance at the 2008 Academy Awards that sat in judgement over her choice not to wear make-up to receive a best supporting actor award. Celebrity culture will not allow any loosening of the mask of fame.

The design of the film's overall aesthetic is dominated by the retro styling witnessed in the art deco home exteriors and the vintage limo that the couple next door are menacingly driven around in. It is a look that is completed with Bowie and Swinton styled as if in a 50s melodrama. Swinton in particular in blonde wig, sunglasses, neck scarf and swing coat seems to be setting up the figure of the suburban domestic goddess in a mode previously inhabited by Doris Day. This defiantly anti temporal way of remembering creates a present enchanted by the past, or as Jameson notes when discussing the neo noir *Body Heat* (Kasdan, 1981):

> [t]his approach to the present by way of the art language of the simulacrum, or of the pastiche of the stereotypical past, endows present reality and the open-ness of present history with the spell and distance of a glossy image.
>
> Jameson, 1999: 21

After establishing the narrative, the song starts and the video begins to dramatize the way that age has created a rift between the once perfect fit between the 'star image' and 'character' that existed in the Bowie film career whereby: 'the roles and/or the performance of a star in a film were taken as revealing the personality of the star (which was corroborated by the stories in the magazines, etc.).' (Dyer 1992, 22). A fit which was exploited to the full in *The Man Who Fell To Earth* and *The Hunger* (1983) directed by Tony Scott. In both these films the interplay between rock star and film role was central, as Bowie's association with androgyny and pallid otherworldliness made him readily identifiable with the alien of *The Man Who Fell To Earth* and the vampire of *The Hunger*. This rift is best observed in a scene where the cardigan-wearing Bowie character gets up from watching the TV with his wife and bangs on the wall as the music made by his young doppelganger and band interrupts the domestic bliss. A tracking shot then carries us into a voyeuristic Hitchcockian split screen, bisected by the adjoining wall, which allows us to observe both interiors within the semi-detached building.

The split screen has often been used as a device by Hollywood to express human duality, particularly via twins (see for example *The Dark Mirror*, 1946, and *Adaptation*, 2002). The process is very similar here as 'Bowie' meets *Bowie* across the brickwork resulting in an epiphany moment for the audience as the 'not quite died' Bowie breaks through the diegesis as the ageing curved spine of the sixty-seven-year-old David Jones is clearly caught in silhouette against the night sky framed in the window behind, his 'body left to rot in a hollow tree'. The two then appear to recognize former and future selves as they both mirror each other's movements and emotions with looks to the heavens to close the sequence and to acknowledge where they both come from. Meanwhile, pandemonium is being released as the couple from next door shift from spectatorship to infiltrating the 'Bowie' household. Turning up outside earlier in a car that matched the 1974 Lincoln Continental stretch limousine used in *The Man Who Fell To Earth*, these aliens now take on a vampiric form, a reprise of John and Miriam Blaylock, the married couple played by Bowie and Catherine Deneuve in *The Hunger*.

John and Miriam preyed on urban clubbers to keep themselves alive, slashing their throats with ancient Egyptian pendants. In the film, John as Miriam's vampire progeny finds himself ageing decades within a few hours and ends up being kept in an attic by Miriam along with her other ex-husbands, as a forever withered corpse-like being, in a fully conscious vegetative state. Returning to 'The Stars (Are Out Tonight)', the theme of stardom as an imperfect immortality, a form of morbid ingenuity, is central to the song in question; 'the stars are always with us, the dead ones and the living'. Replaying rock and roll clichés, domesticity is presented as a form of purgatory. And the younger, newer star couple aided by post production F/X jerkily move Swinton and Bowie through the suburban home haunting and taunting the older couple, and mimicking their every movement, just as lesser stars have of course done with Bowie since at the very least the appearance of Gary Numan in 1979. They then move from controlling Swinton's character as if by strings at the dinner table to unleashing first the housewife's and then Bowie's libido. This process continues and becomes an increasingly obvious indictment of the symbiotic relationship between the generations of the chosen, 'the stars must stick together', until the spectres reanimate the suburban couple with the 'nice life' and the young couple replace them on the sofa in front of the TV.

The movement from a suburban existence for the Bowies is marked by Swinton removing her blonde wig and revealing her trademark short back and sides and by Bowie appearing to reinhabit the persona of Newton by donning a duffle coat like the one he wore as Newton in *The Man Who Fell To Earth* and also on the cover of *Low*. By the final frame the comeback is complete with Bowie and Swinton, who is now make-up less as at the Oscars, taking on the

F/X-induced jerky movements and creeping up behind the young couple in matching dress suits to take their rightful place in the temple of the gods that is the fictional celebrity magazine *Parthenon*. Resurrected by the latest generation of prodigy that refuse to let classic star personas fade away and die, they are caught in a freeze frame with all the characters facing the camera and Bowie menacingly brandishing an Oscar statuette by its head with either anointment or extinction in mind.

Freed from the overt pastiche of 'The Stars (Are Out Tonight)', the ambiguous video for 'Where Are We Now?' would appear to be Bowie's most personally revealing video to date. As with previous videos, Bowie's role was far from passive in the production process. Indeed the director Tony Oursler noted that 'down to the detail he had exact ideas on how the video would look. You know the scenes in the background, the films in the foreground.' Oursler saw his own role as 'walking the video out of his (Bowie's) head and into reality' (Oursler, 2013). Various reviews have spoken about its revelatory and memorial qualities. Neil McCormick in the *Telegraph* for example: 'Bowie describes himself as a "man lost in time" and the song resonates with qualities of melodramatic memory dripping with a sense of time and place and highly personal nostalgia' (McCormick, 2013).

This reading would seem to be borne out by the lyrics that link Bowie with real locations from his period living in West Berlin in the late 70s. The accompanying black and white film upon first viewing appears to be from that time, and through it Bowie's memories appear to be directly projected, appearing as the remembrances of his time as a man of leisure in the city, a 'stroller' or *flâneur*, signifying the wandering that Bowie undertook through the streets during his residency: a dandy in transit giving himself up to the unpredictability of an urban existence:

> he would spend his time overloading his febrile imagination with ghoulish remembrances of the cities grand decadence, exploring East and West Berlin by bike, visiting the Bruke Museum and wandering around Kreuzberg, the gay area which also housed many of the city's other dispossessed – the Turkish immigrants, the homeless, the artist's and the punks.
>
> Buckley, 2005: 268

The objects in the artist's studio, which according to the arrangement of shots (in the fiction), is above a hallway in a Berlin tenement, which range from a large diamond-shaped crystal and a giant ear to a sculpture of a Chinese water carrier and a headless manikin, appear to be placed so as to indirectly comment on the Bowie oeuvre. The silent presence of the woman next to Bowie presents the viewer with further avenues into art-rock's past as the abstract artist (and also Oursler's wife), Jacqueline Humphries with her straight dark hair and brown eyes next to Bowie, offers up strong visual associations from rock's long association with the archetype of the rock couple and appears as a direct allusion to the most famous art-rock coupling in history, John and Yoko. As Ousler notes, Bowie asked for Jacqueline to be next to him throughout because he 'wanted a doppelganger, appendage or mirror character' (Oursler, 2013). The presence of Humphries/'Ono' allows Bowie an alternative to the video's assumed direct address and thus the song becomes a private exchange: 'you never knew that, that I could do that'. The reincarnation of John and Yoko continues when the song structurally revisits the building self-revelation and primal scream of Lennon's 'God', a song Bowie had already acknowledged in 'Afraid' on *Heathen* in 2002, by pairing down this connection to a simple but essential human duality. And to thus throw back Lennon's conclusion that 'I don't believe in Beatles, I just believe in me, Yoko and me' as 'as long as there's me, as long as there's you'. Given the existential question posed by Bowie in the song, it's interesting to note that John and Yoko's first joint exhibition in 1968 at the Robert Fraser Gallery in London was called 'You are here'. When Bowie is finally revealed in the video, he is minus the puppet at the edge of the studio space where the comforting endgame of duality is complicated somewhat and we see he is wearing a t-shirt with the title of the 1970 film *Song of Norway* written across it as a device for remembering the film that girlfriend, and some say 'love of his life', Hermione Farthingale left him to work on 1969. The weight of time and, in particular, emotional experience, then, appears to inform the pensive stare that Bowie holds on the room. 'My brain felt like a warehouse, it had no room to spare' – we then cut to a Bowie point of view shot across the cluttered studio and one is transported back to 1972 and the nostalgic interior monologue of 'Five Years' and Bowie this time as Ziggy desperately conjuring up memories of past acquaintances before the inevitable apocalypse.

I would argue, however, that our craving for personal revelation from celebrity has in this case forced us into readings of subjectivity that may be illusory, and that Bowie is not in a conversation with his muse when he asks 'where are we now?' Rather 'we' are 'us'. Here, in moving away from the tropes of the music video genre, Bowie enters an expansive poetic mode whose only literal barriers are the Berlin district limits themselves. This new imaginative form transmits the memory of the dandy back into the city of his remaking as a nineteenth-century literary archetype, in a modern spin on the Baudelairian *flâneur* made emblematic of urban experience by the writings of Berlin native Walter Benjamin. Bowie is thus a semi-detached urban stroller through 'the remembrance of things past', exhibiting a Baudelairian relationship between the artist and the metropolis, whereby the artist 'marvels at the eternal beauty and amazing harmony of life in the capital cities', and gazes upon Berlin's landscapes – 'landscapes of stone, caressed by the mist or buffeted by the sun' (Baudelaire, 1986, cited in Gilloch, 2002).

In his relationship with the city in the song and the video, Bowie is fulfilling Baudelaire's image of an artist giving 'aesthetic form to the ephemeral sensations and abrupt encounters of the cityscape, [wresting] meaning and painful pleasures from the intoxicating yet impoverished modern condition' (Gilloch, 2002: 199). Bowie here is close to Benjamin's version of the *flâneur* as a sign of the alienation of the city and of capitalism as seen in his own inhabitation of the archetype in his unfinished 'Arcades Project', where he makes social and aesthetic observations during long walks through Paris. A more telling definition for our purpose should maybe come from Benjamin's friend Franz Hessel, the author of 'In Berlin Day and Night in 1929' for whom a twentieth century *flâneur* is:

> the privileged physiognomist of the urban setting, transforming the city into a locus of reading and remembering. The flâneur, then, is heroic in exemplifying contradictory moments in the city; on the one hand the ruination of experience and the fragmentation of memory; on the other, the decipherment of meaning and the recollection of lost moments.
>
> Gilloch, 2002: 214

It's clear from the black and white film that plays throughout the video that this is in fact contemporary Berlin. One can tell this from the graffiti on the remains of the Berlin Wall that reads 'Tacheles' (Yiddish for straight talking). This is the first act of witness from Bowie and it has little to do with personal memory per se. Rather it is there to draw attention to the closing of the Tacheles art squat in the district of Mitte in September 2012.

Tacheles was an artist collective that had existed from the early 90s, and instead of the hegemonic work created by Hirst and Emin in the UK who turned punk style into profit, it was a radical experiment that was creating a 'vision of anarchist Dada dissent' and had 'the atmosphere of some legendary mythic avant garde venue of the past, like the Cabaret Voltaire' (Jones, 2013). The weight of history here reminds us that when the Nazis came to power in Berlin in 1933 virtually all modern art was banned and branded 'degenerate' and 'un-German'. This new frame of ideological reference takes the perspective away from Bowie and onto Berlin as a site of historical discourse. In this sense the song continues with the themes found in the 'Berlin trilogy' of albums, *Low* (1977), *"Heroes"* (1977) and *Lodger* (1979) and in particular the atmosphere found in the instrumental 'Art Decade' from the album *Low*. This song captures the spirit of West Berlin during the Cold War period; isolated and doomed to a brief existence but also a haven for dissenters. And importantly, not just a bolthole for wealthy and famous interlopers, as *Christiane F.* (Edel, 1981) testified with the adaptation of Vera Christiane Felscherinow's harrowing autobiography, which immortalized the counter-cultural credentials of the area in and around Zoo Station. In this film cameo, Bowie is in Thin White Duke guise as the Aryan stage god the eponymous teenage drug addict worships: 'making sure white stains'. West Berlin in particular for example drew in many 'draft dodgers' during its existence because it was not formally part of the FRG and therefore residents were excluded from national service. This non-conformist period is also alluded to in 'Where Are We Now?' by Bowie's reference to 'sitting in the The Dschungel' nightclub. The later lyrics that discuss the crossing of Bose Brucke, the site of the first border crossing to open on 9 November 1989 and the crossing of 20,000 people whose 'fingers are crossed just in case', offer up the comparison between the hope of East Germans then and the reality of the unbridled capital and unification today.

Bowie then goes on to tell us that he caught 'the train from Potsdamer Platz'. Again this counters the notion of straightforward first-person memory as Potsdamer Platz station was closed throughout the Cold War period, as it was in no-man's land between the Wall and a 'ghost station'. Thus, through the phrase 'you never knew that, that I could do that' taken together with the repeated refrain of 'walking the dead', Bowie takes on a spectral presence and becomes our guide into a liminal space. A space between past and present, personal and public history, and the surviving ideological walls between East and West which still exist in the (often guilty) conscience of the artist, and signposted here by Bowie's repeated indirect reference to Cold War Berlin's 'death strip'. Here Bowie as the fragile and ageing wanderer of the spaces in between is retracing the steps of the character Homer from the highly celebrated European arthouse film *Wings of Desire* of 1987, by Wim Wenders, itself the product of a collaboration with an avant-garde artist, this time the novelist and playwright Peter Handke.

Wings of Desire is the story of two angels, Damiel and Cassiel, banished by God to spend eternity roaming the streets of Berlin unseen and unheard by its inhabitants, observing and listening to the diverse thoughts of its people. The two angels explore West Berlin and meet Homer, an elderly storyteller, played by veteran actor Curt Bois, who lives in the central library and is 'neither man nor angel' (Wenders, 1992: 93). Just as Bowie searched for the Weimar Berlin of Isherwood during his residency in the late 70s, Homer wanders through the city as the bearer of Berlin's collective memory, 'walking the dead' through the spaces between East and West Berlin. In Homer's case it is also a very literal Cold War wasteland where he searches for the well remembered, but now demolished, Potsdamer Platz of the pre-Nazi period. Homer repeats over and over 'where is Potsdamer Platz?' while Bowie asks 'where are we now?' Troubled by his memories of World War II, Homer says 'where are my heroes' while Bowie, in 1977, troubled by the Wall, says 'we can be heroes':

> I'm an old man with a broken voice, but the tale still rises from the depths, and the mouth slightly opened, repeats it as clearly, as powerfully. A liturgy for which no one needs to be initiated to the meaning of words and sentences.
>
> Homer, from *Wings of Desire*, translated from the German

With the music video for 'Where Are We Now?', Bowie and the filmmaker Tony Oursler eschew the claims that the film is straight up nostalgia, a politically loaded term associated with conservatism and even fascistic ideologies, and replace the unproblematic longing for the mythical past with a dialectical engagement with the present day that Walter Benjamin might refer to as a historical awakening: not so much walking the dead as waking them. The video allows for this process largely through its ambiguity and relative incoherence. Turning its back on the plot-bound genre formula of 'The Stars (Are Out Tonight)' it refuses to provide explanation and instead lends itself through its episodic visual structure, underscored by the Bowie narration, to poetic documentary and the city symphony and ultimately the domain of the arthouse. This then is a short film categorized as video but communicating via the codes of cinema, 'the sixth art'. Thus when watching the music video as cinema, one reads it via cinema's specific qualities – i.e. the juxtaposition of different locations, the moving camera, framing and the use (or absence) of colour. Through the use of the back projection of Berlin scenes full of iconic subjects, the film grammar (i.e. the tracking shots) and the employment of monochrome film stock, the video evokes *Wings of Desire*. And the kinetic POV afforded us thus increasingly evokes not the perspective of Homer, but that of the angel Damiel played by Bruno Ganz.

Damiel is a visitor from the stars who envies the now-ness of mortality, travelling unseen like a ghost through the city streets, in the crowd but not of it; cloaked in a flat cap, hoodie and shades, the now reclusive Bowie was captured by the paparazzi while shopping with a female aide in New York in October 2012. In this guise in Berlin, back in the city of his re-birth, Bowie moves through the urban spaces like the native of Walter Benjamin's City Portraits Berlin, with 'the motives of one who travels into the past instead of the distance' (Benjamin, cited in Szondi, 1962: 19), yet with the historical omniscience of Benjamin's 'angel of history', who, aware of the chaos of progress behind him, 'would like to stay, awaken the dead, and make whole what has been smashed' (Benjamin, 1929, 1968: 257). The music video, like

Wender's film, follows the trajectory of a fall: Bowie's cinematic first-person narration is back projected and moves to a sedate waltz time signature as it bears witness to the city as site of the Berlin Wall, the fernsehtum (TV tower), the exterior of Bowie and Iggy Pop's apartment on Hauptstrasse in Isherwood's once decadent district of Schöneberg, the Reichstag building and the Berliner Dom (Berlin cathedral) – all file past for our contemplation. Here Bowie's POV again mirrors Damiel's, for he presents as a being able to transcend the time barrier and, rather like the angel, it seems he:

> experiences time less as a linear flow than as a kind of plane on which all of history is gathered as a single event: the angels can move back along an infinite time continuum, without the necessity of the act of remembering, viewing past moments as if they were the present.
>
> Graf, 2002: 129

As in *Wings of Desire*, the video for 'Where Are We Now?' seeks redemption over memorialization with a descent into the sensual world of temporality. And just as Damiel loses his role as an introspective onlooker and recorder of history after his fall to earth, Bowie becomes steadily more earthbound as the song changes from the sedate trance-like waltz to a quickening military march. Here we find Bowie returning home to his studio, down always down, from the artistic heights of the apartment buildings of Hauptstrasse via a highly mobile and 'free' camera that tracks down the stairs out into the hall and then into the interior of the studio space where the puppets sit in front of the screen. The cinematography appears to mimic the highly sinuous camerawork of Henri Alekan in its tracking and probing of the city in the service of celestial omniscience.

The studio, in 'Where Are We Now?' eventually appears miraculously in colour with Bowie also in colour standing against the wall looking in and surveying his earthly existence while that symbol of domesticity, a dog, wags his approval in the foreground. Here again in its switching from monochrome to colour and from dream to reality the video mirrors the construction and trajectory of *Wings of Desire*: 'As long as there's rain' sings Bowie as Damiel in *Wings of Desire* now also perceiving the world in colour realizes that for the first time that he has cut himself during his fall and tastes his own blood. 'As long as there's fire' sings Bowie as Damiel moves across town to the sausage stand frequented by Peter Falk to taste the piping hot coffee that Falk previously eulogized. 'As long as there's me, as long as there's you', sings Bowie as Damiel races over to the Hotel Esplanade to meet his earthly desire, the heavenly trapeze artist Marion 'in the flesh' for the first time. Both films end with redemption being found in a profound humanism that stresses that a celestial existence in any form is less fulfilling than earthly love; a staple cinematic romantic fantasy seen at its most effective and most fantastic perhaps in *A Matter of Life and Death* (Powell and Pressburger, 1946). The song builds now almost ecstatically in celebration of this revelation as the focus moves from the studio and back into the iconography of Berlin via the back projection and out into the realm of the vertical again as the camera tilts upwards and tracks around yet another angel of history as seen atop the Siegessäule victory column. Its existence, pockmarked by shell holes, evidence not of divine intervention per se but of the eternity of a united Berlin: 'as long as there's you, as long as there's me'. For Wenders 'BERLIN' is 'representing THE WORLD' (Wenders, 1992: 74) and the condition of human endurance they both ultimately celebrate and to which the angel, column and city stand as testament:

> One day, in the middle of Berlin, I suddenly became aware of that gleaming figure, 'The Angel of Peace', metamorphosed from being a warlike victory angel into a pacifist . . . [T]here have always been childhood images of angels as invisible, omnipresent observers; there was, so to speak, the old hunger for transcendence.
>
> Wenders, 1992: 77

In conclusion, this chapter has remembered the development of Bowie the visual artist, someone who, more than any other artist of a similar profile, has pushed the envelope to the extremes of the pop video form for over three decades now. In doing so he has been searching for sincerity in a seemingly moribund mechanism of personal expression, manipulating the form into a self-reflective tool of engagement with his own mythos, dispatching former identities and ideologies and then producing more accommodating selves for the 80s and beyond. In two music videos for singles from *The Next Day*, Bowie takes two very different approaches to respond to the ageing process and fame beyond beauty. In 'The Stars (Are Out Tonight)', a pastiche of a film full of richly rewarding intertextual reference points to film roles and Hollywood cinema texts, he reminds us that 'pop will eat itself' as stars are recycled through the next generation of simulacra and/or live on endlessly through the process of comeback. 'Where Are We Now?', his most experimental video to date, breaks with the playful postmodernism of 'The Stars (Are Out Tonight)' and instead situates its nostalgic yearning for the West Berlin of the 70s he inhabited in the plotless monochrome ambiguity of the arthouse, thus allowing the audience the freedom of multiple and endless interpretations as Bowie's ageing city stroller now seeks meaning over action and creates a poetic travelogue through a Berlin now 'lost in time near KaDeWe'.

References

Benjamin, Walter. 1929, 1968. *Thesis on the Philosophy of History*. Translated by Harry Zohn. In Hannah Arendt (ed.) *Illuminations*. New York: Schocken Books.

Buckley, David. 2005. *Strange Fascination: David Bowie, The Definitive Story*. London: Virgin Books.

Dyer, Richard. 1992. *Stars*. London: BFI Publishing.

Gilloch, Graeme. 2002. *Walter Benjamin: Critical Constellations*. Cambridge: Polity Press.

Goodwin, Andrew. 1992. *Dancing in the Distraction Factory: Music Television and Popular Culture*. Minneapolis: University of Minnesota Press.

Graf, Alexander. 2002. *The Cinema of Wim Wenders: The Celluloid Highway*. New York: Columbia University Press.

Jameson, Fredric. 1999. *Postmodernism or The Cultural Logic of Late Capitalism*. New York: Verso.

Jones, Jonathan. 2013. 'The closure of Berlin's Tacheles squat is a sad day for alternative art'. Art Blog, *The Guardian*, October, www.theguardian.com/artanddesign/jonathanjonesblog/2012/sep/05/closure-tacheles-berlin-sad-alternative-art, accessed 15 October 2014.

Kolker, Robert Phillip and Peter Beicken. 1993. *The Films of Wim Wenders. Cinema as Vision and Desire*. Cambridge: Cambridge University Press.

McCormick, Neil. 2013. 'David Bowie Where Are We Now? First Review'. *Daily Telegraph* online, 8 January, www.telegraph.co.uk/culture/music/9787215/David-Bowies-Where-Are-We-Now-first-review.html, accessed 15 October 2014.

Oursler, Tony. 2013. 'David Bowie video director explains "Mystery Woman"'. *Front Row*, 17 January 2013, www.bbc.co.uk/news/entertainment-arts–21056907, accessed 10 May 2014.

Szondi, Peter. 1962. 'Walter Benjamin's City Portraits'. Translated by Harvey Mendelson. In Gary Smith (ed.) *On Walter Benjamin: Critical Essays and Recollections*. Cambridge: MIT Press (1991).

Waldrop, Shelton. 2004. *The Aesthetics of Self-Invention: Oscar Wilde to David Bowie*. Minneapolis and London: University of Minnesota Press.

Wenders, Wim and M. Hofmann (1992) *The Logic of Images: Essays and Conversations*. London: Faber & Faber.

Index